THOMAS BENTON CATRON
and his era

Thomas Benton Catron,
Attorney General of the Territory of New Mexico, 1869–72.

THOMAS
BENTON
CATRON
and his era

Victor Westphall

The University of Arizona Press
Tucson, Arizona

About the Author . . .

VICTOR W. WESTPHALL, longtime devotee of southwestern history, has focused his interest primarily on the last four decades of the nineteenth century. He considers these years obscure historically because available documents have not been read exhaustively, a deficiency he has spent many years correcting. He is known among southwestern historians for his investigation of the public domain in New Mexico and the American Valley murders, and for a definitive study of New Mexico land grants. Westphall holds a Ph.D. in history, and was president of the Historical Society of New Mexico.

THE UNIVERSITY OF ARIZONA PRESS

FOR DAVID

who in his twenty-eight years of life
attained a literary excellence
that will always guide
and inspire me.

Contents

ILLUSTRATIONS

Chronology

1840, October 6:	Thomas Benton Catron born.
1860, July 4:	Graduated from University of Missouri.
1865, May 10:	Paroled from Confederate army.
1866, July 27:	Arrived in Santa Fe.
December 14:	Confirmed district attorney for third judicial district — moved to Mesilla.
1867, June 15:	Admitted to the bar.
1868:	Territorial House of Representatives.
1869, January 12:	Confirmed as attorney general.
1872, March 7:	Commissioned United States attorney.
1878, April 28:	Married Julia Walz.
October 10:	Letter of resignation as United States attorney.
1879, January 20:	Relieved from duty as United States attorney.
1882:	Defeated for Territorial Council.
1884:	To Territorial Council.
1886:	Defeated for Territorial Council.
1888:	To Territorial Council.
1890:	To Territorial Council.
1891, February 8:	Attempt on his life.
1892:	Defeated as delegate to Congress.
1894:	Delegate to Congress.
1895, October 25:	Acquitted in disbarment proceedings.
1896:	Defeated as delegate to Congress.
1898:	To Territorial Council.
1900:	Defeated for Territorial Council.
1904:	To Territorial Council.
1906:	Mayor of Santa Fe.
	Defeated for Territorial Council.
1908:	To Territorial Council.
1910:	Member constitutional convention.
1912:	To United States Senate.
1918:	Defeated for United States Senate.
1921, May 15:	Died.

Preface

Numerous controversies surrounded the life of Thomas Benton Catron, the complexities of which no doubt resulted in the hesitation on the part of previous historians to record the story of his life. Aside from William A. Keleher's excellent sketch in his *Fabulous Frontier,* and three Master's theses respectively by Hefferan, Sluga, and Wooden, the history of Catron's life in New Mexico largely has been ignored. An oral tradition — with many variations — therefore evolved about Catron, who moved to New Mexico after the Civil War, there to become the largest individual landowner in the history of the United States, with the controversial Tierra Amarilla Land Grant among his possessions.

This present book is an attempt to evaluate Catron's life and his era objectively. The prevailing oral stories have been subjected to factual research, and the interpretations given herein have been based on verifiable evidence. Because the nefarious nature heretofore attributed to the man is not generally borne out in the recorded evidence, much of the oral tradition has of necessity been discarded here. It may well be that some persons will deplore this seeming tampering with tradition. Indeed, some already have expressed suspicion that this is a biography arbitrarily designed to present only Catron's better side, thereby pleasing family and friends.

Emphatically, such is not the case! I take full responsibility for the analysis of Catron's relationship to his era, and I here state that every effort has been made to find bona fide evidence of all the various kinds of activities and personality traits attributed to him. Conscious effort toward objectivity has been constantly borne in mind.

I now wish to express my thanks to the University of New Mexico personnel who cooperated fully in my examination of the extensive Catron papers there. I owe special thanks to the late Charles C. Catron for his foresight in making these papers available to a recognized repository without the amateur selective deletions usually attendant to such a bequest, and to his conviction that this act of faith would serve well both history and his father's name.

I have profited much from the help of members of the staffs of the National Archives, Library of Congress, Federal Records Center at Denver, Henry E. Huntington Library, University of New Mexico Library, West Virginia University Library, Vicksburg National Military Park, and Missouri Historical Society. At Santa Fe, I received help from personnel at the Bureau of Land Management, United States Court House, State Records Center and Archives, and Museum of New Mexico library.

In addition, I am appreciative of the assistance of the numerous individuals whose contributions are specifically acknowledged in the text. In particular, I wish to thank Thomas B. Catron II and Thomas B. Catron III, who supplied the photographs used in this book.

Finally, thanks are due the University of Arizona Press for effecting publication of the book.

V.W.

1
Missouri Heritage

The great westward movement, motivated by restlessness in the souls of men and hunger for land, was heralded by the tenuous progress of caravans from Missouri. Thomas Benton Catron's destiny was forged over this Santa Fe Trail to Santa Fe, and to the Territory of New Mexico, where he would become one of the largest land owners in the nation.

In 1821, the same year that Missouri was admitted to the Union, William Becknell organized the expedition that earned him the title "Father of the Santa Fe Trade." Starting at Franklin, Missouri, the eastern terminus of this trade moved west to Independence, and then to Westport Landing. Kansas City, established in 1839, ultimately absorbed Westport Landing. Thus, Catron's home in Lexington, Missouri, located less than thirty miles east of Kansas City, was close to the beginning of the Santa Fe Trail.

On October 6, 1840, when Catron was born, the "hard cider and log cabin" presidential compaign of William Henry Harrison had two months remaining.

The Catrons' cabin was of black walnut, which was plentiful in the western Missouri of those days. Material other than that from the land was in short supply, so the builders used wooden pegs instead of nails, and leather hinges. This construction was typical of that in the region where the Catron homestead was situated, about four miles southeast of Lexington. In 1818, Thomas's grandfather acquired 1,600 acres of land on which he broke the first prairie sod in the county. He also possessed the first shingles and sawed planks. Although the family experienced the privations and discomforts of pioneer life, they aided their neighbors in laying the foundations of the future state of Missouri.

It was here that Thomas's father grew to manhood, working on the farm and serving as apprentice to a bricklayer. In 1833, when he married, he received 530 acres of the family farm. With hard work and intelligence he amassed a competence from stock-raising and tilling of the soil.

From this farm, Thomas gained a sense of the soil, and from his father, uncompromising principles. But from his own observation and thinking came the political philosophy that was a salient characteristic of his later years. His father was an ardent Democrat, but Thomas spent his entire adult life as an equally staunch Republican.

Aside from the environment of his home and its geographic proximity to the beginning of the Santa Fe Trail, the most important influence in his early life was the growing sectional controversy over slavery. As Thomas matured he was called upon to make his own decisions concerning such national events as the Compromise of 1850, the publication of *Uncle Tom's Cabin* in 1852, the Kansas-Nebraska Bill of 1854, John Brown's massacres in 1854 and his raid on Harper's Ferry in 1859, the Lincoln-Douglas debates of 1858, and the division of the Democratic party in 1860.

This decade of national contention was concurrent with Catron's impressionable teen years. The American people had earnest hopes for the Compromise of 1850, but it did not end the slavery dissension. The prosperity of the 1850s stimulated expansion. So long as the frontier moved westward, the recurring problem remained: Should the newly developed areas be slave or free? That question was debated endlessly, wearing nerves thin, until peaceful settlement was impossible. Civil war alone would decide the issue.

John Catron, Father of Thomas Benton Catron.

Particularly significant to young Catron was that he lived close to an important segment of the growing tension — the internecine struggle for Kansas. Immigrants from New England and those from south of the Mason-Dixon line met here, but they would not blend. The divisive element was slavery, and Catron grew up in an atmosphere where compromise was not looked upon favorably. One was either for or against slavery, and public pressure called for a declaration. The nation could not avoid dispute. The Lincoln-Douglas debates were a mirror of unrest throughout the land.

There is no record of Catron's impressions of this period. Because he joined the Southern cause in the Civil War, it must be assumed that he concurred with the sentiments of his father and opposed those of the majority of his neighbors. It is significant, though, that his most important decision after the war was to relinquish the cause for which he had battled, and adopt that of his former enemies. Of this strife he later said:

It would have been terrible had the result been different. The result of that war has added very much to my belief in the interposition of Divine Providence. Providence generally makes everything all right; and in this case it is shown to be so. We, who faced each other on the field as good soldiers, never could entertain a particle of resentment against each other. I have always thought that our country at large ought to be grateful to the South for bringing on the war and having the question of slavery and states rights settled for ever, and settled rightly.[1]

Thomas was the fourth child born to John and Mary Catron; the nine children, in order of birth, were Upheminy Ann, George Monroe, James Fletcher, Thomas Benton, Washington, Margaret Elizabeth, Amanda Caroline, John Jr., and Mary Jane.

Thomas was named for Thomas Hart Benton, famed United States Democratic senator from Missouri. John Catron admired Benton, who served in the Senate for thirty years. The father later became displeased with Senator Benton and changed his son's name to Thomas Jefferson Catron. The youth, at the age of ten, displayed an early independence of spirit by resuming his baptismal name, Thomas Benton Catron. The genealogical pages of the Catron family bible contain erasures attesting to this change.

The original family name of the Catrons was Kettenring. The first Kettenring came from Switzerland and settled in the Rhineland near Herzberg. He was given the name Kettenring because, as a blacksmith, he made a type of log chain whose links would not kink when coiled. *Ketten* means chain; thus, Kettenring means chain-ring. The first recorded home of the Kettenrings was at Rheiupfalz, Bavaria, in Southern Germany.

Thomas's great great grandfather, Christopher (or Christoff) Kettenring, was born about 1720 and moved to Holland near Rotterdam, where he married Susannah Gose. On December 9, 1765, he brought his family to America on the ship *Chance*. He arrived at Lancaster, Pennsylvania, and then moved to Wythe County, Virginia, where he resided until his death in 1793.

Among the children brought to America was Peter Kettenring (1754–1840), who took up his residence in what later became Grayson County, Virginia. He later moved to Wayne County, Kentucky, where sometime before his death he changed his name to Kettering. His wife was Elizabeth Houch, and to this couple in 1781 was born John Catron, the Supreme Court justice.*

A younger brother of Peter Kettenring was Jacob Kettering (1756–1816). The father, Christopher, had changed his name before Jacob was born. Jacob, great grandfather of Thomas Benton Catron, resided in White County, Tennessee, until his death. Here he married Elizabeth Gose, who was related to Maria Gose, mother of President Martin Van Buren.

To Jacob and Elizabeth was born Christopher Kettering (1786–1819). Christopher moved from Grayson County, Virginia, to White County, Tennessee, and then in 1817 to Missouri, where he died in Lafayette County. While in Virginia he married Euphemia Minipraa Jones. Among the children she bore was John Catron (the father, as was becoming the custom, having changed his name to Catron).

John Catron (1812–97), father of Thomas Benton Catron, was born in White County, Tennessee. He was named after his illustrious second cousin, Associate Justice John Catron. In 1817 he came to Missouri Territory with his parents and located in Saline County. Early the following fall, the family moved to Lafayette County, southeast of Lexington. In 1833 John Catron married Mary Bonham Fletcher, a native of Virginia, who settled in Lafayette County the same year the Catron family took up residence there.

Thomas received his early education in rural schools in

---

* Judge Catron (born Kettering) moved from Kentucky to Tennessee in 1812, where he served as the first chief justice (1831–34). He was associate justice of the U.S. Supreme Court from 1837 until his death May 30, 1865. He married Matilda Childers, and adopted a daughter.

Lafayette County. Although the father's formal schooling had been meager, he was interested in the education of his children and often encouraged his son Thomas to read items of interest aloud to the family. Among these items were the speeches of Stephen A. Douglas.

Thomas was considered studious. In 1857 he enrolled at the Masonic College in Lexington, a junior college established by the Masonic Lodge of Missouri.[2] Here he met Stephen Benton Elkins, who was to become the most important single associate of his lifetime. Both stood high in their class. Years later an old resident of Lexington prophetically recalled: "I allus said the country'd hear of Steve Elkins and Tom Catron."[3]

Elkins was born in Perry County, Ohio, September 26, 1841. When three years old he was brought to Missouri by his parents. His father, Philip Duncan Elkins, married Sarah Pickett Withers; Stephen was the eldest of their six children. The family settled at Westport where the father acquired land, owned slaves, and became a man of some affluence in the community. He also became a slave trader. Earlier there had been a strong disposition toward emancipation in the Elkins' family, but the Nat Turner insurrection in 1831 caused a severe reaction, changing the family disposition to bitter pro-slavery feelings. Stephen's father, like Catron's, was an admirer of Thomas Hart Benton and therefore named his son Stephen Benton.

In 1859 Catron and Elkins enrolled at the University of Missouri at Columbia, where they were roommates. The Lincoln-Douglas debates of the previous year had attracted wide attention and were published in book form. These debates, an informal part of the curriculum, were studied carefully and much discussed. Here the pattern was set for an unusual — and often strained — relationship between the roommates; Catron, adhering to the politics of his forebears, sided with Douglas, while Elkins held to the less popular side of the question at Columbia and favored Lincoln.

Throughout their lifelong association they often differed just as fundamentally as in their college days. Despite often bitter differences, they were destined to a lifetime connection that, at best, only approached lasting friendship. More characteristically it became an alliance of convenience that was often stormy and almost never more than cordial. They invariably came to each other's aid when it was mutually advantageous to do so, but they frequently clashed when a crisis had passed. In the end, when life for each was short, the rancors of the past were mostly forgotten and mutual remembrances of their long association proved stronger than past differences.

Through it all, if there was any giving to be done, it was more often than not Elkins who did the giving. A year younger than Catron, he was in many ways the leader of the two. Just as he aligned himself on the winning side in the Civil War, he seemed more often right in his decisions. Their paths were to cross inextricably for more than a half century, during which time probably the biggest concession that Catron made in their mutual relations was to staunchly avow the Republican faith of his colleague.

As the summer of 1860 approached, a division in the Democratic party became apparent. With it there was a growing trend toward secession by the Southern states. In the midst of this divisive atmosphere, on July 4, graduation exercises were held at the University of Missouri. There were nine members in the class, including Catron and Elkins.* Catron's courses had been moral philosophy, natural science, mathematics, and modern language. He received an honorary Master of Arts degree in 1868 and an LLD in 1919.

---

* Other New Mexicans who attended the University of Missouri were Henry L. Waldo and Napoleon B. Laughlin. New Mexicans from Missouri contemporary with Catron were W. H. Brinker, Howard Lee Bickley, Humphrey B. Hamilton, Thomas F. Conway, Otto Askren, Lorion Miller, John I. Hinkle, James F. Hinkle, William T. Thornton, and Charles A. Speiss. Thornton and Speiss became Catron's law partners.

General Sterling Price gave the commencement address in 1860.* Although a Southerner, Price was an ardent Union man, and in his speech he counseled restraint and forbearance from hasty decisions on the festering problems of slavery.

After graduation, the roommates returned home by steamboat, Catron disembarking at Lexington, and Elkins at Westport. That summer Catron helped on his father's farm. In the fall he was hired to teach at a nearby school located on land conveyed to the school board by his father.† Unknown to Catron, Elkins also taught school at the same time in Harrisonville, Missouri, about forty miles southwest of Lexington.

---

* Price came to Missouri in 1830, and was elected to the legislature where he served as Speaker of the House of Representatives. He raised the 2d Missouri Volunteers for the war with Mexico, and served as military governor of New Mexico, returning to Missouri after the Treaty of Guadalupe Hidalgo. In 1852 he was elected governor of the state and held that office for four years.

† One of Catron's students was Anne Limirick, who later married William C. Mead and moved to La Mesa, New Mexico. There Catron helped Mrs. Mead with some legal advice, and she reciprocated with a warm letter of congratulations in 1912, when he was chosen first U.S. senator from New Mexico. Catron to Anne Limirick Mead, February 18, 1898 (C.P. 105, Vol. 14); April 4, 1912 (C.P. 501, Box 10); Mead to Catron, March 31, 1912 (C.P. 501 Box 10).

2
Civil War

As Thos. B. Catron (as he signed his name until age thirty-one, when he shortened it to T. B. Catron) proceeded through his only year as a school teacher, the national situation rapidly deteriorated. In December 1860, South Carolina led the way in secession. By February 1861, when the Confederacy formed, six other states of the lower South followed. Abraham Lincoln was inaugurated on March 4; Fort Sumter was fired upon on April 12; and the four Confederate border states soon followed in secession. The nation was at war. Although Missouri declined to secede, the citizens there soon went about the grim business of choosing sides.

A conflict between the North and the South had been expected for months, but only a few in Missouri had made an irretrievable alignment. People in the southeastern counties and the extreme western portion aligned themselves with the pro-Southern party. Around Lexington, as well as in most of the rest of the state, the majority feeling was for the North.

Only a militant minority stood unrelentingly for the South. Backed by powerful newspaper support, this group included Governor Claiborne F. Jackson, the lieutenant governor, both United States senators, and a majority of the legislature. A larger and more moderate group felt that, while secession might ultimately be necessary, every attempt should be made at peaceable adjustment of difficulties. Among these moderates were former governors Robert M. Stewart and Sterling Price, as well as Alexander M. Doniphan and some influential editors.

Frank P. Blair, Jr., was the brains and ramrod of the unconditional Unionists and was ably supported by General Nathaniel Lyon. Both were veterans of the Mexican War. Blair was appointed United States attorney for New Mexico by Stephen Watts Kearny in 1846 and assisted in compiling the Kearny code of laws.

Trouble in Missouri became imminent when a force, thought to be pro-Confederate, formed at Camp Jackson in St. Louis. The officers and men professed loyalty to the Union, but Lyon, then in command of the newly organized pro-Union force, suspected their motive was to capture the St. Louis arsenal. Accordingly, he surrounded them with superior numbers and forced surrender on May 10. Street fighting followed between Union soldiers and aroused citizens, resulting in twenty-eight deaths. Reports were spread of a massacre of defenseless persons, including women and children.

While this incident was the spark that ignited hostilities, the situation was fundamentally more complex. Involved were national ramifications that had been growing in virulence from before the time that Missouri had become a state. The Know Nothings were in favor with the populace and had recently stirred up strong antiforeign prejudice. Thus the German element in Missouri became the target of persons with secessionist and proslavery inclinations. Significantly, the Catrons, with German antecedents and living in the strongly pro-Union community of Lexington, preserved their secessionist preference.

Following the so-called St. Louis massacre, Governor Jackson issued a proclamation of war and placed the state military force under the command of former Governor Sterling Price. Ultimately about 30,000 from Missouri fought for the South, while 109,000 served the Union army.

Price hoped to avoid a test of arms and came to an agreement with General William S. Harney, who commanded the military department of the West. Harney was a sincere Unionist, but preferred conciliation to force. Price agreed that he would use his troops only to keep order in the state, and Harney promised to reciprocate by not attacking him. Unfortunately, the radical leadership of Blair and Lyon prevailed when Lyon attacked and routed the Confederates at Booneville. Meanwhile, the state capital at Jefferson City was seized by Union forces.

After the initial action by Blair and Lyon, however, the Confederates had the advantage of superior boldness, vigor, and mobility. It appeared possible that the quickly rallying state army would take lower Missouri, capture strongly secessionist Cairo and southern Illinois, sweep Kentucky into the Confederacy, and make even southern Indiana doubtful territory. If they succeeded, the war might be virtually lost for the North.

These matters were known to young Catron as he finished his term of teaching. When his school closed for summer vacation, he enlisted for military service, was elected 2d lieutenant in Captain Hiram Bledsoe's battery, "Missouri State Guard, Confederate States army, June 11, 1861, and was commissioned 2d lieutenant of Company D, 6th Regiment Infantry, 8th Division, Missouri State Guard, C.S.A."[1]

Meanwhile Elkins also finished his school term. For him the anticipated war was particularly trying because, like the Union, the Elkins family was soon to be torn asunder. Stephen concluded that the cause of Abraham Lincoln was right; the Union should not be destroyed. But his father and some of his brothers were of the opposite persuasion and served in the Confederate army. Stephen was assigned to sentinel duty along the Missouri River protecting against bushwhackers (Confederate guerillas). After the fall of Vicksburg, it appeared that the Union troops in Missouri would see only desultory action for the rest of the war, so young Captain Elkins requested relief from his command. The request was granted July 3, 1863.

He found no peace at home as a civilian; feeling still ran high at Westport. From the days of his boyhood he had watched the covered wagons depart for New Mexico and California; now he decided to seek his destiny along the Santa Fe Trail. The wagon train in which he was traveling reportedly took three months to reach the Rio Grande. He probably arrived in New Mexico in November 1863, for a letter was waiting for him in the Santa Fe post office on the fifth of that month.

For Catron the war was long and horrible, although it started out in a romantic way. His assignment to Bledsoe's three-gun battery was an event he could point to with pride for the rest of his life. The service of this outfit was distinguished throughout the war and later became a local legend. Bledsoe said his men had "more merit and bravery and intelligence than you would have found in any mess in the army."[2]

While a great deal more information is available about Bledsoe's battery and the Missouri State Guard in general than about Lieutenant Catron specifically, it can be concluded that with his assignment to a battery of only three guns, whatever happened to the battery also happened to Catron. John C. Moore refers to Bledsoe's battery in his *Confederate Military History*:

> One of Bledsoe's guns was captured by the Missourians in the Mexican war at the battle of Sacramento. It was presented by the general government to the State of Missouri and for years stood on the bluff overlooking the Missouri River at Lexington. . . . There was a considerable percentage of silver in its composition, which gave it a ring when fired that could be distinguished on the field amidst the firing of a hundred ordinary guns. Bledsoe's battery was always in the thickest of the fight, and the soldiers of the State Guard, as well as the Federals, soon came to know "Old Sacramento's" voice. It became so badly grooved from use that it was finally condemned, sent to Memphis to be recast with other guns, and its identity lost.[3]

"Old Sacramento" served as a rallying symbol during many battles in which Catron participated, the first of which was Carthage near the southwest corner of Missouri. Here he received his baptism of fire less than a month following his enlistment. The State Guard and the Union forces were so disposed that neither knew for certain where the other was. They found out on the morning of July 5, 1861, when the Guard troops saw the glint of enemy bayonets across a creek. The Unionists were under the command of Franz Sigel, while the Confederates were commanded by Governor Jackson since General Price was in Arkansas at the time seeking reinforcements. Sigel opened the fight by firing his artillery across the creek, to which Bledsoe's guns replied. Sigel was defeated and driven back to Springfield. There were 40 or 50 Missourians killed and about 120 wounded, while the enemy lost twice that number. These losses, while small, were only a prelude to the horrible slaughter to follow.

Confederate forces were threatening Springfield, with Union soldiers under Lyon between the Confederates and Springfield. On August 10 the opposing forces met at Wilson Creek. Within its limits it was one of the fiercest encounters of the Civil War. Bledsoe placed his battery so as to command the Union position. As the infantry advanced he opened at point blank range. The fight at Bloody Hill lasted five hours, and the dead of both armies lay upon it in piles. Among the slain was the Union commander, Nathaniel Lyon. John C. Moore describes the battle in his *Confederate Military History*: "Never before — considering the numbers engaged — had so bloody a battle been fought on American soil; seldom had a bloodier one been fought on any modern field."[4]

Following the battle of Wilson Creek, General Price took possession of Springfield and set about recruiting, organizing and drilling his army. In less than a month he was able to move toward the Missouri River with a force of about 4,500 men armed with seven pieces of artillery. At Drywood, about fifteen miles east of Fort Scott in Kansas, he encountered several thousand Kansas Jayhawkers and routed them. From here Price marched to Lexington, Catron's home town.

On September 18 the Confederates attacked Lexington in force. Price's army far outnumbered the defenders, and the outcome was never in doubt. The batteries of Bledsoe and others kept up an effective artillery fire; meanwhile, sharp-shooters harrassed the enemy and cut off their water supply. Despite a gallant defense, without water, they were compelled to surrender on September 20.

Catron now left his home town and native state for the duration of the war. Price and his command, forced by superior numbers to flee Missouri, joined other Confederate forces in Arkansas. Finally, at Pea Ridge (Elkhorn Tavern) on March 6, 1862, the Southern armies turned and fought a three-day battle which resulted in their complete defeat. Soon thereafter, the Arkansas troops crossed the Mississippi River into Tennessee. Price, accepting a Confederate commission, crossed with about 8,000 of his men (including Catron).

The Missouri troops reached Corinth, Mississippi, April 11, 1862, only four days after the battle of Shiloh at nearby Pittsburg Landing, Tennessee. A few days later they were placed in camp at Rienzi, twelve miles south of Corinth. Here the work of reorganizing from the state to the Confederate service proceeded. On April 21 Catron was elected 1st lieutenant of Captain Schuyler Lowe's Company (Jackson Battery) Missouri Artillery, C.S.A.

After action at Iuka, Price joined forces with General Earl Van Dorn in a move on Corinth. The attack started on the morning of October 3, with Van Dorn's command holding the right and Price's the left. By sunset the enemy in front of the Missourians had been driven into the town, and the weary Confederates rested for the night. Two hours before dawn Price's artillery wreaked bloody havoc at short range; at daylight the guns were withdrawn. By midmorning the attack resumed, and within twenty minutes the Confederate flag waved bravely over the ramparts of Corinth. Soon Price had penetrated to the center of the town and was in a position to strike at the enemy flank and rear. Gradually though, the horrible fact became clear that the attack on the right had not been made. The enemy was able to withdraw forces from that sector and concentrate on Price. Unsupported, the Missourians were confronted with overwhelming odds and were forced to extricate themselves as best they could. This they accomplished, but only after valiant efforts and grievous losses. In the words of General Maury, General Price — "Old Pap" to his men —

looked on the disorder of his darling troops with unmitigated anguish. Big tears coursed down the old man's bronzed face, and [seldom was] witnessed such a picture of mute despair and grief as his countenance wore when he looked upon the defeat of his magnificent troops.[5]

Price was hard pressed in retreat and, just before night, formed a line with masked artillery supported by infantry. When the enemy reached close range, the artillery opened fire and the infantry charged. The Union forces were checked and pursuit ended for the day.

Another army had been brought by forced marches from Jackson, Tennessee, to intercept Price in front, making it necessary to cross the Tombigbee River and then the Hatchie. The crossing of the first was unopposed, but the enemy was waiting at the second, and Price's army was turned back at Hatchie Bridge. Escape seemed impossible; nevertheless, General Price learned of a little-used road leading to a mill five miles down the Hatchie. Here a dam served as a base for a bridge hastily constructed with logs and timber scrounged on the spot. By midnight the tattered remnant of an army was across and safe for the time.

The battles of Corinth and Hatchie Bridge ended the fighting for Missouri troops during 1862. In February 1863 they encamped near what had been the attractive little city of Grand Gulf, the southern outpost of Vicksburg. Here the monotony of camp life was broken by occasional forays west of the Mississippi River and by action at Oxford and Grenada northeast of Vicksburg.

Lieutenant Catron and his men were with the Missourians who fought with conspicuous valor in a series of battles in May leading to the siege of Vicksburg. Port Gibson was followed by Baker's Creek, Champion Hill, and Big Black River Bridge. Valor was not enough, and the Confederate forces were compelled to make a final stand at Vicksburg.

On the evening of May 18, General Ulysses S. Grant's army appeared in force and drove in the pickets from the outskirts. The weakest spot in the line was a point where the entrenchments, running east from the Mississippi River, intersected Graveyard Road and turned south. The right angle formed by the turn in the line of fortifications could be swept by enemy fire from both sides of the angle. At the point of the angle was a knoll, on the contours of which the Confederates had placed a circular fortification protruding even further into enemy territory. This was known as Stockade Redan Complex.

It was obvious to Grant that this strategic fortification must be subdued if his army were to breach the works. The 1st Missouri Brigade was dispatched to this threatened point, including Lieutenant Catron, in Captain Lowe's battery. The battery had lost its guns at the Black River affair, but had been resupplied. One of the replacements was a 20-pound Parrott rifle known as "Crazy Jane." Just as "Old Sacramento" had been an earlier rallying symbol, "Crazy Jane" now served as the intangible influence.

On May 22, after a terrific four-hour bombardment, Union forces attacked the Vicksburg perimeter with a concentration on Stockade Redan Complex. Heavy losses caused General Grant to issue orders for siege operations to begin.[6]

The last rations — mule meat — were issued on July 2, and all hope of aid from the outside was abandoned. On the 4th, the Confederate forces unconditionally surrendered. Thomas B. Catron, Senior 1st Lieutenant following the wounding of Captain Lowe, was now a Brevet-Captain of Artillery and was paroled on July 9. The surrendered men were quartered at Demopolis, Alabama, and on September 13, 1863, notice was received of the exchange of all prisoners.

Six regiments of infantry and one of dismounted cavalry

were now consolidated into four regiments to be known as the Missouri Brigade. Catron's battery had suffered heavy casualties, so was consolidated with the 3rd Battery Missouri Light Artillery, C.S.A.; Captain William E. Dawson continued in command, with Catron as Senior 1st Lieutenant. Catron assumed command of this battery soon thereafter, and was still in charge at the end of the war.

The extent of losses in Catron's battery before the consolidation are not known, but in three other batteries consolidated into one, there were only 60 men left of the original 375. The whole brigade numbered little more than 2,000 — all that were left of the 8,000 who crossed the Mississippi with General Price.

Lieutenant Catron and his battery were detached from the Missouri Brigade soon after being exchanged and were sent as part of a detachment to reinforce General Braxton Bragg in north Georgia. It is difficult to follow his career at this juncture. One comrade later lamented that, because they became a detached unit, they did not get as much credit as some of the other artillery outfits in the Missouri Brigade. He opined that they should have at least been given credit for what they did do! "We done as much running as any of them."[7]

Lieutenant Catron was in the battle of Chattanooga in November 1863 and rejoined the Missouri Brigade later that year. In January 1864 the Brigade was transferred to Mobile because of a reported mutiny of troops, which proved to be more imaginary than real. In April the Missourians returned to their old camp at Demopolis, but Catron remained in the Mobile area until the end of the war. In the spring of 1864 he was with an expedition into Louisiana and saw action at Kelley's Crossroads. But more important events were shaping up for the war in Alabama.

Mobile, basking like a crocodile on its low and sandy stretch of seacoast, had long been an objective of the Union strategists. By the summer of 1864 it was the only part of the gulf available to blockade runners, and Admiral David Glasgow Farragut prepared to seal this last Confederate bastion of ocean intercourse.

Mobile stands at the head of Mobile Bay, where two low-lying sand points, guarded by Fort Morgan, defended its main entrance. Forts Powell and Gaines protected shallow inlets to the west, but were too distant to be effective in safeguarding the main entrance. Catron was at Fort Morgan. The intrepid Farragut forced a passage past the defenders there, but at the cost of terrible toll of life from the batteries of the fort. On August 23 the obstinate defenders at Fort Morgan, beaten down by a heavy bombardment, were forced to surrender, but not until the guns were spiked, the stores destroyed, and part of the garrison evacuated. Among those who escaped were Lieutenant Catron and his 3d Missouri Battery.

Mobile was no longer strategically important and consequently was unmolested by General Grant until the following spring. In February 1865 the Missouri Brigade was again ordered to Mobile, where it was subsequently rejoined by Catron. Some exchanged prisoners were added to the brigade, bringing its strength to about 400 men. This fragment of the 8,000 who had proudly crossed the Mississippi under General Price were attached to the army of General D. H. Maury, who commanded the Confederate forces at Mobile. Maury, heavily outnumbered, occupied Spanish Fort and Fort Blakely. Here he waited. The noble Missouri Brigade, characterized by General Maury as "the survivors of more than twenty battles, and the finest troops I have ever seen."[8] was stationed at Fort Blakely. Catron was with the garrison at Spanish Fort. The bombardment and assault of these forts from April 9 to 11 resulted in the capture of Mobile.

Spanish Fort fell first, and Lieutenant Catron was among the handful who escaped capture and joined their comrades at Fort Blakely. The Missouri Brigade was so weak in numbers, and the line of their defense so long that it was necessary to deploy men ten yards apart. Against such odds no defense could stand, no matter how stout of heart. Finally the attackers forced their way into the entrenchments; the Missourians were cut off and took to the water. By wading and swimming 150 brave men reached Mobile — the remnant of General Price's once formidable army. When the lost and wounded were assembled, fewer than 800 finally returned to Missouri.

After a last pitiful effort to regroup, the remaining defenders of Mobile retreated wearily to Meridian, Mississippi, 130 long miles away. Here at last, on May 4, 1865, the road of war was ended with the surrender of all Confederate armies east of the Mississippi River.

"Thos. B. Catron, 1st Lt. Comdg. 3rd Mo. Battery,"[9] was paroled May 10, 1865, having survived odds of ten to one. He was now a young man of 24 years; he was five feet nine inches tall, with blue eyes, light hair, and a fair complexion. He listed his occupation as farmer, but he had no farm and could hardly have suspected that one day he would own some two million acres of land.

He was soon to cast his lot with the rough give and take of a raw frontier, for which his military training had fitted him well. Many of his contemporaries had been through the same violent training; it gave rise to a hard and unrelenting way of life among the group who pushed westward after the war. Catron was later to say, "Nobody has any friends out here. Every one looks out for himself."[10]

How strong the influence of the rigorous crucible of war was on him no one can say, but perhaps the experiences of his war years helped to mold the tough exterior that he presented to public view in later years. One conclusion can be drawn — he was never one to back away from a contest of wills or a marshalling of power to gain an objective.

3
New Mexico Newcomer

A week after Lieutenant Catron's parole, he reported and registered at New Orleans. From there he proceeded to the parole camp at Demopolis, Alabama, where he encountered his cousin, William J. Catron. The latter had enlisted as a private in Hiram Bledsoe's battery only a few days prior to the battle of Lexington, probably at the suggestion of his cousin, Tom, who was already in the outfit.[1]

William J. Catron was four years older than Tom. During the 1850s he made three trips from Lexington to Santa Fe in the employ of the freighting firm of Russell, Majors, and Waddell; his accounts of the opportunities available in New Mexico aroused Tom's interest. In their discussions at Demopolis, Tom may have been strengthened in his resolve to try his luck in New Mexico if, indeed, it was not here that the "yen" was acquired.[2]

William J. Catron remained at Demopolis until the spring of 1866, but Tom tarried there only a brief while before returning to his home. Here, with books borrowed from a Lexington attorney, he devoted nearly a year to the study of law. Even while engrossed in this study, he must have known that he could not pursue a legal career in Missouri. Soon after the close of the Civil War, Missouri passed a statute prohibiting anyone who had borne arms against the Union from practicing law, teaching school, or preaching in the state.

It was at this point that Stephen B. Elkins entered into Catron's decision to move to New Mexico. By November 1863 Elkins was located there. Later that year he was admitted to the bar and established a law practice at Mesilla.* He also served as district attorney for the third judicial district. In 1864 he was elected to the House of Representatives of the Territorial legislature from Doña Ana County, which brought him to Santa Fe. By July 1865 he had moved to that city to establish a law practice in all the courts of law and equity in the Territory.

During this time he corresponded with his betrothed in Wellington, Missouri; then, about the middle of April 1866, he departed for the States to be married. On June 5, 1866, he married the talented and well-educated Sarah Jacobs. They started immediately across the plains for Santa Fe. Thomas B. Catron was in the same wagon train.† Oral tradition indicates that on their journey Catron and Elkins mutually resolved to seek a seat in the United States Senate.

Catron was now twenty-six years old and girded with the confidence inspired by four years of war. He had studied law

* Elkins was not immediately permitted to plead cases before the Supreme Court. *Santa Fe Weekly New Mexican,* February 13, 1864, lists Supreme Court lawyers as John S. Watts, G. D. Wheaton, Merrill Ashurst, R. H. Tompkins, C. P. Clever, and J. Houghton.

† *Santa Fe Weekly New Mexican,* July 28, 1866, November 5, 1872; Oscar Doane Lambert, *Stephen Benton Elkins,* 30, says Elkins and Miss Jacobs were married June 10. John Paul Wooden, *Thomas Benton Catron,* says: "William A. Keleher in *Maxwell Land Grant,* p. 152, claims Catron and Elkins came to New Mexico together after Elkins had returned to Missouri on a visit. . . . It would seem that this is simply another of Mr. Keleher's 'good stories.'" This statement is in a footnote, and Wooden does not explain the reason for his deduction. Wooden was as presumptuous here as he was in writing his entire thesis, where it is obvious that he used little material other than that found in two earlier theses on the life of Catron. These are by Vioalle Clark Hefferan and Mary Elizabeth Sluga. Only 16 percent of the 367 footnotes in the Wooden thesis are not to be found in exact (or very similar) form in the Hefferan or Sluga theses, and Wooden's content is entirely similar (and often identical) to that of Hefferan or Sluga. Yet Wooden is disparaging in his analysis of the earlier works from which he copied so liberally.

for nearly a year, but also had more tangible assets. His father had amassed a competence by combining farming with a lucrative business as a mason-contractor; he presented his son with two prairie schooners, each drawn by eight mules. The wagons were loaded with flour which he was able to sell for ten dollars a sack when he arrived in Santa Fe.

Before leaving Missouri, Catron purchased a Spanish grammar which he studied at night by the light of campfires and as he drove his mules during the journey. He was also tutored by Elkins, who had already mastered the language. He studied diligently and had some mastery of the language of his adopted homeland by the time he reached Santa Fe.

This endeavor made sense for one who aspired to power and wealth as Catron did. Spanish was more often than not the language of the law courts, the market place, and the home. To cultivate worthwhile acquaintances and inspire their confidence, it was necessary that he learn Spanish well.

One of Catron's most vivid recollections of the journey was that of an enormous herd of buffalos that they encountered. The train traveled about twenty-two miles a day and took three days to pass through the herd. The animals traveled in bunches of from fifty to a thousand, with spaces between, and could be observed as far as the eye could see. Periodically it was necessary to meet bunches approaching the wagons and to head them off by firing rifles and pistols. At night the wagons were corralled, the mules placed inside the enclosure, and a heavily armed guard placed upon the surrounding prairie to prevent night-traveling buffalos from trampling the train. As they finally left the herd, it stretched out for sixty miles along the Arkansas River. Catron reported, "The whole earth seemed to contain nothing but buffalos, and a very little wagon train drawn by frightened and snorting mules."[3]

Catron arrived in Santa Fe July 27, 1866.* No record is

---

* This is the commonly accepted date of his arrival, although he is reported to have said he arrived early in August (*Washington Herald,* September 6, 1914, Catron scrapbook). Another source indicates the date may have been as early as July 23 (*Santa Fe Weekly New Mexican,* July 28, 1866).

available of his early impressions, but it is reasonable to assume that he quickly noted the political situation in New Mexico. It has been concluded that Catron was opportunistic and decided to join the Republicans because of their party strength in New Mexico. It is said that he told Tom Boggs: "Tom, when I came to New Mexico the Republicans were in power. It seemed to me they were likely to remain in power for a good many years. The only thing left was for me to join them and run them the way I think they ought to be run, and that's what I'm doing."[4]

The explanation is not that simple. His father, a staunch Democrat, was active politically, although he would never consent to hold office. Political issues were sensibly discussed in the Catron home, and the tariff question was not neglected. Thomas early became a protectionist. He had studied economics along with law, which strengthened his protectionist leanings and, along with his perusal of the law, brought him to the decision to leave the political faith of his father. He would become a Republican despite the knowledge that that party had so changed the state organic law as to drive him out of Missouri where he was born.[5]

There was no Republican party as such in New Mexico when Catron arrived there. As a matter of fact, there was no organization, or attempt to organize the Republican party, until the winter of 1867. Prior to the Civil War, New Mexicans were inclined to sympathize with the South against the North in questions emanating from the institution of slavery. Their commercial relations were chiefly with Southereners; army officers arriving in the Territory were mostly from the South, and appointed Territorial officials were mostly Southern sympathizers. The masses were controlled politically by a few leaders who fancied themselves Democrats and who had no admiration for Republicans or Abolitionists. Yet the leading attitude toward national politics was apathy, with only slight favoring of Southern views on general principles. A stronger peculiarity was distrust of Texans.

The Civil War invasion of New Mexico from Texas outweighed Southern susceptibilities, and New Mexicans stood with the North. Energetic Northern leadership was provided during and following the war, resulting eventually in Republican control of New Mexico politics. That ascendancy was not complete until 1873, with the election of a predominantly Republican legislature.[6]

Prior to 1867, political parties were known by the names of their leaders; typically, Gallegos party, Perea party, or Chavez party. In the campaign of 1867, J. Francisco Chavez ran against Charles P. Clever for Territorial delegate to the United States Congress. Chavez adherents claimed that the party supporting him was the Republican party and that Chavez was a Republican and Clever a Democrat. Still, neither candidate ran as a Republican or a Democrat.

That winter William Breeden invited a few prominent Republicans to a conference, and the result was the formation of the Republican Association of the Territory of New Mexico. This group became a power in politics and led the movement toward organization of the Republican party. The convention of 1869 was the first Republican convention in New Mexico. This convention adopted a straight Republican platform, and again nominated Chavez to run for delegate.[7]

Thus it can be said that William Breeden was the father of the Republican party in New Mexico. To that extent he was also the first leader of the party but was not particularly forceful in his leadership, preferring to work behind the scenes as the perennial chairman of the Republican party. In this formative period no one person dominated Republican leadership. While Breeden was regarded by many as the shrewdest politician and ablest lawyer in New Mexico, the way was open for more forceful personalities to lead in particular exigencies as they arose.

The most important political association for both Elkins and Catron in New Mexico was with William Breeden. Each showed willingness and ability to assume party responsibilities as they matured in political wisdom and experience, and

Breeden encouraged them to fill the voids left in political leadership by his tendency to remain in the background. Elkins especially responded to this encouragement. He arrived in New Mexico earlier than Catron and, to a larger degree, got in on the ground floor of the crucial period following the Civil War. Beyond that, he possessed a more natural flair for political leadership. He was diplomatic, while Catron inclined more to blunt frankness. Where Catron would say no, Elkins would say maybe. Edgar A. Walz, Catron's brother-in-law, made this comparison:

> I have often while in New Mexico heard it said that if one asked Mr. Elkins for a favor, he would shake you by the hand, smile on you, pat you on the back and ask you to come again, but he would never grant your wish; that if you asked Catron for a favor, he would bluster, take your head nearly off, but give you what you asked for if it was a reasonable request.[8]

To a remarkable degree Catron's political career followed that of Elkins, who started his law practice at Mesilla and was elected to the Territorial House of Representatives from Doña Ana County. He served as district attorney for the third judicial district, attorney general (only briefly), United States attorney, Territorial delegate to Congress, and United States senator. Catron followed Elkins in each of these political attainments. Only in one particular did their political careers differ materially. Elkins became secretary of war in a national administration, while Catron served numerous terms in the Territorial Council. Each was, upon occasion, a reluctant candidate to political office, and both were more interested in land and wealth than politics. While both enjoyed politics, the political career of each was motivated to a degree by the part that politics could play in developing their respective economic empires.

When Thomas B. Catron arrived in Santa Fe and had disposed of his wagons, teams, and flour, he learned that Merrill Ashurst, a Santa Fe attorney, had been ill for some time and was in need of assistance in his law office. Ashurst was born in

Alabama and had come to Santa Fe in 1851, where he served
as attorney general from 1852 to 1854. He was a convincing
orator, a successful prosecutor, and a man of unusual ability.
While he was not of Catron's newly formed political persuasion, he did offer a job, and Catron came into his employ
soon after arriving in Santa Fe. While in Ashurst's service he
also worked briefly for Kirby Benedict as a scrivener.

Benedict had just been succeeded by John P. Slough as
Territorial chief justice. Benedict had been a candidate for
reappointment and did not take kindly to removal from the
office that he had held for thirteen years. He had just started
to practice law in Santa Fe; however he was handicapped by
a Bowie knife wound in his right hand and so was obliged to
rely on others to write for him. From Benedict, Catron learned
much of the background and tradition of New Mexico as well
as of the people and laws of the Territory.

As Catron went about his legal tasks it became evident
that he needed to perfect a better working knowledge of
Spanish. Accordingly, in the fall of 1866 (probably in September) he left his employment in Santa Fe and took up residence
with the family of Elias Clark at Alcalde in Rio Arriba County.
Clark, the proprietor of a store, was the only member of his
family who spoke English. Catron was called upon to communicate in Spanish and rapidly improved himself in the
language.

It would be interesting to learn whether this crash course
in Spanish was undertaken with the foreknowledge that it
would lead to political appointment. The record in this regard
is not clear, but the timing was such as to indicate that there
might have been a reward waiting for him if he learned his
lessons well. He was soon to be appointed district attorney for
the third judicial district, but the circumstances of this
appointment need explaining.

Governor Robert B. Mitchell had been inaugurated
about the time that Catron arrived in Santa Fe. Less than a
month later Mitchell departed on a tour inspecting mineral

resources in the Territory. Armed with information gleaned on this trip, he departed for the East on November 12, 1866. His purpose was to advertise New Mexico's resources to prospective immigrants. He left shortly before the convening of the Territorial legislature and did not return until March 1, 1867. Mitchell authorized W. F. M. Arny, secretary of the Territory, to act both as secretary and governor while he was away.

With Governor Mitchell's departure on the inspection tour only weeks after Catron's arrival in Santa Fe, there was little time for them to arrive at an understanding about a political appointment. The fact is Catron was appointed district attorney for the third judicial district by Acting Governor Arny. Mitchell, however, may have approved Catron's appointment before he went East. Among Arny's other appointments was that of Stephen B. Elkins for attorney general, to replace Charles P. Clever who had resigned in expectation of being seated as Territorial delegate to Congress. These appointments were confirmed by the Territorial Council on December 14, 1866.[9] The House of Representatives did not view Catron's appointment as favorably as the Council did; it passed a resolution protesting his confirmation because he had been an officer in the Confederate army in the late rebellion.

Soon after his confirmation, Catron departed for Mesilla to be gone for two years, during which time there were repercussions involving the Arny appointments. Early in January 1867, Clever was admitted to his seat as delegate to Congress from New Mexico, although his opponent, the incumbent J. Francisco Chavez, had contested the election as being fraudulent and was continuing his effort to replace Clever as delegate-elect. Chavez, after a long and bitter contest, prevailed.

When Governor Mitchell returned to Santa Fe on March 1, 1867, he made known his intention of canceling some of the appointments made by Acting Governor Arny. Mitchell informed Elkins of his intention to cancel his appointment as attorney general and replace him with Clever. Mitchell had, however, secured for Elkins the post of United States attorney. Elkins had already been confirmed as attorney general and questioned Mitchell's right to make the change. He was tactful in his protest, however, and ultimately accepted the office of United States attorney.

It would seem that Mitchell, in replacing Elkins with Clever as attorney general, was protecting Clever, since there was doubt that he would prevail as delegate. A further complication arose when Merrill Ashurst was defeated by R. M. Stephens as representative to the Territorial legislature, and later replaced Clever as attorney general.

Throughout this political infighting, Catron was able to maintain a middle ground, and his appointment was not questioned by Governor Mitchell. However, Catron was later to be involved in successive controversies that continued almost without respite for the remainder of his life.

He did enjoy relative tranquility while serving as district attorney for the third judicial district at Mesilla. Here he was not admitted to the bar until June 15, 1867, although he could and did appear as attorney in the probate court before his admission. His first case was pleading in broken Spanish a cause for which he received a fee of ten dollars.

At Mesilla he was introduced to the grimy details of the manner in which legal business was carried on, but he did not become an insider. For example, when a wealthy citizen died, it was a case of "all come to the feast." Carpenters would get $30 for a casket taking at most two days to build when wages were a dollar or two a day. Doctors would be paid $150 to certify that a person had died, although they might not have treated that person when he was alive. Clerks of the court might get $200 for recording the transaction. Attorneys in good standing with the probate judge figured a bill and multiplied it by ten or more. Not so Catron. He was said to have become executor of those estates which paid less than twenty cents on the dollar.[10]

While at Mesilla, Catron renewed his active participation in Masonry; he became secretary of the Aztec Lodge at nearby Las Cruces. He had become a Mason during the Civil War while on duty at Mobile, Alabama.

In the fall of 1868, Catron was elected to the House of Representatives for the 18th assembly, which was to meet in Santa Fe from December 7 of that year until February 4, 1869. There was some opposition by the Territorial press to his election. The *Santa Fe Gazette* alleged that he had been a Democrat and had opposed J. Francisco Chavez for delegate to Congress in the preceding election. The *Santa Fe Weekly New Mexican* denied this allegation and maintained that he stood solidly with the Republican party.

While Catron was meeting with the legislature in Santa Fe early in 1869, Attorney General Ashurst, who had been ill for some time, was forced to resign. He would die within the year of cancer.[11] Catron's association with Ashurst, his first employer in Santa Fe, had been brief, but there is no indication that it was other than pleasant. Ashurst nominated Catron for admission to practice law in the New Mexico Supreme Court, effective January 13, 1869.

When Ashurst resigned, upon recommendation of Elkins, Catron was nominated attorney general by Governor Mitchell. The nomination was confirmed by the Council on January 12, 1869, and Mitchell signed his commission (effective February 7, 1869) the following day. Catron was hailed as a young lawyer of much promise, and every confidence was expressed that his appointment would result in universal satisfaction.

Catron did not return to Mesilla to live. On February 8 he assumed the duties of attorney general and prepared to start a law practice in Santa Fe. On March 13, as was the custom in those days, he announced through the local newspapers that he would practice in all the courts of law and equity in the Territory and give special attention to the collection of claims.

It was standard practice in that era for persons holding Territorial or federal offices to practice law. As attorney general, Catron was required to have his office and his residence in Santa Fe, the seat of the Territorial government. He also acted as district attorney for the first judicial district, headquarters of which were in Santa Fe.

In the New Mexico of that day, the offices of United States attorney and attorney general were of considerable importance. The former presented cases involving federal statutes to the grand jury and tried them before the petit jury. The district attorney in each of three districts presented Territorial cases to the same grand jury and tried them before the same petit jury. But the attorney general acted as district attorney for the first judicial district which, at that time, included the counties of Santa Fe, San Miguel, Santa Aña, Mora, Taos, Rio Arriba, and Colfax. In addition it was the duty of the attorney general, when requested, to give his opinion to the legislature, secretary of the Territory, governor, auditor, treasurer, or any district attorney, upon any question of law relating to their respective duties or offices. Each of the three district judges sat in cases within their district involving both Territorial and federal laws. The three district judges made up the Supreme Court, with the judge of the first district being the chief justice.[12]

Early in April 1870, during the administration of Governor William A. Pile, Attorney General Catron played a prominent role in a drama that came to be known as "The Battle of the Archives." Other leading characters were Governor Pile and his appointee as Territorial librarian, Ira M. Bond.

The curtain opened when Catron needed additional space for his office as attorney general and consulted with Bond concerning a room in the library located in the Palace of the Governors. The immediate drawback was that the room was packed with old papers and documents. Governor Pile was consulted; he instructed Bond to preserve such papers as were valuable and to store the remainder in an adjoining room. Bond complied with these instructions, after consulting with local authorities as to which papers were valuable. It would seem that these authorities did not have an adequate sense of historical values. Bond later disposed of the papers declared not valuable. When this disposal became publicly known, there were loud and angry outcries that Bond had sold or given away many valuable papers and documents. Bond attempted to straddle the fence in the resulting furor. First he claimed that the documents sold were without value, then maintained that they had been returned. Finally he advertised for the return of the papers, claiming that they had been removed by mistake as to their value.

Opponents of Governor Pile's administration gleefully seized upon this misadventure and tried to force his resignation. Charges of unlawful destruction of archives by Bond formed the basis for their attacks, but they made other accusations as well. Among these was the imputation that Pile had retained Catron as attorney general, well knowing that he was an unreconstructed Rebel. Governor Pile defended Catron without reservation. He explained that, since the war, his attorney general had supported the reconstructionists in the government and had acted uniformly with the Republican party. Pile claimed that in the discharge of his duties, Catron had been able, faithful, and efficient. Moreover, he was in office when Pile came to New Mexico and had been recommended by Delegate J. Francisco Chavez, United States Attorney Elkins, and Chief Justice Joseph G. Palen.

Governor Pile was also accused of bargaining with New Mexico Democrats to gain their support, whereby he would be selected for a seat in the United States Senate if New Mexico were granted statehood.* Pile, it was claimed, had agreed to split state offices with the Democrats in return for

---

* The statehood movement at this time contemplated New Mexico being admitted to the Union as the State of Lincoln. *Santa Fe Weekly New Mexican,* July 5, 1870.

their support. Attorney General Catron was charged with entering into this conspiracy by conniving with political leaders at a recent Republican Territorial convention.

Both Pile and Catron denied these charges. Whether true or not, Catron was gaining political experience and finding that it was impossible to remain completely aloof from the entangling web of New Mexico politics. Still, all available records indicate that the first half decade of Catron's political career in New Mexico was relatively free from the storms of bitter controversy that characterized most of his adult life.

Catron was now five years removed from the rigors of the Civil War and was already taking on the body weight and rotundity that stayed with him for the rest of his life, despite repeated efforts to lose weight and slim his figure. As a contemporary put it, he now looked the gentleman and had, to a degree, "the air and suavity of a Frenchman."[13]

4
Building an Empire

The two wagonloads of flour Catron brought to New Mexico sold for ten dollars a sack. With these proceeds and that of the wagons and cargo, perhaps $10,000, he embarked on a career of empire building that witnessed his ultimate ownership of nearly as much land as in the states of Delaware and Rhode Island combined. While land was cheap in money-hungry New Mexico when Catron arrived there, his assets were sufficient to acquire no more than one percent of what he ultimately owned.

He early turned to another method of increasing his financial resources before dealing in the land grants that were later to form the bulk of his holdings. During the last days of 1866, while in Mesilla as district attorney for the third judicial district, his commercial activities were not extensive, nor did he acquire property there.* He did, however, loan money to a Mr. Goldbaum, who had the beef contract at Fort Bayard. Goldbaum's contract was annulled, and Catron took over the 170 head of cattle that had been pledged as security

---

* Interview, Adlai Feather, October 18, 1964. Catron paid no income tax for 1867 or 1868, while Elkins paid $3,134.40 for 1867, and $3,400.00 for 1868. *Santa Fe Weekly New Mexican,* July 21, 1868, and May 25, 1869.

for the loan. He then offered them for sale to the military at a lesser price than that called for in Goldbaum's contract.*

This transaction set a pattern that was to prevail throughout Catron's life. The standard interest rate for that day was 12 percent per annum, and often higher if the loan was badly enough needed. It is likely that Catron would have preferred the interest on the loan rather than the cattle, but he had to take the cattle and was faced with the problem of their disposal. Significantly, he was forced into secondary maneuvering to recover his money. During his lifetime he never ceased to make loans for which he was often obliged to take collateral in repayment. Frequently this collateral was potentially of more value than the money loaned but had to be disposed of to realize that value. He sought land, and few if any persons who ever lived in the United States acquired more; nevertheless, this was a mixed blessing because he constantly had to take even more to protect what he already had. As his empire grew, disposal of property in exchange for cash created tremendous problems which led to the ultimate loss of most of the property he owned.

When the session of the Territorial legislature ended in February 1869, Catron assumed his new duties as attorney general and made Santa Fe his home. Again, Elkins seemed to lead in paths that Catron followed. They early turned their attention to acquiring large amounts of land in New Mexico by dealing in land grants.

In all probability, the subject of land grants is the most controversial of any in New Mexico history. The practice of land accumulation had begun before New Mexico came under United States' control[1] and was continued during the years prior to the Civil War. The need for protection on the frontier was great, and an extensive amount of inexpensive

---

* Thomas B. Catron to Colonel Charles McClure, April 22, 1867 (N.A. Consolidated Correspondence File). There is no record of whether the offer was accepted.

land was available. Large grants therefore were made to encourage brave and hardy pioneers to thinly settle the periphery of the principal settlements as a buffer against the marauding of nomadic Indians. These grants were made initially to persons of Spanish ancestry and later to the earliest Yankee newcomers. Some recipients were Henry Connelly, Eathan W. Eaton, Preston Beck, Jr., and Hugh M. Stephenson. Among the purchasers of land grants before the Civil War, the names of Lucien B. Maxwell and Elias Brevoort stand out.

The Treaty of Guadalupe Hidalgo of 1848 guaranteed property rights of former Mexican citizens. Land held by them was of two classes. Most of the 80,000 people who became citizens of the United States upon the annexation of New Mexico were relatively poor, their chief claim to affluence being limited to a small strip of irrigated land along some river or stream. It was not these meager allotments that were generally sought by speculators; they coveted the large grants made by former Spanish and Mexican governments. New arrivals saw an opportunity for rapid gains, and life in the Territory became centered around traffic in these grants.

The process by which the United States would guarantee title to former Mexican citizens was, in theory, relatively simple:

A grant claimant was required to submit his evidence of title to the surveyor general, who held hearings to determine the validity of the claim and then submitted his findings and recommendations to Congress, which body was responsible for the rendering of a final decision. In practice, this was not so simple, since from the first, numerous claimants suspiciously refused to submit their evidence of title. They believed (in many cases so informed by designing persons) that such action would not secure their titles and could lead to unnecessary labor and expense.[2]

Yankee newcomers sometimes took advantage of this situation. Their practice was to exaggerate the complexity of the confirmation process and then offer to serve as attorneys to guide the claims through the intricacies involved. In the absence of cash, land was usually the payment for such services. Most native inhabitants had little understanding of the relative value of this land, so fees frequently were high. Besides this practice, a surprisingly large number of grant interests were bought and sold, almost invariably for small amounts until the middle 1870s, when the proper value of land came to be more widely known.

But it was not the number of grants involved or the traffic in them that was the greatest evil to New Mexico. Rather, it was the enlargement of existing grants. This view was stated clearly by Wilbur F. Stone, associate justice of the Court of Private Land Claims:

> A number of grants have had their boundaries stretched and areas marvelously expanded. But this has been done mostly by Yankee and English purchasers and not by the original Mexican owners. Where boundaries were made by natural landmarks, such as a "white rock," a "red hill," or a "lone tree," another rock, hill, or tree of like description could always be found a league or two farther off, and claimed to be the original landmark described in the grant documents. Thus it has been found — unofficially — by the court that, in the unparalleled climate and under the generous sun of the Rocky Mountains, not only does vegetation thrive and grow to enormous size by irrigation, but that land grants themselves grow immensely — without irrigation.[3]

An amusing instance of the uncertainty of land grant boundaries was a case, being argued for final adjudication, of a grant in the narrow valley of Santa Fe Creek in the mountains above the city. The width extended from the bed of the stream to the *faldas* of the mountains on either side. A *falda* in Spanish means primarily a skirt, as the skirt of a woman's dress. The delicate question of just where the skirt of a mountain is worn was argued for all one day.

Catron, attorney for the claimants, insisted that

> the faldas should be held to be up about timber line, so as to include all of the valuable timber. Hon. W. H. Pope, the assistant United States attorney, contended that such elevation of the faldas was a highly improper interpretation, since it would fix the bottom of the said faldas so high above the foot as to expose the trunks and limbs of the trees,

after the fashion of the knee-plus-ultra skirts of a ballet dancer — a
meaning never intended by the pious Mexicans; that the setting sun
would blush upon such immodest mountains; but that, on the contrary,
the term should be construed to bring the skirts down to the trails of the
foothills, after the style of the decorous ladies who assist the street
sweepers in gathering up microbes from the sidewalk.[4]

The court, after thoughtful consideration, decided that
a falda comparable to the average bicycle skirt was about
proper for mountain use, and decreed the boundary to be a
little above the foot of the slopes, about the region of the calf
pastures, at the line of possible irrigation.

Uncertainty of land titles and boundaries became a detriment to the economy of New Mexico. Prospective settlers
soon learned that Spanish and Mexican grants of land covered
most of the arable areas upon which settlement was possible
without serious danger from Indian attack. In California
private claims were settled soon after American occupation,
but in New Mexico only 48 of 212 claims submitted were
confirmed prior to the adjudications of the Court of Private
Land Claims, 1891–1904. Of this number only 22 were
patented and 8 rejected outright. This left nearly 35,000,000
acres of land (nearly half the total in the Territory) privately
claimed with consequent unsettled titles.

Federal land laws decreed that any claims be reserved from settlement and public disposal until they were adjudicated by the Federal
Government. As a consequence, settlers could never be certain that they
were not settling on land claimed, or that might later be claimed, as a
private grant. This situation was widely known throughout the nation
and resulted in a "deep and acknowledged distrust of land titles in New
Mexico . . ." that retarded immigration and the rapid settlement of the
Territory. Likewise, owners of valid claims could realize only depreci-
ated prices on their property.[5]

Before the work of the land court, it was commonly
believed that many of the grants were illegal, forged, or
fraudulent, and that the court would so find. To the contrary,
the court found that the notorious Peralta Grant involving
James Addison Reavis was the only one of that description.

Despite this plain finding by the court, even today it is widely presumed that there was much fraud in grant titles.

How, then, was it that the Court of Private Land Claims validated only 1,934,986 acres of claims out of the 34,653,340 acres submitted for adjudication? The answer lies, to a large extent, in the aforementioned stretching of boundaries. Beyond that, a number of grants were made by officials without proper authority to do so, although the grants were made in good faith:

> Under such conditions many grants, made perhaps a century before the court was established, had existed with titles undisputed by the people and by the Government under which they were granted, and in strict equity were justly entitled to be held good, but had to be rejected by the court under the limiting provisions of the statute creating the court, which required proof of strict legal authority in the granting powers, and a rigid compliance with law in the form and manner of its execution.[6]

Most persons who concern themselves with the history of land grants in New Mexico lay undue stress on purported fraudulent manipulations of persons who dealt in these grants. The record should be set straight. To repeat, the Court of Private Land Claims did not find fraud in grant titles. It did, however, detect extensive stretching of grant boundaries. Reprehensible as this practice was, the far greater crime was that of the United States Congress in allowing grant titles to remain for so long in an unsettled condition, thus inviting the practice of enlarging grants. The repeated plea, in official reports, of virtually every concerned public servant in the Territory (and in Washington) for many years bears testimony that this was a disturbing state of affairs to New Mexicans.

It is claimed that Catron caused titles to be fraudulently created, yet the Court of Private Land Claims found no evidence of this practice — and there seems to be virtually universal lack of complaint with the work of that body. As any intelligent person would, who desired that his title not be questioned, Catron seems to have scrutinized carefully and successfully the strength of titles to land in which he acquired interests. This assertion is validated by examination of the grants in which Catron had an interest, or owned outright, titles to which were settled by the Court of Private Land Claims. As nearly as can be ascertained, these were thirteen in number, with a total of 1,602,922.16 acres claimed. The court validated twelve of these for 317,085.29 acres. The Estancia Grant of 415,036 acres was the only one totally rejected.

Elkins and Catron first turned their attention to the Mora Grant. On September 28, 1835, there was granted to seventy-six citizens of the Republic of Mexico a tract of land known as the Town of Mora Grant. Title to the land was held jointly and in undivided interests, a customary practice that made it impossible for later purchasers to give title to any specific portion of a grant without first acquiring title to the entire grant. The petitioners were known as José Tapia et al., and on October 20 of that year the grantees were duly and lawfully placed in possession of the land.

On June 20, 1859, a request for confirmation of the grant was filed with the surveyor general of New Mexico; on July 1, he approved the claim and recommended its confirmation by Congress. On July 21, 1860, the grant was confirmed as recommended by the surveyor general, and in July of the following year he entered into a contract with Deputy Surveyor Thomas Means for the survey of the claim.

The settlements flourished, and by 1860 a thousand settlers lived within the boundaries of the grant. The culture there was traditional: the settlers lived in villages and farmed a small tract nearby. In most rural communities in New Mexico, the raising of sheep and goats was at least as important as the raising of crops, but there was more emphasis in these settlements on grains and fruits. The Santa Fe Trail passed through the grant, and Fort Union was within its confines. The native farmers found a ready sale for their products at the fort. This establishment needed supplies for more than its own use because here was located a supply center for other military posts in the Southwest. It also supplied provisions for caravans passing over the Santa Fe Trail. Mora, destroyed in the revolution of 1847, was rebuilt following the establishment of Fort Union in 1852. To serve the officers and men at the fort, there were the usual saloons, dance halls, and houses of prostitution of a typical frontier community.

The value of the grant became apparent to many residents of New Mexico. Among these was Elkins, who late in the 1860s was called upon to represent a Mora Grant resident in a criminal case. In payment of his fee he received a deed to part of his client's undivided interest in the grant. With this as a start, he acquired additional interests by purchase. Catron joined him in these purchases.

By November 18, 1870, they acquired sixteen interests in the grant, all in the name of Elkins. They then entered into a contract with Samuel S. Smoot, land speculator, and E. N. Darling, United States surveyor. Catron prepared the contract in which parties agreed to purchase all of the grant from the heirs and assigns of the original seventy-six grantees. Provision was made for the signature of a fifth party, Surveyor General T. Rush Spencer. In return for a one-fifth share in the venture, Spencer agreed to assume the responsibility of selling the grant to Eastern parties. Spencer not only failed to sell the grant but also did not sign the contract until two days before he died on June 19, 1872.[7]

Spencer's failure to sign the contract became a factor in later lengthy litigation. Speculation arose that this oversight was because of his official position as surveyor general. He had approved the original survey and, on July 1, 1871, transmitted to the General Land Office in Washington a petition for patent by the claimants of the grant. Attorneys for the claimants were Elkins and Catron. On July 24, Commissioner Willis Drummond informed Spencer that he had examined the application and saw no immediate reason why it should not be approved. But a controversy had been underway for several years as to the validity of the original survey; consequently, the patent was not immediately issued.

On December 5, 1871, Smoot contracted to sell a one-sixth share in the venture to William Blackmore, an English speculator then engaged in acquiring land in New Mexico. Smoot agreed to receive $5,000, with $1,000 on account and the balance in sixty days.

In this negotiation with Blackmore, Smoot violated his agreement with his associates to purchase and sell the grant jointly and in its entirety.[8] Furthermore, his promise to deliver not less than 138,000 acres was impossible. Catron and his associates had been able to purchase only part of the interest in the grant, and Smoot's portion was one-fifth of the total purchased. More important, Smoot owned none of the grant in his own name, since all of the purchases were held undivided in Elkins' name.

Since Elkins and Catron had supplied the interests in the grant that they purchased earlier, it was agreed that Smoot and Darling should furnish the money for additional aquisitions. Coincidentally or otherwise, the $5,000 they pledged was the identical amount named in Smoot's agreement with Blackmore.

The plan followed in making these purchases, made entirely by Catron at his own expense and on his own time, was to allow the various grantees and their descendants from whom the purchases were made to retain their home and a small amount of land for a garden and farm. Prices paid ranged from $6 to $300 per interest, tending toward the smaller amount. Catron later declared that he paid an average of less than $100 for each interest that he purchased.[9]

Catron has been accused of immoral, if not illegal, practices in connection with land grants that he acquired. It is said that in the Mora Grant dealings he told grantees it would be necessary to deed all land (except that actually being cultivated) to him in order to arrange proper partition of lands. There was then, it is claimed, a contract drawn up promising that, with the exception of land to go to Catron as fee, all land would be returned to the grantees. This contract was not notarized and, therefore, inadmissible as evidence. While lack of notarization would not have affected admissibility, it is further claimed that land was never returned to the owners and, since the contracts were void, they could not get it back. It has been said that copies of the contracts as well as the deeds bearing witness to the practice are in existence, but none have been presented for examination.

There is one document at hand bearing vaguely on the type of transaction in question. In 1903, Marcelino Martinez addressed a letter to Elkins which referred to a contract dated August 27, 1872, made by Catron as agent of Elkins, promising a quit-claim deed to 800 *varas* square (roughly, a quarter section) of land. This contract was with Severiano Martinez, who died in 1901. In 1903 his son Marcelino requested the promised deed or, more to the point, wished to have Elkins pay him $600 for the land.[10] The parcel in question was undoubtedly one of those retained by the grantee as a farm, and not the larger surrounding amount that was purchased and held in Elkins' name. There is no record as to whether Elkins and Catron paid Marcelino Martinez the money requested or gave him a deed in lieu thereof.

Another claim is that Catron took advantage of the ignorance of grantees in negotiating purchases and paid only a fraction of what the land was worth. The fact remains that the price paid for the land was consistently low until the middle 1870s, when there came to be a more general appreciation of land values. For example, in 1871 Jesus Lujan sold the Eaton grant of 81,032.67 acres to Nicolas Pino for eighteen dollars cash.[11] Low as it was, this is a fair indication of the price paid for land grants at the time. The price is remarkable, however, because it was evidently for the entire grant. This presents another factor in the prevailing low price, which was that almost all land grant purchases were for undivided interests. Thus they did no one much good unless the entire grant was acquired or the various interests partitioned, which Catron was to do.

By August 15, 1876, when the Mora Grant was patented, the price for which interests could be purchased increased greatly. For example, Catron learned that the interest of Ramon Abreu would cost $4,000, which was generally indicative of the price increases at the time. He reported this price to his associates, who authorized him to make the purchase. Later they refused to reimburse Catron, whereupon he declared that all future purchases by him would be made in his own name. This circumstance, along with the death of Spencer, inclined Catron to the opinion that the partnership was no longer binding except as to lands already purchased. As a consequence, Elkins and Catron were named attorneys to partition, in the name of Elkins, the holdings among the partners. Elkins subsequently was not available in New Mexico, so handling the suit was left entirely to Catron.[12] This partition suit became extremely involved and was attended by much animosity. Catron was repeatedly threatened with violence while attending to the suit. According to oral tradition, he was once compelled to leave Mora disguised in woman's clothing because certain of the townspeople objected to his role in the proceedings.

In 1885 Darling and Smoot conveyed their interests to Benjamin F. Butler. Butler paid only a small amount down and was sued for the balance of the purchase price. Catron also agreed to sell Butler his interests in the original partnership for $70,000, but Butler failed to comply with the contract and Catron regained his interests. During these transactions Butler successfully ignored the interests of Surveyor General Spencer on the ground that he had not sold the grant as agreed. Elkins' interests were acquired by Adelbart Ames.

By the time these transactions ended, about sixteen of the seventy-six interests in the grant remained to be gathered in. Catron owned a fraction over twenty-three interests (about

240,000 acres) while Ames and Butler owned the remaining thirty-seven interests. Butler conveyed his portion of the grant to the Union Land and Grazing Company.

In 1888 Butler tried to get control of the pending partition suit. All of the interests still stood in the name of Elkins. Butler applied for a power of attorney, which Elkins gave to him on the grounds that Butler had purchased all of the interests. This caused a rift between Catron and Elkins. Catron took the position that, while Butler had deeds for the various interests, he had not paid for them and therefore did not own them. Butler succeeded in having O. D. Barrett replace Catron as attorney for the partition suit. In 1890 Butler attempted to sell the interests he claimed, consisting of the unpaid-for interests of Darling, Smoot, and Catron. Darling sued, and Catron continued to press his case in the partition suit. By 1893 Butler had died. His heirs agreed to reinstate Catron as attorney and to pay him the $25,000 he claimed for past services.[13]

Now followed a series of complicated negotiations in which the Butler heirs could not agree, and Adelbart Ames proved to be hardheaded beyond belief. M. S. Baldwin was hired to conduct these negotiations and, if possible, to sell the interests of all. One possible sale fell through because Ames insisted on $250,000 when $200,000 was offered for his interests. He later lowered his price to $150,000. One proposal was to organize all of the interests under the Fort Union Pastoral Company. This suggestion was dropped when Ames insisted that Catron receive one-fifth of the stock, with himself and the Butler heirs retaining the remainder. This was disproportionate to the interests owned, but Ames maintained that the proportion was fair because of the cost of a fence for which Catron had not shared in paying. Catron suggested that the fence be paid for out of first earnings of the company, but Ames was adamant.[14]

In 1895 Catron agreed to take his share of the grant from the portion north of the thirty-sixth parallel, while Ames and the Butler heirs made their selection from south of that line. Baldwin continued in an unsuccessful attempt to sell the entire grant.

As the years passed, it became more difficult to sell the Mora Grant. Squatters encroached on the land, and valuable timber was cut in large quantities by persons with no authority to do so. The partition suit dragged on, and whenever it came to a possible sale of the entire grant, the interested parties could never agree on prices and terms. At one time or another Catron entered into negotiations for the sale of his share for prices as high as three-quarters of a million dollars, but there was always some obstacle standing in the way of a sale. He also unavailingly attempted to obtain various loans as high as $250,000 secured with his interests in the grant. In 1902 he mortgaged the property to Numa Reymond, a Las Cruces merchant, for a loan of $31,720, and experienced difficulty in repaying even this amount.*

In 1909 Catron turned the grant over to his son, Charles, on an option. Charles C. Catron learned that there was a tremendous amount of work involved in clearing up titles to the grant. He also came to grips with the squatter problem and found it not only difficult but dangerous as well. In 1911 Bob Sammon, Catron agent for collection of royalties, was killed. The identity of the murderer was never learned. Charles C. Catron was later informed that he had also been marked for murder, but the conspirators had never been able to get him alone as they had poor old Bob Sammon.[15] Understandably, the younger Catron experienced difficulty in finding a replacement for Sammon. After extensive correspondence he entered into a contract with Adolpho Sandoval for a salary of $50 per month and 15 percent of all moneys collected from leases, timber royalties, or other revenue

---

* Catron to Neill B. Field, March 20, 1911 (C.P. 105, Vol. 30). Insofar as can be learned, Catron owed Reymond some amount continuously from as early as February 1, 1883 (C.P. 103, Box 2).

derived from the grant. Sandoval spent the first two weeks of his employment on a drunk in Mora. When Charles learned of this he immediately terminated Sandoval's contract, which left him in the position of having for some time to personally make collections.

The Mora Grant yielded some revenue, every cent of which was put back into the business for expenses and for clearing of titles so the land could be disposed of. By 1912 Charles C. Catron was attempting to sell 1,176,809 acres of land grants in which he or his father had interests. These were the Ojo del Espiritu Santo, Antonio Ortiz, Piedra Lumbre, Mora, and Anton Chico. The Tierra Amarilla Grant had been sold in 1909. None were sold in time to save the Mora Grant. On February 27, 1913, it was sold to Frank Roy, of Las Vegas, on a tax sale.[16] Both father and son struggled valiantly to raise the money with which to redeem the grant, but to no avail. The partition suit instituted by Catron in 1879 was still on the docket of the district court of Mora County.

While the Mora Grant was the first in which Catron acquired interests, his largest single possession was the Tierra Amarilla Grant. The latter involved even more of his time than any other, and efforts to realize on its potential probably caused him more anguish than anything else in his life.

The grant was made in 1832 on petition of Manuel Martinez, who had six sons and two daughters. These constituted the direct heirs; the grant was later conveyed in eight parts. Francisco Martinez, a son, petitioned for confirmation of the grant. On September 10, 1856, Surveyor General William Pelham recommended to Congress that the grant be confirmed. He found that Francisco Martinez had been in quiet and peaceable possession of the land for twenty-two years. He determined that the grant was bounded on the north by the Navaho River, on the south by the Nutrias River, on the east by the mountain range, and on the west by the mouth of the Laguna de los Caballos. The grant was confirmed by act of Congress, approved June 21, 1860, and surveyed by Sawyer and McBroom under contract with Surveyor General Henry M. Atkinson, dated April 15, 1876.

Numerous conveyances of interests were made prior to the survey for relatively small considerations. For example, in 1871, Jose Manuel Martinez sold his one interest to Elkins for $100.[17] As time passed, purchase prices increased markedly, even before the survey. On December 9, 1874, Jose Chavez and wife sold a 5/36 interest to Elias Brevoort for $8,500. The following day Brevoort conveyed this 5/36 interest to William Pinkerton for $15,277.70. On February 8, 1881, Pinkerton, for a consideration of $25,000, delivered this same interest to Catron.

On February 21, 1881, patent was issued for 594,515.55 acres of land located in New Mexico and Colorado. Elkins later maintained that he had spent much time and money in helping to secure the patent. He was, at the time of this assertion, quibbling with Catron over which had rendered the greater service to the other over the past several years. Catron countered by reminding Elkins of an earlier statement that all he had done was to write a note to the chief clerk in the land office in Washington who then had the patent issued. Catron asserted that Elkins, according to his own statement, was employed by William Pinkerton in arranging for the patent. Catron affirmed that, at the time the patent was issued, he owned less than a hundredth part of the grant. He was in error; by that time he had acquired nearly one-third of the interests, including Pinkerton's 5/36 portion which was conveyed to him two weeks before the patent was issued.[18] Both agreed, however, that Elkins had been of some service in having the patent issued.

Catron's first purchase of an interest in the grant was made in 1874 from Felix D. Martinez. With at least forty-two conveyances, by 1893 he acquired all interests in the grant.

For these he paid nearly $200,000,* largely with borrowed money.

It has been popularly supposed that Catron virtually stole much of the land that he acquired in the form of land grants. This is not substantiated in the case of the Tierra Amarilla. Land grants were sold for minimal amounts in the 1860s and the first few years of the 1870s, but prospective sellers seem to have realized the potential value of property by the middle 1870s. Persons who were initially satisfied with the price they received later thought they had been bilked when the economy of the Territory became more affluent, and the price of land increased.

While Catron's first purchase of an interest in the Tierra Amarilla Grant was made in 1874, it was not until 1881 and 1882 that he acquired the larger and more costly interests. At this time he entered into deals involving promissory notes. In 1882, to consolidate these debts, he bonded the property with the Mercantile Trust Company of New York for $200,000, the bonds to bear 7 percent interest and be payable in 1892. The contract proposed that the money was to be used for brood cattle, other livestock, and machinery; nevertheless, the money was not utilized for these purposes to any large extent. While the record is not entirely clear, it is evident that most of the money was used to consolidate debts in acquiring the property, and to make further purchases of interests not owned by Catron at the time the bonds were issued. It is probably not a coincidence that the amount of

---

Abstract and Deeds (C.P. 305, Box 1); John H. Knaebel to Attorney General of the United States, March 25, 1893 (C.P. 305, Box 1). Of the forty-two conveyances (copies of the originals) no purchase price was stipulated on nine. For twelve, the price was one dollar and other considerations. The total consideration stated on the other twenty-one deeds was $87,660. Deeds on which other considerations was stipulated were from, among others, Elkins, Thomas D. Burns, Wilmot E. Broad, and D. B. Koch. They were made at a relatively late date, and for probably more than the average. By any reasonable process of interpolation, Knaebel's figure of nearly $200,000 seems substantiated. Because of many complicated involvements, it is probable that Catron himself did not know precisely the total that he paid for all interests in the grant.

the bonds was about the same as the amount Catron paid
for the grant.[19] This arrangement started a series of debts
that plagued Catron until the day he died.

Among the persons from whom Catron purchased interests was Wilmot E. Broad, who came to play an important
role in his affairs. Broad arrived in New Mexico from Chicago
in 1876, as president of the New Mexico Stock and Agricultural Association, the office of which was at 130 Dearborn
Street. The enterprise was incorporated under the laws of
Illinois for the purpose of colonizing, developing, and improv-
ing lands in New Mexico and Colorado for stock raising,
agricultural, and mining purposes.[20]

On February 9, 1877, Broad purchased 1/8 of the interests
in the Tierra Amarilla Grant from Elias Brevoort for one
dollar and other considerations. Presumably a promissory note
was involved. Brevoort had purchased the interests from
Robert and Hugh Campbell in 1874 for $3,500, sold them
to James F. Johnson and Bernard Koch in 1875 for $5,000,
and repurchased them from Johnson and Koch in 1876 for
$6,500. After Broad's purchase he set about trying to establish
a colony of enterprising American citizens. He could not,
however, overcome the problem of undivided interests.[21]

Broad sold his interests to Catron on April 20, 1882, for
one dollar and other considerations.[22] In addition to his own
affairs, as early as 1876 Broad was associated with Catron as
agent for acquiring interests in the Tierra Amarilla Grant.*
He later became full-time manager of the grant.

In 1883 Catron signed notes for Broad in order for him
to enter into a partnership with Pascal Craig in the Monero
Coal and Coke Company. When the note came due a year
later Broad was unable to pay, and Catron had to make good
to the extent of about $66,000, including interest and later

Affidavit in application by Catron for a loan, September 26, 1903 (C.P. 305, Box
1). At this time Broad said he was fifty-four years of age and had been Catron's agent
for the past twenty-seven years. This would place their association back to 1876. Prior
to that year, Catron had acquired only one interest in the grant.

litigation with Craig. Catron was also guarantor of notes in
the name of the partnership. In the process Catron was forced
to take over the Monero Coal and Coke Company, which
proved to be a losing venture.

As the situation developed, Broad's position as manager
of the grant proved to be one of virtual debt servitude. He
received $100 per month, half of which he paid to Catron on
the indebtedness of himself and Craig. Catron conceded that
Broad, as his agent, generally did a good job of looking after
the property. He did not, however, hesitate to remind Broad
that 12 percent money, compounded, doubles itself about
every six years and six months. Thus, as the years turned into
decades, Broad's debt became astronomical. He could have
wiped out his indebtedness by selling the grant for Catron.
Despite diligent efforts he was never able to do this, partially
because every time there was a prospect of a sale Catron
wanted more money than was offered. Still, Catron badly
needed to sell the grant. In 1896 Catron offered to pay Broad
$125,000 and release the latter from all obligations if Broad
sold it at a price that would realize Catron $1,350,000. In
1901 Broad reminded Catron of the arrangement, and Catron
heatedly replied that he would be an infernal idiot to make
the same proposition after four years had passed with consequent increase of interest on Broad's debt.[23] He did, though,
agree to pay Broad $112,000 on the same terms.

Wilmot E. Broad died in 1907 at the age of 58, his debt
still largely unpaid. In Catron's letter to Frank W. Broad
acknowledging the death of his father, he allowed the brusk
side of his nature to intermingle with his expression of sympathy. He told Frank that he regretted the death of his
father very much and sympathized with the family in their
loss. He then asked Frank to immediately take care of certain
taxes with money collected by his father and warned him
not to let the money collected for rentals be mixed with the
money of his father's estate. He concluded the letter, "I shall
miss your father very much."[24]

Frank Broad now became Catron's agent for the grant. When something less than a year had passed, Frank asked for a $100 increase in salary, which would make his pay $250 a month. He promised that he would make it up by increasing the rentals. Catron replied that he was not willing to pay all the rentals to an agent and that he would not increase his salary anything whatever. He placed Broad on the defensive by claiming that Broad had been paying little attention to matters connected with the grant; he expressed a desire to confer with him about his duties. Moreover, Catron brought up the matter of Frank's father's large debt.[25] Frank Broad, however, continued as agent for the grant in the same bickering sort of way as had been the fate of his father.

Final solutions were left to the second generation on both sides, when Charles C. Catron took over active management of the grant. Three months after his father's death, Charles C. Catron offered to settle the entire claim against the Broad estate for $10,000 cash. Although this was less than a fifth of what he was sure he could recover on a judgment, he needed immediate cash to settle obligations left by his father.[26]

In 1885, with the start of Grover Cleveland's first administration, there commenced nearly a decade of controversy in which the patent to the Tierra Amarilla Grant was attacked. Commissioner of the General Land Office William A. J. Sparks, and Surveyor General of New Mexico George W. Julian vigorously assailed land grant titles in New Mexico. The Tierra Amarilla Grant was among those censured. The grant had been surveyed at the direction of Surveyor General Henry M. Atkinson. While accusations were brought that the grant was larger in extent than intended by the grantors, no imputation of fraud was brought against Atkinson.

The trouble started when certain persons represented to the surveyor general of Colorado that, based on the Wheeler and Hayden geological survey, there was an excess of about sixty thousand acres in the grant because of an improper survey of the eastern boundary.[27] The identity of these certain parties is not revealed, but it may reasonably be assumed that one of them was Jacob H. Crist who, over a period of years, sought to stir up settlers on the grant in order to have the patent set aside. It is known that he was in communication with Surveyor General Julian in the matter,[28] and it is not unreasonable to assume that he also was in touch with the surveyor general of Colorado.

As a result of this threat to the ownership of his property, on November 21, 1885, Catron entered into an agreement with James M. Freeman, a Denver attorney, giving Freeman the responsibility of seeing that the patent to the grant not be disturbed in case suit should be brought by the United States government to vacate the patent. Catron agreed to pay Freeman $45,000 if he prevailed against such a suit.[29]

As was frequently the case in such matters, negotiations proceeded slowly. On November 26, 1886, Surveyor General Julian was instructed to investigate the charges brought by the surveyor general of Colorado. On March 28, 1887, Julian reported that not only was the case of the surveyor general of Colorado well founded but also there were three other good reasons why the patent should be vacated. The patented survey, Julian maintained, included the pasture, woods, and watering places which, under the grant, were left common to all with the fee reserved by the Mexican government. Furthermore, the grant was made under the colonization law of 1824 and, therefore, should be restricted to eleven square leagues. Julian also alleged that Congress was left entirely in the fog as to what land was meant to be included in the grant at the time that it was confirmed. Julian concluded: "The Government would be recreant in its trust if it should suffer five or six hundred thousand acres of its Public Domain to be stolen, without a judicial inquiry into the theft."[30]

In 1889, with the incoming administration of Benjamin Harrison, Freeman thought he had the case about wrapped up. He found, though, that it would be necessary to use

$20,000 of his fee from Catron in payment to certain parties. On April 15 Freeman reported that in about thirty days Secretary of the Interior John W. Noble would sign a decision favorable to Catron in the case. He wanted to make sure that his client would have the money immediately available to pay the fee when this was done.[31]

As it happened, Noble did not sign the decision, and the case dragged on for several years longer. Earlier in April, Elkins had informed Catron of a circumstance that might mean trouble. Noble had a grudge against Catron that went back to about 1869, when Catron was attorney general. Noble was beaten in a lawsuit tried before the New Mexico Supreme Court in which Elkins was his opponent. This was the only case in which Noble was ever involved in New Mexico; still, he was compelled to pay thirteen dollars for a license to practice in the Territory. Catron claimed that he himself was in Colorado at the time and someone else must have told Noble of the license requirement and warned him that he had better take one out.[32]

Catron wrote to Noble seeking clarification of the misunderstanding. Word had come to his attention, Catron stated, that Noble would like to kick him because he had not treated him in a gentlemanly manner when he was in New Mexico. Catron then painstakingly reviewed the situation and requested that Noble refresh his memory. He hoped to be excluded from any ill-feeling on the part of Noble for anything that had happened in New Mexico.[33]

Noble promptly answered. The statement that he would like to kick Catron, he said, was untrue in word and spirit. He had said, in a conversation carried on in a laughing tone, that he had been compelled to take out a license to practice in one case, that he had received his license in Spanish, and that he and Catron had been on opposite sides in the Civil War.[34] As subsequent events were to prove, Noble's protestation of friendliness was only a nicety.

Clarification of the case involving the validity of the

patent to the Tierra Amarilla Grant remained in abeyance. Understandably, this hampered Catron's efforts to sell the property. Envy may have played a part in Noble's failure to act in the matter. Word was around that Catron was getting in excess of $50,000 a year royalty from the grant. Catron protested that this was a fourfold exaggeration, that he scarcely got enough to pay taxes.[35] Royalty statements from Wilmot E. Broad, Catron's agent on the grant, indicate that the gross income some months approached $8,000. At other times it was scarcely $1,000 a month. Perhaps the gross approached $50,000 a year at times, but it is unlikely that it averaged that amount the years that Catron owned the grant.*

It was common knowledge among subordinates in Noble's office in Washington that, if the case were brought to the courts, it could hardly be decided other than in favor of Catron. It was equally well known that the suspension was to spite Catron.

During the earlier Cleveland administration, a law clerk in the Department of the Interior had prepared an opinion favorable to Catron. In 1892 Catron prevailed on J. C. Hill, a friend and also a clerk, to procure a copy of this favorable opinion. The purpose was to let Noble know, in some circumspect manner, that the opinion existed. Hill gave a copy of the report to another clerk, who entrusted it to a third party. By this time the purpose of the maneuver was not understood, and the opinion was presented directly to Noble without further explanation. Hill had thought he was doing Noble a favor by letting him know that even persons in the previous administration had considered Catron's case legally sound. Noble thought otherwise. He looked upon Hill's

---

* In 1907, Catron claimed, in connection with a possible sale of the grant, that it had averaged over $40,000 yearly income from timber and grazing privileges since 1885. Catron to A. C. Foster, March 24, 1907 (C.P. 103, Box 28). In 1894 it was claimed that he had been paid over $400,000 cash from timber royalties since 1885. *Santa Fe Weekly New Mexican Review,* November 1, 1894. Both of these claims probably are somewhat exaggerated.

intervention as insubordination and relegated him to a lesser job that took him away from his home.

Elkins and Richard C. Kerens, who had been instrumental in Harrison's election, now undertook to intercede directly with the president. Kerens was associated with Elkins in the railroad business in West Virginia and, like Catron and Elkins, was formerly from Missouri. Furthermore, he was a member of the Republican National Executive Committee. Harrison, however, was called away hurriedly by the illness of his wife, and the matter was not immediately settled.

Assistant Attorney General Shields prepared an elaborate opinion as to why a suit to vacate patent to the Tierra Amarilla Grant could not be maintained. Noble ignored this opinion. Just before he left office in March 1893 he requested that the attorney general bring suit to vacate the patent. He was secretive in this action and informed neither Shields nor the docket clerk.

James M. Freeman, who still represented Catron in the case, now enlisted the aid of John H. Knaebel and C. C. Clements in preparation of a letter to the attorney general, pointing out why a suit could not be maintained if brought. Despite this well-reasoned letter, it was not until February 14, 1894, that a decision favorable to Catron was finally signed by Secretary of the Interior Hoke Smith, Noble's successor.[36]

This ended nearly a decade of petty prosecution that, according to Catron's own statement, kept him in constant dread.[37] He had confidence that he would prevail if the case were brought to trial, but he had been constantly frustrated when the decision was held up year after year without his being able to do anything about it.

Freeman now wanted his fee of $45,000, but Catron paid no heed to the requests for payment. As a matter of fact, he did not have the money or any way of getting it unless he sold some property. Other attorneys, perhaps realizing

Catron's discomfiture, interceded to attain a meeting of minds between Freeman and Catron. One was John H. Knaebel, who knew Catron's monetary condition. He pointed out that Freeman felt offended and hurt because he thought Catron treated him with unkind silence. Freeman had spent about $20,000 out of pocket on the business and was short of money. Knaebel suggested that Catron at least give Freeman satisfactory security.

At the same time Knaebel had an axe of his own to grind. He had only lately learned of the contract with Freeman and chided Catron about it: "In view of what I was doing, this contract read like a satire on my simplicity, for I shall always believe that I did more than any body else to win the case."[38]

In response to Knaebel's mediation, Catron offered Freeman 22,500 acres of the northern part of the Tierra Amarilla Grant.[39] After further negotiation it was decided to utilize the northernmost 60,000 acres to form the Banded Peak Land and Mining Company. Catron retained half of the stock in the corporation, and Freeman received the other half except for a small share given to Knaebel for drawing up the charter and organizing the new corporation. The venture never prospered.

As a result of his relations with Catron, Freeman joined the growing band of persons who attempted to sell the Tierra Amarilla Grant, but he was no more successful than the others. The complications in trying to sell it were astounding. Catron entered into negotiations for the sale far too numerous even to mention here. In 1883 he arranged an agreement with E. Von Jeinsen of Germany for the sale of 580,000 acres of the grant for $900,000 and one-tenth of the company stock to be issued upon completion of the sale. The deal fell through because the parties represented by Von Jeinsen would pay only $800,000.[40]

For a number of years the grant did not sell because Catron insisted on a price that the market would not bear.

Perhaps a reason for his stubborn insistence on too high a price was that he could not bear to part with this possession; it was the jewel in the crown of all he owned. Not only were there price increases, the price fluctuated from time to time. He even had different prices outstanding to various persons at the same time.

His more or less standard asking price was $1,250,000 until 1891 when Adolph F. Bandelier learned of some London people who might be interested in purchasing the grant. Catron then asked $1,400,000. Negotiations were carried on through Reginald Oestrom, a friend of Bandelier. Oestrom offered $1,350,000 on behalf of his clients, with one-half of the purchase price to be taken in a company to be formed to develop the property. Catron refused this offer, and Oestrom asked for a three-months option to work out an acceptable arrangement. Catron was willing to give this option but at a price of $1,500,000. Statehood talk, current at the time, led him to believe that the value of the property would surely double if New Mexico became a state. Oestrom was unable to complete a deal because the increased price was more than his people would pay.

It is impossible to convey the complexity of the negotiations that followed over the years. Only by going over the actual documents is the vast scope of bargaining revealed. Any reader who would do this would almost certainly wish to go back through the time of history and chastise Catron severely for each of the opportunities for a sale that came and slipped away.

When the Oestrom-Bandelier negotiations fell through, Catron held his price for a time at $1,500,000 for 580,000 acres. In 1894 the area for sale was reduced to 520,000 acres because of the 60,000 acres removed to form the Banded Peak Land and Mining Company. Catron wanted $1,455,000 for the reduced amount of land. But in 1895 the price was reduced to $1,040,000, only to climb to $1,750,000 by 1897.

In 1901 John D. Rockefeller, "Rockyfeller" as Catron was informed, sent a representative to secretly examine the grant. Jay Gould and "Buffalo Bill" Cody were also interested.

That year his price to a group trying to sell the property (including James M. Freeman, Wilmot E. Broad, and Hal Sayre of Denver) was $1,700,000. Almost concurrently he authorized Adolph J. Jarmuth, also of Denver, to sell the grant for $1,075,000. In 1902 he entered into fruitless negotiations to sell Elkins a half interest for $325,000. That same year, through Elkins' contacts, some Boers from Africa became interested. Negotiations continued with them for several years, during which time Catron authorized Hal Sayre to sell them the property for $1,350,000, but to no avail.

In 1902 one party complained that the grant had been hawked about so much it was useless to try to handle it unless someone was encountered who had not heard of the various negotiations. In July Catron suffered a particularly humiliating experience. William O. Manson learned that Catron was desperately in need of $250,000 to meet the deadline of a note payable. Through Adolph J. Jarmuth, he offered Catron precisely the required amount. Jarmuth reported that Manson might go as high as $500,000, but that would be the limit.

Catron broke off with Jarmuth for a time but in December renewed negotiations with him. Jarmuth arranged for a loan of $250,000 on the grant with the Continental Trust Company of Denver. In return, Catron gave Jarmuth an option to sell the property for $925,000. Catron reserved the right to sell the grant himself but agreed to pay Jarmuth $125,000 if he did so.

Within less than a year Eugene H. Wilson of New York City wrote to Catron that he understood the price to be $2,600,000 for the 520,000 acres. With what certainly must have been tongue in cheek, Catron wrote that he was correctly informed.[41] At the same time his price to O. P. Bowman, of Toledo, Ohio, was $1,750,000.

About this time Hal Sayre indicated that he knew Catron had offered the property for $900,000 and wondered how he could be expected to sell it for $1,750,000. Catron denied vigorously that he had ever offered the grant at the price quoted by Sayre, but he did not mention the $925,000 arrangement with Jarmuth.

In 1905 Catron attempted to borrow money on more advantageous terms than the loan from the Continental Trust Company and asked Governor Miguel A. Otero to recommend the property. Otero complied: "The relations between Mr. Catron and myself are not of the most cordial nature, but the property speaks for itself, and without hesitation I recommend that you make the loan."[42]

In March 1907 Catron gave an option to sell the grant for $1,925,000 to R. W. Hadden of Pittsburgh. The land remained unsold, and early in 1909 the situation became critical. The Continental Trust Company was threatening foreclosure. Catron, now sixty-nine years old, had hoped to retire several years earlier. Faced with this desperate crisis, he took to the road personally in one last effort to sell the grant. His situation was so well known in financial circles throughout the nation that the cards were stacked against him. Even under such conditions he was tough and resourceful. He recognized that he would have to sacrifice; his goal was to keep the sacrifice to a minimum. He sold the grant in May to a Minneapolis group headed by Ogden A. Confer in a transaction arranged by William C. Van Gilder. He received $495,000 in cash — about the total amount of his indebtedness at the time. Out of this amount he paid Van Gilder's commission of $20,000, and the usual expense of closing, as well as $15,000 by way of compromise with O. B. Crum, who alleged that he was entitled to a commission.

In addition to the cash, Catron received a building allegedly worth $175,000 on which there was a mortgage of $85,000, as well as $88,000 of telephone company stock in Iowa worth not much. He also accepted 40,000 acres of land in Oregon, represented to be worth $10 an acre but which he thought could be valued at no more than $5 an acre. It was estimated at the time that about $850,000 was represented in the entire settlement.[43] It was the old story of too much equity and not enough cash. Furthermore, it was nearly a year before all details of the transaction were finally arranged. Catron still owned the Oregon land when he died.

During the final stages of Catron's struggle to sell the Tierra Amarilla Grant, Mrs. Catron was in her final illness. She had hoped to recover so they could travel together, but she died on November 8, 1909.

Two persons, more than any others, hurt Catron in his business and financial dealings; they were Charles H. Elmendorf (in relation to the American Valley Company) and Wilson Waddingham. Catron met Waddingham in the spring of 1870, just after the latter had participated in the sale of the Maxwell Land Grant to an English syndicate.[44] Waddingham became as near a close personal friend as Catron ever had; in 1888 he accompanied Waddingham on a trip to Europe. From the beginning of their association he was Waddingham's lawyer, and they never quarreled. Their professional arrangements were often on a verbal basis.* Catron took care of Waddingham's affairs when the latter was frequently gone from the Territory.

The antecedents of an unfortunate circumstance for Catron involving Waddingham started in 1882, when Catron bonded the Tierra Amarilla Grant. The bonds were payable in 1892, and in that year, evidently to meet accrued interest payments, he entered into an arrangement whereby Waddingham borrowed $100,000 from the Alliance Trust Company of Dundee, Scotland, using bonds of the Tierra Amarilla

---

*Catron and Wilson Waddingham apparently never had a formal settling of their respective accounts during Waddingham's lifetime. At the time of Waddingham's death, Catron could show unpaid bills dating back to 1871. Catron to E. G. Stoddard, August 18, 1899 (C.P. 105, Vol. 16).

Grant as security. The money from the loan was split equally between them.

In another piece of business in 1885, Catron conveyed the 225,000 acres of his interest in the Antonio Ortiz and Anton Chico Grants to Waddingham for seventy-five cents an acre. Waddingham then owed Catron (after certain adjustments) $159,964.30, but this amount was not paid at the time.[45]

Thus Waddingham had Catron's deeds to the two grants, and also had the Tierra Amarilla Grant encumbered with a mortgage to the Alliance Trust Company. This involvement frightened Catron. The holdings of both men were largely acquired by the use of borrowed money. Catron, although he trusted Waddingham, was afraid his friend might not be able to cover the loan when due and that his bonds, secured by a mortage on the Tierra Amarilla Grant, might be in jeopardy. He urged that the loan be covered by some other security, but this Waddingham never accomplished.[46]

A further entanglement occurred in 1893, when Catron secured from Waddingham the use of the United States Land and Colonization Company. His purpose was to transfer the Tierra Amarilla Grant to this company in an attempt to raise $500,000 in bonds.[47]

By all accounts Waddingham was a persuasive operator, but it is hard to believe that he could have talked Catron into another deal that started in 1897. Waddingham told Catron that he could sell 520,000 acres of the Tierra Amarilla Grant (which was in the name of the United States Land and Colonization Company) for $1,300,000, or $2.50 an acre. To facilitate the sale he wanted to change the name to the Southwestern Lumber and Railway Company. He also wanted to reduce the capital stock by half — to $1,250,000 — about the amount of the proposed sale of the grant. To expedite these arrangements he asked Catron for the stock of the United States Land and Colonization Company. Waddingham offered reasons why it was desirable to make these changes, and Catron consented.[48]

The following year Waddingham informed Catron that he had renegotiated the loan with the Alliance Trust Company, reducing it to $50,000 and continuing to use the bonds of the Tierra Amarilla Grant as security.[49] He did not, however, mention a great deal more that he had done.

When Wilson Waddingham died on May 16, 1899, from a stroke of apoplexy, there came to light almost immediately certain information concerning his business activities, which were international in scope. Catron had supposed that Waddingham owned about 1,700,000 acres of land, that he was worth about two million dollars, with debts of seven or eight hundred thousand dollars.[50] This supposition was not correct; settlement of his estate involved harried efforts to sell enough real estate to pay his debts.

Within a few days after Waddingham's death, Catron was obliged to suspect that matters between them were not as had been represented. Still, Catron believed that something would show up among Waddingham's papers indicating that he had somehow protected Catron. As the administrators probed into matters concerning the estate, details of duplicity came to light. Within a month Catron was surprised beyond measure to learn that Waddingham had caused $200,000 of new bonds to be issued to the Southwestern Lumber and Railway Company. He had used only $50,000 of the new issue as security to the Alliance Trust Company and had covered personal obligations with the remainder. This left Catron liable for all debts secured by the bonds. Others were comparably duped. John H. Knaebel, for example, felt that he had been hurt even worse than Catron.[51]

Waddingham's estate was not probated until April 27, 1903, and settlement involved many complications and much time. To raise cash for a pressing bill, the Armendariz Grant was sold at a sacrifice. In satisfaction of his claim, Catron encountered his old nemesis of being obliged to take part payment in land rather than cash. He agreed to pay off all of Waddingham's debts caused by manipulations directly involving himself. In exchange he was to receive 490,000 acres of the Antonio Ortiz and Anton Chico Grants at fifty cents an acre, which amounted to $245,000. The total amount that he paid in Waddingham debts was about $291,000; the balance of $46,000 came in dividends from the estate. In addition, the difference between Catron's and Waddingham's respective debts to each other was calculated at nearly $129,000 in favor of Catron, which amount he also received in dividends from the estate. Thus, he paid out $291,000 in exchange for a promise of $175,000 and the two grants.[52]

The important thing is that he had to make his payment relatively soon after Waddingham's death and did not receive any remuneration during the five years occupied in settling the estate. These were crucial years during which Catron was hurt badly by having this money tied up.

Negotiations for the settlement were lengthened in large measure because of delaying tactics by the two Waddingham wives. The first, Mary Emma Waddingham, who had been granted a divorce in 1889, had legitimate claims which Catron had to pay and which he was not fully able to accomplish until 1907.[53] The second Mrs. Waddingham, Nannie B., had not nearly the claim she thought she was entitled to. Nevertheless, she was able to stretch her demands to the limit: "The widow, as you know, is pretty; she wiped away several tears as did her counsel. The judge being a bachelor was visibly affected."[54]

Throughout the harrowing experience of making the best of a bad situation, Catron was reluctant to believe that Waddingham had deliberately deceived him. Even when this was evident, he seems to have been more hurt than bitter that his friend had victimized him. Thus, when it was brought out that Waddingham, in connection with cattle deals, had induced Robert Martin to sign letters in blank and had then written letters over the signatures to obtain credit on his notes, Catron could not believe that it was true. Still, he had to admit that Waddingham's conduct toward him was unauthorized and highly improper. He said: "I hate to give credence to these statements, they are so unlike Mr. Waddingham as I knew him prior to his death, that it is painful for me even to repeat it . . ." He finally came to admit that Waddingham had compromised him beyond measure.[55]

Others were not as patient with Waddingham. John H. Knaebel pointed out that it seemed to be his favorite amusement to play chess through an automaton.[56]

Throughout the settlement of the estate Catron realized that there could be no benefit in it except to get rid of his worry, trouble, and embarrassment. As late as 1912 he was still paying small remaining amounts in connection with the settlement. He felt that he had been compelled to sacrifice the Tierra Amarilla Grant because of the situation and that he had lost more than a million dollars by Mr. Waddingham.[57]

It would seem that Catron's involvement with Wilson Waddingham might have made him a little cautious about whom he trusted in the future. The fact seems to be that he was a lifelong unfailing optimist in his outlook toward the integrity of persons he encountered in a business way. This may have been partially because one complicated business involvement led to another at such a harrying pace that he had not the time to properly investigate persons with whom he had business dealings. On the other hand, others were usually duped along with Catron. It seems to have been his fate to become involved with more than his share of slick operators. So it was that, while he was still picking up the pieces of the Waddingham foozle, he encountered another conniving sharper.

By 1905 Catron had received a three-fourths interest in the Antonio Ortiz Grant consequent to the final settlement of the Waddingham estate. The other quarter interest was owned by Julius Day of Derby, Connecticut. The grant embraced 163,921.68 acres, but only about 155,000 were merchantable because of adverse claims. On July 1, 1908, Catron contracted to sell this land to Don A. MounDay of Topeka,

Kansas. Catron agreed to receive $4 an acre and to supply partial releases of title as MounDay sold portions of the land. MounDay bargained to pay $20,000 a month the first year and the balance of the contract the second year. He was president of the American Sugar Manufacturing and Refining Company and promised to build a large refinery in the center of the tract following its irrigation and occupancy by beet farmers. He also assured that he would have a railway built into the area. As it turned out these were merely promotion gimmicks; he made only cursory attempts to secure the necessary irrigation water and none at all to build a railroad.

MounDay, over six feet tall and weighing 240 pounds, had cultivated a loud voice with which he could easily be heard within a radius of 60 feet on the street or in a building making noisy comments or boosting his proposition. His wife, Lou, was cooly calculating and was said to be the real brains of the operation.[58]

MounDay had an Oklahoma corporation, and one by the same name in New Mexico. There was no relation between them, yet he was interested in both. The Oklahoma company sold the land, although it never owned a foot of ground in New Mexico nor was it ever in a position to give a warranty deed to any land. He was said to have had 45 agents in 15 different states who sold 40,000 acres of land at $40 an acre, from which it was estimated that he realized from $300,000 to $500,000. Yet it appears that all Catron ever got out of his contract with MounDay was $120 for 30 acres of land.

When Catron sold to MounDay, he contracted with Julius Day for his quarter interest in the Ortiz Grant to be included in the deal. His ability to pay Day was dependent upon payments from MounDay. When these payments were not made as agreed, Catron forfeited the $40,000 that he had already paid to Day because he was unable to complete the balance of the contract.[59]

Meanwhile, MounDay stalled with every clever stratagem he could devise. He claimed that title to the grant was imperfect and that his clients did not understand the title because it emanated from a Spanish grant. He even endeavored to have the terms of the agreement changed so he could sell the best part of the land, and leave Catron holding the rest.[60] All the while, he was selling land without warranting title or supplying irrigation water. He even sold large quantities of land after his option contract with Catron had clearly expired.

It is hard to understand why Catron gave MounDay so much time to exercise the terms of the contract. At an early date MounDay forfeited any rights he had. Even while he was waiting on MounDay, Catron was offered $250,000 cash for the property but held out for $387,000, and the deal fell through.[61] It is possible that the clever and persuasive Moun-Day prevailed upon Catron to believe he would still produce under the terms of the original $620,000 contract. MounDay duped hundreds of people in at least fifteen states, many of them prominent public figures, including United States Senator Charles Curtis.

In 1913 MounDay and his wife fell afoul of the laws of the United States and the Blue Sky statute of the state of Kansas. They were arrested, charged with using the United States mails to defraud, and convicted.[62]

Early in 1871 Catron entered into the first of several mining ventures that he became connected with during his lifetime. Articles of incorporation were filed by a group including, besides Catron, Lehman Spiegelberg, Elkins, R. B. Willison, Charles B. Thayer, and William A. Pile. The company proposed to operate in the new silver mines at Ralston and Cienega.[63]

Other mines that Catron owned outright, or in which he had an interest, included Ambrosia, Anaconda, Aztec, Bonanza, Banded Peak Land and Mining Company, Cerrillos Coal and Iron Company, Good Hope, Hanover, Juanita, Last Chance, Monero Coal and Coke Company, Mora Copper Mining Company, New Mexico Mining Company, Pacific

Gold Company, and San Pedro. While these mines occupied a great deal of his time, they were, in the aggregate, financially unremunerative.*

Another facet of Catron's varied career in New Mexico was that of a banker. He participated in the purchase of the First National Bank in Santa Fe from Lucien B. Maxwell. Actually, Catron was a relatively minor stockholder with 1,050 shares as opposed to 2,730 shares owned by Elkins and 2,450 by Jose Leandro Perea. Others had lesser amounts. Elkins was the first president with Perea vice president, W. W. Griffin cashier, and S. B. Wheelock assistant cashier. Catron was on the board of directors.[64] Maxwell had started the bank with proceeds from the sale of the Maxwell Land Grant. Elkins and his associates had planned to start another bank, and Maxwell sold out to them rather than face the competition. Then too, he had suffered financial reverses with the bank because of poor management.

Another Catron banking venture is significant because it augmented the rigorous financial difficulties he experienced during the 1890s. Early in 1891 J. S. Sniffen organized the Socorro National Bank with himself as vice president, Luis M. Baca president, and R. A. Jones cashier. Sniffen wrote to Catron explaining that, because of stringency in money matters, the stockholders were experiencing difficulty in raising money to pay for the stock they had agreed to purchase. He requested that Catron join with them as a stockholder. Catron complied, with an initial investment of $5,000. The bank soon found itself in trouble financially because it made several uncollectable loans. To protect his own investment Catron made further advances of cash — a total of $18,000 — all of which he eventually lost.

When the bank reached an untenable financial position, Sniffen abruptly left for Florence, Arizona. Catron, in an

---

* There is a great deal of informative data concerning these mines in Catron's correspondence. He also had mining interests in Mexico.

attempt to salvage what he could, assumed presidency of the bank. He was unable to recoup his loss and was involved in unpleasant relations with bank examiners and litigation with creditors until 1900. During this time his rapport with Sniffen was far from cordial; his correspondence was about as openly derogatory as is possible of expression in the English language, typically: "I am in possession of a remarkable letter from you. If there was anything on earth to convince me that you are a mere child, that letter would do it."[65]

Besides mining and banking, Catron became involved in New Mexico's other major industry — ranching. His most important undertaking in that business — the American Valley Company — is related in other chapters, but there were others. In 1882 he was an incorporator, along with Henry M. Atkinson and John H. Thomson, of the Boston and New Mexico Cattle Company. In an earlier ranching enterprise — the Carrizozo Ranch which he owned from 1878 through 1882 — he employed his brother-in-law, Edgar A. Walz, as manager (see chapter 5).

When Walz completed this employment he borrowed $5,000 from the First National Bank in Santa Fe (with Catron as co-signer) as well as $10,000 from Catron personally. He invested this money in a mining claim in Socorro County and land in Lincoln County, upon which were located springs which he hoped to use as a nucleus for a ranching operation of his own. His plans did not materalize as anticipated, and he was not able to fully repay the loans until 1900, thus adding to Catron's financial discomfiture.*

Catron was also associated in the Tularosa Land and Cattle Company which originated in 1885 with a partnership including John H. Riley, William L. Rynerson, and

---

* In 1892, Walz moved to Chicago where he founded the National Debtor Record Company, the function of which was to supply hotels with the names and descriptions of persons who should not be entitled to credit. The following year, he moved to New York where he established a similar organization under the name of the Hotelmen's Confidential Agency.

Pantaleon Sandoval. Catron acquired an interest on December 31, 1889, when Sandoval's share was transferred to Riley, Rynerson, and himself as individuals.[66] The company was incorporated on March 29, 1890, with Rynerson, Riley, Catron, Albert L. Christy, and Henry J. Cuniffe as incorporators. Rynerson died in 1893, and his interest was acquired by Riley and Catron. A purpose of the company was "To purchase, lease, buy and sell water rights, and charge rental and toll therefor."*

Application of this purpose resulted in later lengthy litigation. In 1904 Catron received a writ of injunction from the law firm of Albert B. Fall and Horton Moore, which represented the Tularosa Community Ditch Company. Upon inquiry, Catron learned that there was an agreement between Riley and Fall in the matter.

> The understanding between Judge Fall and myself was to this effect. That the Indians were using a large amount of water that they were not entitled to and that he would bring a suit for the water users of Tularosa against the Indians and all others up the canon (including ourselves in a friendly way) and that you would aid him draw up the papers. That while the suit was pending we would endeavor to purchase water rights and consolidate them and fight the Indians for the water they were using and we would arrange an amicable arrangement by which Judge Fall you and I would make some money out of it.†

The case dragged on with one ramification or another through 1914. Meanwhile, in 1910, Riley and Catron agreed to sell to the Tularosa water rights owners, represented by W. D. Tipton and George Curry, all of their land along the

---

Articles of Incorporation (C. P. 608, Vol. 1). The location was "on both sides of the Rio Tularosa (Tularosa River) to commence at Tularosa at or near the west side of the Mescalero Apache Indian Reservation and extending down said Rio Tularosa on either side thereof and extending out to, and embracing all lands which can be reached and irrigated thereby; and also including all ravines and cañons to any distance on either side thereof which can be dammed or made into reservoirs. The terminus of said canals and ditches shall be at or near a point or points about ten miles west of the town of Tularosa."

†John H. Riley to Catron, January 4, 1905 (C.P. 103, Box 22). Riley had moved to Colorado Springs in 1896.

Tularosa River except the home ranch near the town of Tularosa. For this they received fifty of the water rights of the Tularosa Community Ditch Company valued, at the time, at $1,000 each.*

It seems to be a part of human nature for some people in any era to attach ascriptions of dishonesty to the financial practices of persons who attain wealth. This certainly was no exception in the case of Catron. It seems evident that few of his contemporaries realized the extent to which he was land poor and the difficulties which beset him in acquiring enough cash to meet his obligations. This was particularly true in the matter of taxes on his property. He was constantly charged with being a tax dodger. It should be pointed out that it was extremely difficult, if not impossible, to assess taxes on undivided interests in land grants; consequently, it became the legal practice to assess such property to "unknown owners."† Since a majority of grants were so undivided, this was the biggest tax problem of the Territory. It is unjust to condemn Catron or any other land owner of that era for taking advantage of the law as it then stood. True, Catron strove by all legal means available to keep his taxes down on all property owned by him individually. Even so, more often than not he was behind in the payment of taxes because he did not have the money to pay them. As a matter of fact, his inability to pay taxes on time was a constant source of worry to him because he was left open to tax judgments on his property.

People of his time took no pity on him because of his difficulties, nor did he ask them to; he largely ignored the sniping against him. Typical of these attacks was in 1894

---

*Curry, *George Curry, 1861–1947: An Autobiography,* 111; *Agreement,* August 20, 1910 (C.P. 103, Box 36). The agreement also called for $57,000 in cash, but it is not clear if it was finally consummated in this form. There is evidence of some cash consideration because Catron reportedly received about $20,000 from sale of some of his Tularosa holdings. Frank Lavan to Thom Catron, October 3, 1911 (C.P. 101, Vol. 13).

†Catron to Assessor of Bernalillo County, April 27, 1902 (C.P. 105, Vol. 19). There are numerous comparable letters.

when he was accused of returning assessments on the Tierra Amarilla Grant during the twelve previous years, which called for the payment of only about $15,000 when it was felt that the amount should have been closer to $108,000.[67]

He was also accused of driving people from their homes who had settled on land that he acquired. The law stipulated that land obtained by legitimate settlers be segregated from land grants. Catron apparently was scrupulous in adherence to this law. In fact, there are numerous instances in which he arranged for squatters with no legitimate claim to retain the land upon which they lived. One source of his political power was the friendly relations he maintained with the native people.

But at least some people realized the problem of being a large land owner in this era when it was relatively easy to acquire land but extremely difficult to obtain cash in connection with deals involving that land. One of these, T. A. Finical, wrote to Catron:

> I think it would be a good idea for some of you large real estate owners to deed some of your lands to some of us poor devils, so that we might continue to be kept poor by paying taxes on them. To that extent I am a socialist, if you don't think so, try me.[68]

During his lifetime Catron owned entirely, or had an interest in, at least thirty-four land grants. These were Alamitos, Agua Negra, Anton Chico, Armendariz, Baca Location #1, Baca Location #2, Bartolome Fernandez, Beck, Bosque del Apache, Canada de Cochiti, Caja del Rio, Canada de los Alamos, Canon de Chama, Canon del Agua, Cebolla, Cebolleta, Eaton, Estancia, Gabaldon, Huertas, Juana Lopez, La Majada, Lamy, Los Luceros, Mora, Nicolas de Chavez, Ojo del Espiritu Santo, Ortiz, Piedra Lumbre, San Pedro, Sangre de Cristo, Santa Teresa, Tecolete, and Tierra Amarilla.

The combined acreage of these grants was nearly 6,000,-000, and Catron owned, at one time or another, in excess of 3,000,000 acres of this land. It is impossible to calculate how much real property he owned at any one time, but it was probably no less than 2,000,000 acres. As a matter of fact, in all likelihood he did not himself know at any given time the extent of his holdings. For example, in 1888 he was dealing with some English clients concerning the Los Luceros Grant of 126,024.53 acres just west of Taos. The following year he learned that he was himself the owner of that grant.[69]

Catron also represented clients in at least sixty-three land grant cases in New Mexico with holdings comprising more than 3,000,000 acres of land, as well as cases in Arizona and Colorado, including the Conejos claim in Colorado of about 2,500,000 acres.[70] There seems little doubt that he was not only the largest individual landholder in the history of the United States but also represented clients, as an attorney, in litigation over more land than any other person in that history.

Catron also owned about eight thousand acres in patented preemption and homestead claims. As was the practice in that day before wells and artificial storage tanks, this patented land was strategically located in areas controlling natural water supply. For grazing purposes, the control of water provided domination of large areas of surrounding land. It is impossible to determine accurately the amount of land he controlled in this way, but it surely was in excess of three million acres.* He also owned property in Mexico, California, Oregon, Colorado, Arizona, Kansas, and Missouri.

Like the amount of his land, the extent of his wealth is difficult to calculate. It was mostly in real estate, the value of which fluctuated widely and depended entirely on a purchaser to realize any value at all. An undivided interest in a land grant might be as low as thirty cents an acre, while well-located land with a merchantable title could command $3 an acre. As early as 1889, he conservatively estimated his net worth as 1.5 million dollars and his annual income from real property as fifty thousand dollars.

---

*The land owned by the American Valley Company alone controlled between two and three million acres of range.

Income from his law practice fluctuated widely but was not as high as might be supposed. His net income from this source in 1903, assuming all collections were made, was about $7,000.* This was a period, though, in which he was plagued with financial difficulties from the American Valley Company, settlement of the Wilson Waddingham estate, and failure to sell the Tierra Amarilla and other land grants. While financial records are fragmentary, indications are that his earnings, both from commercial venture and his law practice, hit a peak about 1890. From then on he was harassed almost unbearably by financial problems that hit him from all quarters. So much of his time was occupied trying to salvage his empire that his legal practice suffered. Earnings from his law practice in the early 1890s were undoubtedly higher — perhaps much higher.

Paradoxically Catron's career as a businessman was ultimately hampered by too much trusting of his fellow men, coupled with an empire-oriented aversion to selling land. In fairness, his business was so vast, sprawling, and complex that, on a frontier where communication was elementary, it was extremely difficult to keep abreast of developments. Throughout his business career he was constantly pressed to safeguard his investments. This deployment of time, energy, and talent would have consumed the full capacity of an individual with less drive and stamina. As it was, commercial pursuits, of necessity, occupied a relatively small portion of his attention. If it came to a matter of arithmetical proportion, it would not be far amiss to surmise that his time was occupied about equally with business, law practice, and politics. Somehow, with the faculty that especially busy people seem to have, he was able to enfold into his tempo of living segments of apparently unavailable minutes and hours for public service, philanthropy, cultural pursuits, and wide general reading.

---

* *Catron-Gortner Financial Statement* (C.P. 101, Vol. 7). Catron received ⅔, Gortner ⅓.

5
Lincoln County Imbroglio

The earliest relations of Thomas Benton Catron in Lincoln County are surrounded with mystery. A foremost authority on Lincoln County history has said: "I could weep when I think of the destructive fire of 1888. . . ." He was referring to the burning of Catron's law office. Among the items to escape that fire, which might illuminate the enigma if corroborated by other data, are some receipts signed by Lawrence G. Murphy at Fort Stanton in 1868 for merchandise received from C. Brown & Co. of Santa Fe. The receipts were signed about the time Catron moved to Santa Fe from Mesilla. Any presumption as to why these receipts appear in his papers would be only conjecture. One possible conclusion is that he met Murphy and others from Lincoln County in Santa Fe where merchants were a source of supplies for Fort Stanton and its environs.[1]

The first request for surveys by actual settlers in New Mexico came from this region in 1855, where pioneers moved in following the establishment of the fort earlier that year. William Pelham, the first surveyor general of New Mexico, reluctantly decided against surveys here because of the isolation of the area, danger from Indian attack, and the difficulty of crossing the San Andres Mountains with surveying lines from the Rio Grande Valley. As a consequence, no surveys were made in the Fort Stanton area until 1867.[2]

During this interval the fort was abandoned for a time during the Civil War. When it was reestablished the area was quickly settled by cattlemen and sheepmen and by farmers attracted by the fine farmland along the streams. Far removed from more settled sections of the Territory, law here became largely what the residents made it.

Among the early settlers were Lawrence G. Murphy, Emil A. Fritz, and James J. Dolan, all of whom had served at Fort Stanton and were mustered out of the army at Santa Fe in 1866. That year Murphy and Fritz established a store adjacent to Fort Stanton. Two years later they — along with Paul Dowlin and Saturnino Baca — took out the first homesteads in the vicinity. In 1869 William Brady also entered a homestead.* These pioneers took pride in their early arrival and had officers of the law on their side in the conflict with newcomers that came to be known as the Lincoln County War. Thus, favoritism for the well established became a problem mitigating against impartial enforcement of law.

In 1867 Dr. Joseph H. Blazer wandered into the region and traded a freighting outfit for a sawmill at Mescalero, thereafter known as Blazer's Mill. That year, also, John Simpson Chisum drove his herd of hundreds of cattle into the vast area of public domain along the Pecos River that had before been used only by the Comanches and other Plains Indians for grazing horses and stolen cattle. Within a few years Chisum built up a great cattle outfit and enjoyed a lucrative business in contracts to supply beef for reservation Indians and military posts in New Mexico and Arizona. An early problem for Chisum was protecting the immense range he claimed from intruders.

Among those whose herds Chisum thought increased

---

* Registers and Receivers, *Abstracts of Entries* (N.A.). Murphy, Fritz, and Dowlin also made earliest entries under the preemption act.

more rapidly than could be accounted for by the laws of nature were those of Lawrence G. Murphy. Even as Chisum formed his empire along the Pecos, Murphy, in partnership with Emil Fritz under the name of L. G. Murphy & Co., expanded from his mercantile business near Fort Stanton and acquired other interests such as cattle ranching and farming. Murphy was aggressive and soon controlled most of the business interests in the region. As early as 1871 army officials feared that Fritz and Murphy would gain control over all the hay in the region and that the army therefore would be forced to buy on Fritz and Murphy's terms.[3] Murphy owned the only store and had the financial means to extend credit. If farmers and ranchers wanted this credit, they were forced to buy from him at exorbitant prices. He also controlled most of the wagon trains, so producers were compelled to sell their goods to him at his prices. Accordingly, he came to enjoy virtually dictatorial power over the countryside. William Brady and other sheriffs were Murphy men and helped to sway the balance of power to him.

Emil A. Fritz became ill and in June 1873 left for Germany, where he died the following year. In September 1873 Murphy was evicted from Fort Stanton because of a quarrel involving one of his employees, James J. Dolan, and an officer of the post. Murphy sold his business as post trader to Paul Dowlin & Company and moved to the town of Lincoln where he opened a new store and continued his economic domination of the neighborhood. Poor health forced him to take Dolan into his business at this time. Another associate, John H. Riley, entered the firm in November 1876.

Riley is first heard of in the vicinity of Lincoln in 1872, when he sold 350 cows and 12 horses to Murphy. Riley accepted the entire purchase price in notes and probably took an interest in the business in 1876 as payment.[4]

Riley's role with the firm was that of a cattle dealer. For a number of years he had been a supplier of beef on government contracts. His relations with his associates were not cordial; Riley was a confirmed Republican, while Murphy was a Democrat, and Dolan was either upon occasion. Other differences were more fundamental. Riley would condone such practices as stampeding fat cattle that were being delivered following sale, and then replacing them with skinny animals before they were returned following the stampede. But he balked when it came to dealing in stolen cattle, refusing to handle cattle pilfered by the notorious John Kinney. It was this sort of disagreement that contributed to the eventual dissolution of the firm.

In March 1875 Alexander A. McSween came to Lincoln, and the stage was set for future violence. McSween was a lawyer who had been trained for the Presbyterian ministry; consequently he would not touch alcohol or wear a gun. His compunctions against physical violence did not prevent him from being ambitious and aggressive however. His law practice soon brought him into conflict with Murphy, in some instances as the legal representative of John S. Chisum. But he was not content merely to practice law. Besides acquiring an interest in a ranch, he started a bank and opened a store to challenge Murphy's trade monopoly. Chisum probably supplied the financial backing for the store. McSween was jealous of Murphy's economic and political power and sought to replace him as a leader in the community. His methods were contentious, and in this pioneer region if one pushed he could expect to be pushed back. Wearing a gun was a symbol warning others that a pushing contest must be kept within limits. To many of the old guard in the community, McSween seemed a hypocrite who hid behind an unseemly protective façade with his refusal to wear a gun.

Also in 1875, Catron, in connection with his duties as United States attorney, came into conflict with Chisum when he filed several minor suits against him in federal court. These were for small amounts, mostly licenses and tobacco taxes. Also, in the next few years, Catron became involved as a private attorney in cases against Chisum. While Chisum was generally considered to be a wealthy man, his financial affairs, due to heavy borrowing and bad investments, were in critical condition. Catron was hired by various creditors in collection cases.

Catron's involvements in Lincoln County have been misunderstood; at no time was he personally in the region. Between his official duties, his law practice, and his business interests, he was an extremely busy man. It is not likely that he had time to manipulate the strings of minor puppets in remote Lincoln County. There is every indication that his lifelong practice of lending money in situations where he was forced to take collateral in repayment involved him in the struggle that was beginning. Catron's suits against Chisum did not invite friendship with him or with his ally, McSween. On the other hand, there was no reason for a close relationship with Murphy except in a business way. In fact, there was reason for Catron to be repelled by Murphy, a Democrat who practiced his politics with vigor but not always with commendable scruples. For example, in the election for delegate to Congress in 1875, Murphy, using his authority as probate judge, threw out seventy votes for Stephen B. Elkins, Republican candidate for delegate.[5]

It has been a historical supposition that the Lincoln County troubles were abetted by the Republican Santa Fe Ring through persecution of McSween and his adherents, and championing the Murphy-Dolan cause. There is some basis for this deduction, yet McSween was evidently a Republican while Murphy was certainly a Democrat. In an era when a person's politics frequently determined his business associates, affairs in Lincoln County strangely crossed party lines. Economic considerations seem to have been the determining factor in the factional alignments.

In 1876 a number of events affected these factional relationships and touched on the fringes of Catron's connection with activities in the area. In May, Governor Axtell visited Lincoln, borrowed $1,800 from John H. Riley, and returned to Santa Fe with Riley. In July Frederick C. Godfroy assumed the post of agent for the Mescalero Apaches at the reservation established in 1873 south of Fort Stanton. In August Lawrence G. Murphy and William Brady were nominated and unanimously chosen to represent the Democratic party from Lincoln County in the Territorial convention to be held in Santa Fe later that month. Juan B. Patron was similarly selected as the Republican convention delegate, and Alexander A. McSween was secretary of the Republican electors.[6]

In November Axtell repaid the money he had borrowed from Riley, and Riley entered the firm of L. G. Murphy & Co. It was about this time that Catron loaned money to the Murphy firm and to Lawrence G. Murphy personally. As far as is known, this was his first business interest in Lincoln County.

Also in November John Henry Tunstall arrived in Lincoln. Tunstall came from a wealthy English family and was eager to make a fortune with cattle in the expanding American West. He had earlier met Alexander A. McSween in Santa Fe, and they now became closely allied in business. Tunstall furnished financial backing that enabled McSween to make more extensive inroads on the economic monopoly that had been enjoyed by L. G. Murphy & Co. Tunstall made no secret of his intention to use his wealth in securing power and did not scruple at sharp practices along the way. He acquired land with illegal manipulations of land laws. Not all others in the community were lily white in this regard, but Tunstall was a foreigner who even wrote home about his machinations.

The growing tension was helped along by a dispute over insurance money on a $10,000 policy taken out by Emil A. Fritz, former Murphy partner, who had died while on a visit to Germany. The policy was turned over to McSween for collection with the understanding that his fee would not exceed $2,500. Because of difficult legal technicalities, the insurance company delayed in making payment. McSween traveled to New York in pursuance of the collection and claimed that he was obliged to pay the $2,500 to attorneys in that city and to spend an additional $4,095 for further expenses. The heirs of Emil Fritz believed this fee to be excessive and consulted Murphy with their problem. Murphy retained Catron and William L. Rynerson to recover the money. These attorneys obtained a judgment against McSween for the amount of the policy less the $2,500 which the court allowed McSween for his fee.

McSween refused to pay the judgment, and his property was attached. Tunstall's holdings were also attached on the representation that he had an interest in McSween's affairs. There was no legal basis for including Tunstall in the action, because a contemplated partnership between the two was not to take effect until May 1878. McSween continued to resist payment and was indicted on a charge of embezzlement. Warrants were then issued for the arrest of both McSween and Tunstall.

Partisan lines were now quickly drawn throughout the neighborhood. McSween had acquired many friends, including John Chisum and a few other large cattle growers. Murphy, Dolan, and Riley were also popular, particularly with the smaller cattle and sheep growers to whom they had been generous in extending credit. When Murphy and Dolan entered into the controversy, these smaller operators lined up solidly behind them.

McSween, when the indictment for embezzlement was returned against him, hired gunmen to protect himself from arrest. Among these was Billy the Kid, who became the leader of the McSween forces.

The Murphy-Dolan group also recruited gunmen who seem to have been plentiful in the area. Included in this fighting force was Jesse Evans, a friend of Billy the Kid. The two had come to Lincoln late in 1877 and found employment at the Chisum ranch. Evans became friendly with Jimmie Dolan and placed his gun at Dolan's disposal; nevertheless, he remained friendly with the Kid throughout the ensuing depredations and killings.

Meanwhile, on April 20, 1877, Murphy severed his connection with the company bearing his name, leaving Dolan and Riley to continue under the name of Jas. J. Dolan & Co. A year later, in ill health and desiring to leave Lincoln County, Murphy advertised his Carrizozo ranch for sale cheap for cash. The ranch contained twenty square miles of excellent pasture with abundant water. He left Lincoln on May 10, 1878, and died in Santa Fe on October 20 of ·that year at the age of forty-seven years. Before his death he renewed a note to Catron pledging his Carrizozo ranch as additional security.[7] When Murphy died Catron took possession of the ranch and in 1882 sold it to James A. Alcock for $175,000.*

On January 12, 1878, James J. Dolan and John H. Riley executed a mortgage deed conveying to Catron forty acres of land in Lincoln together with their house, store, and all personal property, including a herd of about 2,000 cattle at Seven Rivers. The loan from Catron had been needed to pay Spiegelberg brothers in Santa Fe an amount owed for supplies. The firm also owed the Fritz estate $48,000 and Tunstall's Lincoln County Bank $1,000 additional. The business was still solvent, but evidently overextended on credit, and the owners were unable to meet the obligation of their note to Catron.[8]

On April 23, Jas. J. Dolan & Co. announced temporary suspension of business and on May 1 the formal dissolution of their company. Edgar A. Walz, Catron's brother-in-law, took over the business. Walz had arrived in Santa Fe from Minnesota about the first of the year, and Catron trusted him with full power of attorney in handling this difficult and potentially dangerous assignment. Catron's law partner, William T.

---

* Catron to James A. Waymire, May 11, 1891 (C.P. 105, Vol. 3). The amount has been variously reported elsewhere: Edgar A. Walz, *Retrospections*, p. 8 ($175,000); William A. Keleher, *Violence in Lincoln County*, p. 347 ($170,000); and Keleher, *Fabulous Frontier*, p. 114 ($225,000).

Thornton, journeyed to Lincoln to arrange legal details of the settlement.[9]

On January 5, 1877, Roswell Smith (under power of attorney to Van C. Smith) had executed a mortgage to Catron on property within the present city of Roswell to secure the sum of $1,000 loaned by Catron. On September 24, 1877, Smith conveyed this property to Catron by warranty deed. This land gave Catron headquarters for the cattle received from Dolan and Riley.*

Concurrent with Catron's acquisition of the Lincoln property, fuel was being fed to the flame of violence that was soon to flare up there. In a letter of January 18, 1878, addressed to the editor of the *Mesilla Independent,* John Henry Tunstall wrote in a partisan manner for his friend and associate Alexander A. McSween. Tunstall accused Sheriff William Brady of failure to turn over to the Territorial treasurer an amount in excess of $2,500 collected in taxes. James J. Dolan answered Tunstall's letter in the January 29 issue of the *Independent.* He pointed out that Sheriff Brady, because of sickness in the family, had been unable to appear in Santa Fe in time to settle his account with the Territory; nevertheless, Brady could show proper receipts from the Territorial treasurer of his account. And so he could. Catron had paid the money on behalf of Brady with proceeds of Indian Department vouchers made out to John H. Riley and forwarded to the First National Bank in Santa Fe for deposit.[10]

Tunstall had crossed swords with Dolan, and it had earlier been proven that this could have fatal results. On the morning of February 6 Tunstall and his party were in camp on a return journey from Mesilla. Jimmie Dolan and Jesse Evans, guns in hand, approached the camp. Dolan asked Tunstall if he was ready to fight and settle their differences.

---

*Samuel Atkinson to Catron, May 28, 1901 (C.P. 103, Box 12). In 1882 Catron transferred this property to Patrick F. Garrett, and later it was conveyed to James J. Hagerman.

Tunstall, who by this time should have known the difference between the code of the formal duel and the less ceremonious shoot-out practiced on the American frontier, inquired if this was a challenge to a duel. Dolan again pressed his demand for a less pompous settlement; however, a deputy sheriff present with Dolan stepped into the prospective line of fire and thus prevented the affair of honor. Along with some words intended to deter Tunstall from writing further inflammatory letters to the *Independent,* Dolan stated just prior to his departure, "You won't fight this morning, you damned coward, but I'll get you soon."[11]

Shortly thereafter McSween tried to arrange surety for his appearance bond in connection with charges of embezzlement against him. On February 11 he executed the bond and delivered it by registered letter to fellow Republican, District Attorney W. L. Rynerson. His enemies had evidently put pressure on persons willing to go on the bond; it was refused. Jose Montano was one of the volunteers on the bond. Later he informed McSween of a threat made by Dolan — that, if Montano became surety for McSween's bond, he would have him prosecuted by United States Attorney Catron for cutting timber on public land. This was a charge to which few persons of that day could plead innocent; nevertheless, it would have been Catron's duty to prosecute Montano if a grand jury presented an indictment.

On February 18, 1878, Sheriff Brady sent a deputy, William S. Morton, and a posse to serve the attachment on Tunstall and to arrest him. Reportedly, Tunstall was warned of the approaching party and left his ranch for Lincoln. When Morton and his men reached the ranch and found Tunstall gone, they followed, overtook him, and shot him down. It was a cowardly murder probably planned by no one in advance, but it gave rise to much speculation, then and since, of a sinister plot involving not only Dolan and Riley, but also Sheriff Brady, United States Attorney Catron, and District Attorney Rynerson.

When Tunstall's companions — who had escaped — reached Lincoln with their story, it caused much excitement at the McSween home. It is said that John H. Riley stopped by to see what the commotion was. To show that he was unarmed, he removed his coat. Reportedly, a small memorandum book fell from his pocket and was later picked up and handed to McSween. The story goes that in this book were the cipher names of certain of Riley's associates:

T. B. Catron	"Grapes"
L. G. Murphy	"Box"
Maj. Godfroy	"Hampton"
Indians	"Trees"
W. L. Rynerson	"Oyster"
1st Nat. Bank, Santa Fe	"Terror"
2nd Nat. Bank, Santa Fe	"Fearful"

Most accounts imply a menacing inference to this code. If the situation and the times are taken in context, there is nothing unusual about Riley's possession of a cipher code, as codes frequently were used in communications intended to be private. Catron, for example, used such a code on numerous occasions. Following is an example in a transmission to Wilson Waddingham:

Claudicant Dame Saveloy Frache Fiveate Dollars Drawcansir Gravey and Fowling Drawcansir himself Dame Walloon Gravey Wareful Warily peeress Fowling capitulary Bacchanal Your Niece Acerous.

Translation:

I have telegraphic communication with Dame in which he says one thousand four hundred dollars is due Gravey and five hundred dollars is due himself Dame will wait as long as possible Gravey in want of money wants you if possible to pay five hundred dollars cash balance your note will be accepted.[12]

Along with the code, a letter of February 14 from Rynerson to Dolan and Riley — reputed by many to be a forgery — is said to have been in the pages of Riley's memorandum book. The letter said in part:

I believe that Tunstall is in with the swindles with the rogue McSween. They have the money belonging to the Fritz estate and they must be made to give it up. It must be made hot for them all the hotter the better especially is this necessary now that it has been discovered that there is no hell. . . . Shake that McSween outfit up till it shells out and squares up and then shake it out of Lincoln. I will aid you to punish the scoundrels all I can. . . .[13]

While Rynerson was hot tempered and pugnacious, analysis of his letter to Dolan and Riley — whether or not a forgery — reveals ño indication that it was an incitation to murder as claimed by his opposition.

Shortly after Tunstall's death, Sheriff Brady wrote a letter giving United States Attorney Catron details of the slaying. Catron referred the letter to Governor Axtell with recommendation that the President of the United States be informed of conditions in Lincoln County and that he be requested to authorize the use of federal troops to aid Territorial authorities in maintaining the public peace.[14] Axtell followed Catron's advice; furthermore, he immediately left for Lincoln in person. Here he found a dispute over jurisdiction of local law enforcement. The McSween adherents, despairing of action from the openly partisan Sheriff Brady, turned to Justice of the Peace John B. Wilson, who issued warrants for the arrest of Tunstall's murderers. Brady, weak and vacillating, was caught in a cross fire because some of the warrants were for his own deputies.

Governor Axtell had to make a decision. From a standpoint of establishing jurisdiction, there was some logic in his proclamation of March 9 that only District Judge Warren H. Bristol and Sheriff Brady had the right to enforce law in Lincoln County. Axtell was notoriously obstinate and showed a notable lack of diplomacy in his methods. With questionable legality he declared that the appointment of Justice of the Peace Wilson by the Board of County Commissioners was good for nothing.

Governor Axtell was either wildly foolhardy or he sadly misjudged the length of the fuse attached to the powder keg

that was Lincoln County at the time. It was widely known
that he had borrowed money from John H. Riley on a previous
visit. Although the loan had been repaid, it was firmly believed
(and openly stated) by McSween adherents that the governor
favored their opponents because he was under obligation to
them. Despite the atmosphere of barely contained resentment
in Lincoln, Axtell returned to Santa Fe and blithely announced that the trouble between the Dolan and McSween
parties was quieting down.[15] If Axtell honestly expected that
his executive fiat would preserve the peace, he was tragically
mistaken. By championing Brady's authority, he signed the
sheriff's death warrant.

The thwarted McSween adherents now went outside the
law, as decreed by Governor Axtell, in the guise of "Regulators." Two of the murderers of Tunstall were captured and
shot down. On April 1 Sheriff Brady and a deputy, George
Hindman, were shot from ambush and killed instantly. Billy
the Kid led the attack aided, it was charged, by McSween
partisans. Open warfare followed.

A majority of the Lincoln County commissioners at this
time were friendly to McSween and appointed John Copeland
to succeed Brady as sheriff. He was sheriff for but little more
than a month, but this period was significant for the affairs of
Catron in the neighborhood.

On April 23, 1878, a communication from the office of
Colonel Edward Hatch in Santa Fe to army headquarters at
Fort Leavenworth stated that the presence of troops at Lincoln
would be necessary for some time to come. This judgment was
based largely on information obtained from United States
Attorney Catron.[16] His advice was sound because the military
was the only force respected there at the time. He was aware
of unrest in the area; moreover, he had a mortgage on the
property of Dolan and Riley. His motive may have been to
keep the peace or to protect his loan collateral. Sensibly, he
could have hoped for both. Indeed, it soon became evident
that his property needed protection.

On May 1 Edgar A. Walz formally took over the Dolan and Riley business. That same day, men in charge of Catron's cattle on the Pecos were warned by Regulators that unless they left the ranch and cattle they would be killed.[17]

At this time John H. Riley had a contract with Indian Agent Frederick C. Godfroy for supplying the Mescalero Indian reservation with beef. He had a similar contract with the military post. Evidently he had agreed to purchase the cattle acquired by Catron in connection with the transfer of the Dolan and Riley assets to him.* Catron's cattle were on the Pecos, and horses were needed to make delivery. The Regulators' warning of May 1 for the herders in charge of the cattle to leave was not heeded. About the middle of May, Riley traveled to Seven Rivers to supervise driving a herd of cattle to the reservation. Upon his arrival he learned that the entire herd of twenty-seven horses had been forcibly driven off by a party of nineteen men claiming to be a sheriff's posse. In the process they killed one man and wounded two others, then drove off Catron's 2,000 cattle and mixed them in with the vast Chisum herd. The group was headed by Doc Scurlock, who claimed to be a deputy, and included Billy the Kid as well as others responsible for the death of Sheriff Brady.†

---

* There was persistent rumor at the time (still perpetuated about one hundred years later) that Catron was interested in government beef contracts. On September 11, 1878, he denied this connection in answer to questions submitted to him by Frank Warner Angel. Catron explained that he had sold cattle to William Rosenthal, who had such contracts, and what Rosenthal did with the cattle was none of his business. In a letter of 1891, however, Catron refers to Edgar A. Walz as a nominal contractor on government contracts for Indian supplies. The contracts were in Walz' name, but Catron did not clarify his own position in the contractual procedure. The implication, though, was that Walz felt Catron owed him money in the transaction. Catron to James A. Waymire, May 11, 1891 (C.P. 105, Vol. 31).

† Riley to Dudley, May 19, 1878 (N.A.R.G. 94) identifies "Kid" as one of the party who stole Catron's horses and cattle. Dudley to Acting Asst. Adj. Gen. May 25, 1878 (N.A.R.G. 94) says: "I am informed by parties, one of the contractors among the number, that Hunter alias Chisum, McSween or others, have driven some fifteen hundred head of Riley and Dolan's cattle, or Catron's cattle (whoever owns them) into Chisum's herd, which numbers forty, sixty, or more thousand head." There are enough other references to this incident in N.A.R.G. 94 to make it seem reasonably certain that this information was rather common knowledge at the time.

They were actually employees of McSween and Chisum, and their purpose was to hamper Riley in fulfilling his contract with Godfroy.

Riley informed Colonel Nathan A. M. Dudley, who had assumed command at Fort Stanton on April 5, that without the stolen horses he would be unable to fulfill the beef contracts; he requested the aid of soldiers in their recovery. He also notified Indian Agent Godfroy of his predicament, and Godfroy likewise requested military aid because he needed supplies for the June 4 issue. Dudley had heard and believed that there was some question as to the ownership of the horses and cattle; therefore, he did not deem it proper to authorize troops to aid in their recovery (they unquestionably belonged to Catron). He also had information that Wm. Dowlin & Co., post traders, had offered to sell Riley enough cattle to keep his contract. Finally, he was informed that Riley was accompanied by some twenty armed men and believed that if the cattle were his he ought to be able to recover them.

Dudley did not seem to heed the implication of such an attitude in fostering further violence.[18] The fact is that Riley's men were outnumbered by McSween and Chisum forces (estimated at from 50 to 100) and were forced to flee to avoid capture. Riley was firmly convinced that capture meant death.

Because Catron's cattle near Roswell had been scattered, it was impossible for Riley to satisfy his contract with purchases from this source. Walz and Thornton, in behalf of Catron, evidently realized the hopelessness of trying to round up and move the cattle on the Pecos in time for Godfroy's June 4 deadline. Both consented that Riley purchase cattle from Wm. Dowlin & Co. Walz later recovered and moved Catron's cattle to the Carrizozo ranch, acquired by the latter in the autumn of that year.[19]

When Thornton heard that Catron's horses had been stolen, he demanded an explanation from Sheriff Copeland.

On May 24, the sheriff denied that any of the thieves were deputies and claimed that he was in no way responsible for the theft. Copeland was removed from office on May 28; Catron might be accused of vengefully causing the removal, except that he did not learn of the loss of his horses and cattle until May 30.[20]

The fact is that Copeland's appointment had been unpalatable to the anti-McSween faction, so James J. Dolan and others had visited Santa Fe with a complaint to Governor Axtell. The governor used as an excuse for removing Copeland the fact that he had failed to file his bond within the required thirty days. Axtell, however, surely knew that the reason for Copeland's tardiness was that the tax lists had not been prepared because of disturbance in Lincoln County. The bond was correlated with the amount of taxes to be collected, so it was impossible for Copeland to file his bond. Axtell appointed George W. Peppin, a Dolan-Riley partisan, to replace Copeland.

Immediately upon receipt of Thornton's letter informing him of the loss of his stock, Catron wrote to Governor Axtell. Understandably, he was irritated by the theft of his property; nevertheless, if one refrains from torturing statements into desired points of view, it is apparent that he recognized his duty as a federal official when he again urged that the military be requested to keep peace. Had his advice been heeded, much bloodshed might have been averted. He said:

> I also learn that all the stockmen on the lower Pecos living near my cattle have been compelled to abandon their stock and go to the mountains where they are now awaiting an attack. There seems to be no authority in the county of Lincoln to compel people to keep the peace or obey the law, and there seems to be an utter disregard of all law in the county as well as life and private rights. I would most respectfully request that some steps be taken to disarm all parties carrying arms, and that the military be instructed to see that they all keep the peace.
> I am informed that the sheriff keeps with his deputies large posses armed who are one of the factions only and who take occasion at all

time to kill persons and take the property of the other faction whenever they get an opportunity. There is no power from what I can learn that can keep the peace in that country, except the military, of whom both parties have a healthy dread.[21]

By this time a newcomer had arrived in Lincoln Town. Frank Warner Angel was sent by Washington officials to investigate the death of John H. Tunstall, and the conduct of Governor Axtell and other Territorial officials. He arrived in Lincoln on May 14 and took numerous affidavits of persons involved in the growing feud.*

The new sheriff, Peppin, had no more success in controlling lawlessness than had his predecessor. While the month of June passed quietly, the potential for civil disturbance was augmented by an act of Congress prohibiting the use of federal troops in civil matters in the Territory without the express permission of the President. This act was approved on the eighteenth and passed on through military channels. Territorial officials had recognized that only military force could keep order in strife-torn Lincoln County. The new order was an open invitation to increased violence.

Among the outlaw element that now rushed to Lincoln County to take part in the expected fray and, hopefully, to share in the spoils of victory, was a band headed by the notorious outlaw from the Mesilla area, John Kinney. He arrived in Lincoln on June 22, 1878.

Kinney appears in New Mexico history, alternating between respectability and flagrant cattle thievery. Catron's law partner, William T. Thornton, later defended Kinney before the law for larceny of cattle. From this connection, apparently, grew a legend that Catron was responsible for Kinney's participation in the Lincoln County troubles. If any Territorial official is to be charged with this recruitment of an outlaw element, it must be District Attorney Rynerson. It is equally possible, though, that Kinney sought to take

---

* The results of Angel's investigations are presented in chapter 7.

advantage of chaotic conditions in order to purloin cattle in the area. In April of the following year, he opened a meat market in Mesilla.[22]

Prior to Kinney's arrival in Lincoln, Sheriff Peppin had attached him and his gang to the sheriff's posse. Governor Axtell later held the position that, while he did not approve of Kinney acting with the sheriff, he could not blame Peppin, when attacked, for taking into his service all who offered.[23] This was one of Axtell's more obvious rationalizations and hardly to be excused on the part of a Territorial governor. For a sheriff to have a gang of thieves in his constabulary was questionable, and it served the further purpose of seeming to make the McSween faction martyrs preyed upon by acknowledged outlaws.

There were those in Lincoln who thought — or at least pretended to think — that Catron supported Kinney and his cohorts, and this writer cannot claim of certain knowledge that he did not. Those who could say for certain are long since dead. The present weight of evidence and logic, however, indicates that he simply owned property in the area and wanted it protected — a perfectly reasonable desire. Conversely, it does not seem sensible to accept without reservation the information conveyed by a hired gunman caught up in the emotional atmosphere of civil turmoil. With this explanation the reader is invited to judge for himself the historical merit of a letter of July 13, received by Edgar A. Walz, in the handwriting of Charles Bowdre, but signed "Regulator."

Sir, we are all aware that your brother-in-law, T. B. Catron sustains the Murphy Kinney party and take this method of informing you that if any property belonging to the residents of this county is stolen or destroyed, Mr. Catron's property will be dealt with as nearly as can be in the way in which the party he sustains deals with the property stolen or destroyed by them.

We returned Mr. Thornton the horses we took for the purpose of keeping the Murphy party from pursuing us, with the promise from him that the horses should not again be used for that purpose. Now we know that the identical horses returned are used by the party with whom you are all clearly identified.

We know that the Tunstall estate cattle are pledged to Kinney and party. If they are taken a similar number will be taken from your brother. It is our object and efforts to protect property, but the man who plans destruction shall have destruction measured against him. Steal from the poorest or richest American or Mexican, and the full measure of that injury you do shall be visited upon the property of Mr. Catron.

This murderous band is harbored by you as your guests and with the consent of Mr. Catron occupies your property.

Regulator.[24]

Walz later stoutly maintained that his intention was strictly to protect Catron's interest, and that neither he nor his employer had any intention of taking part in the controversy. This would have been the course of any prudent person set down in the midst of civil war, and there is no reason to believe that he was not prudent. It was said of him:

Edgar A. Walz left for Lincoln County Monday last after a couple of weeks sojourn among friends and relatives in Santa Fe. Although it might seem to some like going into the valley of death he feels no fear, as he thinks he has convinced both parties that he wishes to tend strictly to his own business. No fights in his if you please.[25]

As that eminent authority on Lincoln County, William A. Keleher, has graphically stated:

July 19, 1878, was a day of wrath and reckoning in Lincoln. Several days preceding that dread day, scores of mounted men, carrying a tried-and-true weapon, whether six-shooter, rifle or shotgun, and armed with all available ammunition, rode toward Lincoln, the county seat of Lincoln County. No need to ask the name of the place of rendezvous, or to inquire into the purpose of traveling toward a common destination. Instinctively, each man seemed to know the objective was Lincoln; and that there would be fighting after reaching there. . . . Everybody seemed to know, without being told, that the time had come for a showdown between the McSween and Dolan and Riley forces.[26]

The oft-told account of the battle of Lincoln, culminating with the burning of the McSween house and the slaying of Alexander A. McSween and others on July 19, need not be told here. Significant to the Catron story, though, is the part played by Colonel Nathan A. M. Dudley.

Dudley was prohibited from active participation in the Lincoln dispute by the recent Congressional Act forbidding military intervention in civil affairs. But on July 16 Berry Robinson, a soldier in Dudley's command, was fired upon while bringing a message to Lincoln. Sheriff Peppin informed Dudley of this incident in the second of two letters (Dudley had declined to loan him a howitzer in answer to the first).

Daylight of July 19 witnessed a stalemate between McSween and anti-McSween forces. Dudley now used the Robinson incident as an excuse to interfere, as he later expressed it, to protect helpless women and children. In a matter of hours after the arrival of Dudley's strong force, the tide of battle veered toward Sheriff Peppin's party. Shortly after their arrival in Lincoln, Dudley's staff officers persuaded a reluctant justice of the peace, John B. Wilson, to issue a warrant for the arrest of McSween and others, charging assault with intent to kill Berry Robinson. With this assurance that they were acting within the law, Peppin and his deputies proceeded with bloody subjugation of the beleagured Mc-Sween party.

It was later charged by McSween advocates that Colonel Dudley's men, along with those of Sheriff Peppin, looted the store of the deceased John Tunstall. Dudley indicated otherwise. Edgar A. Walz, he reported, had visited the Tunstall store on July 21 and found four or five wagons in front of it with a number of Mexicans loading goods from the store. Walz asked Mrs. McSween why she allowed pilfering of the property of her late husband's deceased friend and associate. She is said to have replied that she had nothing to do with the matter. Walz and David M. Easton then told the Mexicans that they ought to restore the goods or they would be liable for stealing. A portion of the stock was returned.[27] Dudley used this incident to hint at a lack of interest on the part of Mrs. McSween toward her deceased husband's affairs.

Little more than a month after McSween's death, implications cropped up in Colonel Dudley's official reports that

Susan McSween was rapidly recovering from any grief she may have felt at the death of her husband. His version was that Jim French was in town almost every night, leaving early in the morning, and stopping at the house where Mrs. McSween lived.[28]

On July 19, 1879, she marked the first anniversary of her husband's death by filing suit against Colonel Dudley alleging arson in connection with the burning of her husband's house, as well as defamation of character, and asking for $25,000 in damages.[29]

One specification, later withdrawn, complained that Dudley had annulled the contract of David Easton for the delivery of corn at Fort Stanton because Easton refused to make affidavit reflecting on the character and chastity of Mrs. McSween.[30]

Easton, along with Edgar Walz, was Catron's agent, representing him in business interests in the area. These included, besides the property acquired from Dolan and Riley, a brewery located at Fort Stanton.[31] Catron's relationship with Easton brought him into conflict with Colonel Dudley. Dudley inferred that Catron was somehow connected with Easton's contract for military stores at Fort Stanton.

In 1871 Dudley had been tried by court martial in Arizona for offenses including drunkenness. On November 26, 1877, while in command at Fort Union, he was again court martialed and relieved from command. Catron represented Dudley in the proceedings and probably was instrumental in saving him from a more severe penalty. It has been conjectured that Dudley was grateful for this and followed Catron's advice on how to proceed in his new command at Fort Stanton.[32] The fact is, the two clashed emphatically at the time.

Dudley claimed that his troubles while in command at Fort Stanton were partially an outgrowth of honest effort to serve the government. In this capacity he had become obnoxious to certain prominent parties connected with the Santa Fe Ring, among them a swarm of sore-headed contractors. These contractors had taken exception to his official actions because the actions clashed with their pecuniary interests. He said, for example, that he had refused to allow the post quartermaster to receive some 4,000 pounds of inferior quality Mexican corn furnished by Staab & Co., Santa Fe contractors, when their written bonded contract called for merchantable American corn. He maintained that the market value of the American corn was nearly double that of the Mexican product.

Dudley singled Catron out particularly. He said he had refused to comply with Catron's insulting written demand at the time Catron's official conduct was being investigated by Frank Warner Angel, that he go blind and certify to the United States attorney general that certain parties who had made affidavits against Catron were unreliable and unprincipled men.[33] While there is no present record of this alleged demand by Catron, Dudley's displeasure is evident; but he seems to have been displeased with about everybody and everything.

Dudley characterized Catron as an all-powerful unscrupulous lawyer whose displeasure he had incurred by his official actions. Dudley had heard, he maintained, that Catron had threatened to drive him out of the service by volunteering his legal aid, if not employed to prosecute him.[34]

As a matter of fact, Catron's law partner Thornton had assisted Henry L. Waldo in April 1879 to successfully defend Dudley before a board of inquiry which had investigated his conduct as commanding officer at Fort Stanton.[35]

On December 6, 1879, Susan McSween's case charging Dudley with arson and libel was tried at Mesilla. United States Attorney Sidney M. Barnes was assigned to defend Dudley, while Ira E. Leonard presented the case for the prosecution. Catron, despite Dudley's earlier intimation, had no part in the trial, during which Susan McSween, the leading prosecution witness, failed to appear. Dudley was acquited by a jury that deliberated only a few minutes.[36]

By January 1881 the business acquired from Dolan and Riley was closed out by Catron's agent Walz, and Catron sold the store building to Lincoln County. After his sale of the Carrizozo ranch the following year, he had no appreciable business interests left in Lincoln County.[37] He owned property there for only half a decade, but these years encompassed the bitter feuding that is probably more widely known than any other facet of New Mexico history. If one examines the record of his affairs in that time and place objectively, it can be seen that he does not fit well the role of conniving manipulator that tradition has assessed to him. Furthermore, there is little reasonable basis for claiming in the pages of history that he supported partisan intervention in the quarrel.[38] He owned property there and wanted it protected, but he also gave sensible advice calculated to keep the peace in that strife-torn community. It is evident, though, that neither side in the fighting wanted peace except on their terms — perhaps this is the basic reason there is fighting anywhere at any time — so the turbulence had to run its course.

6
Partisan Repercussions

Thomas Benton Catron was present when the Republican party in New Mexico was organized in the winter of 1867 and when the epithet "Santa Fe Ring" was applied to its leaders. It was Catron's fate to become the acknowledged head of both party and ring, although he did not seek the leadership. His outspokenness made him many enemies who deplored his leadership and fought against it, but he possessed one qualification — he was willing to work harder than any contemporary. His production of letters was staggering, enabling him to keep close contact with persons throughout the Territory. In his letters, as in speaking, he characteristically swayed people by force and logic rather than personal charm, but he was also resourceful and brilliant. He could, and did, employ personal persuasiveness if reason did not suffice. Repeatedly, people came to him for leadership because he was the only person willing to pay the price in effort and money to achieve mutually desired political and economic goals.

In the history of New Mexico, there is no person concerning whom such extensive oral tradition has grown as Catron. Most of this tradition is adverse. Thus it is that his relation with the Santa Fe Ring has taken on connotations of ringleader rather than leader. A contemporary wrote in 1911:

Catron was the boss of the Territory from 1865 to 1900 and is probably still the most unscrupulous man in the Southwest. His methods of whole-sale assassination and blackmail are [notorious]. His frown has waned of late years but he still runs the gang in this country.[1]

In a letter in 1965, the author was informed: "If you tell the truth about this scoundrel, it would be highly unpalatable to [his sons and grandsons]."[2]

Much of this traducement was promulgated by Catron's political enemies, in many instances over circumstances related to monetary debts owed him and not paid by his debtors. Unfortunately for historical writing, Catron's office burned in 1888 and with it most of his correspondence. However, his papers from that date until his death are largely intact and simply do not bear out the nefarious imputations.

Some detractors have said that he was too smart to be caught and probably destroyed the incriminating evidence. This possibility is unlikely because his affairs were so complicated that it was hard enough to keep them orderly, let alone keep a crooked record straight. More important, he was an inveterate collector and never intentionally destroyed any records. Much of his correspondence is chronologically numbered and indexed and shows no evidence of his sorting out information that might later prove detrimental to him. He tended to disregard his detractors; his affairs were so complicated that it would have been impossible for him to do otherwise.

The term *Santa Fe Ring* is closely linked in historical tradition with Republican politics in the post-Civil-War period and probably excites the romantic imagination of more people than any other words in New Mexico history. The appellation is little understood, and to the popular fancy brings imaginings of a sinister organization with members dedicated to unqualified promotion of their own selfish interests. In familiar tradition it is accompanied by connotations of violence, deception, deceit, fraud, and other nefarious implications.

The expression was a natural product of the times which was the era of the Robber Barons and "Boss" Tweed. In New Mexico, as nationally, a *ring* was a group of persons with common political and economic interests that conflicted with those of other individuals or combinations. The Santa Fe Ring had no fixed membership or formal organization; members were Republican leaders who would scarcely have been aware of their alleged affiliation, without reminders from Democratic counterparts. Conversely, Republicans labeled Democrats as members of rings, but never originated as colorful or durable a term as Santa Fe Ring.

The wording came into use with the organization of the Republican party in the Territory. From the first, it was a phrase used by Democrats in malicious reference to Republicans whom they wished to traduce. It was originated to counteract the strength provided by Republican party unity. In time it was also used by Democrats in referring to other Democrats who acted in concert with Republicans, particularly for mutual economic gain. Such cooperation was the surest way for a Democrat to be labeled a member of the Santa Fe Ring.

Other rings were referred to throughout New Mexico; however, the Santa Fe Ring was reputed to be the controlling influence over others throughout the Territory. This was only partially true. There was no network of control in an organized sense; there was mutual cooperation but only in specific instances for particular events or projects.

Litigation over the Maxwell Land Grant first launched the Santa Fe Ring into notoriety. It is ironic that Catron's connection with the grant was relatively minor, yet this was the start of the tradition that labeled him as the leader of ring activities in the Territory.

The original grant was secured from Governor Manuel Armijo on January 11, 1841, by Guadalupe Miranda and Charles Hipolite Trotier de Beaubien. Starting in 1858 the land comprising the grant was purchased by Lucien B. Maxwell. By the end of the Civil War, Maxwell had become one of the most prominent men in northern New Mexico. His rich and undeveloped empire attracted the attention of capitalists who sought to negotiate a purchase. The most serious of these was a group including Senator Jerome B. Chaffee, a Colorado mine owner; George M. Chilcott, Colorado congressman; Charles F. Holly of Cimarron, mining man and lawyer; Wilson Waddingham, entrepeneur; and Stephen B. Elkins, who became attorney for the company. On May 26, 1869, they acquired an option from Lucien and Luz Maxwell to purchase all of the estate except one thousand acres comprising the home ranch at Cimarron. A superseding option was made on January 28, 1870. Maxwell received $10,000 for the option and agreed to a sales price of $1,350,000 for approximately 2,000,000 acres of land.

On December 3, 1869, Secretary of the Interior Jacob D. Cox had ruled that the grant should be limited to twenty-two square leagues or 97,000 acres, but Chaffee and his associates continued their negotiations for purchase. Furthermore, on January 5, 1870, they contracted with William W. Griffin of Santa Fe to continue his survey of the grant, which survey had been interrupted by the ruling of Secretary Cox. Chaffee received Griffin's field notes and survey plates, and filed them with the General Land Office in Washington. Before this filing, Chaffee arranged for approval of the survey by Surveyor General T. Rush Spencer who was, conveniently, an official of the grant company. Griffin's survey called for the 2,000,000 acres, more or less, of the sale to the Chaffee syndicate.

Meanwhile, Senator Chaffee and his associates were involved in lengthy negotiations with a number of English capitalists headed by John Collinson of London. This group wanted the property, but foreigners were not authorized to hold real estate in New Mexico. To evade this complication, the Englishmen chose three prominent New Mexicans to "front" for them and to file for incorporation as the Maxwell

Land Grant and Railway Company. These men were William A. Pile, governor of New Mexico; T. Rush Spencer, surveyor general of the Territory; and John S. Watts, former Territorial chief justice.

On April 30, 1870, Collinson's syndicate took up the option, and on May 12 the articles of incorporation were acknowledged by the secretary of the Territory. Shortly thereafter members of a newly elected board of directors held their first meeting. In addition to the three incorporators the board included General William J. Palmer, railroad builder, and Miguel A. Otero, father of the later Territorial governor of New Mexico. Within the year a large loan was floated on the Amsterdam market, and the company commenced surveying and subdividing the grant with a view to selling the land to new settlers.[3]

But there were already settlers on the grant, and they posed a serious problem. The difficulty had existed when Maxwell owned the property. He had partially solved the problem by arranging with most of the settlers to pay for their farms in produce. Most of the miners consented to pay for the privilege of mining. Some refused to recognize his title, but Maxwell had not been inclined to press the issue. In any case, his rents were nominal. The Englishmen respected agreements made by Maxwell but were firm in asserting their rights where no agreements existed.

At first polite notices were sent to squatters to either make proper arrangements with the company or move out. When this failed, ejectment proceedings were brought by Elkins as attorney for the Maxwell Land Grant and Railway Company. Catron was attorney general for the Territory and, as such, acted as district attorney for the first judicial district which included Colfax County where the grant was located. In this capacity he had official duties in connection with the ejectment suits.

Attempts to eject settlers from the grant were resisted; on October 27, 1870, a serious riot broke out at Elizabethtown. Elkins telegraphed Governor Pile requesting that troops be ordered to suppress the disturbances which, it was feared, would result in destruction of the town by fire. This was only one of several serious commotions that followed.

Catron came in for a share of the blame in connection with the eviction proceedings. He claimed, with justification, that he was only acting in his official capacity as attorney general.* He was not, at this time, connected in any official way with the Maxwell Company.

A month earlier, on September 17, 1870, Elkins had resigned as United States attorney, ostensibly because of increasing professional business, but he may have wished to avoid any seeming conflict of interests. In his letter of resignation to United States Attorney General A. T. Ackerman, Elkins recommended that he be succeeded by Thomas B. Catron. Elkins' recommendation was endorsed by J. Francisco Chavez, Territorial delegate from New Mexico. Chavez pointed out:

> Mr. Catron has all the qualifications being one of the most prominent young lawyers in this community and possessed of a personal character of the highest order. He is besides a fine Spanish scholar, a prerequisite without which a U.S. District Attorney in this Territory would be simply a farce.[4]

But the enthusiastic recommendation of Elkins and Chavez was not shared by all persons in the Territory, including some who claimed to be Republicans. On September 26, 1870, a letter was sent to the United States attorney general protesting the appointment of Catron as United States attorney. The letter was signed by, among others, Alexander P. Sullivan, editor of the *Santa Fe Post*; Henry Wetter, Territorial secretary; and L. Spiegelberg of Spiegelberg Brothers. They advanced as their opinion that Catron was an unreconstructed Rebel and continued:

---

* *Santa Fe Weekly New Mexican*, May 2, 1871. About this time Elkins' home in Santa Fe was burglarized. This may have been retaliation for his part in bringing the eviction suits.

we protest against rewarding with official honors and emoluments a man like Thomas B. Catron whose bitter hostility to the Union is unchanged and who has never given utterance to a single sound or did a single act to retrieve his past conduct, or prove any devotion to the Union or any willingness to be other than its enemy in the future.[5]

This letter appears to be prejudiced and unfair. Whatever faults Catron may have had after he came to New Mexico, disloyalty to the United States or the Republican party could not be claimed among them. But the letter created enough doubt in the mind of the attorney general for Catron's appointment to be held up. On October 20, 1870, Singleton M. Ashenfelter was granted a temporary commission as United States attorney.[6]

Alexander P. Sullivan and his coterie were a decided minority in opposition to Catron's appointment. When this opposition became known, virtually every official in the Territory, as well as numerous private citizens, rushed to Catron's support; typically:

There is no man in New Mexico to whom the interests of the government could be more safely confided, in the position of United States District Attorney, than Mr. Catron, while the present incumbent of the office is utterly incompetent.[7]

An event now transpired that manifested a struggle for political power in the Territory, involving Catron and his bid to be named United States attorney. On Saturday, December 30, 1871, an act was introduced into the Territorial legislature that, with unseemly haste, was hurried through both houses. This bill transferred Chief Justice Joseph G. Palen from the first to the third judicial district. Palen had been appointed chief justice on April 15, 1869, by President Grant. There is little question that he was a man of integrity, though headstrong to the point of prejudice. He became a particular friend of William Breeden, and the two, along with Elkins and Catron, were repeatedly and vehemently accused by enemy newspapers of largely controlling the Territorial courts. They were just as staunchly defended by a friendly press.

The bill was engineered by Sullivan and Henry Wetter. Both were under pressure of indictment at the time and evidently hoped to secure a more facile judge for the first district in the person of D. B. Johnson of the third district. Johnson was represented as a drinking debauchee in whose hands Sullivan and Wetter evidently thought they would be quite safe. Behind the scenes this was a move on the part of the Democratic party to curb the growing power of the upstart Republican leaders known collectively, even then, as the Santa Fe Ring. At the same time there were reports of a powerful Democratic money ring, and there was persistent clamoring for Secretary Wetter to divulge what supplies were purchased and services rendered with $5,110 of public money paid by him to a Santa Fe mercantile firm. Sullivan and Wetter were, at the time, backed by S. Seligman & Brother; Spiegelberg Brothers; Mayer Kyser; Guttman, Friedman & Co.; and A. Staab; all merchants. Attorney General Catron was in a position to bring indictments and Judge Palen to sit in judgment. The money ring apparently determined to get rid of Chief Justice Palen.[8]

On January 4, 1872, the bill was returned to the House, where it originated, without approval by Governor Marsh Giddings. In his veto message, Giddings stated that the bill was in violation of law and that it had been secured by false statements to members of the legislature. He then reviewed the legal questions involved in an impartial, candid, and able manner.

On receipt of this message, the opponents of Chief Justice Palen adopted the desperate measure of taking over the House after it was adjourned. In order to obtain the requisite two-thirds majority to pass the bill over the governor's veto, members voted to expell three Republicans and admit three Democrats. They also filled a vacancy caused by death with another Democrat, as well as resorting to other lawless and revolutionary maneuvers. The speaker and two members were arrested and held in confinement until released on a writ of habeas corpus sued out by Attorney General Catron in the Supreme Court. The legislative mob became so riotous that the deposed speaker of the House, Milnor Rudolph, called upon General Gordon Granger, commanding the United States military district in New Mexico, for the military to preserve order. Governor Giddings added his endorsement to this request.

The House suspended further deliberations until January 22, when the Supreme Court ruled that the attempt to take over the House of Representatives was illegal and void. Forces of the United States marshal's office, reinforced by United States soldiers, stood by to see that there was no further interference. The Republican majority passed a resolution expunging from the record and nullifying all proceedings of the revolutionary Democratic minority.[9]

This legislative fiasco was repeatedly dragged from the limbo of past lore, as Catron grew to a position of political power in New Mexico, and was refurbished to attack his integrity. For example, in 1895, when an effort was being made to disbar him from the legal profession in New Mexico, an article was printed in the *Las Vegas Independent Democrat* that was based on information from the *Las Vegas Optic* of September 2, 1884. Catron was called the corrupt partner of a venal judge. The article continued:

T. B. Catron's reputation, now being "smirched" by evidence that he was a briber and too dishonest even to practice law in New Mexico, was made more than twenty-five years ago, and in 1872 it was so bad that United States troops were called out at Santa Fe to prevent the outraged people of that town from hanging him. At that time . . . the Santa Fe Ring was in its prime. Thomas B. Catron was Attorney General, James [should be Joseph G.] Palen was United States Judge, and Steve Elkins was general manager of all the deviltry.

The article accused Catron and Elkins of sharing plunder with Judge Palen so that it was impossible for any other attorney to win a case in his court. Paraphrased, the article continues:

This corrupt combination exasperated the people, who presented petitions for Palen's removal. These petitions were headed off by Elkins, so the legislature passed a bill assigning Palen to another district. The Ring's governor vetoed the bill, so a popular movement was organized to pass it over the veto. Catron and Elkins bought off a number of legislators including August Kirchner. Elkins promised him a favorable decision in a certain suit should Palen not be removed. Elkins also promised to cancel a $780 mortgage on the property of Pascual Baca for his vote. At the hour for the gathering of the assembly the town was wild with excitement, so the sheriff called upon General Gordon Granger for troops to prevent the people from assassinating Catron, Elkins, Palen, and Breeden on the spot. Elkins was afraid to let the matter come to a vote, so instructed his tool, Speaker Milnor Rudolph, to adjourn the House before a quorum was present. Rudolph did so, then wandered off outside the town threatening to kill whoever pursued him. The sheriff swore in old Jesus Baca, who had the reputation of being a "killer," as deputy, and instructed him to bring Rudolph back. He found the speaker and, taking him by the ear, led him to the legislative chamber. In the confusion it was impossible to muster enough members to transact business until the hour for final adjournment arrived. Before the legislature could be reconvened, Judge Palen died. It was believed that he committed suicide to avoid the exposure and punishment that were sure to follow his transfer to another district.

The obvious outright lies in this article are apparent. For example, Chief Justice Palen remained in office for an additional four years. During this time he suffered continued criticism by Democratic newspapers and was as staunchly defended by the Republican press. Palen paid little heed to his detractors, and his judgments and decrees grew in favor. By the time of his death — December 21, 1875 — he was generally recognized as one of the ablest and most unimpeachable judges ever to preside in New Mexico.*

---

* Arie A. Poldervaart, *Black-robed Justice*, pp. 95–96; *Santa Fe Weekly New Mexican,* January 25, 1876. United States Attorney Catron and Attorney General William Breeden were among those in a committee of the bar to draw up resolutions commending the late chief justice. Catron served as a pallbearer at his funeral.

Throughout the attempt to humiliate Chief Justic Palen, Catron continued his efforts to be named United States attorney. His enemies countered by means of an affidavit made by August Kirchner on February 1, 1872, a copy of which was sent to United States Senator Lyman Trumbull, chairman of the judiciary committee. In the affidavit, Kirchner swore that Catron and Elkins had approached him and prevailed upon him to buy legislative votes in an effort to leave Palen undisturbed.

Catron immediately prepared an affidavit attacking the Kirchner affidavit. He admitted that he had called on Kirchner, on January 2, 1872, at Kirchner's request. Kirchner, Catron maintained, had professed to consider the legislation just passed removing Chief Justice Palen to the third district an outrage and had wondered what could be done to defeat the bill. Catron assured Kirchner that, in connection with his duties as attorney general, he had seen a resolution requesting a veto signed by enough legislators to sustain that veto. Furthermore, he had been consulted by Governor Marsh Giddings — who was preparing a veto message — as to the legality of the legislation just passed. Under these circumstances, Catron maintained, it would have been pointless for him to have requested Kirchner to buy legislative votes; moreover, he categorically denied that he had done so.[10]

In support of Catron, Governor Giddings and Chief Justice Palen wired the United States attorney general:

To defeat Catron's confirmation a grossly false affidavit has been sent to Senator. Catron is able honest upright and undoubtedly the best man for the place. Please say this before the President and Senator Trumbull.[11]

Others also stood by Catron. Among these was W. W. McFarland of the New York law firm of Barlow, La Roque, and McFarland. He assured Attorney General George H. Williams that he had no personal interest in the matter except to promote the welfare of the United States and the people of New Mexico. McFarland stated that Catron, along with Elkins, was at the head of the legal profession in New Mexico and beyond doubt the best man available to represent the United States in legal matters in the Territory.[12]

Early in March 1872, Catron was appointed United States attorney by President Grant. It was reported that, as attorney general, he had exhibited unusual ability and was one of the best prosecuting officers ever to hold that office:

He is a man of very positive nature and force of character, fearless in the discharge of his duties, and a terror to evil doers. . . . His appointment by the President is just recognition of Mr. Catron's ability, legal learning and eminent fitness for the office for which he is named, as well as his earnestness, activity and unswerving fidelity as a republican.[13]

Within a month after his appointment, Catron brought an indictment against Henry Wetter for converting public funds to his own use. In July, Alexander P. Sullivan was indicted for embezzlement.[14] But these indictments did not end further attacks by Catron's enemies. There were other attempts to remove him and Chief Justice Palen from office.

To combat this sniping, Governor Marsh Giddings again wrote to the United States attorney general. He prefaced his remarks by reminding the attorney general of his unswerving devotion to the Republican party and the national administration, pointing out that he had been one of the five who framed the first Republican platform. In defense of Palen and Catron, Giddings indicated that they and their many and influential friends were of the better classes of citizens who had given immense aid when nothing but their help could have saved the Territory from anarchy after a minority had attempted to take over the legislature. Catron, he particularized, had been infamously attacked at the time of his confirmation, but August Kirchner, who had made an affidavit against him, later made another affidavit admitting his error, mistake, and untruthfulness.[15]

If Catron considered that these matters in the early years of his public career were troublesome, he would have been horrified had he been able to look into the future. He was sailing on relatively tranquil seas compared to the deluge of controversial attacks upon him that were to follow. Among these were the growing storm clouds of vituperation from Colfax County. The Maxwell Company continued to be the focal point of trouble there.

On October 24, 1872, the annual meeting of the company was held at Cimarron with John Collinson presiding. Elkins was elected president of the board of directors for the ensuing year, and William R. Morley, a young railway engineer, was chosen as vice-president and executive officer. Other directors were Dr. R. H. Longwill, H. M. Porter, and J. B. Maingay of Rotterdam.[16]

On February 4, 1873, Morley informed President Elkins that the settlers were becoming discouraged and that, in his opinion, a few suits would settle the whole situation. Accordingly, more ejectment suits were filed, which only drove the settlers to further rebellion. Morley at last realized that a long hard fight was in prospect. He called to his assistance Frank Springer, a young attorney who had attended college with him. Springer arrived in New Mexico late in February 1873 at a time when anarchy threatened. In April a public meeting was held in Cimarron to protest alleged swindles by the Maxwell Land Grant and Railway Company. Acting as one of the counsel for the settlers was Melvin W. Mills, who later switched his allegiance to the group opposing the settlers.[17]

At the annual meeting of the company in October 1873, Elkins was continued as president. A month earlier he had been elected as delegate to Congress from New Mexico.[18] Since Elkins would be in Washington, Catron was made a director of the company so he could serve as their attorney. As United States attorney, he had no contact with eviction of settlers which was a district court matter involving the Territorial attorney general, William Breeden.

While it has popularly been supposed that Catron joined Elkins as a law partner soon after he arrived in New Mexico, it was not until January 1874 that this patrnership was made, and then, because Elkins would be away from the Territory. This involved Catron for the first time directly in the affairs of the Maxwell Company. Henry L. Waldo was selected by Elkins to handle cases in which Catron was adversely employed.

In 1874 the secretary of the interior declared the Maxwell Land Grant to be public domain; the commissioner of the general land office, in a letter of January 28, ordered the surveyor general of New Mexico to extend the public surveys over it; however, the survey was delayed for lack of funds.[19] By the following summer the Maxwell Company was bankrupt and not even able to pay 1874 taxes. Elkins now resigned as president, leaving William R. Morley, Secretary Harry Whigham, and Frank Springer in charge. Catron cast his lot with Elkins. This was the beginning of friction between Morley and Springer on one side and Elkins, Catron, Mills, and Longwill on the other. One facet of this contention is involved in the continuing history of the Maxwell Land Grant.

In September 1876, the district court rendered judgments against the company for taxes due. Payment was not made, so the property was auctioned on December 16 to Melvin W. Mills for $16,479.46. The money for purchase of the tax deed was raised by a Santa Fe group headed by Catron. On July 19, 1877, Mills deeded the property to Catron for $20,000.[20]

It has been said that this was a move by Catron to keep the claim of the Maxwell Company alive.[21] There seems little doubt, however, that this was a maneuver by Catron to acquire the property for himself and his group. They hoped that the period of redemption would end before the Amsterdam bondholders redeemed the property, but Catron was paid $20,961.85 raised by an assessment on the bonds and stock of the company. The stock and bondholder committee now charged the past management with fraud, but excluded Morley, Whigham, and Springer, whom they praised for loyalty to the company's interest.

New hope for persons interested in the grant was provided by a United States Supreme Court decision in October 1876, in the case of *John G. Tameling v. The United States Freehold & Emigration Company.* The land involved in the decision was derived from the Sangre de Cristo Grant title which the Supreme Court decreed was valid, even though it exceeded the eleven square leagues of the Mexican colonization law. The court decided that Congressional confirmation passed title as effectively as though a patent had been issued. Using this decision for authority, Secretary of the Interior Carl Schurz decreed that patent would be issued to grants confirmed by Congress even though they exceeded eleven square leagues.

Under a survey appropriation approved March 3, 1877, Surveyor General Henry M. Atkinson employed William W. Griffin and Charles H. Fitch to survey the Maxwell Grant. Commissioner J. A. Williamson refused to approve the contract because Griffin had been employed in 1870 by the Maxwell Land Grant and Railway Company to survey the grant. Atkinson awarded a contract to John T. Elkins and Robert G. Marmon. John T. Elkins was a brother of the former president of the grant company, Stephen B. Elkins, who was also one of the sureties of the bond guaranteeing completion of the contract.

This has been construed as a circumstance favorable to the Maxwell Company. It should be remembered, though, that S. B. Elkins had resigned as president and was at odds with Morley and Springer, who were retained to run the affairs of the company. S. B. Elkins' main interest was in securing back salary. More to the point of censure, John T. Elkins and Marmon took only twenty-one days for a survey that probably would have required two months of careful work for competent performance. The 1,714,764.94 acres of land called for in the survey naturally delighted the grant owners and displeased the disillusioned settlers on the grant. It was felt that the people of Colfax County had been taken in by John Elkins.[22]

On June 5, 1878, the property went into the hands of

William T. Thornton as receiver. This move was requested by John Collinson, who had instituted legal proceedings. Thornton had become a partner of Catron in January. In view of Catron's earlier effort to acquire ownership of the grant, it might be supposed that Collinson would avoid further involvement with his firm. Receivership, however, involved only the receiver to act as legal custodian of the property while parties involved in litigation resolved their differences. The worst that can be said of Thornton's receivership was that the property suffered from neglect. This was understandable, since there was no money available to properly develop the grant. Thornton's receivership ended in 1880 when the property was sold under foreclosure in behalf of the first-mortgage bondholders. The buyer was Maxwell Land Grant Co., organized under the laws of Holland, and headed by Frank R. Sherwin. Patent to the grant was issued under orders of Secretary of the Interior Carl Schurz, on May 19, 1879. Catron was later employed, in routine law matters connected with the grant, into the 1900s.

Aside from his term in the House from Doña Ana County shortly after his arrival in New Mexico, Catron was not active in Republican party activities until the 1873 election for delegate to Congress. In the Republican convention he represented delegates Melvin W. Mills and Frank Springer from Colfax County as well as delegates from Valencia County. He was appointed a member of the committee to select one person from each county to serve on the Central Executive Committee of the Republican party in New Mexico. There was evidence for some months prior to the convention that Catron's fellow attorney and business associate, S. B. Elkins, would be the choice for delegate of Republicans throughout New Mexico. Contemporary reports indicate that he was a reluctant candidate because of his private affairs and professional business; nevertheless, when it came to the convention, he was nominated by acclamation on the first ballot with no other person being named.[23] He was elected by 3,829 votes — the largest number in any election to that time.

Allegedly, Elkins became a delegate to advance the cause in Washington of the Maxwell Land Grant and Railway Company. It is true that he introduced a number of bills designed to clarify the land grant muddle in New Mexico. One was for confirmed grants to be surveyed at the public expense, which would have been a boon to the Maxwell Company. It is, nevertheless, unrealistic to maintain that his efforts were calculated to benefit this company alone. Other grants were involved, as well as the economic development of the Territory. Land grants were an economic potential in New Mexico. As long as titles remained unclear, and boundaries vague, prosperity in New Mexico would be hindered.

In the election campaigning Elkins was accused of making money, by implication, from unscrupulous business deals. Elkins' friends countered that his opponent, Jose M. Gallegos, also liked to make money, strictly by political maneuvering however.[24]

In 1875 Elkins was again elected delegate to Congress. He was in Europe at the time of his nomination. Of this election, his opponents said:

Immediately after the election the friends of Elkins admitted his defeat, but upon second thought they concluded it would be better to manipulate the returns when they commenced publishing a series of "official counts." As fast as Democratic counties were heard from, there would be new "official" counts on the returns of Republican counties, which would increase the Elkins' majority up to any required number. So that at the present writing, although a month has elapsed since the election and three separate official counts" have been published, no one knows whether certain counties have yet ceased to vote for Elkins.[25]

The election was contested and Elkins prevailed.

Following the 1873 election, charges were also leveled at Catron. It was alleged that many persons in San Miguel and Mora Counties were arrested and accused of illegal trading with Comanche Indians and were then placed under bond and forced to appear for trial at Santa Fe. Upon payment of fees to United States Attorney Catron, and agreement on their part to vote for Elkins, they were released. Again, it was claimed that 600 suits were brought by Catron against persons mostly living in Taos County for living on Indian lands. All but two of the suits were dismissed. It was charged that the suits were brought for the twofold purpose of getting fees for the prosecution and whipping in votes for Elkins.[26]

The story of New Mexico politics at this time drearily recites charges and countercharges of chicanery in securing votes. To claim that no votes were influenced by questionable tactics would be untenable; however, that these charges against Catron are unfounded is demonstrable.

In 1873 he was requested by the commissioner of Indian affairs to bring suit against persons thought to be illegally residing on lands of the Pueblo Indians. He refused to act without instructions from the secretary of the interior because there would have been more than 1,000 suits. Upon receipt of instruction, Catron requested that the principle offenders be named. Subsequently, 204 cases were tried in district court upon a question of the right of the Indians to sell or lease their lands. It was decided that the Indians had this right, and that most of the settlers were on the land in question by virtue of sale or lease. Catron then took out a writ of error in one case and an appeal in another to the Supreme Court of New Mexico, where the decision of the district court was upheld. The United States Supreme Court, in turn, upheld its counterpart in the Territory.[27]

The charges against Catron partially stemmed from his growing feud with Springer and Morley in Colfax County. What had been differences of opinion in business matters broadened to include politics and personal interests. Morley was to leave the Maxwell Company within a few years to become chief construction engineer of the Santa Fe Railroad, while Springer was connected with the company until his death in 1927. During their association in Colfax County,

Springer and Morley jointly ran the *Cimarron News and Press*. As their dispute with Catron became more virulent, they used this paper to air their views and added fuel to the bitter fire. Little things played a big part. The dispute was more particularly between Catron and Morley, and Springer sided with his associate. As is so often the case between strong-willed men, neither would examine the side of the other in the light of impartial judgment. Their connections became enmeshed with the more encompassing passions of controversy involving the entire county. Here was involved bloodshed and uncontrolled storms of recrimination. It was inevitable that their personal identification become a part of the larger tempest.

Morley pursued a straightforward course devoid of subtlety. He was an angry young man and cared little who knew it, least of all Catron. Springer, though, was more of an enigma. His entire role with the Maxwell Company and embroilment in Colfax County is difficult to assess. Morley had much of the bluntness of Catron, while Springer's approach to the solution of problems was more like that of "smooth" Steve Elkins, as the latter was contemporarily described. Springer was that unusual person who could successfully play both ends against the middle. He was loyal to his trust in management of the Maxwell Company while assigning to himself the role of champion of the settlers on the grant — this at a time when the grant was the natural enemy of the settlers.

The end result is that Catron acquired the role of villain in oral tradition surrounding Colfax County troubles, while he had relatively little connection with the grant or affairs in the county. Springer comes off better in that tradition, with few understanding completely what his role was. His story of the troubles there, as related in an affidavit to Frank Warner Angel, makes little direct reference to Catron; Springer singled out Governor S. B. Axtell for condemnation more particularly than any other individual. Nevertheless, it is a rare account by an intelligent observer based on firsthand observation and is summarized in Appendix 2.

While Catron's contretemps in Colfax County — and they were fundamental to his public career — started in disagreements with Morley and Springer, their culmination can be attributed more to one person than any other: Mary E. McPherson, mother-in-law of William R. Morley, and mother of Morley's wife, Ada.

In the spring of 1875 the sister of William R. Morley mailed a letter at the post office in Cimarron. This was one of the most momentous events in the life of Catron during the entire decade of the 1870s because it was of importance in ending his career as United States attorney. In those days at Cimarron the letter drop was a box on a table. A few minutes after the letter was dropped into the box, Morley's wife, the former Ada McPherson, hurried into the post office and said that the letter had been mailed by mistake. Without waiting she ran to the box, selected one letter and left the office. The postmaster, John B. McCulloch, immediately called on Mrs. Morley and accused her of taking the letter. She first admitted that she had done so; then she denied her admission.

Some little talk was had about the matter during the next few days. Finally Morley, who was not McCulloch's friend, openly defied the postmaster by threatening to prosecute him for neglect of his duty in reference to the letter. McCulloch then wrote to United States Attorney Catron, informing him of the facts, and requested that he be summoned before the United States grand jury at Santa Fe. Catron complied with this request, and an indictment against Mrs. Morley resulted from the postmaster's testimony.

The indictment was made in July, and a warrant for the arrest of Mrs. Morley was presented to United States Marshal John Pratt in August. Marshal Pratt did not immediately serve the warrant because of a trip East. Catron, having learned that Mrs. Morley was pregnant, requested that the warrant not be served because her reaction might harm the unborn child. The son, Ray Morley, was born on March 17, 1876. Mrs. Morley left for a trip to the East in April or May and did not return until the following winter, thus being absent during the next term of court. Meanwhile, Catron, at the request of Postmaster McCulloch, dropped the case.[28]

McCulloch was probably embarrassed by the circumstance. Admitting that Morley was his enemy, he may well have not become involved had it not been for the defiant attitude of Mrs. Morley and her husband. In that era of chivalry toward women, Catron must certainly have realized that it was not to his advantage to either present or maintain the indictment. In fairness, it must be recognized that it was not his prerogative to suspend the matter with no official reason for doing so.

But there may have been another reason for McCulloch's decision not to press the case. A year earlier redoubtable Clay Allison — with the quick temper and quicker gun — had dumped William R. Morley's printing press into the river. The next morning he strode into the wrecked printing office where he was unexpectedly confronted by the irate and distraught Ada Morley. He suffered her scolding with genuine embarrassment, presented money to pay for another printing press, and concluded, "I don't fight women." It is reported that true to his word, when he heard of the indictment against Mrs. Morley, he exclaimed, "Bring that woman to trial and not a man will come out of the courtroom alive."[29]

In later years the Morleys always thought that they had successfully defied authority with their righteous stand against a frivolous charge and had lived under the cloud of the indictment until it ran the course of the statute of limitations. There is no question, though, that the charge was dropped.[30]

Early in 1877 Mrs. Mary E. McPherson, mother of Ada Morley, complained to Attorney General Alfonso Taft. She prefaced her complaint by stating that she had only come to visit her daughter but had remained to protect her. In regard to the indictment against her daughter, she claimed that United States Attorney Catron had brought charges in a fit of personal spite. Her version was that William R. Morley was given the use of a buggy in connection with his employment by the Maxwell Company. This buggy had been used to bring Catron and others to a term of court at Cimarron. Mrs. McPherson maintained that Catron wanted the use of the buggy at a time when Mrs. Morley was using it to fulfill a previous engagement, and that Catron had vowed he would get even with her.[31]

It seems incongruous that so trivial a complaint could be used as a springboard to launch an attack as serious as hers proved to be to Catron. She lamented that he used his official position to oppress the innocent instead of punishing the guilty; that he shook indictments over the heads of people until they promised to vote for Elkins; that court was adjourned while he pursued this method of electioneering; and that one could avoid indictment by feeing Catron. She had heard, she claimed, that she was to be indicted for libel in connection with her reporting conditions to the Board of Missions of the Methodist Church in New York City. She then implied that Catron was, in some way, responsible for more serious happenings in Colfax County. These included the punitive removal of courts from Colfax County to Taos County; the assassination of Rev. Thomas J. Tolby; the freeing from jail of all those supposed to be implicated in the murder; the indictment of those searching out the assassins; and the leaguing together of all U. S. officials to oppress the people.[32]

To do all these things would have required more official power on the part of Catron than he possibly could have possessed. Not the least of these talents would have been the ability to call into play at will the forces of both federal and territorial courts. His duties and privileges as United States attorney were circumscribed by law; moreover, it was not within his province to prosecute violations of Territorial law.

Catron was called upon by Attorney General Alfonso Taft to answer Mrs. McPherson's charges. He denied as absolutely false any statement on his part that Mrs. Morley had insulted him or that he intended to punish her in connection with the use of any buggy. To the contrary, he had been approached by a friend of Mrs. Morley who had requested that an indictment be prevented, and he then had told the person that the case was a matter for Postmaster McCulloch and the grand jury. He denied that he had used his official position to oppress anyone instead of punishing the guilty; that he shook indictments over the heads of any persons for any purpose; or that he had ever received a fee to prevent an indictment. He explained that he could have had nothing to do with any suit against Mrs. McPherson for libel, since it was a Territorial offense. He added that this was the first time he had heard of the matter. As to the reason for the removal of courts from Colfax County to Taos County, Catron declared that several men had been hung or shot by armed mobs, with no effort toward prevention being made by the people of Colfax County. To the contrary, the same was in substance encouraged by William R. Morley, son-in-law of Mrs. McPherson, who was the editor of the newspaper in the county. Catron further explained that no United States business was conducted in the courts of either county, and that he had no official connection with the same except as an attorney who practiced therein. All of his official business as U. S. attorney was confined to the U. S. branch of the court in said district held in Santa Fe (Attorney General William Breeden was responsible for prosecution of Territorial matters in the counties). Furthermore, he had not been a member of the legislature that had caused the removal of the court to Taos County, nor had he had anything to do with the matter.[33]

Catron reported that the murder of Rev. Tolby had twice been thoroughly investigated without a scintilla of evidence pointing toward a single U. S. official. Some persons indicted for the murder were still at large because officers had been unable to arrest them, and others had left the country. The Reverend Oscar P. McMains, Tolby's successor, had been so enthusiastic in searching out the murderers that he was instrumental in lynching a man who had been indicted. Catron concluded by declaring as utterly false any allegation that U. S. officials were leagued together in any manner so that the people suffered or that there was any combination among them for any purpose whatever.[34]

William R. Morley somehow learned the contents of Catron's explanation to Attorney General Taft and wrote to Taft defending his position and that of his wife. He defied Catron to prove that he had, through his newspaper, encouraged disorder or murder in Colfax County. In regard to the indictment brought against his wife, Morley continued his defiance when he maintained that she had at all times been ready to stand trial but that she had never been arrested. He contended that Catron had seen to it that the arrest was not made because the indictment had been brought for malicious motives, and a trial of Mrs. Morley would reveal his crime and corruption. Morley continued:

I respectfully request that your office will call upon Mr. Catron to explain why he has so long failed in his duty to prosecute the cause and charge that unless he gives good and sufficient reasons that he is unfit for a public official.[35]

It seems evident that Morley was not aware of Postmaster McCulloch's request that the charges against Mrs. Morley be withdrawn, or else that he was attempting to again call the attention of the attorney general to the fact that his wife had not been tried under the indictment brought against her. His lament probably did not carry much weight.

Numerous persons other than Mrs. McPherson and Morley addressed letters to Washington complaining about the conduct of officials in New Mexico, particularly in regard to reports of unrest and violence in Lincoln and Colfax Counties.[36] The letter of Mary E. McPherson, however, was especially directed toward Catron.

As a result of these letters, Frank Warner Angel was sent from Washington to investigate. His inquiry was first conducted in Lincoln County. He then took testimony from numerous persons in Colfax County. The statement most influential in shaping Angel's eventual report in its entirety was made by Frank Springer on August 9, 1878.[37] Springer's testimony, along with the earlier allegations of Mary E. McPherson, W. R. Morley, and others, formed the basis for later extensive interrogatories presented by Angel to Catron for answer. Mrs. McPherson's militant stand was the beginning of circumstances eventually resulting in Catron's resignation as United States attorney.

7
Angel Report

Conditions of crime and lawlessness prompting the investigation by Frank Warner Angel and his report on conduct of officials in New Mexico had their genesis in the years following the Civil War. The situation had become serious by the time Samuel B. Axtell became governor of New Mexico on July 30, 1875.

Axtell, a Republican, was a man of great dignity and positive opinions who had been a congressman from California and, briefly, Territorial governor of Utah. In New Mexico it was rumored that he was a Mormon bishop who had remained in Utah only long enough to perfect a plan for making New Mexico a Mormon colony. Particularly, he was suspected of seeking to have the Maxwell Grant declared public domain so that Latter-day Saints could settle thereon.

Soon after his arrival in New Mexico, he became known as "Obispo," Spanish for Bishop. The name remained with him throughout his stay in the Territory, despite his denial and those of Mormon officials. It looked suspicious that he had left the governorship of Utah after only ninety days. The fact is that he had become involved in a serious political squabble in Utah. The death of New Mexico Governor Marsh Giddings, in June 1875, made it possible for Washington to extricate him from what seemed an untenable situation. Ironically, New Mexico was not the place for him to avoid contention. In the making were more serious involvements than those he had abandoned.

Axtell neither understood nor appreciated New Mexicans and their problems. He arrived at a time when a spring of contentious events was winding at an accelerating pace. Neither the governor nor the governed seem to have seen that the only way for the spring to become unwound was to break, unless strong remedial action was taken. Crime was rampant in many parts of the Territory. Governor Axtell was called upon to apprehend and punish the guilty, but there was little he could do within the framework of existing government other than offer the traditional $500 reward in particularly atrocious murder cases and hope the reward money would be made available by the next legislature. There were few arrests and fewer convictions. Even indictments were hard to procure because people would not come forth with information. Jurors were reluctant to convict, frequently for fear of reprisal. More important, the vast hiding grounds of sparsely populated areas made apprehension of criminals difficult and frequently impossible. By process of natural attraction, a criminal element gravitated to the region.

Two other fundamental factors caused growing unrest in New Mexico: political contention and the unsettled state of land ownership in the Territory. Democrats had enjoyed political dominance prior to the Civil War. After 1865 an influx of newcomers greatly strengthened the Republican party, and in a remarkably short time it took over leadership in the Territory. This growing strength was resisted by Democrats. Lack of effective libel laws encouraged increasingly vituperative statements, accusations, and recrimination in the public press by all concerned. Various derogatory expressions were coined on both sides, the most enduring being "Santa Fe Ring." The leading newspaper at the time, and throughout the Territorial period, was the *Santa Fe New Mexican*.

Published by the brilliant team of William Manderfield and T. J. Tucker, it supported the leaders of the Republican party. The administration of Governor Axtell came at a time when the newspaper battle was at its height. It would have been difficult for him to remain strictly neutral in this "war of words," and it was natural that he favored the administration that had appointed him to office.

The chaotic status of land ownership, particularly that of large grants of land, had long been a problem in New Mexico. The administration of Governor Axtell started when contention over land titles was reaching a high point. Here was a situation unparalleled in the history of the United States. At one time nearly half the land in New Mexico — the best land — was claimed as a private grant. In large areas, prospective purchasers could not be certain of land titles; this situation was a detriment to the economy of the Territory, touching the life of every citizen in New Mexico.

These involvements would have been troublesome even for an able governor, and Axtell cannot be accorded that distinction. His approach, weak and vacillating, was not adequate; law and order gave way to open rebellion against authority, especially in Lincoln and Colfax counties.

In Lincoln County, the murder of John Henry Tunstall on February 18, 1878, caused repercussions at home and abroad. Tunstall was a British subject, and a request for explanation and indemnity was not long in arriving. Soon after Tunstall's death, his father, John Partridge Tunstall, made a demand through proper channels for a complete investigation of his son's death, as well as a prompt and satisfactory report of the facts surrounding the slaying. The senior Tunstall, a prominent London merchant, was a man of prestige and influence. His demand was presented to Secretary of State F. W. Seward and turned over to the attorney general of the United States. On March 18, 1878, United States Attorney Catron was ordered to make prompt inquiry into all circumstances attending the murder and to report fully with a statement of what measures had been or could be taken to bring to punishment the parties guilty of the crime.[1]

No record has been found that Catron immediately replied. His failure to answer has been used by past authors (including this writer) as an indication that he was embarrassed by his own involvements in Lincoln County.[2] The whole truth calls for a more complete answer than this simple explanation. National and Territorial officials alike were stunned by involvement with the British government. Lack of action in the case was the rule rather than the exception. Within two weeks after Tunstall's death, Governor Axtell vainly requested military aid to keep the peace in Lincoln County. This was obviously the only authority that the quarreling factions would respect. Catron repeatedly urged military support, both in an official capacity, and as a private citizen who desired that his interests in the area be protected.

Despite national and international repercussions, Tunstall's murder was a violation of Territorial law and not a crime calling for prosecution by the United States government. Less than a year earlier, Catron had been called upon by the United States Attorney General to suspend proceedings in the case of the Reverend Oscar P. McMains, then being tried for murder. Catron had made it evident to his superior that all he could do legally was to call on the attorney general of the Territory for this action.[3]

When Catron was ordered to report on Tunstall's murder, William Breeden was attorney general. Less than a week later he resigned. The reason for his resignation is not clear. As chairman of the executive committee of the Republican party in New Mexico, he was the recognized head of that party.[4] For some time he had been carrying on a battle of words in the public press against attackers of the Santa Fe Ring and had repeatedly called for all who claimed specific evidence of wrongdoing by persons allegedly belonging to that group to publicly state their case. Despite his persistent challenges, only vague and insinuating generalities continued to be published. It is possible that he desired to be free of public office in order to more effectively combat these attacks on the Santa Fe Ring which were, in reality, aimed at the Republican party.

By a quirk of historical fate, the climatic embarrassment of the Santa Fe Ring was accompanied, in April 1878, by the death of "Boss" Tweed, the archetype of ringleaders. Republicans, while still ascendant politically, were clearly on the defensive in matters connected with Colfax and Lincoln counties. They were in power and, rightly or wrongly, were blamed for chaotic conditions there. In fairness, it must be stated that chaos had resulted from factors beyond mere political control.

Breeden's successor, Henry L. Waldo, was a Democrat who had the happy faculty of getting along well with persons of both political faiths. Despite some accusations that he acted in concert with the Santa Fe Ring, he generally enjoyed a reputation of impeccable honesty with Democrats and Republicans alike.

Washington officials continued to ignore authorization of troops to prevent further violence. Instead, they sent Frank Warner Angel to investigate the death of Tunstall and the conduct of Governor Axtell and other Territorial officials. Angel arrived in Santa Fe early in May 1878, where he called on United States Attorney Catron and other United States officials to assure them that they would have every opportunity to answer any charges that might be brought as a result of his investigation. He left for Lincoln on May 10 and arrived there four days later.[5]

In Lincoln, Angel secured the affidavits of numerous persons and witnessed for himself the violent emotions of people in the neighborhood. These emotions would soon result in the famous affray in Lincoln on July 19, 1878, when the McSween house was burned and several persons killed.

While in Lincoln, Angel requested Attorney General Charles Devens to send copies of reports Catron had rendered to the justice department. He was interested in the number of cases reported and fees collected.[6] He was evidently assembling information as a basis for interrogatories later presented to Catron.

By July 16, 1878, Angel had completed his investigation in Lincoln County and was in Santa Fe awaiting funds so he could proceed to Las Vegas and Cimarron to take additional testimony.[7]

On the basis of what he had learned in Lincoln County, Angel concluded that the death of John Tunstall was not brought about through the lawless and corrupt conduct of United States officials in the Territory of New Mexico. He recommended that the governor be given such assistance as would enable him to enforce the laws.[8] Governor Axtell, at the suggestion of Catron, had requested such aid eight months earlier.

There was soon to be a drastic change in Angel's attitude toward the matters of his investigation. Frank Springer was in correspondence with Governor Axtell. The former accused him of deliberately conniving to cause his death and that of associates by arranging for the arrest of R. C. Allison in Colfax County a year earlier under conditions that would have caused troops to shoot bystanders as well as Allison. During the course of this correspondence Axtell was evasive in his replies to Springer, only regretting that any ambiguity in his letters had caused Springer to believe that harm was intended him.[9]

Angel was evidently not aware of Springer's communications with Axtell. While in Santa Fe he told the governor that he had no charges to make against him. This judgment was to be reversed abruptly when he took the testimony of Frank Springer in Cimarron on August 9, 1878. Springer's affidavit in hand, he hurried back to Santa Fe the following day and prepared a list of thirty-one interrogatories for Governor Axtell to answer. So complete was his change in attitude that he caused the questions to be delivered to Axtell on

August 11 (although that day was Sunday) and gave him only twenty-four hours to answer. Angel enclosed Springer's original affidavit as a partial basis of information upon which the interrogatories were propounded. While Springer's affidavit was confined largely to information about Colfax County, Angel's interrogatories to Axtell dealt mainly with matters in Lincoln County. Evidently Springer's account had changed Angel's mind all along the line.[10]

On Monday Axtell evasively replied, concluding his letter:

You have been a long time in the Territory, and you told me when you returned from Lincoln that there was not the scratch of a pen against me; under what influence has this crop sprung up so suddenly? When you have completed your charges I will answer them within a reasonable time, either to you here or to the Department at Washington. If you choose to stand as my accuser, well and good; if not, then give me the name or names of the parties who make these charges. I am anxious to do right, and I have been taught that a part of doing right is not to submit to a wrong.[11]

Angel promptly replied. He had thought that Axtell had no objections to being investigated, but now believed otherwise. As to the time limit of twenty-four hours, Angel said that if he were the accused he would not want even that long to answer. He did, nevertheless, subject to the approval of the secretary of the interior, give Axtell thirty days to respond.[12]

Frank Warner Angel left Santa Fe on August 17, 1878, and arrived in New York City on August 24. Soon thereafter he was summoned to Washington by President Rutherford B. Hayes to report informally. On September 4, Secretary of the Interior Carl Schurz suspended Axtell and appointed Lew Wallace as his successor. There was some lamenting in New Mexico newspapers that Axtell was dismissed without a hearing. The truth is that on August 13, 1878, Angel gave Governor Axtell thirty days in which to answer charges. Axtell did not reply with a sworn statement. Just before Angel reported to President Hayes, he received a newspaper article, not even signed, which was Axtell's reply to charges against him. By the time Angel made his formal report on October 3, 1878, he saw no reason for changing anything he had earlier reported to the president.[13]

Angel had also gathered evidence concerning the official conduct of Catron. He sent a number of affidavits to Catron from Cimarron shortly before he left that place for Santa Fe on August 10. Along with the affidavits, his letter requested that Catron appear before him to be examined. Catron replied, expressing confidence that he could explain every allegation so perfectly that it would convince every candid mind that there was no reasonable foundation for the charges. Because the affidavits were indefinite as to times, places and individuals, he felt that he would have to get facts from the records which would be difficult to do in less than sixty days. He requested that Angel submit his examination in the form of interrogatories and indicated that he would cheerfully and willingly answer at as early a date as practicable. This arrangement was agreeable to Angel, except that he would grant only thirty days to answer the affidavits already in Catron's possession and the interrogatories which he enclosed.[14]

Catron insisted that he be given sixty days in which to make his answers and enlisted Elkins to help him to that end. He pointed out to Angel and to Attorney General Charles Devens that politics were running so high that he was experiencing difficulty in securing affidavits. Prominent Democrats told him frankly that they were making the charges against him part of their campaign. Then, too, his private and legal business was so extensive that he and his clients would suffer pecuniary loss if he were forced to rush his defense. This line of discussion was not wise strategy. It was typical of Catron that he sometimes failed to view his problems in the light that others might see them. Angel believed that his excuse of a Democratic measure to prevent his obtaining affidavits was all humbug and that Catron merely wanted more time to circulate a petition certifying as to his character and ability. Devens, for his part, was irked that Catron appeared not to have considered answering charges of sufficient importance to take precedence over his private matters.[15]

On September 11, 1878, Catron prepared his answers to Angel's interrogatories and mailed them the following day. This was just within the thirty days time stipulated by Angel, but he continued to mail affidavits for several days and requested that they be considered before any charges were made against him.

One of the unanswered, and apparently unanswerable, questions of history is whether Angel ever made a formal report on charges against Catron. A careful search of the National Archives discloses no report. Likewise, there is no record of the affidavits submitted to Catron for answer, nor of those in his defense.[16] The interrogatories, though, are at hand. Another circumstance, however, clouds the issue.

In 1892 Catron was running for delegate to the United States Congress. Word came to him that his political opponents intended to secure a copy of Angel's report on charges against him to use for political mudslinging. Catron wrote to S. B. Elkins, then secretary of war, requesting him to see that the attorney general did not issue a copy of the report to anyone. Catron stated that he had never seen the report and knew nothing of its contents, but supposed it to be something false. Elkins assured Catron that the attorney general would comply with his wish. The following year Catron requested that Elkins secure the report and destroy it. Elkins replied that he had caused diligent search to be made in the attorney general's department for Angel's report but that it could not be found.[17]

This raises the question: Did Angel ever make a formal report on charges against Catron? It is evident that he intended to do so before he received Catron's answers to interrogatories.[18] Catron's cogent and reasonable answers to Angel's questions must have stood in his favor. He successfully explained away the facts and sworn statements every allegation made against him.

Angel's questioning was thorough and searching. Catron wrote out each of the eighty-nine questions followed by his answer in fifty-nine pages of testimony. Angel was especially interested in Catron's relation to land grants, government contracts, witness certificates, and low ratio of convictions compared to indictments for various federal offenses.

Catron admitted that he had interests in land grants, but he explained that these were almost entirely in confirmed and patented grants, nearly all of which he had acquired before he was appointed United States attorney, and that all had been bought and paid for in good faith. He maintained that he had never appeared in any grant case seeking confirmation of title, except as owner or part owner, and knew of no law that prevented him from protecting his own interest.

At one point, Angel wanted to know if Catron did not consider it his duty as United States attorney to protect the government rather than the land grabbers who were claiming the Ortiz Grant. Catron explained that he had served as counsel for that grant in behalf of the owners, including himself, but only in a contest case in which their ownership was questioned by claimants of a conflicting grant. Catron did not think he rated the appellation of land grabber, and he allowed that Angel probably was applying that hard name to the contesting claimants in the contest suit. Catron would not admit to any belief that the title to the Ortiz Grant was fraudulent. To the contrary, he had thoroughly investigated the title and believed, as he believed in his existence, that it was a good grant. In any case, he had bought and paid for his interest in good faith before being appointed United States attorney.

In other questioning, Angel wondered if Catron had ever sold an interest in the Uña de Gato Grant to Stephen W. Dorsey. Catron clarified that line of questioning by stating that Manuel A. Otero was the sole claimant to the entire grant. He denied that he or his firm had ever been retained to protect Dorsey's interest in the grant and affirmed that, to his knowledge, Dorsey owned no interest.

Catron had been accused of causing numerous persons to be indicted for illegally living on Indian lands and then not prosecuting upon payment of fees and promise that the indicted persons would vote for Stephen Elkins as delegate to Congress in the election of 1873. In this instance, Catron clarified obvious malicious rumor and showed how he had done his duty to the fullest by taking facets of the case to the United States Supreme Court (see Chapter 6).

Angel was also suspicious about the low number of convictions for violations of internal revenue laws. There were, Catron, explained, numerous credible reasons, among them, that witnesses would frequently testify to grand juries when they were afraid to testify in court and would either avoid attending court or testify adversely there. Furthermore, there was violent prejudice against the internal revenue laws in the Territory. Without even the few successful prosecutions, the job of the collector would have been a great deal more difficult.

Catron denied that he was interested in government contracts as principal or otherwise, or that he employed his brother-in-law, Edgar A. Walz, as a cover to handle such transactions. To clarify, he stated that he was under contract with William Rosenthal to supply 3,000 head of cattle which, he understood, Rosenthal intended to turn in on the contract at the San Carlos Indian Agency. What Rosenthal did with the cattle, Catron maintained, was none of his business.*

Angel apparently had information that $2,500 had been deposited to Catron's account at the First National Bank in Santa Fe in connection with a transaction involving witness

---

* In a letter of 1891, Catron refers to Edgar A. Walz as a nominal contractor on government contracts for Indian supplies. The contracts were in Walz' name, but Catron did not clarify his own position in the contractural procedure. The implication, though, was that Walz felt Catron owed him money in the transaction. Catron to James A. Waymire, May 11, 1891 (C.P. 105, Vol. 31).

certificates. Catron declared that he had borrowed the money from the bank for a Mr. Barela of Mesilla, using the certificates as collateral. The transaction was a convenience to Barela, from which Catron derived no benefit. He affirmed that he had been offered both juror and witness certificates but had refused to purchase them.

In earlier conversation with Angel, Catron denied that he had kept witnesses from testifying before him. Angel, apparently, wanted this denial under oath and repeated the question in the interrogatories. Catron repeated this denial and stated that any such information conveyed to Angel was an infamous and malicious falsehood.

It is possible that, because Catron so thoroughly explained his case, Angel decided not to carry the matter against him further and did not make a formal report. As stated, no report has been found. Still, Angel specifically refers to a report on Surveyor General Henry M. Atkinson — in fact, favorably — and this report cannot be found either. Regardless, despite absence of any record that Catron was asked to resign, it is reasonable to assume that some type of mutual agreement existed indicating it was best for him to do so.

Angel made his report concerning Governor Axtell on October 3 and followed on October 7 with his statement on troubles in Lincoln County and the death of John H. Tunstall. On October 10, 1878, Catron resigned. He said: "In accordance with a purpose long entertained, I hereby tender my resignation as United States Attorney for New Mexico, to take effect November 10th, 1878." [19]

Elkins claimed that Catron's dismissal was ordered and an indictment talked of strongly. Elkins maintained that it was only through his efforts that Catron was saved from dismissal. At the time, the former law partners were quarreling over Catron's alleged attempt to force Elkins' resignation as president of the First National Bank in Santa Fe. Catron claimed that Elkins had stood in the way of the bank loaning him money, while Elkins maintained he had urged that as much money be loaned to Catron as the interest of the bank would permit. There were also questions concerning their respective ownership of land in the Territory.[20] Under these circumstances it would have been natural for Elkins to stress his part in aiding Catron in order to put the latter on the defensive. Elkins' correspondence with the Interior Department at the time indicates that he was helpful but that he probably exaggerated the importance of his services.

Another circumstance indicates that Catron did not leave office under pressure. He was scheduled to resign on November 10, but court at Mesilla was to commence and Attorney General Devens requested that he delay in order that the work there would not be interrupted. Catron complied and suggested that his resignation take place as soon after November 30 as his successor could be qualified. It was not until January 20, 1879, that he was relieved by Sidney M. Barnes.[21]

Barnes was injured by a fall from a sleeping-car berth while journeying to the scene of his new duties; he was confined to his room for several days. During this time Catron showed him every courtesy and cooperation in assisting him. It was upon Catron's motion that Barnes was admitted a member of the bar in New Mexico.[22]

In retrospect, it can be said that Catron's resignation as United States attorney was one of the few things in later years concerning which he was personally defensive. He wished it understood that his conduct had not been such as to warrant censure.

8
Julia

Thomas Benton Catron was thirty-seven years old before he was married. There is only one recorded hint of why he reached this relatively mature age before taking this step — a letter of June 13, 1867, received by him while he was at Mesilla less than eleven months following his arrival in New Mexico. It is unusual that this missive should be preserved when all other of his correspondence of that period has been destroyed.

Santa Fe, N.M.
June 13, 1867

Friend Tom,

I will hardly consider this a reply to your lengthy and highly interesting letter received some time since. I am not well enough to write but a few lines. I know you are anxious to hear of Bettie, & I have been wanting very much to write, not that I have any cheering news to communicate, but to prevent you from taking any hasty steps in this matter. I have not received a line from her, have you, if so & you think courtesy demands & answer, be very careful, write a formal letter do not intimate your feelings — do not commit yourself. I know Mr. Catron that you are honest and conscientious & I would not willingly have your affections trifled with. *Bettie*, I *know* to be a heartless coquette — *perfectly* heartless, & for the friendship existing between you and Steve and that I feel for you myself I warn you to beware. Take my advice as that of a true friend, but if you now go further in this matter, you cannot blame me if you are deceived. I know more than you probably think I do. I cannot write more now. My regards to Mr. Willie and lady. I remain very truly & respectfully your friend.

Sallie Elkins*

---

* Sallie Elkins to Catron, June 13, 1867 (C.P. 803, Box 1). Sallie Elkins may have been a cousin or an aunt of S. B. Elkins visiting him in Santa Fe at the time. Elkins later had a daughter named Sallie.

Who was Bettie? Her identity is not known, but she was likely a girl Catron knew in Missouri. How deep was his fondness for Bettie? The letter from Sallie Elkins indicates it may have been more than a passing fancy. Was unrequited love for Bettie the reason he did not marry for another decade? This question cannot be answered with certainty, or even with probability, but it might have been. It would be only conjecture to surmise what effect his relationship with Bettie had on his character, but the fact remains that in his adult years he was characteristically grave and reserved, even gruff and forbidding at times, in his contacts with others than his closest friends and family.

On the evening of May 5, 1877, Catron reached Santa Fe on the eastern coach. He brought with him as his bride one of Minnesota's "most accomplished daughters,"[1] the former Julia A. Walz of Mankato. She had been born in Springfield, Ohio, in March 1857 and soon thereafter moved to Minnesota.

Catron met Julia in 1875 while she was teaching school at Mesilla and he was serving the Territory as United States attorney. They liked each other and were soon engaged to be married. Before their marriage, though, Julia returned for a third year at Oberlin College in Ohio; and then, as a gift from her betrothed, she visited the Centennial Exposition at Philadelphia. They were married on April 28, 1877, at Mankato, Minnesota, and journeyed directly to Santa Fe, where they lived for a time with the family of W. W. Griffin.*

On February 4, 1878, their family was increased to three with the birth of a twelve-pound son whom they named John. It was their desire to have a large family of children. They

---

* Vioalle Clark Hefferan, *Thomas Benton Catron*, p. 12. When Wilson Waddingham heard that Catron was married, knowing that S. B. Elkins had tried to arrange a match between Catron and his sister-in-law, Ollie Davis, he sent Mrs. Catron a set of library furniture for a wedding present with the initials O. D. C. inscribed on the table.

had six, but one died in childbirth and another, Mary, in infancy. Three other children were born to them: Charles C. in 1879, Thom in 1888, and Fletcher in 1890.

Catron said of his wife's relations to her sons:

She made many trips abroad, taking our children with her and placed them in schools and educated them in different languages, that they might be better able to meet the requirements of life and perform their duties to themselves and the public. She impressed on them honor and honesty in their dealings and conduct, and was always proud of their attainments and demeanor. *

For a number of years Jennie Walz, daughter of Julia's brother, Will, of El Paso, lived with her aunt and uncle almost as a daughter; in fact, they sometimes referred to her as Jennie Walz Catron. Her Uncle Tom was her favorite relative, and he reciprocated her affection. Except for his acknowledgement as her uncle, his letters to her when she later studied music at Wellesley could certainly be understood as coming from a loving and thoughtful father to his appreciative daughter. Jennie corresponded with her "Uncle Tom" for all his life, even after she became Jennie Walz Turner.[2]

Before his marriage to Julia, Catron had no regular place of abode; he roomed and boarded with various families. This regime was more or less continued for a time with his family. In 1880, while they were making plans for their own home, they set up housekeeping in rented quarters known as the McFerran building. In the spring of 1883, their own house was started, and when completed in September at a cost of $70,000, was considered the finest in the Territory. Julia, a beautiful cultured woman and a gracious hostess, made their home the social and cultural center of Santa Fe. Her husband left management of the household to Julia, even to such matters as caretakers and workmen for repairs. In this home

---

* Remarks by Catron at his wife's funeral. Charles was born in New Haven, Connecticut; the other three in Santa Fe. On March 6, 1922, Thom legally changed his name to Thomas B. Catron II.

Catron was, in some respects, somewhat of an anomaly. Never fastidious in attire, he contrasted sharply with gentle Julia in matters of personal appearance. But in the realm of the mind, they held a common bond.

Julia was a loyal friend of Santa Fe and New Mexico. In projects for the common good, she was content to work in the ranks and throw her whole ability and energy into their successful consummation. At her funeral Catron said:

> Her love for our people extended to the whole Territory; she worked for the advancement of education of all the people of New Mexico and its prosperity; she helped and aided whenever she could find a deserving person or anyone on whom she could bestow her efforts; she observed in her travels and gathered ideas that she might turn to her advantage. She was not a gossip, but when trouble occurred among her friends she was most apt to favor the weaker party; her sympathy went to all.

She was fond of travel and music — she was a fine vocalist — but her home was her greatest joy. She lavished on it unstintingly of her time and energy to make it a place of beauty and quiet repose. Catron's contribution to this home was the finest library in the Southwest. With Julia's aid he worked for a decade making this collection. One of his leading acquisitions was the library of Father Augustine Fischer of Mexico. This purchase, made in 1890, was arranged through Adolph F. Bandelier and Catron's brother-in-law, Will Walz of El Paso. The library consisted of some three thousand volumes, four or five hundred of which were old manuscript collections considered exceedingly valuable. The books were purchased for his own professional use and for the Historical Society of New Mexico.*

---

* Catron to a Mr. Clarke, April 2, 1890 (C.P. 105, Vol. 3). Catron also contributed numerous other books to the Historical Society of New Mexico. His law library was also considered the finest in the Southwest and was used extensively by other lawyers in New Mexico. His personal library was later donated to the University of New Mexico, and much of his law library was acquired by the Huntington Library in California.

Catron was also interested in obtaining the famous Herbert Howe Bancroft collection. Having acquired the library of Father Fischer, he felt compelled to build his hobby into a complete array of all books and documents referring to New Mexico. On page 20 of Bancroft's *History of Arizona and New Mexico,* he found a reference to 1,756 pages of manuscript material pertaining to New Mexico history. Catron inquired of Bancroft whether he would be willing to send these items to New Mexico so they could be copied. He guaranteed that he would return them unsoiled and in as good condition as when received. The alternative was to send a man to California to do the copying, and Catron wished to avoid this expense.

Bancroft's office answered:

> In reply to your letter of July 2d. Mr. Bancroft thinks it would be a long and laborious process to copy all the material on New Mexico, or Spanish America. There is much more as important to you as the book you speak of. He has no catalogue except in MS, and comprising two volumes, each eighteen or twenty inches square and two or three inches thick. He suggests, as his historical work is now practically finished, that you buy his library, consisting of some 50,000 volumes, more or less, including maps, Mss., pamphlets, and bound books. He will sell for less than the cost of collecting, not to mention the fact that a large part of his collection never can be duplicated at any price.*

Catron did not reply to Bancroft's letter; evidently he did not have money available then to make the purchase. But even without the Bancroft collection, Catron's library was impressive for that time in New Mexico.†

Catron's preoccupation with books was manifested in a determination to give his sons the finest education available. When they were at home, he customarily hired tutors to

---

* The History Company (by H. Bishop Hannbly) to Catron, July 7, 1890 (C.P. 102, Box 8). No price was mentioned, but even the cost of collecting Bancroft's library must have been considerable.

† Robert C. Gortner to his parents, February 11, 1891 (C.P. 109, Vol. 1). Gortner said of the library: "It is a fine one and contains many old & valuable volumes."

teach them. In 1890, when Jennie Walz and John were twelve years old, Charles eleven, Thom two, and Fletcher a few months old, Catron inquired of his brother George in Lexington, Missouri, about a possible teacher to replace one who had left unexpectedly. George informed his brother of a young man named W. E. Coons, a graduate of the University of Missouri and an experienced teacher. George believed that Coons was somewhere in New Mexico.[3]

It happened that Catron knew Coons was in Silver City and wrote to him. He desired a teacher, he said, who could prepare his sons for Yale or Harvard. His object was that they be taught to think and analyze and be thoroughly prepared for college courses.[4] After due consideration and negotiation, Coons was engaged at a salary of sixty-five dollars for each calendar month, as well as room and board. In addition, Coons was to have the benefit of Catron's library and his aid in the study of law.

While Coons did not suppose he would differ with Catron in the matter, in the interest of harmonious relations, he wished it explicitly understood that he was in no sense to be a nurse to the children. Catron readily agreed to this stipulation because he had a German governess who, with Mrs. Catron, attended "to that business."[5]

Coons proved thoroughly competent. In June 1891, after he had completed one year of instructing the children and had been diligently studying law, Catron made him a partner in his law firm to replace John H. Knaebel who had left in December of the previous year. Throughout his life, Catron seems to have been impressed by people connected with education. Catron's correspondence indicates that he was visibly impressed by the young professorial Mr. Coons and was personally fond of him.

Within a few months after associating with Catron, Coons was offered a position as chief clerk for the Department of Education of the state of Missouri. The Superintendent of Education of the state informed him:

I have thought of every educator in the State of Missouri. I would rather have you than any one else. I not only admire, to the highest degree, your ability, your system, your sincerity, and your loyalty; but prize you most highly as a friend.[6]

But Coons remained with Catron. Their relationship was one of the finest in Catron's lifetime, and the untimely death of W. E. Coons late in 1893 was distressing to Catron both personally and in a business way.

To replace Coons as a teacher for his children, Catron arranged with R. P. Ingram, a recent graduate of the University of Missouri, who had been recommended by Coons. Julia and her husband at this time considered having their children educated in Mexico for a year so they could acquire a sound understanding of the Spanish language. After consideration, they decided instead that Julia would take them to Spain for that purpose. They hoped that Mrs. Catron could, at the same time, secure medical assistance for the severe deafness that had come upon her. She left in September with her four sons, her niece Jennie Walz, a governess, and instructor R. P. Ingram.*

They settled in Malaga, Spain. Ingram promptly informed the father of arrangements for educating the children. Thom and Fletcher were too young for formal classes, but each day for John, Charles, and Jennie was scheduled from 6:00 A.M. to 9:30 P.M., and included periods for meals, recreation, study, exercise, and rest. Their grades in arithmetic, spelling, reading, grammar, history, and Latin were based on thorough written examinations. Also studied, but not graded in as formal a way, were Spanish and German. Young as they were, Thom and Fletcher participated in these language sessions. John and Jennie, besides their regular classes, took lessons on violin and piano.[7]

When the year in Spain was completed in September 1892, Catron hoped that his family would return to Santa Fe

_____

* Julia had made an earlier trip to Europe in 1883.

and that his sons would continue their education with Mr. Ingram as their teacher. It was his wish that other pupils be enrolled in the classes so that his own children would have the benefit of wider association. But Julia apparently liked life abroad and persuaded her husband otherwise. She placed John and Charles at Phillip's Academy in Exeter, New Hampshire, and returned to Europe with Thom and Fletcher. This began a nomadic way of life for Julia that continued until her death. The initial purpose was to educate the children, but, when this purpose was accomplished, it became evident that travel had become for her a way of life. From that time until she died, Catron rarely saw his family. During this time he struggled heroically to keep them in funds.

Julia returned to the United States for the summer of 1893, but her doctors informed her that she needed absolute rest for a period of six months, so she again went to Europe. She returned in September 1894 to enroll Thom and Fletcher in a school at New Haven, Connecticut. Catron sent two ten-year-old mortgage notes for her signature, for which part of the security was their home. Catron expressed hope that he would soon be able to take up these notes and be released from debt.[8]

Julia continued to reside in New Haven, with only occasional visits to Santa Fe. During that time, in 1897, she again returned to Europe with Fletcher and Thom. Upon returning in 1898, she enrolled Thom at Wentworth Academy in Lexington, Missouri, for a period of two years.

In 1895, Catron had become Territorial delegate to Congress from New Mexico, an office that gave him the privilege of making appointments to West Point and Annapolis. He wrote to Julia that he thought of appointing Charlie as first at Annapolis and John as his alternate, then appointing John as first at West Point and Charlie as his alternate.[9]

In the same letter he stated to Julia that he was having more trouble meeting his obligations than he had ever had

before in his life. His idea regarding disposition of service
academy appointments to his sons was probably, at least in
part, dictated by a desire to relieve himself of the heavy strain
on his financial resources. Some of his constituents in New
Mexico, however, did not take kindly to the idea.

By this time there were growing signs that the cloistered
life of education by tutors and lack of a father's association
and discipline was having its effect on the Catron boys. It is
not uncommon for youths to reach college age and find the
world they live in has suddenly become a different place than
they had formerly realized. Fortunately, these situations
usually turn out all right, and it was so with Catron's sons.
But the process, as it sometimes is in varying degrees, was
somewhat painful.

Charles suffered from malaria in the East and in 1896
enrolled at Stanford University in California. He could not,
therefore, attend a service academy. At Stanford he received
some conditional grades, dropped out for a time, and journeyed to Santa Fe. He returned to Stanford, however, and did
commendable work in his studies. He transferred to the University of Chicago and graduated there in 1901.

John attended Annapolis in 1896, West Point in 1897,
and Yale in 1898. Catron was informed that John was doing
inadequate scholastic work at Yale because his attendance was
irregular. Placed on probation and facing possible dismissal,
John telegraphed his father: "Dropped today: shall ask you
for no more: and am going to shift for myself. . . ." [10]

The father had considered his son's expenditures excessive in the past, but he immediately sent more money and
wrote that the idea of shifting for himself was foolish. He
suggested that John join his mother in Germany and attend
a school there. Catron explained the situation to his brother,
George:

John left Yale simply because he was too lazy to study and would
not study, but became quite extravagant. He is now in Germany and

will take up his studies there. It is my purpose to give him another opportunity at Yale, after he has learned to be economical and to apply himself to his studies.[11]

Catron also informed his brother of Charles' progress at Stanford:

> Charlie seems to be doing exceedingly well at Leland Stanford University — much better than any year heretofore. Last year he about equalled John's record at Yale, but this year he has entirely reformed his methods, keeps down his expenses, and keeps up with his classes very well. I think he is all right.[12]

Within a few months Catron secured for John a commission as 2nd lieutenant in a battalion of New Mexico Territorial volunteers. John rose to 1st lieutenant and served with distinction. For a while he considered joining the regular army but decided instead on a career in civil engineering. He attended the Colorado School of Mines at Golden for a time and then transferred to Columbia University in New York, where he graduated in 1905.

During these years Julia continued her travels. She returned to Santa Fe for a time in 1900 but became sick with erysipelas. Her doctor thought she should go to a lower altitude — Chicago perhaps, or even somewhat further east. Julia's husband hoped she would be able to return in about three months, but it was not to be; Julia was off to Europe again. During this stay, Thom and Fletcher were enrolled in schools variously at Zurich and Geneva in Switzerland and Malaga and Valencia in Spain.

During all this time Catron accepted his wife's arrangements stoically with only occasional hints that he might like to have his family settled down so he could see them a little more often:

> I am glad you are going to put the boys in school at Geneva; get a good school for them, be sure that Tom keeps up his Latin and if they have a Greek department, that he take some Greek also and that he keeps along all right in mathematics. Arrange for them to stay the year and not be jumping back and forth from one place to another. It can do

them no good to be in school in three or four different places during the year.[13]

During the lengthy intervals when his sons were away, Catron wrote them long and detailed letters constantly urging that they apply themselves diligently to their studies and to not waste time on amusements or luxuries. His advice was always practical, but perhaps he did not realize that it probably repeated much that the boys heard daily from their teachers. Thus he urged Thom to diligently practice his handwriting. He pointed out that it was a simple thing like not crossing t's and dotting i's that had been one of the causes of John's failing at Annapolis.[14]

With a little forebearance, it can be understood that a very busy father, aged sixty-three, who had seen his sons for only brief periods in their lifetimes, might not understand the things a boy would like most to hear. He considered sports as pastimes that mostly just interfered with study. When Charles was fifteen, he received an admonition from his father in this regard:

> I notice that you say you have made application to enter a foot-ball nine. I do not much like this. I would rather you had not done it. It was a foot ball team which caused the death of your uncle Charlie. However, if you have gained admission to it, go ahead with the understanding that it is not to be expensive.[15]

Catron's confusion as to the number of players on a football team was not a typographical error; he did not understand these things.

Years later, his youngest son became a star baseball player for the University of Chicago. Fletcher Catron added his bit to the legend of Amos Alonzo Stagg as an athletic coach: "Tell Charley that old man Stagg can certainly bawl fellows out but he is also a peach of a coach."[16]

Fletcher, as had Charles before him, received a letter indicating that his father did not know much about sports:

> I have just noticed a report of a base ball game in which you participated on the [side] of the University of Chicago against the University

of Illinois. I do not know enough about the game to determine whether or not your playing was good or bad, nor do I care much, except to this extent that if you are not a satisfactory player you ought not to keep yourself on the team when better material might be had.[17]

Catron, it would seem, was in no way indicating that his son might not be a satisfactory player; he was simply pointing out a fundamental justice as it appeared to him. He did not seem to understand that it was for the coach rather than Fletcher to decide whether or not his play was satisfactory.

At an earlier date, Fletcher was cautioned by his father:

After you get this letter, if you will sit down and go to work hard on your geometry, you will surely be able to pass, but you will have to stop base ball, foot ball and every other kind of ball and devote yourself for a month . . . to your studies.[18]

In 1903 Catron tried to exact a promise from Bernard S. Rodey, Territorial delegate to Congress from New Mexico, that he would appoint Thom to West Point. Rodey was reluctant to commit himself in advance, particularly since his own son might be of age when it came time to make a decision. Catron persisted, and Rodey wrote: "Just keep still and I will name the boy, but if you go howling around Santa Fe about it, it will bring a lot of candidates out and embarrass me."[19]

Catron very much appreciated Rodey's favor, but he did not like to be called a "howler." He wrote:

I am in possession of your letter of January 21st. and note what you say in it in reference to my son, and for your purposes and intentions as expressed therein, I am grateful. . . .

Now I wish to take notice of the character of the letter you have written me. I do not like its tone. I am entitled to a letter of a different tone from the one which you wrote. You speak about me going howling around Santa Fe about the matter and the fact it will bring a lot of other candidates and embarrass you. I have never mentioned the matter to a soul on earth except to my wife and to my boy. I do not want to accomplish just what you say and I think I have sense enough without your designating me as a man "howling" around Santa Fe. However, I wish to thank you very much for the information you have given me. . . . My former letters showed you why I was anxious about the matter; I am now perfectly content and satisfied.[20]

In June 1904 Julia returned from Europe so Thom could prepare for West Point. That summer she and the family camped out on the Tierra Amarilla Grant. Two of the party each killed a porcupine, so they named their location Camp Porcupine Hollow. To avoid the mosquitoes, they were obliged to get away from the really good fishing, but, as Julia wrote her husband, they did not mind that. Her letter was addressed to "Papa Dear" and signed "With love, Mamma." This was typical of the mode of addressing and closing of their respective letters (the sons customarily addressed their father in their letters to him as "Papa" or "Father"). She closed her letter saying, "We all wish you would come up and visit us."[21]

As usual, Julia's husband was too busy; moreover, that form of relaxation did not particularly appeal to him. Reading was his chief diversion, although he enjoyed solitaire and pinochle. For some ten years he and Julia played a continued pinochle game with no score closed and no money involved. Catron resented losing at a game, so others could not interest him in such pastimes as poker.

During much of Catron's life, his contemporaries noted that he lacked humor. The constant financial pressure of his entire adult lifetime had been enough to make any person somewhat less than cheerful. Still, it was conceded that he was a gracious host and genial companion in his own home or among friends. He also possessed a natural kind of humor:

> I received the cow after she had been on the car 48 hours. She was evidently loose in the car, thrown about in every direction; she was not given any water sure, because after I got her and could get her quieted down so she would drink she drank 5 bucket fulls. When she reached here she was out of humor and furious. . . . She gave very little milk when we received her, but now she is doing better; she is improving, but of course we are all strange to her and the place is strange. I presume after a while she will get good natured and then she will get along better and eat blue grass and also give probably more milk.[22]

Another example of Catron's humor illustrates the subtle type of joke he preferred:

This reminds me very much of a story which is told of Gov. Tabor
and a Jew in Colorado, who were playing seven-up. The hands showed
that the Jew had four kings. The Jew remarked that he would like to
bet at poker on the hand. A queen was turned up for trump. Tabor
said to him, if you will allow me to take up that Queen, I will bet you.
The Jew said, all right. Tabor took up the Queen; they commenced to
bet; the Jew bet every cent he had in the world and every piece of property and every obligation he had in the world. When they showed down
their hands Tabor had four aces. The remark of the Jew was, "Mr.
Tabor, I would just like to know what the hell you wanted of that
Queen?" [23]

Thom entered West Point in 1905 and graduated four
years later. Fletcher accompanied his mother for another year
of school in Europe during 1906 and 1907, then continued his
education at New Haven, Connecticut, until he entered the
University of Chicago in 1909. He graduated there within
the customary four years and then remained to complete the
work for his law degree.

When Julia came back to Santa Fe from Europe in 1907,
she was in increasingly ill health. For years she and her husband had planned to travel together, and now all arrangements were completed for a trip around the world. When
the time came to depart, however, Catron decided that business pressures were too great. He sent his wife on alone,
hoping to catch up with her later. This he was unable to do,
so Julia decided to abandon her trip and come home with
hopes that they could start another trip together. Catron wrote
to her in Manila:

I am very sorry that you could not have gone on around the world.
I think you might have done so had you made a little more effort, but
somehow or other you got it into your head that you ought to come
back and try to make another trip. That will be allright, if we have got
the money and I get my matters in shape so that we can leave, but I do
not think you ought to bank too much on it. I think you have spent
almost enough time away from home. . . .[24]

Julia arrived in Santa Fe in May of 1908. Catron informed his brother: "Julia arrived at home day before yesterday and will be here from now on." [25] Her illness was much

worse now, but in September she decided to visit her son, John, in Los Angeles. When it came time for her to return in December, her husband had to borrow the money for her journey. He explained to Charles, "Mama will need more money than I have to my credit."[26]

In May of 1909 Catron was in Chicago trying to make arrangements for the sale of the Tierra Amarilla Grant. Charles wrote, "Mother is about the same. She is sleeping a little better nights. She hopes that you will succeed and get everything straightened out so that the two of you can travel a little bit."[27]

But her hope was not to be. Her illness lingered on, and she died on the eighth day of November, 1909.

9
American Valley Company

    An event in the spring of 1881 on a frontier settlement in New Mexico evolved into circumstances of far-reaching consequence in the life of Catron, although he was not then even aware of the occurrence. At that time John P. Casey brought his herd of cattle from Albuquerque to the valley of Largo Creek south of what later would be called Quemado and north of Gallo Mountain. He had reconnoitered here the previous autumn and noted that the area was unsurpassed in its natural advantages for raising cattle. For reasons that are lost to history, he named his haven the "American Valley" and set about carving out a cattle kingdom.

    The first step in the Casey planning was to arrange for surveying of townships so land entries could be filed on areas controlling water. This was done by depositing money in the land office at Santa Fe, which could later be used as part payment for lands entered under the land laws. It was required by law that actual settlers reside in a township for it to be surveyed. This requirement was partially fulfilled by early settlers in the region; for the rest, it was ignored. The entire area was surveyed from March through August, 1881.*

---

* Casey's initial interest was in the two townships controlling the water along Largo Creek. The survey deposit for T.2S, R.16W was made in the name of Bisente Naranjo on February 25, 1882 (a Naratigo's ranch is shown on the original survey plat). The deposit for T.1S, R.16W was made in the name of Joaquin Alire on April 1, 1882. S.G.R. 8/25/82, 47 Cong., 2 Sess., H.E.D. No. 1, 572, 583 (2099). Either these people filed in good faith and were dispossessed by prior filings in the name of Casey's employees or else they acted in collusion with Casey and Surveyor General Henry M Atkinson.

During this time Casey formed a verbal partnership with Henry M. Atkinson, the surveyor general of the Territory. Atkinson brought from Nebraska to the Territory a long and distinguished career in public office. In New Mexico, however, he became a controversial figure, and his public service must be characterized, in some details, as outright malfeasance in office. Atkinson was considered a good man to have as a partner in the Casey scheming because through him they could get possession of the land in the American Valley regardless of who settled it. He provided plats of the area long before they were approved or filed in the land office at Santa Fe, while Casey secured the range by fixing up entries to cover the water in the area.

Casey and Atkinson now made plans to gain control over as much land as possible, regulate the water rights, and then sell their interests to Eastern capitalists for a substantial profit. They planned to arrange this sale through John A. Logan, a United States senator from Illinois.

Logan, later an aspirant to the presidency (he settled for vice-president under James G. Blaine and was defeated in the election of 1884) had raised an Illinois regiment in the Civil War and risen to the rank of major general. General Logan, who was interested in getting in on the cattle boom then in progress, was a good friend of S. B. Elkins, Catron's former law partner. Casey's and Atkinson's contact with Logan was made through Elkins, with Catron the intermediary. Catron was associated with Atkinson, along with John H. Thomson, in the January 1882 incorporation of the Boston and New Mexico Cattle Company.

In the summer of 1882 Logan visited Atkinson and Casey in New Mexico, and plans were discussed for development of the American Valley property. To carry out these plans it would be necessary for Casey to travel extensively in the East, and it was essential that someone be on hand to manage affairs at the ranch. In September, Casey and Atkinson sold a one-third interest to W. C. Moore, who had been employed by

Casey for some time. Moore did not immediately fulfill the terms of the agreement and was given an extension of time.

W. C. Moore was from the LX ranch of the Texas panhandle, where he was generally called Outlaw Bill Moore in recognition of his light-fingered way with cattle. He had come to Texas from Wyoming a jump ahead of the law for killing a Negro coachman. A previous escapade had brought him to Wyoming when he killed his brother-in-law in California.

Control over most of the land on both sides of Largo Creek was attained from October through December 1882 by homestead and preemption entries in the name of Casey's employees. Meanwhile, he and his associates were eyeing the territory to the north, in the area of the Mexican village of Rito, as an addition to the grazing land under control. Rito was located about four miles east of present Quemado. There were just six springs in the vicinity, and to add the land controlling this water to their holdings along the Largo would give them dominion over almost 1,600 square miles of grazing land.

In theory it was necessary for the survey plats to be filed in the land office before settlers could submit papers to claim the land they had settled upon. Atkinson held back these plats long enough for Casey to arrange with his employees to file on the desired land, title of which was ultimately conveyed to Casey. These filings were made early in 1883.*

The three partners had now secured the land with water controlling the range in an area nearly forty miles square. But to make it even more interesting to prospective purchasers, they had scouted out the country on the periphery of their range. By securing control of about an additional 3,400 acres of land with water on it, they could gain dominion over more than three million acres of prime grazing land (T.8N through T.2S and R.10W through R.21W). If they also secured

---

*Interview, Celestino Padilla, April 18, 1960. Mr. Padilla was 87 years old at this time, and the interview was conducted through his daughter. His father, Jose Francisco Padilla, lived to be 115. Interview, Frank Armijo, April 18, 1960. *Field Note Books* and *Survey Plats* of the area (B.L.M.).

the water at Gallo Spring, it would provide an additional foot-hold for expansion south of Gallo Mountain. In the parlance of the times, all they wanted was what joined them.

Control over this amount of land was a lucrative prospect. According to Casey, in October 1882, Catron, who was attorney for the firm, requested that he be let in on the ranch at what he called a bedrock price. Casey partially consented with the proviso that the deal be approved by Surveyor General Atkinson. Later Casey spoke to Atkinson, who would not give his approval because he was afraid there would be a clash, politically and otherwise, between Logan and the locally powerful Catron. Moreover, Casey claimed, it was Atkinson's opinion that Catron would be in favor of retaining the property and would stand in the way of plans to dispose of the ranch. Furthermore, he was afraid that Catron's interpretation of a bedrock price would mean his influence and their capital. Casey's version indicates that it was agreed they would let the matter drop and, if Catron approached Atkinson about sharing an interest in their holdings, Atkinson would put the blame on Casey saying that the latter would not consent.[1]

Late in 1882 Judge Holderman of the St. Louis National stockyards came out to examine the ranch and was well satisfied with the property. Holderman proposed to give them $425,000 for the company if they would take half cash and half stock in payment. This proposition pleased Atkinson; however, he considered it prudent to hold off and see what could be done in Chicago. Accordingly, the management of the ranch was turned over to W. C. Moore, while Casey left for Washington to lay the matter before General Logan. Shortly after his arrival Casey received a letter from a Mr. Newman of St. Louis stating that he was greatly pleased with Judge Holderman's report and proposed to guarantee the sale of stock in a joint stock company. This company proposed to pay $800,000, with $100,000 down.

After reading the letter Logan excitedly remarked that he knew the ranch was a big thing but did not realize there was any such sum as this in it. He suggested that when Congress adjourned he would contact his friend C. C. Campbell who was connected with the stockyards in Chicago. He felt that if St. Louis parties could afford that price, Chicago people could do better.

John P. Casey and General Logan arrived in Chicago from Washington on April 10, 1883, and Logan immediately contacted Campbell. The latter laid the possibility of purchasing the ranch before Cyrus Coy, attorney for the stockyards. Consequent to this negotiation, Campbell and Coy accompanied Casey to New Mexico to look over the ranch, arriving there on the eighth of May.[2]

On the morning of May 10, a party of visitors set out on the trail south over Gallo Mountain in the process of inspecting the ranch. Their purpose was to examine the country in the vicinity of Gallo Spring which, it was hoped, could be included in the prospective sale. A portion of the party passed about a mile east of a house at Gallo Spring, out of sight of it, and rode in a southerly direction for two or three miles before retracing their way to rejoin the rest of the party. Unbeknown to them, at the very hour they passed the house, a sorrowful party was engaged in burying Alexis Grossetete and Robert Elsinger who had been murdered on May 6 and whose bodies only that day had been found for burial.

Late in 1881 these young settlers had moved in at Gallo Spring across Gallo Mountain south from the budding empire of John P. Casey. Alexis Grossetete was the eldest son of Mrs. Clotilde Grossetete, who migrated to New Mexico from Lawrence, Kansas, in 1881. Mrs. Grossetete, whose maiden name was Xavier, arrived in the United States from France in 1840. Two years later August Grossetete arrived, and they were married soon thereafter. The young couple settled and farmed near a small town in Pennsylvania, where two of their children were born. They then moved to Lawrence, where their family increased to four sons and four daughters, and where August met his death by accidental drowning.

Durango, Colorado, was a stop for the Grossetete family on their way to Socorro, New Mexico; here Alexis formed a partnership with Robert Elsinger, formerly from Illinois, a young man of about his own age of twenty-four. Elsinger accompanied the family to Socorro and, with Alexis, settled at the Gallo. They had little money and encountered many hardships; nevertheless, by hard work and perseverance they built a stone house with a shingle roof and acquired some property. As soon as they felt secure in their new home, late in 1882, they sent for Mrs. Grossetete and the three younger brothers, Fred, Alfred, and Gus.

Grossetete and Elsinger had been at the Gallo for less than half a year when trouble started. In May 1882, Township 3S., Range 17W., where they had settled, was surveyed. Since the partners were the only settlers in the township and had not deposited money with the land office in Santa Fe, they must have wondered who had provided the funds for the survey.*

Puzzlement in this regard was dispelled later that month when John P. Casey and a party of horsemen paid Grossetete and Elsinger a visit. Casey offered to buy their preemption rights and became threatening when they refused to sell. Casey, however, was busy consolidating his interests north of Gallo Mountain, and it was another year before these threats were backed with action.

Subsequently, on the strength of affidavits by Daniel H. McAllister, a Casey employee, five men were indicted for the murder of Grossetete and Elsinger. These were W. C. Moore, James Courtright, James McIntyre, Mueller Scott, and James Casey. All were employees of the American Valley Company. James Casey was a brother of John P. Casey; Courtright and McIntyre were professional gunmen hired only a few days earlier by W. C. Moore; Scott had recently replaced McAllister as ranch foreman. McAllister claimed that he had accompanied the group but had not actually participated in the slaying.

On May 25, 1883, James Casey and Mueller Scott were

---

* *Survey Plat* T. 3S, R. 17W (B.L.M.). The deposit for the survey of this township was paid in the name of Juan Jose Careary; since this name appears nowhere else in the record, it may have been a fictitious name entered by John P. Casey and Surveyor General Atkinson.

taken into custody for the murder of Grossetete and Elsinger. On the same day John P. Casey was arrested on five charges of cattle stealing and brand changing. Moore, Courtright, and McIntyre learned of the arrests and hastily left New Mexico. Moore somehow had learned a day earlier that a warrant was out for his arrest and, as later claimed by John P. Casey, quickly sold the cattle belonging to himself, Casey, and Atkinson to Catron, giving a bill of sale in the transaction.

Catron subsequently disputed this point. He said that after Casey's brother James was arrested, Casey had requested Catron to take up a note for $6,000, which a man by the name of Anderson had against John Casey and Moore. To secure the note, Casey and Moore had given a bill of sale for their cattle. A $4,000 note to the San Miguel National Bank was also secured by Casey and Moore cattle.[3]

Catron maintained that this was his first connection with the company, which it probably was. The circumstance under which the bill of sale was lifted is substantiated only by the conflicting statements of Casey and Catron. Regardless, this was the start of a long and bitter feud between them.

On May 26 John P. Casey engaged Sidney M. Barnes, Charles H. Gildersleeve, J. Francisco Chavez, and John H. Knaebel to defend him against charges brought by the grand jury. The following morning D. W. McIntosh attached several head of mules and horses and a wagon belonging to John P. Casey, for a board bill of $265. Two days later the firm of Cordale and Peterson also ran an attachment on the mules and horses for a stabling bill of $300. These were Albuquerque merchants. The bills had been presented to Casey, who said he could not pay them, but refused to secure the debts. The attachments followed.*

John P. Casey was in serious financial trouble. On May

Albuquerque Morning Journal, May 27 and May 29, 1883. There is some indication that the firm of Catron, Thornton, and Clancy was also engaged by Casey, but they seem never to have represented him.

28 he mortgaged his one-third interest in the American Valley Company to Surveyor General Atkinson. Atkinson had advanced $6,660 to Casey and had signed notes for about $25,000 more.[4] On June 1 Catron also assumed some of the debts of the firm.

On June 10 Catron and General Logan were reported in close conversation on the train from Santa Fe to Albuquerque.[5] John P. Casey was on the same train. At Lamy Junction he was, according to his statement, approached by a man who said W. C. Moore had given him a bill of sale for the cattle belonging to Atkinson, Casey, and Moore, and that he was on his way to take possession of the stock (Casey implied that Catron had hired the man and used this method of warning him that the cattle were going to be possessed).

Casey reported the circumstance to Atkinson, who informed him that Catron had promised to lift the bill of sale in exchange for Moore's interest in the company. Moore had not paid for the interest, while Catron had settled some of the debts of the firm. Casey saw no way out and agreed to the transaction. He was planning a trip to Chicago in connection with the sale of the property; he agreed to find Moore and have him sign the deed.

Moore was reported to be in Dodge City, Kansas, where he had gone to see his wife, who had returned to her parents, Dr. and Mrs. T. J. Wright. After learning that Moore had gone to Montana, Casey continued on to Chicago without stopping in Kansas City.*

By June 20, 1883, Casey was in Chicago, where he was unable to make final arrangements for the sale of the ranch. He was, however, able to arrange for Cyrus Coy and C. C. Campbell to visit the American Valley ranch again, with an even more representative group of Eastern capitalists.[6] They

---

Albuquerque Morning Journal, June 6, 1883; John P. Casey, *Statement;* El Caso Ranch, *Abstract of Title, passim.* There was a report that Moore had been heard from in Kansas City where he issued checks that a Santa Fe bank refused to accept.

arrived at the ranch on September 12. A few days earlier, H. H. Eddy, a special agent of the General Land Office in Washington, had reached there to make widespread inspections of fraudulent land entries in the Territory. This included the American Valley ranch on which Eddy reported the illegality of a number of entries made in behalf of the American Valley Company.[7]

While it is not recorded that Casey's visitors became aware of Eddy's presence, it is likely that they did. At the same time, discussion was widespread concerning the pending trials for the murder of Grossetete and Elsinger. Perhaps Casey's friends were intimidated by either or both of these circumstances; at any rate, they were not heard from again.

The first trial of James Casey and Mueller Scott for the murder of Robert Elsinger commenced in Albuquerque on October 9, 1883, on a change of venue from Socorro. The venue was probably changed because a vigilante committee had been organized at Socorro in 1880, and there was bitter feeling against the defendants. The trial ended in a hung jury, reportedly eleven to one for conviction. Oral tradition indicates that $2.50 bought the one holdout.

The second trial, for the murder of Alexis Grossetete, started on October 18 and also ended in a hung jury. In this case the chief prosecution witness, Daniel H. McAllister, so hopelessly contradicted himself that it was reasonable for doubt to exist in the minds of some of the jurors.

In November 1883 Casey learned that W. C. Moore was in Deer Lodge, Montana, and sent the deed to him for his signature. Moore returned the signed deed, which was also signed by Mrs. Moore who was still in Dodge City.[8]

For all practical purposes Casey, heavily indebted to both Atkinson and Catron, was now out of the company. Catron and Atkinson continued to consolidate the ranch holdings. In April 1885 Atkinson gave Casey notice of foreclosure; on April 30, Catron (for himself and other creditors of John P. Casey) purchased Casey's one-third interest in the business.

Henry M. Atkinson was mortgagee and trustee for the transaction.*

Atkinson and Catron now hired Peter Burleson, formerly
a sheriff of Colfax County, to run the ranch. Burleson was
renowned for blunt tactics and a violent temper. A year later
he had shot and seriously wounded Tim Driscoll, foreman of
the Palo Blanco Cattle Company, in an altercation involving
too much poker and too much pistol.[9] He was soon to be at
odds with John P. Casey.

Casey no longer owned an interest in the American Valley
property, but he continued to reside at his home on the forks
of the Largo — probably because Atkinson still owed him
money in connection with the settlement.

In February 1886 Casey quarreled with Burleson and was
pistol whipped in the resulting fight. Catron wrote to Casey
requesting that the latter meet him in Socorro to come to an
understanding in the matter. Casey was confined to his bed
because of the beating from Burleson, and Mrs. Casey met
Catron instead. She returned with a letter from Catron to
Burleson informing him that Mrs. Casey seemed fearful that
he would murder her husband and family. Catron ordered
Burleson to kill no one unless forced to do so in self defense;
to avoid all difficulties and disputes if possible; and not to
molest or disturb Casey or his family. Two days later Casey
received a leter from Burleson which probably explains the
cause of the quarrel. Burleson wrote: "I forbid you from killing any more beef, as you have no right to kill them, if you do
so I will treat you as a thief."[10]

On August 2, 1886, the American Valley Company was
incorporated by Catron, Henry M. Atkinson (no longer surveyor general), William B. Slaughter, and Henry L. Warren.

---

* El Caso Ranch, *Abstract of Title*, pp. 32, 33. The deed was dated December
22, 1885, and filed August 10, 1886. Casey claimed that on June 6, 1884, he entered
into an equal partnership with Atkinson, Catron, and Logan, and that Catron later
refused to refund money owed to Logan. There were also hints in various newspapers
that Logan had invested; nevertheless, there is no substantial evidence that Logan
ever participated financially in the venture.

Warren was a stockholder for organizational purposes only. Slaughter had moved his herds into the area from Texas in 1882, a year after the arrival of John P. Casey. Slaughter came to dominate a large area of grazing land by gaining ownership of land controlling water. To relate how he did this would be to repeat essentially the account of Casey's tactics.

Slaughter's interests became aligned with those of Catron and Atkinson in a series of contested land cases extending from 1885 through 1888 — cases that apparently were all decided in favor of Slaughter and the American Valley Company. Typical of these cases was that of Slaughter vs. Jose F. Padia over homestead entry number 1836. The entry of Padia was cancelled, and Slaughter was allowed a preference right on the entry. Padia stoutly, though unavailingly, maintained that he had not been informed of the date of the hearing, and that advantage had been taken of his ignorance of the English language to suppress his testimony and "fix things."[11]

Two Washington attorneys hired in connection with the settlement of land titles were Van H. Manning and D. A. Chambers. Local representatives were G. L. Brooks and Max Frost. Frost, a former register of the land office in Santa Fe, had been charged with malfeasance in office and, in March 1885, was permitted to resign. There was no uncertainty in Catron's mind that Frost was guilty as charged and indicted; in fact, he later reported to Elkins that Frost "was convicted and sentenced to the penitentiary, got a new trial, stole the indictments and escaped. Nobody doubted his guilt."[12]

Catron was no friend of Frost. As a matter of fact they later became bitter enemies, but he evidently recognized Frost's qualifications for these contest cases. Frost had firsthand knowledge of the intricacies involved and could provide an edge for his clients.

The American Valley Company issued 500 shares of stock at $1,000 for $500,000 capitalization. Atkinson and Catron subscribed to $132,000 while Slaughter undertook $367,000 worth of stock. Atkinson and Catron agreed to convey, by warranty deed, 4,300 acres of land covering the water rights owned by them and to quitclaim all incomplete land interests that they owned in the area. They also agreed to convey to the corporation by bill of sale all cattle, bulls, and horses — amounting to 1,400 head or more — as well as tools, saddles, and harnesses belonging to them on the ranch. Slaughter agreed to transfer to the corporation 4,000 acres of entered land as well as all incomplete land interests owned or controlled by him. He also bargained to turn over 9,500 head or more of cattle and all bulls as well as 80 ranch horses, 4 wagons and sets of harness, and ranch camp outfit complete.[13]

Efforts were now made to secure valid title to all incomplete land interests so that the American Valley Company eventually comprised some 12,000 acres of patented land controlling the water and range to the extent of between two and three million acres of land.

> The ranch company controlled most of the water in several townships; the idea being by absolutely controlling the water right thus to command the range adjoining; but the plans were never fully carried out.[14]

Henry M. Atkinson died in October 1886, and management of the ranch was largely turned over to Slaughter. John A. Logan died in December of the same year.

On November 26, 1886, John P. Casey, Ellen Casey, and John P. Casey, Jr., for a consideration of $10,000, conveyed to Catron by warranty deed all of their interests whatsoever in the American Valley property. Atkinson owed Casey $10,000 as a result of the foreclosure in April 1885. Of this amount $1,000 was to pay Col. Sidney M. Barnes, who had been one of the trial attorneys in the defense of James Casey and Mueller Scott in their trial for the murder of Grossetete and Elsinger. Atkinson also owed Casey an additional $6,000 on notes that he had signed guaranteeing payment to other lawyers in that case and which, in the transaction, it was agreed Atkinson would pay. As an equal owner with Atkinson in the business, Catron assumed these obligations and also paid Casey an additional $5,000, part of which was for services rendered by Casey personally in working up the titles to the American Valley properties, and part to D. A. Chambers, a Washington attorney, for services in that same connection.[15]

John P. Casey continued to reside at his home on the forks of the Largo until March 1887, when he moved to Las Cruces. Catron still hired him to assist in working up title to various pieces of land in the American Valley.[16] Meanwhile, Catron had not completed payment of the agreed amount to Casey. The latter refused to turn over the deed to his interest, while Catron repeatedly insisted that he do so. Catron's continued plea in the matter was that he needed the deed to use in raising the money to pay Casey. Catron insisted that Casey should trust him because he would need his continued assistance in perfecting land titles. It is probable that Catron was short of cash, because he attempted to borrow $2,000 from S. M. Folsom of Albuquerque to pay Casey.[17]

By December 29, 1887, Catron completed his payment to Casey — the deed was filed on that date — nevertheless their feud continued. Within a week Catron wrote to Chihuahua trying to establish Casey's forgery of a deed in another land matter. Their differences were carried into the courts,[18] and Casey continued to harass Catron. As time passed, however, this harrying became petty and trivial. As late as 1900 Casey acquired a parcel of land in the American Valley of no practical value to himself but of some value to Catron. To acquire this land from Casey, Catron used a third party so that Casey was not aware of the identity of the real purchaser.[19]

But it was in another way that Casey hurt Catron more seriously. In 1892 Catron became a candidate for Congressional delegate. His Democratic opponents worked through Casey with a plan to hamstring Catron at the polls. The scheme was to have Casey release a statement just before the election claiming that Catron had paid a bill of $350 for horses rented at Socorro by Moore, Courtright, and McIntyre for transportation to the American Valley a few days before

Alexis Grossetete and Robert Elsinger were slain. Catron learned of the conspiracy and squelched it by threatening suit. He readily admitted having paid a bill to the livery stable in Socorro but explained that this payment was made in settlement of the company's bills long after the debt was incurred.*

A whispering campaign started by John P. Casey on the streets of Las Cruces insinuating that Catron was implicated in the murders was an important factor in Catron's defeat in the following election.

The innuendo continues to the present time in legend perpetuated by oral transmission. For example, one version told to the author has it that a certain party was in a hotel room in Magdalena and overheard Catron in an adjoining room tell the alleged murderers where to go and what to do. This infamous account goes on to say that Catron had rented a team and buggy from Trimble's livery stable in Albuquerque and drove so hard on the return journey that he killed one of the horses and had to pay for it.

The originator of this fairy tale — his identity has long been forgotten in the process of repeated telling — evidently overlooked the fact that Catron habitually traveled by train. It is ridiculous to suppose that he would abandon his customary mode of travel in favor of skulking over the countryside in an uncomfortable buggy. There is, of course not a shred of evidence to support this ignominious account; it is repeated here only to show the base tactics employed by Catron's opponents in resisting him.

Catron's problems in connection with the American Valley Company were not limited to those involving John P. Casey. Another centered around settlement of the estate of Henry M. Atkinson. Atkinson had died suddenly, and his affairs, particularly those connected with the American Valley venture, were thoroughly tangled. He was financially over-

---

*Catron to W. L. Rynerson and Catron to Neill B. Field, September 22, 1892 (C.P. 105, Vol. 5); John P. Casey, *Statement*. Casey's statement is dated October 15, 1892, and apparently is related to the one that was intended for publication.

extended, and his untimely death tied up available potential assets. As a consequence his wife, Ada, was forced to return to Lincoln, Nebraska, where she resumed her profession as a schoolteacher. This had been her employment prior to her marriage to Atkinson. The position of surveyor general in New Mexico was comparable in importance to that of Territorial governor, and as wife of the surveyor general, Mrs. Atkinson had enjoyed a position of eminence. Atkinson was also a burgeoning entrepreneur, which provided some affluence. As a schoolteacher Mrs. Atkinson was poorly paid and had scant funds to raise her children. She no longer received money from the American Valley Company, since it failed to prosper. In 1892 she requested Catron's aid in securing a position in Washington through Elkins. No position was available, so she continued to reside in Lincoln.[20]

Mrs. Atkinson's legal representative in New Mexico was Frank W. Clancy. In 1893 a controversy arose over the relative merits of the accounts left by Atkinson and those kept by Catron. Because of his relations with Catron as a former law partner, Clancy was reluctant to enter into the dispute and turned Mrs. Atkinson's account over to Neill B. Field.[21] Field accepted stock in the American Valley Company in payment of fees. In the process of settlement, he became president of the company.

Field and Catron quarreled bitterly over some stock Catron claimed Atkinson had turned over to him prior to his death. Catron, however, never had the stock transferred to his name and requested Field to make the transfer. Field refused because he thought there might be some doubt as to the ownership of the stock, and he wanted to protect Mrs. Atkinson.

The matter degenerated into a personal vendetta in which neither Field nor Catron would budge. Mrs. Atkinson stood by helplessly while the two attorneys bickered. Typical of their heated exchanges, Field wrote:

Now Mr. Catron, it is folly to talk of friendship between you and me. You ought to know me well enough to know that no man can mistreat me and retain my friendship. I want to say to you, Mr. Catron, once and for all, that I am exceedingly sick of your method of doing business and I do not propose to put up with it.[22]

Catron replied:

You have worked yourself into a fever in this matter unnecessarily. You have used language toward me which is unmerited and unwarranted.[23]

Final settlement of Atkinson's estate dragged on for years.

Under William B. Slaughter's management the ranch did not prosper:

Owing to dry seasons and severe winters, the losses of the company's stock were very great. Mr. Slaughter moved a great many of the cattle, some to Texas; some to Montana; in fact at one time, he must have had cattle in at least five states and territories. At that time cattle were very low and expenses under such condition were very heavy. The losses were great and W. B. Slaughter personally became heavily involved. The consequence was the company suffered in every direction. In 1893, when it was decided to sell the cattle less than 4,000 were sold including those gathered and the remnant. The stockholders of the company [now more numerous than the original incorporators] received dividends or distributions amounting in all to $11.00 per share. This dividend was derived from the sales made. The litigations to which the company was subjected, largely on account of Mr. Slaughter's personal embarrassments, were expensive and much more unfavorable than was expected. The Montana business especially being almost an entire loss, partly on account of the failure of the bank, which held the funds involved.[24]

The American Valley now became virtually abandoned. It would have been well for Catron had he withdrawn from the project; nevertheless, he stubbornly held on, and his involvement became a heavy burden until the day he died.

10
American Valley Company
Revived

By 1899 the American Valley Company, under the management of William B. Slaughter, had failed. The interest of the former Surveyor General Henry M. Atkinson in the company was still unsettled, and it was a rueful day in the life of Catron when Charles H. Elmendorf was sent from Nebraska to represent Mrs. Atkinson in the final settlement of the estate. Elmendorf, who was rated an expert accountant, had cattle interests in Nebraska. In May 1899 he was introduced to Catron by a letter from Frank W. Clancy, a former Catron law partner.[1] This began a relationship that evolved into one as stormy as any in Catron's turbulent career.

Elmendorf was introduced to Catron on May 19 and by June 16 was able to report to Mrs. Atkinson that he had come to a settlement with him. "Mr. Catron," Elmendorf stated, "on his part has shown a spirit of fairness very agreeable and somewhat unexpected."[2]

By this time Elmendorf was able to clear up substantially other items not yet settled in connection with the Atkinson estate. These included an interest in the Antonio Baca land grant, the Galena Chief mining claim, and a lot in Santa Fe. He also informed Mrs. Atkinson that the San Miguel del Bado Grant title had failed and nothing would likely be realized from that source. There remained but to dispose of Mrs. Atkin-

[166]

son's share of the land in the American Valley Company. This was advertised for sale in August 1900 and purchased by Catron. He also purchased her share of stock in the company.

Catron was impressed with Elmendorf's businesslike approach in the Atkinson settlement, so decided to hire him for various tasks connected with the floundering company. Late in June 1899 he sent Elmendorf to make an inspection of the American Valley lands.[3] Elmendorf found the area to be virtually deserted. Living there were only a few Mexicans, including the Somora, Padilla, and Romero families. J. V. Morrison was hired as guide for the eight day trip. They rode from Datil to Rito Quemado, up Largo Creek, across to Agua Fria Creek, thence southwest for a time before turning east at Horse Springs. During the entire ride they did not see two hundred head of cattle. Dry weather and short grass made it evident to Elmendorf that the country was not suitable for a permanent cattle range because of periodic droughts, so he recommended that the range be utilized as a sheep ranch; Catron concurred.[4]

Elmendorf further suggested that efforts be made to gain control over absolutely all the water in the area. This could be done by perfecting title to lands in question — by outright purchase, by utilizing land scrip purchased for the purpose, and by leasing areas otherwise unobtainable. Catron agreed, and Elmendorf energetically set about acquiring strategic land. Only rarely did he pay more than $2.00 an acre for land controlling water, never more than $2.50 for particularly desired areas.[5] The price of land scrip was higher — usually $4.00 an acre — because it could be located with the register of the land office, in strategic areas not otherwise available, in the name of Catron as entryman.[6] Elmendorf carried on a whirlwind campaign of personal contacts and letter writing. Much of his correspondence was with persons who did not reside in New Mexico. His standard approach was the logical reasoning that the country was virtually deserted and that small pieces of land were of little value to scattered individuals. Always he was calm, reasonable, and courteous. His methods were successful; in a remarkably short time he made extensive purchases or leases.

Some persons had "squatted" on lands purchased by Elmendorf. In these cases his attitude was one of patience and kindness, but no-nonsense firmness. To foreman John E. Ryan, he wrote:

I want you to be very decided but very friendly and you can state to all the parties that unless they get off peaceably, we will commence action for possession and damages which will make them costs and trouble and which we wish to avoid if possible.[7]

The Padilla family presented particular difficulties. Elmendorf wrote:

I think they are a very dangerous outfit, and I do not wish to have any trouble with them; but we must get them off the property and now is the time to do it. Please write me very plainly what they say. Be very kind but very firm.[8]

Another matter handled by Elmendorf was the purchase for Catron of miscellaneous outstanding shares of American Valley Company stock. Like the land, ownership of this stock was widely scattered; it required energy and ingenuity to locate the owners and make the purchases. He was able to secure this stock for prices ranging from seventy-five cents to three dollars per share.

As in the case of land acquisitions, his purchasing technique was logical. One letter is typical.

As you have but a small amount of stock and Mr. Catron desires to purchase it all, he authorizes me to say that he will pay you $3.00 per share which is, as I have before stated, the most that any one has received. I have no hesitancy in advising you to accept this amount as I believe it to be more than you would receive were the company wound up and the assets distributed pro rata.[9]

Elmendorf was also involved in settlement of W. B. Slaughter's interest in the concern. In his management Slaughter had become heavily indebted by allowing his personal affairs to become mixed with those of the company; consequently in 1898 the other stockholders brought suit to attach his shares of the stock. This suit was sustained. In the final settlement, in 1900, Slaughter received $3,000 for his entire interest. Most of the negotiations prior to the settlement were carried out by Elmendorf. That same year Slaughter received a final discharge in bankruptcy.

By the end of 1899 Elmendorf's record of accomplishment in New Mexico was impressive. Catron had long sought a way to recoup his losses in the American Valley venture and decided to utilize Elmendorf's talents to that end. In the first month of the new century Catron entered into a business agreement with him. His reasons for doing so seemed sound at the time. Elmendorf was level headed and calm. He seemed to possess sound business judgment and had an excellent knowledge of the intricacies of corporate finance. Furthermore, he was willing to accept responsibility, confident of his own ability, and not inclined to bother others with details of management.

Still, affairs of the new venture did not prosper. It is impossible to name any simple cause for ultimate failure. The plan was too complex from the beginning; Elmendorf's time was too divided between local management and Eastern financial arrangements; loans were difficult to procure at crucial times; and cordial relations between Catron and Elmendorf broke down early. Catron became mistrustful and berating; Elmendorf reciprocated with quiet but steadfast defiance. Catron undoubtedly became overly critical about details; but more important, he displayed in full force a lifelong habit of maintaining an unbending position in negotiating prices of land and details of financial arrangements. At times this attitude undoubtedly hampered Elmendorf in his negotiations. On the other hand, Elmendorf was visionary and impractical in his stubborn insistence of too rapid expansion of the business. The result was a tangled skein of transactions that

became too involved ever to be untangled. Through it all
Catron heaped upon Elmendorf coals of bitter criticism and
insulting invective. Elmendorf accepted criticism and insult
alike and only infrequently fought back with relatively less
virulent verbal attacks.

In Catron's arrangement there is one factor that he
should have considered more carefully: Elmendorf had no
money. But he apparently had brains and initiative, which
Catron evidently thought was enough. Catron agreed to a
three-fifths interest in the new concern and Elmendorf two-
fifths. Elmendorf was to be paid a salary as manager, and they
were to be paid from the profits in proportion to their respective interests.

At the time Catron was owed $41,000 by the company
as the result of transactions prior to the death of Atkinson. He
had also paid John P. Casey $15,000 and had expended
$19,000 in connection with the Antonio Sandoval (Bosque del
Apache) Grant which had been included for sale or development in the agreement with Elmendorf. To help out the new
venture, he agreed to be credited with only $45,000 of the
$75,000 owed him. It was understood that this amount, plus
any future expenditures by Catron, would be paid before
Elmendorf shared in the profits.[10]

The first step in their joint venture was to apply for a
loan of $10,000 for four months from the First National Bank
in Santa Fe. To substantiate their loan application, they
claimed ownership of 7,091 acres of land and leases on 1,920
additional acres. They also planned to script 1,500 acres
more. This, together with additional purchases, as well as
other land on which title was being cleared, would give them
about 12,000 acres of patented land controlling the water
and range to the extent of between two and three million
acres of land.

Of the 5,000 shares of stock of the original company,
3,978 had been issued; they controlled 3,426 shares of this.
They planned to purchase the remaining 552 shares at a price

of not over $3.00 per share and then issue all the stock of the company. Their plan was to bond the company for a sufficient amount to pay all indebtedness, including the requested $10,000 loan, then make all necessary improvements and purchase sheep to stock the ranch. Money for the bonds, they assured, would be available as soon as transfer of the real estate could be fully accomplished. The $10,000 loan was to be used to purchase the required script, to buy outstanding shares of stock, to make initial purchases of sheep, and for the contemplated costs of reorganization. The loan was granted.[11]

Elmendorf now turned his attention to purchasing sheep. The winter and spring of 1900 were very dry, and there was possibility of drought with consequent loss of sheep. Catron suggested that they defer their purchases, so it was June before Elmendorf bought about 12,000 sheep in San Angelo, Texas.[12] After engaging the necessary herders and starting the sheep toward New Mexico, he resumed his attempt to place the bonds of the American Valley Company. This proved more difficult than he anticipated. Due dates for obligations were fast approaching, though, and Catron was becoming uneasy. Elmendorf had capably performed tasks in New Mexico, but he had been unduly optimistic about negotiating with Eastern capitalists to arrange the necessary money. At the same time a complication arose in connection with the Bosque del Apache Grant.

This grant of 60,117.39 acres was located on both sides of the Rio Grande some dozen miles south of Socorro. It was patented to Antonio Sandoval on March 21, 1877, but was sold in 1871 to John Collinson and S. B. Elkins before issuance of patent. Collinson and Elkins were associated in affairs of the Maxwell Grant at the time of their purchase. Collinson put up the money to buy the property and received two-thirds interest. He agreed to wait until the grant was sold before receiving payment from Elkins for the remainder.[13]

Starting in 1872, Catron acted as agent in management of the grant, for which he was to share equally in Elkins' interest. Catron engaged various persons, among them Elfego Baca and Holm O. Bursum, to oversee leasing the property, but the leases never even paid for taxes and expenses. Catron had obligated himself to pay the taxes and protect the property. The original agreement ran only until 1885, yet Catron continued to pay the taxes and expenses; consequently, he had money due him. Collinson refused to reimburse him for money expended, so he sued Collinson for $19,000.

Meanwhile, Catron consummated his arrangement with Elmendorf and decided to purchase Collinson's interest. The contract with Collinson called for $35,000 total consideration with $5,000 down and the balance free from all claims within three months.[14] Catron made the deal with Collinson on the assurance that Elmendorf could sell the grant within the three months allowed for final payment. This Elmendorf was unable to do, and his failure was the beginning of years of bitter relations between himself and Catron.

June 30, 1900, was the due date of the loan to the First National Bank in Santa Fe, but by then Elmendorf had barely commenced negotiations in connection with the sale of the bonds. This called for an extension of time from the bank and made necessary a series of loans and loan extensions that constantly plagued Catron and harried Elmendorf in his efforts to sell the bonds.*

A note to Elkins was particularly troublesome. Early in 1901 Elmendorf borrowed $2,000 from Elkins for which he agreed to give as security one-tenth of the capital stock fully paid and nonassessable.[15] At that time Elmendorf thought he was about to close the sale of a large amount of the stock and that Elkins' loan would see him through until the deal was closed. Catron blamed Elmendorf for making a bad deal with

---

* Involved, besides the Santa Fe bank, were the Bank of Commerce in Albuquerque, the First National Bank in Albuquerque, the First National Bank of Silver City, the National Bank of Commerce in Kansas City, the Waco (Texas) State Bank, and the New Haven County National Bank of New Haven, Connecticut. Some individuals involved were S. B. Elkins, Miss Emma Waddingham, Gustave Becker, W. H. Herrick, and a Mrs. Perea.

Elkins; Elkins blamed Catron for urging the loan; Catron claimed he had not pressured Elkins in the matter; and Elkins repeatedly threatened to sue Elmendorf for recovery of the money loaned. Numerous other creditors clamored for payment. Failure to make payments brought a series of threats of suit, litigation, judgments, and making of emergency loans to meet obligations.*

Meanwhile Elmendorf continued to have trouble selling the bonds. He learned that businessmen were inclined to wait in money matters until after the 1900 election. There seemed little doubt that William McKinley would be reelected and that financial conditions would remain undisturbed. The men Elmendorf was trying to do business with, though, were a conservative sort and held off in money matters until the event was fully decided. There was a general feeling that if William Jennings Bryan should be elected there would be a general tightening of the money market if not actual panic. It was felt that the sheep business was dependent upon the political situation.[16]

Another trouble was that title to some of the property had not yet been perfected. This reflected on the validity of the bonds, and Elmendorf was forced to delay his efforts to sell them in order to attend to land titles. Catron grew critical and Elmendorf complained:

> You seem to be severely criticising me for supposed delays. Allow me to say that there has not been an hour of delay on my part in anything. I do not wish to place myself on the defensive, or allow you so to place me, but will state for your information that I have done everything about this matter that I think any one can do.[17]

---

* Catron was the most heavily involved financially. There was also the payment to John Collinson for the Bosque del Apache Grant. Others were J. Korber and Company; Grunsfeld Brothers; Allaire, Miera & Company; Peck Dry Goods Company; and the Friedman Shoe Company. An example of an emergency loan was the case of Mrs. Perea. Catron borrowed $4,000 from her on February 15, 1906, for thirty days. The money was procured to avoid execution of judgment on a note by Gustave Becker. At the end of thirty days, Mrs. Perea granted an extension of fifteen days, but said she must then have the money without fail because she had obligations to meet at that time. Catron to Elmendorf, March 28, 1906 (C.P. 105, Vol. 24).

On March 1, 1901, the American Valley Company gave a trust deed to the Continental Trust Company of Denver to secure payment of two hundred bonds of $1,000 each issued to secure payment to that company. With the security of the bonds now in the hands of a reputable trust company, Elmendorf set out with renewed energy to effect their sale. By May, negotiations were under way that even Catron felt would bring results. Eastern interests represented by a Mr. Nichols desired, however, to examine the property before consummating a deal. Catron was confident that they would find the security to be worth at least $400,000, and perhaps half a million.[18]

This negotiation dragged on for months. In August the weather in the East was such that people fled from the heat in all directions and were unwilling to discuss Elmendorf's proposition until the temperature moderated. Catron renewed his criticism, and Elmendorf wrote:

> You at least imply that I do not have your interests at heart as well as my own. Such is not the case — I went into this undertaking for our joint profit and while the profits to you are to be in every way much greater than mine can possibly be, I have not stopped to consider that fact, but have been, am now, and shall continue working for complete success of our enterprize — and am as I ever have been confident of success.[19]

In September the assassination of President McKinley caused jitters in financial circles; consequently, the negotiations cooled off and finally fell through.[20]

Another half year passed, and Catron, now thoroughly exasperated, wrote:

> You have been working on this for a year and a half, practically accomplishing nothing. I hope you will do something now. I must either get some money through the sale, or call the Board together and sell out the property absolutely. I will not delay much longer. You have obtained money from me on assurance that it would be repaid very soon, and you have failed, as a consequence I am unable to meet obligations, and will be compelled to make sacrifices amounting to some hundreds of thousands of dollars. You must either get me some money or I must act. There must be no further delay.[21]

Three weeks later Catron wrote to his wife: "Mr. Elmendorf has done nothing yet says he expects to do so soon, but I have about lost confidence in him.[22]

Catron's letter to his wife followed a particularly humiliating experience. Elmendorf had arranged with a Mr. Brent to look over the Bosque del Apache Grant with a view to possibly making a loan with bonds as surety. Brent arrived, but Elmendorf was not on hand to show him the property. Catron did not know the details of the possible transaction; nevertheless, he had to break into his own busy schedule to show Brent around. Brent was not communicative, simply saying he would report to his company and advise Catron as to their decision. When it came time for Brent's departure, he borrowed thirty dollars from Catron for railroad fare back east, promising to return the money promptly. Instead, Brent said he had directed Elmendorf to pay Catron. Coming at a time when Catron was repeatedly sending Elmendorf various amounts for expenses, his irritation at the transaction is understandable.

Catron expressed his general displeasure:

The indebtedness due to other people or to me does not seem to bother you at all. There must be a change in this regard in your manner of doing. I cannot afford to be dogged by these various creditors of the company simply because I have signed notes on your assurance that the money would be forthcoming and I would not be bothered. Instead of getting it from the parties or in the manner you expected I have been compelled to put up most of it to save myself from greater loss and the company also.[23]

The summer of 1902 passed, and in October Catron resumed his disapproving:

The $13,000.00 which was sent to you was not company money, it was my money and no-one's else and as you did not use the $3,000.00 of it, I think that ought to be sent back to me. However, I do not care about making any noise about that just now. Should you get your matter through, I presume the whole thing will be settled without further annoyance, but I assure you now that I am being very much annoyed and pressed for moneys which I have paid in order to assist this American Valley matter along and which I should have used then for other purposes and had I used them for other purposes, I would not today be at all troubled, but on the contrary would have money to spare. [October 25, 1902]

In December 1902 Elmendorf asked if Catron would be disposed to sell his interest in the American Valley Company. Certain of Elmendorf's friends had expressed willingness to buy if Catron would sell at a reasonable figure. Elmendorf did not attempt to explain why he thought he could find purchasers for Catron's interest when he could not sell the bonds or arrange a loan.

Further correspondence followed concerning a possible sale of Catron's interest. Meanwhile, by 1903, Elmendorf's expenses were running as high as $30,000 per year. Catron protested:

I am not at all pleased with the way you are doing business. You are making that ranch cost four times more than it ought to. . . . I have been putting up money for this ranch business until the ranch owes me at least $80,000.00 beyond what has been paid to me, when interest is counted upon the amount.[24]

By now it would seem that Catron sought to obtain action by the sheer persistence of his letters:

Why cannot you write and tell me what is being done? . . . You must attend to them and not allow me to be annoyed by them. You go away from here and these people do not know where you are and do not pay any attention to you, neither do they consider you sufficiently responsible to be bothered about it. [February 3, 1903]

Early in February 1903 Catron proposed that he would accept $105,000 for his interest in the American Valley Company, providing he would be released from all notes, bonds obligations and indebtedness for which he was endorser or otherwise liable.[25]

Matters continued on their troubled way. A week later Catron wrote:

I cannot understand or comprehend how it is that you have no money with which to pay expenses. Evidently the expenses of the company during the last twelve months have been greater than the full value of the sheep on it, if I am to understand that all the moneys which you have not used in paying notes of the company and in paying for sheep, have been used by you by way of paying expenses. [February 13, 1903]

By now Catron's protests were on a weekly schedule:

I cannot understand your way of doing business. You certainly cause me more trouble than any man I have had anything to do with. Your way of doing business is different from anyone I have ever struck in my life. You seem to care nothing about your obligations. . . . I have been injured fully $100,000.00 by the way in which you have attended to the business of the American Valley Co. [February 23, 1903]

Two days later Catron added a postscript:

I must insist that you get me out of this business at once; I am absolutely on nettles in every connection that I have with you; your way of doing business is so different from mine that I do not wish to go along with you any longer. I wish to be out of this without making any sacrifice or without losing money or making you lose any. [February 25, 1903]

Another three days passed and Catron wrote:

It seems to me that I can never get anything out of you unless you want me to pay some money. I suppose that it is the only inducement for it and it is very seldom that I get it even then. [February 28, 1903]

Elmendorf replied with one of his infrequent and typically generalized communications:

On arriving here I found waiting for me your telegram of the 5th and immediately replied that I am expecting to get everything closed the coming week. I am doing everything I can in this matter but am meeting with obstacles all along the road. However, I am determined to put it through, and I have met most of the unfavorable conditions.[26]

Catron did not consider this information as at all satisfactory. He wrote:

You are certainly the most remarkable man that I have ever had anything to do with. . . . When I went into this transaction I did it with the assurance that you could easily float the scheme and get the money that was necessary to carry it through. . . . The thing has run along on your assurances; we have carried the Company along from day to day by making new notes and shifting from pillar to post.[27]

Elmendorf continued to be evasive and to write only in general terms:

I think your criticisms are very unjust to me. I am doing everything that is possible to do to close the transaction at hand, and shall be able to do so, although I have had many unexpected obstacles to overcome; but your attitude has not made it any easier, I assure you.[28]

Meanwhile, correspondence continued concerning the possibility of Catron selling his interest. His major reason for desiring to sell, as he expressed it, was to be disassociated from Elmendorf. On July 1, 1903, they agreed that Catron was owed — in addition to the value of his bonds — $113,073 as of that date. On September 8 the Socorro Company was incorporated, and on September 24 it received a warranty deed to the assets of the American Valley Company.[29] Title to these assets was escrowed with the Fidelity Trust Company of Kansas City, Missouri, pending sale of new bonds. Catron was issued new bonds in proportion to his interest in the old company. It was well into the following year, however, before Elmendorf completed even the organizational work and could set about raising money in connection with the new transaction.

Through the summer and fall of 1903 negotiations were under way for Catron to take the Kemper building in Kansas City as part payment of the money owed him. Elmendorf and his associates insisted that Catron take the building in at $100,000 equity valuation. Catron was convinced that the equity was worth no more than $75,000; still, he was willing to deal, hoping the property would increase in value so he could eventually recoup his loss. But the sale fell through; in fact, it is doubtful that it was ever more than a delaying tactic on the part of Elmendorf and his friends.

By 1904 the situation had not improved and Catron so informed Elmendorf:

You have no conception of the amount of annoyance and inconvenience to which I have been placed by being deprived of the money which I have placed in this American Valley Co. to help you carry out your scheme which you proposed. . . . You have made all kinds of promises, [but] have up to this date put up nothing and done nothing except to secure the sale of 30 bonds at 82½ when you had absolutely agreed to sell the bonds at par and turn the money in.[30]

Throughout these transactions Catron served the Socorro Company in various legal matters. He sent Elmendorf a bill for services rendered, and Elmendorf complained that the bill was a little too high. Catron replied:

You will see that every bit of income I have has been hypothecated to carry on this business and after I have done that, you have the impertinence to tell me that you think the account I sent you is a little too high.[31]

A week later Catron was still hot under the collar and wrote:

For three years you have been telling me that you are on the eve of consummating and completing this business so as to relieve me from the strain which you have placed upon me by getting me to invest all my means in this transaction on the faith of your promises and agreements and assertions. You have been from time to time making promises not only to me but to the banks and other individuals, of closing up this business and paying up the indebtedness. Every one of your promises up to this date have failed.[32]

Elmendorf seldom reacted to Catron's criticism with any show of anger. Occasionally he did assert himself a little more firmly than normal, for example:

I have not promised to write to you every day for the rest of my natural life. I do expect to keep you fully informed and wish to do so. . . . I will endeavor to furnish you as complete information from day to day and from time to time as such information is obtainable.*

Catron presented his fifth annual summation of Elmendorf's deficiencies a little wearily. Evidently he was being worn down by trying to think of new ways to express his displeasure:

You have now been at this matter for over 5 years and today you have no more assurance as you gave me five years ago, in fact not as much. . . . [You] seem to be unable or unwilling to do anything towards crowding the matter along. This is probably because I am the only person who will be directly injured and you apparently do not care how much I am injured.[33]

---

*Elmendorf to Catron, November 29, 1904 (C.P. 103, Box 21). Despite his promise, Elmendorf continued to write only infrequently and evasively.

By September 1905 Elmendorf managed to reply to Catron's invective with a little asperity:

> Your manner of continued fault finding makes it very hard for me to properly attend to my business. I have not accomplished anything like as much as I would like to have accomplished in connection with the New Mexico proposition, but I think you might at least give me credit for effort. I have at all times tried to please you and meet your views so far as I could. Some of your demands seem to me to be exceedingly childish and unreasonable, and I am chagrined at times that you seem to give me credit for so little sense or business intelligence.[34]

In January 1906 Catron was owed $197,936.59 above the value of his bonds. He agreed to take the Gibraltar building in Kansas City in lieu of $110,000 of this amount, leaving $87,936.59 which represented the balance of the amount he had paid out in cash, or for which he had signed notes obligating him personally. He further agreed to assume a first mortgage of $65,000 and a second mortgage of $25,000; worse, he loaned Elmendorf his bonds for the purpose of raising additional capital. Elmendorf, in turn, agreed to clear up the obligations of the Socorro Company, including the amount still owed to Catron.[35]

But Elmendorf did not succeed in paying off the Socorro Company debts, which left Catron still liable on numerous company incumbrances. As the years passed Catron tried to get back the bonds he had loaned to Elmendorf, but the latter had pledged them in further transactions and was unable to return them. Elmendorf claimed that Catron had agreed to release these bonds to the company in order to raise additional money. Catron justifiably maintained that he had agreed to release the bonds only if the debts for which he had signed were entirely settled and he was released from all obligations.

To summarize, Catron took over the heavily mortgaged Gibraltar building; was still owed $87,936.59 by the Socorro Company; and was not released from obligations of the company. Furthermore, he could not get back his bonds to realize a return from this source.

To make matters worse the Gibraltar building was badly run down and in poor repute with tenants and prospective tenants. Catron immediately had to pay out large amounts to repair the building. Even then the receipts were not sufficient to make payments and pay fixed expenses. Catron showed his displeasure in a letter to Elmendorf:

> I am not willing to take any more chips in whetstones in payment, and I shall take steps to realize upon the bonds I hold unless something is done promptly.*

By December 1907 the amount owed Catron had increased to \$118,658.12, of which amount he agreed to take \$102,000 in various stocks and notes. The notes were largely uncollectable and the stocks turned sour. For example, \$24,000 of the stock was in the Bank of Commerce in Kansas City, and the bank failed. An amount of \$40,000 was represented by stock in the Swofford Brothers Dry Goods Company, also of Kansas City. This concern likewise failed, and J. J. Swofford was indicted by a federal grand jury on three counts of using the United States mail to defraud purchasers of stock in the company.[36]

Meanwhile, Elmendorf had largely turned the affairs of the Socorro Company over to Judge C. H. Stoll of Lexington, Kentucky, for reorganization and development of the property. By now the affairs of the concern were so thoroughly enmeshed in litigation and complicated stock exchanges that it proved impossible to straighten it out. Catron had repeatedly threatened to place the company in receivership, but it was Judge Stoll who finally took this action in June 1909. Elmendorf moved to Los Angeles and claimed to have salvaged virtually nothing for himself.†

---

* Catron to Elmendorf, December 22, 1906 (C.P. 105, Vol. 25). This would have been difficult to do because Catron had loaned the bonds to Elmendorf who had tied them up as security in various transactions.

† Elmendorf to Catron, July 1, 1909 (C.P. 103, Box 34). Elmendorf later returned to New Mexico.

There followed a struggle to avoid foreclosure of mortgages so the bond holders could prevent partition of the property. It was their purpose to jointly reorganize and attempt to develop and sell the whole property. In order to do this they were obliged to pay further assessments for costs of litigation in the receivership proceedings.[37]

Finally, on July 4, 1911, the property of the Socorro Company was sold at Socorro under foreclosure of deed of trust to the bond holders.[38] On August 4, 1911, a syndicate of part of the bond holders, including Catron, purchased the property at a sale held, likewise, in Socorro.[39] The company was now reorganized as the Sandoval Grant Company. Ramifications of this venture were still a problem when Catron died in 1921. Likewise, the Gibraltar building remained unsold and unprofitable.

11
Recouping Political
Fortunes

The decade of the 1870s had been for T. B. Catron a period of service in appointive office as attorney general and United States attorney until his resignation from the latter office which became effective in 1879. During the 1880s his political life centered largely around the Territorial council.

In both these periods the matter of railroad transportation to New Mexico was of paramount importance in the lives of all citizens of the Territory. The former decade was one of waiting, the latter one of fruition and railroad expansion through the Territory that brought New Mexico out of a period of depression and started an era of increased prosperity and expansion. It was this period of optimism and relative economic prosperity that commenced the decade of Catron's legislative career.

But the arrival of the railroad was not a cure-all for New Mexico's woes. The gravest economic problem continued to be the unsettled state of titles to land grants. Governor Lionel A. Sheldon reported:

New Mexico is largely plastered with grants of land, real or pretended, made by Spanish and Mexican Governments. By law these grants are segregated from the public domain, and must continue in a condition of practical mortmain until final action is taken to determine their validity.[1]

He further explained that titles had been manipulated and surveys erroneously made to an extent that these grants seemed to be endowed with India-rubber qualities. No one would attempt to acquire land in the vicinity of these grants for fear the stretching process would apply.*

The advent of railroad transportation arrived upon the heels of an unprecedented era of lawlessness in New Mexico. Trouble in Lincoln and Colfax counties stole the headlines, but in no part of the Territory were life and property completely safe. Indian depredations were a recurring problem. Travel either on or behind a horse rendered the wayfarer vulnerable to brigandage. The vast unsettled areas provided perfect hiding places and made apprehension of criminals difficult. It was not until 1883 that Governor Sheldon was able to report:

> The desperado and thieving element has substantially disappeared, and nothing more is heard of *vigilantes* or lynch law. Animals upon the ranches are not much disturbed, and people may travel over the Territory generally unarmed, with little danger of being held up and robbed. The courts are able and efficient, officers generally perform their duties well, criminals are usually captured, and convictions, when deserved, are quite certain at the hands of juries. Thirty militia companies are organized, armed, officered by good men, under excellent discipline, and as favorably located over the Territory as the condition of population will permit. These companies have rendered most important service aiding the civil authorities to capture and punish offenders, in preserving peace and order, and in protecting the people against Indian raids. Having the support of the good people, the Government is abun-

------

*G.N.M. 9/6/83, 48 Cong., 1 Sess., *H.E.D.* No. 1, p. 555 (2191). Before the adjudications of the Court of Private Land Claims — 1891–1904 — it was commonly believed that many grants were illegal, forged, and fraudulent, and that the court would so find. To the contrary, the court found that the notorious Peralta Reavis case was the only one of this description. The court did find, however, a great deal of enlargement of grant boundaries. See Chapter 4.

dantly able to administer and execute the laws, and to give protection for life and property in every part of the Territory.*

The appointment of Lew Wallace as Territorial Governor in 1878 — in at least a partially abortive attempt to curb lawlessness — had been accompanied by wholesale dismissal and resignation of Republican officials, among them United States Attorney Catron. It became evident, though, that these removals scarcely diminished Republican political power in New Mexico. The result was a renewed Democratic attack on the Santa Fe Ring that reached crescendo proportions as the election of 1880 approached, and Catron came to be singled out as the leader of that organization. During his tenure as United States attorney, he had become a power in New Mexico Republican politics. Working unobtrusively behind the scenes, his opinions became ever more sought after and respected.

In that era there was no effective libel law, and it became almost habitual to say and write things about other persons that would be unheard of today. This was particularly true of newspaper writers. By far the most of this vilification centered around politics, with Democratic and Republican parties as focal points for mutual recrimination. So in viewing the politics of that day, one must weigh accusation against imputation and diatribe against invective. If these become too ridiculous, one can only have a good laugh at the ludicrous and preposterous foibles of the day. It is difficult for the writer as well as the reader to observe these ground rules, but let us both try. Thus it is, particularly, that the famous — or infa-

---

*G.N.M. 9/6/83, 48 Cong., 1 Sess., *H.E.D.* No. 1, pp. 551–552 (2191). This condition was relatively true of the year of Governor Sheldon's report; nevertheless, much unapprehended lawlessness still occurred in later years. There is some question concerning the motives of at least some of the militia companies. One commanded by Albert J. Fountain was accused (perhaps without justification) of needlessly taking human life. Some members of one organized in the American Valley (near present Quemado) almost certainly used their official position as a cover for rustling cattle.

mous — Santa Fe Ring must be examined with circumspection. This is not to say that people didn't take their politics seriously — they did, more so than today. The fact is they had less to take seriously then than we have in our present time.

As had been the case in earlier years, charges of infamous conduct were inclined to be general rather than specific. Typically:

> The Santa Fe Ring is the most corrupt combination that ever cursed any country or community.
> It has controlled the machinery of the Republican party in this Territory for the past twelve years.
> It has vilified, oppressed or otherwise sought to ruin every man who had the independence and hardihood to oppose its corrupt schemes.
> It has grown fat upon the prostitution of the party it controls.
> It has used its power in the courts to defend its criminal tools from merited punishment.
> It has retained its power by wholesale bribery and intimidation of voters.
> It has threatened innocent men with prosecution in the courts, should they dare to oppose it.
> It has promised indicted criminals immunity from punishment if they would assist it to retain its power.
> The people of this county and every county will be benefitted by its overthrow.
> It can be overthrown by defeating its candidates at the approaching election.
> Voting the Republican ticket is no test of a man's Republicanism in New Mexico.
> Every well-informed Republican who loves principal above mere party name and who desires an honest administration of public affairs in this Territory will assist to overthrow the Santa Fe Ring by depositing his ballot against its candidate next Tuesday.[2]

The *Santa Fe New Mexican* was accused of being the mouthpiece of the Santa Fe Ring. This newspaper facetiously pointed out that the Ring was accused of being to blame for the low price of wool, disease among cattle, failure of crops, all careless legislation, and for all illegal acts in the Territory. William Breeden, chairman of the Republican party, renewed his plea of earlier years that names and facts be stated so that these illegal practices, if they did exist, could be corrected.*

The most important elective office then was Territorial delegate to Congress. Catron was singled out as the boss of Ring activities because he championed Tranquilino Luna, the Republican candidate for that office. Luna's Democratic opponent was Miguel A. Otero, I. The drama of the coming election was likened unto a puppet show with Catron manipulating the wires assisted by the *Santa Fe New Mexican* and lesser leaders in the Republican party. The rank and file of Republican voters, it was charged, would have no part to play beyond depositing a straight ticket in a ballot box on election day. "They are not expected to think, speak, or have an opinion. Indeed, how can they, being puppets?"[3]

An appeal was made to Republican voters to join with Democrats in dealing the Santa Fe Ring a crushing blow. Candidate Luna was not generally singled out personally for attack. He was conceded to be otherwise a good man; his crime was in being backed by Catron and the Santa Fe Ring. Every attempt was made to link the name of this organization with infamy. As election day neared, Otero, who had been a strong Confederate sympathizer in the Civil War, attacked Catron personally on his war record. He charged that the Republican party in New Mexico was "led by men who fought against the Union; men who had done all they could to destroy the Union; and failing in that, they had banded together to *rot the Union* and oppress the people."[4]

Despite these tactics, Luna was elected over Otero; however, charges of fraud were leveled at Luna's supporters, charges that were repeated in the election of 1882 when Luna defeated Francisco A. Manzanares for delegate. Manzanares contested the election and was sustained on the grounds of

Santa Fe Weekly New Mexican Review, October 11, 1880. This newspaper, on November 22, 1880, stated: "There are in New Mexico three Republican newspapers, four Democratic, six independent, three devoted to mining news and one to religion. This list is correct unless some of the Democratic newspapers have suspended since yesterday."

illegal votes, particularly from Valencia County where the
returns as submitted by the secretary of the Territory gave
Luna a majority of 4,127 — far more votes, it was charged,
than the county had inhabitants.[5]

This was an exaggeration. Valencia County had over
13,000 inhabitants at the time, but an investigation by the
federal government revealed that people in several of the
mountain villages had voted three or four times in their zeal
for Luna's candidacy. At Rito Quemado there were but some
30 voters, yet 257 votes were returned, all for Luna.[6] Solomon
Luna, political leader in the Valencia County, and friend of
Catron, was blamed for the transgressions of his political
followers.[7]

Luna's biographer says of the accusation:

> In integrity of character Mr. Luna was considered by those who
> knew him intimately, as being above reproach. There are evidences,
> however, that some groups, most of them perhaps, his political oppo-
> nents, who thought him, or rather the Republican politicians in general,
> not too high principled to "vote the sheep. . . ." Probably in those days
> of high political passions, when "business ran politics and politics ran
> business". . . it would not have been surprising if a Republican boss,
> convinced of the protective power of his party, would consider its
> success worthy of this fraudulent method of polling votes.[8]

Miguel A. Otero, II, who sometimes outdid even the
most rabid old time newspapermen in his bias, wrote: "Of
course, I cannot blame Mr. Luna, nor do I believe he was
smart enough to concoct these gigantic steals, but he was well
groomed by the 'Santa Fe Ring,' the real machine controlling
the political situation in New Mexico. . . ."[9]

Mr. Otero's slur against his countryman was hardly
deserved or warranted. Solomon Luna was so astute and
powerful a politician that it was said of him at the constitutional convention of 1910: "he needed only to lift a finger
or his eyebrows, to stop any proposal which he deemed against
the best interest of his people, his party, or the proposed new
state."[10]

In this same election Catron was defeated for the Territorial Senate by Henry L. Warren by a margin of twelve

votes.[11] Aside from a term in the Territorial House in 1868, this was Catron's first attempt to secure elective office. Warren was a strong candidate; nevertheless it is probable that virulent attack by the Democratic press played a part in his defeat. He had strongly backed the appointment of former Governor Samuel B. Axtell as chief justice of the Territorial Supreme Court. Axtell was unpopular with many people in New Mexico, and Catron was condemned for championing his appointment. In the campaign, Catron was characterized as the leader of the "thirty-third degree ringsters." [12]

While it is likely that masonic allegiance played a part in the unity of Republican leaders, this was an element that was not often played up by the press of either party because using this line of attack could easily revert unfavorably against the attacker. That it was used against Catron is an indication that his political opponents were driven to use every measure to combat him. By now it was recognized that he was the real power in the Republican party. It was feared that he would wield even greater power as a member of the Council.

By now a new force had entered the political scene in New Mexico. The arrival of railroad transportation created boom conditions in such railroad towns as Las Vegas, Albuquerque, Socorro, Deming, and Silver City. Citizens in these places, reacting to their new economic importance, began a push for political stature. This was particularly true of Albuquerque, where businessmen and lawyers started a campaign to remove the capital from Santa Fe to Albuquerque. It was in this setting that the legislature met in February 1884.

Catron had been elected to represent Santa Fe County in the Council, defeating Henry L. Warren by a majority of nine votes. But Warren adherents claimed that a large number of railroad hands, who had just arrived in the county, had voted for Catron and were not qualified to vote. They were also other contested seats in the Council.[13]

With the contested positions in the Council and the location of the capital at stake, the delegates assembled at

Santa Fe in an atmosphere of feverish excitement. J. Francisco Chavez, formerly delegate to Congress and perennial delegate to the Territorial Council from Valencia County, led a group favoring removal of the capital. As the time approached for the Council to convene, Secretary William G. Ritch, in accordance with legal precedent, prepared to take the gavel and call the members to order preparatory to swearing them in. He found the chair occupied by Chavez who, in defiance of proper authority proceeded to himself swear in such members as would recognize him.[14]

Secretary Ritch, denied the Council chamber by force, now proceeded to the governor's office to swear in such Council members as presented themselves. Ritch declined to act on the question of swearing in the contested members, including Catron, because it was not clear which contestants were entitled to seats. The Council then organized and elected a president. Upon motion, T. B. Catron of Santa Fe County, and C. C. McComas and J. M. Montoya of Bernalillo County, were declared entitled prima facie to seats.[15] It was under these extraordinary circumstances that Catron commenced his legislative career in the Council.

The Chavez "Rump" Council members continued to occupy the legislative hall night and day, sleeping on chairs and having meals brought to them. The situation created a furor in the newspapers, with zealous enthusiasts on both sides. The Chavez adherents admitted that Secretary Ritch was empowered by law to swear in members of the Council but denied his authority to designate persons to whom the oath should be administered. In this contention they overlooked the fact that Ritch had avoided seating members involved in contests until these members were approved by the duly organized Council itself. The Chavez group continued to occupy the regular meeting place and, unavailingly, appealed their case to Washington.

Governor Lionel A. Sheldon, who was hooted strenuously by Democratic newspapers for supporting the regular Council, reported officially that the law, happily, was such that subversion of popular rights could be prevented. No one had denied the privilege of a refractory element to refuse taking seats in the Council; yet, the remainder was sufficient in numbers to constitute a duly qualified and legally constituted legislative body.[16]

The regular Council proceeded about its business amidst a storm of remonstrance from opposition newspapers. The outpouring of words centered around the seating of Catron. It is recognition of his ability and leadership that the convening legislators were repeatedly labeled the Catron Council — an unusual tribute to his fledgling term in office. However, the Santa Fe Ring was censured. It was said:

> The Ring must soon discover that the time has passed in New Mexico when men can be herded like so many sheep and be made to move at the wave of the hand in violation of law, and every precedent known to the laws governing free people.[17]

As showing the extent to which opponents of Catron thought him capable of influencing legislators, a story was told at the time:

> This morning a couple of supporters of the rump council were discussing the situation when one asked the other if he had heard of the departure of Mr. [Santiago] Valdez for his home, and if he knew the import of it. The other replied that he had not, "but," added he, as a dreadful suspicion took possession of him, "guess it is a effort to break up the rump. I'll bet two to one Tom Catron is at the bottom of it." The fact is Mr. Valdez was called from the midst of the rump council by a letter announcing the confinement of his wife.[18]

An examination of the legislative proceedings presented in newspapers from week to week reveals that Catron did take an active, though hardly overwhelming, part in the actions of the legislature.

During the course of the legislative debating, it was charged that the grand juries of Santa Fe had for many years been creatures of Catron and the Santa Fe Ring.[19] Catron and Trinidad Alarid were accused of approaching Jesus Sena

Baca, clerk of the Chavez Council, with an offer of $1,000 if he would sign a certain document without seeing its contents.

The *Santa Fe New Mexican* branded this story a malicious lie, but the stories continued. It was even asserted that Catron was with the Confederate guerrilla leader, Charles W. Quantrell, in Kansas. Catron's detractors went on to say that the stubs of his checkbooks were as full of evidence as a hound pup was full of bark and that it had cost members of the Santa Fe Ring $20,000 in their attempt to steal the legislature.[20]

Defenders of Catron countered by bringing to light the activities of a New Town Ring in Albuquerque which was then in the process of sending memorials to the United States Congress supporting the Chavez Council. Catron supporters supposed that the Albuquerque coterie would, as a matter of course, be careful to avoid all mention of the fifteen hundred fraudulent votes with which the ballot boxes of that place were stuffed at the preceding election, or the questionable tactics used in offering money for legislative votes.[21]

A striking example of manipulation at the polls was discovered by Governor Sheldon, who had lived in New Orleans. When he examined the poll books showing the list of those who had voted in precinct no. 12 in Albuquerque, he was surprised to find the names of some two hundred persons he had known in New Orleans. Further examination revealed that the names had evidently been copied from the New Orleans city register. Charles Montaldo, a Democratic member of the Chavez Council from Albuquerque, had also formerly lived in New Orleans where he had represented the third ward of that city in the legislature. These circumstances seemed more than coincidental, so Sheldon questioned the legality of Montaldo's position in the New Mexico legislature.*

Santa Fe Weekly New Mexican Review and Livestock Journal, March 27, 1884. Ralph E. Twitchell, *Leading Facts of New Mexican History,* Vol. 2, p. 493, says: "In Bernalillo County, under the leadership of Charles Montaldo, of Albuquerque, a fraudulent registration was consummated and hundreds of illegal votes were cast or counted in the new town where he lived."

The Reverend Oscar P. McMains introduced a memorial in the House of Delegates censuring Catron, Surveyor General Henry M. Atkinson, Elkins, and others for alleged theft of land grants. The fifth specification of this resolution maintained that the interior department surveyed about 800,000 acres more than the original grantees of the Mora Grant claimed, and that it was generally understood that Catron and Elkins were the illegal claimants of this 800,000 acres of land.[22]

McMains' supporters maintained that his speech introducing the memorial was widely acclaimed:

His reference to Tom Catron and the territorial courts, which aided and abetted the land steals that have been going on for the last twenty years, was received with deafening applause and showed conclusively that the house is becoming deeply interested in putting a stop to the disgraceful and dishonest work of the ring.*

Those in opposition to McMains challenged him to repeat his allegations in a court of law where he would be removed from the protection afforded by the rules of the House. It was explained:

He whined that he was misrepresented by Hon. Santiago Valdez when that gentleman asked that his slanderous assertion in regard to the honesty of the people of the territory be placed on record, and now boldly proclaims as thieves men who have no chance to reply. Dearly beloved parson, your political race is run in this territory. If you are a candidate for re-election at the next election you will be buried so deep that there will be no resurrection.[23]

As anticipated, a bill was introduced calling for the erection of a capitol building in Santa Fe. There were loud cries of anguished opposition and much lobbying by those who advocated the moving of the capitol to Albuquerque, but the measure was enacted into law.†

Albuquerque Daily Democrat, March 15, 1884. The resolution was killed in the legislature. *Santa Fe Weekly New Mexican Review and Livestock Journal,* May 8, 1884.

† Twitchell, *Leading Facts of New Mexican History,* Vol. 2, pp. 493, 494, records that "Don Diego Archuleta, a member from Rio Arriba county, was taken to the house of representatives while suffering from a severe attack of pneumonia. His vote was necessary to pass the bill. The exposure incident to this performance caused his death a few days later."

The *Santa Fe New Mexican,* in answer to claims that the
Territory could not afford this expense, pointed out that the
money expended by Albuquerque alone to defeat the bill
would have more than paid the first year's interest on the
bonds to be issued for construction of the building.* The
issue of removing the capitol from Santa Fe continued to be
fought over for the rest of the century. In 1892 the capitol
building, with many valuable records and public documents,
was destroyed by fire rumored to have been of incendiary
origin.

The legislature finished its session, but the quarrel continued throughout the Territory, with an evident rupture
existing within the Republican party. Others took up the
cudgel carried by the Chavez Council against the Santa Fe
Ring. Among these was Albert J. Fountain of Mesilla.

Fountain had quietly become a local political power; now
his influence widened. The legislature's enactments seemed
unfair and disproportionate to him and others in the southern
part of the Territory. It had made large appropriations for
the new capitol building and penitentiary, as well as for a
school in Santa Fe to be operated by the Sisters of Charity,
and for a new hospital in that city. Also appropriated was
money for a new court house at Las Vegas. But requests for
money to build facilities in other counties were ignored. Particularly galling to Fountain's bailiwick was the creation of
Sierra County taken from western Doña Ana County.

Fountain, encouraged by southern New Mexico partisans, now declared war on the Santa Fe Ring. Santa Fe politicians had for several years picked the Republican candidate
for delegate to Congress. Fountain decided to challenge their
selection at the upcoming Santa Fe convention. He laid his
plan before the Doña Ana County convention in mid-August,

Santa Fe Weekly New Mexican Review, March 27, 1884. Building of a penitentiary was also authorized by this legislature.

and his proposal received solid backing. William L. Rynerson a prominent Las Cruces attorney, was selected as the
candidate of this convention for delegate.[24]

Fountain visited other Republican county conventions
and received a number of pledges of support for Rynerson;
accordingly, he came to the Territorial convention at Santa
Fe late in August with considerable strength. Earlier, a number of others had been talked about as possible candidates
including Catron, William Breeden, J. Francisco Chavez,
Lorenzo Lopez, Mariano S. Otero, and L. Bradford Prince.[25]
By the time of the convention, however, the selection had
narrowed to Rynerson and Prince. The delegates met in an
atmosphere of reasonable friendliness that belied the animosities that were soon to follow.

When the convention was called to order by Chairman
William Breeden, it developed that there was a double delegation from San Miguel County. Amid such confusion that
Breeden found it difficult to maintain order, Rynerson's
friends demanded that the delegation headed by Eugenio
Romero be recognized. At this juncture I. S. Tiffany of the
Socorro delegation introduced a resolution that all contested
delegates be excluded from the convention until their cases
could be acted upon by the committee on credentials. This
resolution caused further debate in which William H. H.
Llewellyn, David M. Easton, John H. Riley, and others maintained that the central executive committee had already
decided that the Romero delegation should be admitted as
opposed to the Lopez delegation. Loud calls for the chairman
to call the roll were heard amid greater confusion than ever.
Chairman Breeden now ruled that the convention took
precedence over the central executive committee in the prem-
ises. J. Francisco Chavez had called for a vote to table the
Tiffany resolution. The vote was taken, resulting in forty-eight
against Chavez' motion and forty-two in favor. This was at
once regarded as a triumph for the Prince supporters. A

motion was then carried to exclude contested delegates until they had been passed upon by the credentials committee.[26]

Right then Rynerson was not in attendance at the convention, but his friends arose from their seats and walked out. These were the full delegation from Lincoln, Valencia, and Doña Ana counties, and members from Grant County as well as the Romero faction from San Miguel County. Thirty-six delegates left the convention at this time and were joined by three others later. Santiago Baca, of Bernalillo County, now presented the name of L. Bradford Prince in nomination to the remaining delegates. F. A. Thompson of Socorro County seconded the nomination, and Prince was duly elected.[27]

That evening the Rynerson coterie met in a separate convention. Albert J. Fountain explained the purpose and objectives of the meeting and nominated Tranquilino Luna as chairman. Luna was unanimously elected and called for nominations for delegate. J. Francisco Chavez eulogized William L. Rynerson; David M. Easton spoke similarly for Rynerson and then presented his name in nomination. Albert J. Fountain seconded the nomination, and Rynerson was elected.[28]

The split in the Republican party was now complete. Efforts to patch up the quarrel ended in failure, and the rival candidates departed their respective conventions determined to fight to the bitter end for their cause.

The *Santa Fe New Mexican* maintained that Rynerson's defection was engineered by J. Francisco Chavez in a move to aid Anthony Joseph, the Democratic candidate for delegate to Congress. The wily Chavez is reputed to have said he could do better by organizing a bolt than by supporting Joseph openly. Chavez was always expected to support Joseph regardless of party affiliations, and a split in the Republican party understandably would be useful to that end. It was contended that Rynerson and his friends were used as cats' paws to aid the Democrats. The *New Mexican* concluded: "We do not often agree with Colonel Chavez, but that he is exceedingly smart no one can deny."*

What part did Catron play in these proceedings? He ended up in the unenviable position of being blamed by both sides. A. M. Gibson, Fountain's biographer, declares that Catron was largely responsible for the whole fuss because he was the leader of the Santa Fe Ring that was "bent on various mischief, particularly that of monopolizing party benevolence for clique members." Likewise, Catron supposedly led a movement prior to the convention to have Prince endorsed with no nomination from the floor. Gibson states that this movement was disputed between Fountain and Catron in a meeting of the central executive committee, but this is impossible because neither Fountain nor Catron were members of that committee. William Breeden was the member from Santa Fe County and John H. Riley from Doña Ana County.[29] This, of course, does not imply that Catron could not have led such a movement in some other general way.

On the other side of the coin, in later years L. Bradford Prince singled Catron out as being responsible for Rynerson's nomination. Prince maintained that he had been nominated for Congress in opposition to the Ring, whereupon its adherents bolted from the party and set Rynerson up as a bolting candidate. Prince claimed that Catron, Stephen W. Dorsey, J. Francisco Chavez, Tranquilino Luna, George W. Prichard, Eugenio Romero, and John H. Riley were the leading spirits in the bolt. Furthermore, Prince declared that everyone knew Catron was secretly the life of the Rynerson movement although he did not publicly espouse that cause.

Prince was somewhat contradictory in his accusation. While stating that Catron *caused* the split, he also asserted that

---

Santa Fe Weekly New Mexican Review and Livestock Journal, September 4, 1884. Antonio Joseph was sometimes called Anthony; he was so referred to in this article.

Catron could have *stopped* Rynerson's bid short had he chosen to do so, but that he preferred to see a Democrat elected rather than a Republican candidate.*

What can be deduced from this babel of claims and counterclaims? It seems evident that Catron's position in the controversy was at least one of importance, but where *did* he stand on the issue? He was unquestionably no friend of Prince and later was associated with Rynerson and Riley in business, although he did not always agree with them either in politics or in a business way. Since there is no substantial evidence that he actively backed Rynerson, it is probable that Prince was right in that part of his contention claiming Catron did not exert himself to stop Rynerson's defection. It is likely that he allowed political passions to run their course. In all fairness, it seems reasonable to expect that for one man alone to have swayed the political destiny of that convention would be asking too much.

The Democrats, of course, saw in the Republican split an excellent chance to win. The population of the Territory had increased substantially following the advent of railroad transportation in 1880, and many of the new settlers were Democrats. In the 1884 election Grover Cleveland became the first Democratic President elected since 1856. In New Mexico the Democratic candidate for delegate, Antonio Joseph, was elected; nevertheless, his selection can be attributed to the Republican split because Rynerson and Prince together received about three thousand more votes than did Joseph.†

But Republican party members soon had something else to fight about, rather than squabbling among themselves,

---

* Undated manuscript in Prince's handwriting (Prince Collection, State Records Center, Santa Fe). George Curry, *Autobiography,* p. 47, goes even further than Prince when he states that Catron bolted the convention, took with him a large number of delegates, and nominated Rynerson in the rump convention.

† In succeeding elections, Joseph continued to win in his own right. The Republicans united behind Catron in 1892 to contest Joseph's supremacy. It was not until 1894, however, that Joseph was demoted by the Republicans, with Catron again their standard bearer.

when President Cleveland appointed Edmund G. Ross as
governor of New Mexico. Ross was no stranger to controversy
when he assumed the governorship in June 1885. His place in
American history was assured in 1868 by his stubborn refusal
as a Kansas senator to vote for the impeachment of Andrew
Johnson. His vote was dramatic because it was crucial to the
retention of Johnson in office, and it was reprehensible to his
constituents in Kansas because they had instructed him to vote
with the radicals against Johnson. From that moment Ross
was a ruined man politically in Kansas. After decisive defeat
for the governorship of Kansas in 1880, he moved to Albuquerque in 1882.

That Ross was an honorable man cannot easily be questioned; but, stubborn and opinionated, he was unable to maintain any sort of harmony during his political career in New
Mexico. He had ideals that were commendable, but he lacked
ability to implement them. To put it bluntly, he simply did
not command the respect of the people with whom he had to
work. In this respect, even his inaugural left him open to the
jibes of cruel observers of personal foibles. To carry out a
venerable Aztec tradition pertaining to the coming of Montezuma at sunrise, he took the oath of office at that hour. He
referred to himself as a Democratic Montezuma who would
bring victory and triumph to New Mexico. From that day he
was known as "Montezuma Ross," and the simile was not a
kindly one.

Ross was a reformer, and the one thing he thought needed
reforming more than others was the Santa Fe Ring. The
trouble was he found difficulty locating a handle with which
to grasp that nebulous entity. To his chagrin he learned that
important people within his own party were tainted with what
he considered the stigma of Ring association. Chief of these
was Charles H. Gildersleeve, chairman of the Democratic
Central Committee, and Antonio Joseph, delegate to Congress. That these two gentlemen largely controlled the patronage did not enhance his relationship with them. The one

person with whom he found he could work in reasonable harmony was Surveyor General George W. Julian, a fellow reformer hand picked by President Cleveland to clean up alleged land fraud in the Territory.

When Governor Sheldon was replaced by Ross, he had taken advantage of a Territorial court ruling of 1880, declaring that incumbents of Territorial office could hold their position for two years after appointment or until the biennial legislature met again to confirm their successors. Sheldon, knowing that he was to be replaced by a Democrat, sought to assure some Republican continuity by appointing these officials just before he left office. Most obstructionist of these to the administration of Governor Ross was Attorney General William Breeden, who had held that office since 1881 and was reappointed by Sheldon. In November 1885, Governor Ross fired Breeden, alleging misconduct in office, and offered the position to William T. Thornton, Catron's law partner. Thornton had earlier sought the governorship. In exchange for the attorney generalship, Ross held forth the condition that Thornton end his partnership with Catron. This Thornton refused to do, and Ross appointed Napoleon B. Laughlin instead. Breeden, however, was upheld over Laughlin by the Territorial Supreme Court.*

Governor Ross also tried to lure away another Catron partner. Early in 1886 John J. Cockerel, son of Senator Cockerel of Missouri, was about to become associated with the law firm of Catron, Thornton, and Clancy. Ross is reported to have told young Cockerel that he was making a serious mistake in joining this firm because its members knew no law, had no practice, and were of no account generally. Ross then offered Cockerel the position of assistant attorney general, providing he would influence his father favorably in the United States Senate. But Cockerel informed the governor

---

*Santa Fe Weekly New Mexican and Livestock Journal, January 14, 1886. Breeden continued as attorney general until 1889.

that his father's vote could not be influenced in that manner and that he was perfectly satisfied to be associated with the strong firm of Catron, Thornton, and Clancy.[30]

Napoleon B. Laughlin, unsuccessful in his bid for the attorney generalship, turned to the legislature. In 1886 he successfully contested the seat in the Council held by Catron, receiving a majority of 273 votes.[31] There were charges of fraud at the polls, but Catron offered no objection. The fact is that he had expressed some reluctance to becoming a candidate. This was a period of optimum growth in his land holdings and legal practice; he was tremendously busy with these activities.

The legislature that convened in December 1886 had only a slight Republican majority, but members were controlled by a caucus system and were successful in hampering Ross at every turn. What is more, a bar association had been formed earlier in 1886 and, whenever the legislature considered a bill, it was sent to the association for approval before being acted upon. This meant that the bar association — which was essentially the Santa Fe Ring — effectively controlled the legislature.

Ross chafed under this arrangement but could do nothing about it. While Catron was often assailed as leader of the Ring, he held that position by virtue of ability as a common spokesman for others interested in common goals. Ross learned that economic factors frequently outweighed political implications in the thinking of Ring members. Furthermore, as in the case of Catron and Thornton, law firms frequently encompassed both political parties. Henry L. Waldo called himself a Democrat but was a law partner of William Breeden and was often sympathetic to Republican causes. Moreover, he was in many instances recognized as a Ring member. He had the happy faculty of getting along well with most everyone; he qualifies as an example of why the nefarious implications attributed to Ring activities were oftentimes only in the eyes of the beholder.

This dual relationship more than anything else explains the enigma of the Santa Fe Ring. It was groupings in constant flux of persons whose common interests brought them together for mutual action on specific problems that arose from time to time. Thoroughly democratic in its way, it was a devilish thing to fight for those who wanted to lash out at something they could get hold of.

During the summer of 1888 Catron accompanied Wilson Waddingham on a trip to Europe. Catron returned in September with evident renewed energy for the political wars and determination to regain a seat in the Council. He was also particularly interested in the election for delegate to Congress. Antonio Joseph, a Democrat, had been securely entrenched in that office since 1884, when the split between Rynerson and Prince had assured his election. This was particularly irritating to Republicans because they were sure in their own minds that the Territory was strongly Republican.

J. W. Dwyer had been the Republican candidate to oppose Joseph in 1886 in a campaign managed by Stephen W. Dorsey. It was generally understood that Dwyer was Dorsey's man and that the election was to be carried by money. Catron held that Dwyer made a poor impression on voters during the campaign and lost votes by his appearances. Furthermore, Catron believed that had Dorsey remained at home and not attempted to do anything he would undoubtedly have been elected.[32]

As Catron returned from Europe, Republicans were casting about for a candidate they felt could beat Joseph. Mariano S. Otero had been elected delegate in 1878; it was decided to nominate him again. Catron was confident Otero was a strong and popular candidate and that this choice was an excellent one.[33]

Catron was appealed to — as he always was — for money to support the Republican campaign in a letter telling of the political circumstances at the time:

> The present campaign for Delegate in New Mexico is of great importance to the Party as well as to the Territory.... We have for

several terms been defeated, although our Party is in undoubted majority in the Territory.

This should not occur again but to prevent it requires a vigorous
campaign. Our candidate is all that can be asked; able, popular and
energetic. . . . [He] is willing to do his part but we must remember
that there is but one general candidate and it would be wrong to tax
him too heavily; others who are interested in the result must do their
part.[34]

With another Catron letter, it requires but little reading
between the lines to learn a great deal about the electioneering methods of the day:

I have asked you to put up $150.00 in money, not in carneros
[sheep]. I did not tell you not to use carneros in the balance of your
matters. What I intended was, to raise a fund of $1000.00, but I did
not intend that that should be the only fund that was raised. . . . What I,
and the Republican party asks of you is, that you do everything for the
ticket, and that you spend not only money, but also carneros where
you can make them of use. I only have the interest of the party at
heart, while with you, your reputation, as well as the Party, is at stake.
I ask you to do your best.[35]

A letter received by Catron from a Santa Fe printer is
enlightening concerning methods sometimes used at the polls:

Herewith find samples of Patent Election Stickers, which I am
furnishing for the coming election. You will see at a glance how good
a thing they are in saving trouble in changing names. I have furnished
them for the past three elections and they give perfect satisfaction. A
personal friend in the opposite party can sometimes use them to great
advantage for you. Price per 1,000, $2.25 prepaid.

I make a specialty of election work and tickets. Parties in one
county for which I furnished colored tickets two years ago kept it secret
till election morning, then notified every one to vote the right color,
and as it was too late then to get out an imitation, elected their entire
ticket.[36]

In the election of that year (1888) Antonio Joseph again
prevailed by defeating Mariano S. Otero. In later years L.
Bradford Prince put the blame on Catron, claiming that he
had done nothing to aid Otero; that, in fact, he worked for
Joseph.[37] It is doubtful that Catron was ever aware of Prince's
accusation. For his part, he felt that Otero would easily have

been elected except for one circumstance. In connection with an effort then being made for statehood, a minority report of the Republican members of the committee on Territories in the House of Representatives had slandered and vilified the people of New Mexico. Joseph used this report with excellent effect in his campaign by making the people believe that Republicans had abused them while he had defended them.

In the legislature, Republicans came up with a commanding two-thirds vote in both houses. Despite Catron's fear that he might have spent too much money in other parts of the Territory and not enough in mending his own fences, he was elected by a narrow majority over A. Seligman in a contested election. The original returns had been counted as one more vote for Seligman than for Catron. He explained the circumstances of the voting:

> On the day of the election every Democratic voter wore a badge showing he was a Deputy Sheriff, and carried a pistol and club. The Republicans were absolutely terrorized and bull-dozed, and large numbers of fraudulent Democratic votes were cast.[38]

The legislative session of 1889 was even more strenuous and successful in its antagonism toward the administration of Governor Ross than its immediate predecessor:

> The leader in the upper house, a parliamentarian with few equals and no superiors, Col. Chavez, and the leader of the house of representatives, Col. Albert J. Fountain, guided by a republican caucus, controlled legislation in a manner never before paralleled in a New Mexico legislature. One hundred and forty-five laws were passed, nearly every one of which was first passed upon and recommended by a committee of the New Mexico Bar Association, of which Edward L. Bartlet and Frank W. Clancy were members. Governor Ross used his veto power on nearly every measure, but in each instance the power of the republican leaders was brought into play and the vetoes were not sustained.[39]

An important enactment of the 1889 legislature created the University of New Mexico at Albuquerque, the School of Mines at Socorro, and the New Mexico College of Agriculture and Mechanical Arts at Las Cruces. It was natural that all the counties wanted something in the distribution. Catron, of course, hoped that Santa Fe would be favored. The people at Las Cruces were especially desirous of having the agricultural college. Numa Reymond to whom Catron, incidentally, owed money, urged that he support their wishes. Reymond informed Catron that the folks in his area were more interested in this proposition than he had ever seen them in anything before. Reymond warned Catron that if he cared politically for the southern part of the Territory he had better get the agricultural college located there.*

Heeding Reymond's warning, Catron agreed with William L. Rynerson and John H. Riley that he would push for the agricultural college to be placed at Las Cruces if they would encourage the location of the university at Santa Fe. Meanwhile, persons from Bernalillo County contacted Rynerson and Riley who, without any notice to Catron, agreed to favor locating the university at Albuquerque and, under no circumstances, at Santa Fe. To break the deadlock, Catron's opposition went to the House and attempted to kill every bill favored by him that was pending there. By way of compromise, the Bernalillo and Doña Ana County groups agreed that plans for a normal school at Bernalillo would be dropped and that the appropriation for the entire measure would be cut one-third. Catron was furious with Riley and Rynerson, for he felt that they had double-crossed him. He termed Riley, who he thought seemed to control Rynerson, as the most treacherous man he had ever met.†

In connection with the dispute over location of the colleges, Catron's antagonists widely circulated a story that he

---

*Numa Reymond to Catron, February 10, 1889 (C.P. 102, Box 2). In 1893 the New Mexico Normal University was established at Las Vegas, the New Mexico Military Institute at Roswell, and the Normal School at Silver City.

†Catron to S. B. Elkins, February 9, 1889 (C.P. 105, Vol. 2). Rynerson, Riley, and Catron were later in business together and got along reasonably well, though never with full accord.

opposed a school bill introduced by Russell A. Kistler of Las Vegas and that he had voted to strike out a nonsectarian clause. These allegations were widely distributed in the newspapers of the Territory and, through them, have found their way into modern accounts.[40]

Catron branded this a lie. He explained that he voted to amend this school law so as to make it operative. As originally written, it called for each school district to levy its own tax in a way that gave nonresidents no protection — he was always careful to encourage newcomers — and by which rich districts would have plenty of money, while poor districts would suffer. He insisted that the bill be amended so that the tax was collected at the general level and distributed among the districts according to the proportion of children in each district. The bill, as amended, passed in the Council by a vote of eight to four, and Catron voted with the majority.[41]

During this session of the legislature, there was much discussion in New Mexico regarding the probable successor of Governor Ross. Melvin W. Mills, from whom Catron repeatedly sought political advice, believed that L. Bradford Prince, J. W. Dwyer, and Alexander L. Morrison were the leading candidates, with Prince probably having the most strength. Catron did not like either Prince or Morrison personally. Morrison was a strong Catholic, but Catron had no objection to either his religion or his candidacy. Prince, he believed, would be the best of the lot, but he preferred either of them to Dwyer.*

Dwyer had been beaten by Joseph for delegate to Congress in 1886, and, to excuse his defeat, had charged it to Catron. He thought that Dwyer's stand was unjust because he himself had been a candidate on the ticket for the Council and, while he had spent his time and money in the election,

---

* Catron to Elkins, February 9, 1889 (C.P. 105, Vol. 2). Morrison was one of many persons with whom Catron had difficulties over money owed him. In later years, though, when Catron served in the United States Senate, Morrison was one of his staunchest supporters.

was beaten along with Dwyer. It would be most unfortunate, Catron believed, to have Dwyer appointed governor because he would simply be a tool of Stephen W. Dorsey who was still widely remembered in connection with the Star Route mail frauds.*

Despite considerable opposition from members of the Republican party — notably A. L. Morrison, Solomon Luna, and Max Frost — in the spring of 1889 Prince was appointed governor by President Harrison.[42] Many New Mexicans could not understand the appointment, but Prince had the backing of Eastern financial interests as well as a majority of businessmen in New Mexico.

Prince's relations with the first legislature of his administration were good in contrast to those of his predecessor. In December 1890 Governor Prince, in his message to this session, called attention to the need of a bill for a modern school system as its most important consideration. Catron introduced a bill in the Council that, despite ridicule by some newspapers, was praised by school people. The bill that was finally adopted, however, was framed by L. R. E. Paullin of the House and was hailed as marking a new era in the educational history of New Mexico.

During this session of the legislature enmities that had been building for years came to fruition and resulted in the two most dramatic occurrences of Catron's political career — an attempt on his life and a struggle to disbar him from the legal profession.

Ibid. L. Bradford Prince also blamed Catron for Dwyer's defeat.

12
Borrego Murder Case

A complex and lengthy series of political intrigues, which came to be focused on what was contemporarily known as the Borrego murder case, threatened the legal career and, indeed, the life of Thomas Benton Catron. To understand the antecedents of this case, it is helpful to know about an organization that came to be called the Alliance League and, with more infamous connotations, the Button Gang. The coalition referred to was neither, although it was called both. The contemporary terminology was Knights of Liberty.

In 1890 Terrence V. Powderly's national labor confederation, the Knights of Labor, was gaining a foothold in Santa Fe. Quite a number of Republicans had become members and desired to quit. They were forbidden to do so, and a few were severely beaten when they did withdraw. Accordingly, there was organized a Republican group called the Knights of Liberty, which had the original purpose of mutual support for protection of members who might be attacked or abused. The objectives came to be largely political and in the interests of the Republican party in support of the political campaign of that year. It was a secret organization only in that it had a sign and password by means of which outsiders could be kept from the gatherings. Meetings were confined to members, but no one was forbidden to tell what took place in the affiliation.

For purposes of identification, members wore an emblem which was a button representing two men shaking hands — hence the cognomen "Button Society."

Numbered among the approximate hundred members were Catron, Ralph Emerson Twitchell, Max Frost, Charles A. Spiess, Gus O'Brien, Robert C. Gortner, and other prominent Republicans. Their political opponents blamed these leaders for starting the organization, but it is more likely that it had its inception with the man in the street and came to include the acknowledged Republican leaders of the day. Among the rank and file were Francisco Gonzales y Borrego, his brother Antonio, Lauriano Alarid, Patricio Valencia, and Hipolito Vigil.

Probably in the beginning the intent of members was to act in a law-abiding fashion; however, this ideal was doomed by spontaneous grounding of the organization's roots among those of limited privilege in social attainments. There existed the element of mutual protection which early assumed implications of meeting violence with further violence.

The Democrats had a similar secret society in opposition to that of the Republicans, and it is academic to question which started first. The fact is that they existed side by side. It is even possible that, to an extent, they grew out of mutual differences and hatreds between various members of the Republican and Democratic parties.

These Santa Fe factions had precedent in similar groups in other parts of the Territory. Chief of these was the United Peoples Party of San Miguel County. The real power behind the scenes was the Society of Bandits of New Mexico. Closely allied was the better known group called White Caps. Members of these combinations were as tough a bunch of badmen as could likely be found outside a penitentiary. Crimes were committed with impunity because peace officers were in league with organized criminals. Furthermore, while ostensibly local in makeup, members were affiliated with the Knights of Labor, at that time attracting some mention in the press of the Territory. The chief target of their depredations was the large cattle companies of San Miguel, Mora, and Guadalupe counties. Cattle and horse stealing became their stock in trade, fence cutting their trademark, arson their hobby, and murder their chief political weapon.[1]

In San Miguel County, Catron, together with such associates as O. D. Barrett, Benjamin F. Butler, and Wilson Waddingham, was particularly singled out by the Knights of Labor and the United Peoples Party. The special cause of their displeasure was that large holdings of land grants were claimed in Mora, San Miguel, and Guadalupe counties. Approximately half the area of these counties was embraced in the Mora, Las Vegas, Antonio Ortiz, Preston Beck, Antonchico, Perea, Agua Negra, Pablo Montoya, and Baca land grants.

There were those who felt that the economic development of the grants was a service to the Territory; others looked upon the new owners as exploiters. In former times, under peonage, the economic system centered around a few large Spanish-Mexican families who controlled these grants and, consequently, most of the people. Formerly, these areas were largely untapped sources of economic potential with nebulous boundaries and even more vague status symbols of power. Some persons grew resentful when they did not share more directly when boundaries were actually surveyed and steps taken by new owners to develop the economic possibilities of these grants.

Over the years Catron's political and economic strength was derived largely from good relations with native New Mexicans. Here, however, members of the United Peoples Party felt that Territorial leaders of both Republican and Democratic parties joined in exploiting the poor.

The attitude of these people toward the new regime of political leaders was summed up by Jose Valdez, a master workman of the Knights of Labor, writing in behalf of the local committee on correspondence to Terrence V. Powderly:

They have for years controlled the legislatures, courts and county affairs, and prostituted all of these sources of power to gratify their venal, mercenary propensities and vain ambitions. Party names in this territory have never been or meant anything but sounding catchwords. Political leaders have never been anything but leaders of personal clan followings. Each leader quarelling or coalescing with others as suited his ambitions and personal interests. The mass of poor people have been bull-dozed, cajoled and their votes bought directly and indirectly, and after having been secured by such means, the laws passed by these leaders appear purposely designed to keep them in ignorance, under easy control, and, in some instances, to systematically rob them by means of the courts and legal processes.[2]

Tumult in San Miguel County increased to the point that by July 1890 Catron's property was endangered. He received a polite request from the White Caps to take down his fences which were "damaging the unhappy people."[3] It was a foregone conclusion that fence cutting would follow promptly. Catron appealed to Terrence V. Powderly but received only an evasive reply. He then applied other pressures, and Governor L. Bradford Prince was directed by Washington officials to make a full report on White Cap activities in New Mexico.[4]

Catron also wrote to his friend Wilson Waddingham at Kansas City, informing him that the *Las Vegas Optic* was encouraging the White Caps and discouraging men with capital. The *Optic* was calling Catron a land grabber and was spreading lies about his actions. Furthermore, this newspaper was actually defending the fence cutters and thereby reducing land values. The *Optic,* Catron remembered, owed Waddingham about $1,500 on a mortgage, and he urged Waddingham to put an immediate stop to its support of the opposition.[5]

Eventually law and order prevailed in San Miguel County, and such White Cap leaders as were able moved elsewhere to spread their nihilistic philosophy. Juan Jose Herrera migrated to Albuquerque where he established the White Cap newspaper *El Defensor del Pueblo*. It was reported that Herrera made his move at the solicitation of the Territorial Democratic Committee and that William Burr Childers put up the cash to see Herrera's newspaper published.[6] Childers later became one of the leaders in an attempt to disbar Catron from the legal profession.

Examples of lawlessness in San Miguel County exerted a malignant influence on a receptive element in neighboring Santa Fe, where a venomous cup of political tea had long been brewing. Control of the county and city of Santa Fe had been lost by leaders of the Republican party for several years. The success of the Democrats was largely due to the popularity and influence of Romulo Martinez and Francisco Chavez. In 1885, Martinez, sheriff of Santa Fe County, was appointed United States marshal, and Deputy Sheriff Chavez was elevated to sheriff. Chavez now became the most powerful politician in Santa Fe County.

A resident of Santa Fe at this time was Faustin Ortiz, whose murder instigated a deplorable series of slayings perpetrated by motives of retaliation and revenge, with participants skulking behind Republican and Democratic party labels.

In the spring of 1890 Ortiz mysteriously disappeared; his body, covered with fatal wounds, was later unearthed from a shallow grave in Arroyo Mascareños near the point where the arroyo was crossed by the tracks of the Denver and Rio Grande Railroad in Santa Fe. The *Rio Grande Republican* reported that:

> Ortiz possessed some of the qualifications of a bad man, carried a long knife and a revolver, was something of a ward politician and was supposed to be able to take care of himself, even in Santa Fe, but the poor fellow went under, just the same. Santa Fe is a hard town, politically.[7]

It was charged that Romulo Martinez, together with Sheriff Chavez and certain of his deputies, was responsible for the death of Faustin Ortiz. More specifically, it was believed that Estaquio Padilla and Juan Ortiz had lured Faustin Ortiz to the county jail on a pretext and then murdered and buried him. An indictment was brought against Romulo Martinez and his confederates but was quashed on a technicality and later unsuccessfully appealed by the prosecution.

In August, following the indictment of Romulo Martinez, Catron received a startling letter from one S. Davis, of Galisteo, stating that Susano Ortiz knew all about the killing of Faustin Ortiz. While he had not participated in the slaying, he had been at the meeting when arrangements were made. Susano Ortiz alleged he knew how much had been offered at that same meeting to kill Catron. Indeed, money had been offered a year or two earlier to murder Catron. Susano Ortiz promised that if he were protected from the head men, all Democrats, he would let the cat out of the bag for the "Recompence." Ortiz did, however, want a few dollars in advance to get someone where he wanted him, and allowed as how it would be satisfactory if Catron took this advance out of the recompense.[8] Warnings of danger to Catron's life were not uncommon, but he never believed that anyone would have the courage to try to kill him, so he ignored the communication.

As events transpired, he might well have heeded these threats to his life. During the evening of February 5, 1891, while the legislature was in session, a Council committee meeting was being held in his office in the Griffin building on the northeast corner of Palace and Washington avenues. Catron was standing at a desk facing a window opening on the street, when a charge of buckshot was fired through the window. Evidently the would-be assassins had not seen Joseph A. Ancheta leaning against the window frame, and a part of the buckshot struck him in the neck and left shoulder. A shot from a rifle was also fired through the window. The persons who fired the shots were mounted and escaped in the darkness. Upon the desk in front of Catron were a number of legal papers. Two of the buckshot struck these papers, but Catron escaped injury.

Catron accepted this attempt on his life with relative outward calm. After all, a few buckshot and a single rifle ball were hardly in a class with the terrible fusillades he had endured, for example, when his battery participated in the successful defense of the stockade redan complex which was the focal point of attack in the crucial federal assault during the battle of Vicksburg. Still, he was understandably jumpy for a time. Robert C. Gortner, his stenographer at the time and later his law partner, noticed his restiveness and commented that he would probably have do like the czar and get himself a cast-iron coach to ride around in. Catron did not decline the offer of his stenographer to walk home with him in the nights following the shooting. On one of these twilight strolls they were approaching the military headquarters and a soldier with a gun jumped out of the shadow. "Don Tomas," Gortner reported, with the impious humor that evidently endeared him to his employer, "came pretty near making a wild break for the hills."[9]

In the days following, Catron received a flood of letters congratulating him on his narrow escape. Among the messages was one from Melvin W. Mills, Catron's friend and political ally. Mills was particularly concerned for Catron's safety. He was alarmed lest the "inside combination" persist in their homicidal intent, but hoped that the big reward would scare the "murdering sons of bitches."[10]

Catron also received letters with information as to the possible identity of the culprits. One of these was from Wilmot E. Broad, his manager of the Tierra Amarilla Grant. Broad reported that Refugio Martinez and his brother-in-law, Rallos Archuleta, both sworn Catron enemies, had been in Santa Fe at the time of the shooting. Archuleta, according to Broad, was a leader of the White Cap organization, and Martinez was loco and dangerous.[11] Another tip was from Elfego Baca, who had been with a relative who was in attendance at the legislature in Santa Fe a week prior to the shooting. The relative overheard a conversation indicating that if Catron did not vote as desired on certain legislation, a group of men planned to kill him.[12]

But perhaps the most significant clue as to the identity of the attempted killers was contained in a letter from Thomas Branigan. In June 1890 Branigan was in a restaurant in Albuquerque and overheard a conversation of Romulo Martinez, a former United States marshal and among those indicted for the murder of Faustin Ortiz. Martinez cursed Catron bitterly and mentioned that he was damned sorry he had dissuaded a certain man from trying to kill him. Branigan did not remember the name of the man, but it was someone with whom Catron had experienced trouble in connection with the Chama Grant.[13]

For whom specifically were the shots intended? Some Democrats claimed that senators Joseph A. Ancheta and Elias Stover were the intended victims because they had voted for nearly all measures with the Democrats and against the Santa Fe Ring. Republicans maintained that the shots must certainly have been intended for senators Catron and Pedro Perea because they had received threatening letters. Of the four, Stover and Perea were the least likly to have been intended victims.* Ancheta was a cheerful and witty young man from Silver City, newly elected; scarcely enough time had passed for him to acquire political enemies. At the time no motive for assassinating Ancheta could be found, while Catron had been warned that his life was in danger, so it was largely assumed that the shots were intended for Catron.

The day after the murder attempt a unanimously passed joint resolution of the legislature authorized Governor L. Bradford Prince to offer a $10,000 reward for the arrest and conviction of the guilty persons. Although Ancheta recovered from his wounds, detectives were hired in a fruitless endeavor to apprehend the culprits. Governor Prince called in the famous Pinkerton agency for assistance, and Charles A. Siringo was assigned to the case. After nearly six months of sleuthing,

---

Kingston Weekly Shaft, February 21, 1891. William A. Keleher, *Fabulous Frontier,* p. 134, points out that Albert B. Fall later claimed Jacob H. Crist inspired the assassination attempt.

Siringo was unable to penetrate into the leadership of the White Caps where he believed the identity of the culprits could be learned. His investigation did, however, convince him that Catron was the intended victim. Prince also briefly employed three other investigators identified as "E," "G," and "X." * One of these, R. Ewing, reported he was following a lead indicating that White Caps were the guilty parties. Ewing lamented that he could not follow up this tip because Governor Prince, who was no friend of Catron's, was reluctant to spend more money on the case.[14]

Some four years later Estaquio Padilla (who had been indicted for the murder of Faustin Ortiz) and Leandro Sena were arrested for the attempted assassination of Catron and Ancheta. The statute of limitations had run out, however, and no convictions were ever obtained. At that time Jose Amado Martinez, a confidant of the alleged conspirators, confirmed under oath that Catron rather than Ancheta was the intended victim.

While it was never legally proved, it was apparent Catron was the intended victim of the combination that had allegedly assassinated Faustin Ortiz. In August 1891 the case against this motley array, including Romulo Martinez, which had been appealed by the prosecution, came on for trial at the district court in Albuquerque. The case involved the constitutionality of a jury law passed in 1889 under which the indictments were found against the defendants in July 1890. The prosecution, which Catron shared with Solicitor General Edward Leland Bartlett, lost the case. Neill B. Field was attorney for the defendants.[15]

Almost at the same time there occurred another murder — that of Sylvestre Gallegos — and clarity warrants explaining the background of this homicide.

---

* C. A. Siringo to Governor Prince, July 8, 1891 (Prince Papers, Ancheta shooting folder, State Records Center, Santa Fe). It is here stated that the Pinkerton agency was paid $2,360, while the other investigators received $280.

Among the political adherents of Sheriff Francisco Chavez were Sylvestre Gallegos and Francisco Gonzales y Borrego. Borrego was elected coroner in 1890, at which time the office also included the ex-officio role of Santa Fe chief of police. But the following year Santa Fe incorporated as a city, and the chief of police was named by the mayor. The new mayor was William T. Thornton, elected July 2, 1891, as the nominee of both political parties.

Thornton, a native of Missouri, was born February 9, 1843. He served as a private in the Confederate army and came to Santa Fe in 1877; the following year he became the junior partner in the law firm of Catron and Thornton. The partnership was dissolved in 1882, partly because of financial differences.[16] More important, perhaps, Catron was a staunch Republican, while Thornton was an equally fervent Democrat. But most important, Catron could not abide Thornton's strong penchant for gambling. On March 26, 1881, Catron exacted from him an agreement that should either partner play cards for money, that partner was to pay to the other his entire interest in fees earned by the firm for the year in which he so played.[17] Since Thornton's gambling was later notorious, it is evident the agreement did not have the affect desired by Catron. The partnership ended in an atmosphere of some acrimony. Thornton was a leader in the subsequent effort to disbar Catron, and they became bitter enemies.

When Thornton, as mayor, appointed the chief of police, the coroner's office became of little value. Francisco Gonzales y Borrego was unable to secure another position from his Democratic friends. Considering himself imposed upon, he tendered his resignation to the board of county commissioners. The board refused to accept his resignation, so he declared that he was henceforth Republican in politics. At the same time, acting upon the advice of Catron, he asked that his resignation be withdrawn. The board, noting the change in his political affiliation, now accepted the resignation and appointed Sylvestre Gallegos in his place.

Shortly thereafter at a public dance in a hall on San Francisco Street in Santa Fe, Borrego was in attendance, continuing to exercise the duties of coroner. Gallegos appeared with several henchmen and ordered Borrego to turn over his coroner's star. The latter refused, taking the position that he had retrieved his resignation from the wastebasket when originally refused by the commissioners and, therefore, was still coroner. Gallegos then invited Borrego into the street to settle the matter. The challenge was accepted, and Sylvestre Gallegos was killed in the ensuing fight.

Immediately after the killing, Francisco Gonzales y Borrego was jailed and shackled to a buried log. Pending a trial, he was beaten by the jailer, Juan Pablo Dominguez, a friend of the slain Sylvestre Gallegos. The prisoner appealed to Sheriff Chavez against the conduct of the jailer, and Chavez is said to have replied that Borrego had received better treatment than he deserved. Borrego protested further, and Chavez reportedly beat him over the head with a pistol. Francisco Gonzales y Borrego swore that he would be revenged for this vicious thrashing.

In the trial that followed, with Catron as his attorney, Borrego successfully pleaded self-defense. Bloodshed now ceased for a time in Santa Fe, but it was only the lull before the storm.

At about ten o'clock on the evening of Sunday, May 29, 1892, Francisco Chavez, who had resigned as sheriff, was mercilessly gunned down while going from the city to his home across the Rio Santa Fe. The assassins lay in wait at the crossing of the Denver and Rio Grande railway bridge and killed Chavez while he was passing over the bridge. His body was pierced by four bullets, and circumstances indicated that he was the victim of a conspiracy in which a number of persons were implicated. The mother of Faustin Ortiz, who had constantly clamored to have the murderers of her son brought to justice, now ceased her outcries.

The following Thursday evening about eight o'clock, Juan Pablo Dominguez, in evident retaliation for the slaying of Francisco Chavez, attempted to ambush Francisco Gonzales y Borrego but was a trifle slow pulling the trigger of his pistol and was killed by his intended victim. Borrego languished in jail until his trial during the summer of 1893, at which time Catron was again his attorney. Borrego pleaded self-defense and was acquitted.

Circumstances involving Catron seriously came closer to fruition in April of 1893 when Mayor William T. Thornton was appointed Territorial governor. Catron later steadfastly maintained that Thornton's appointment presaged a series of political maneuvers with himself as the target for personal persecution and with the governor becoming the most active person in the prosecution.[18]

A series of unusual events gives credence to this contention. By the middle of June, Jacob H. Crist became district attorney for the first judicial district, and Governor Thornton personally fired Charles M. Conklin as sheriff of Santa Fe County in favor of William P. Cunningham. The Governor's first excuse for removing Conklin was that he had failed to account for funds collected. It soon became apparent that this reason only thinly disguised Thornton's desire to have his own man become sheriff. The *Santa Fe New Mexican* particularized that Conklin was the only sheriff for years past who had settled his accounts promptly and fully. By contrast, Conklin's predecessor, Francisco Chavez, had resigned in September 1891 when the fact of his large shortage became too apparent. Nearly three years after he was murdered, official investigation revealed a shortage of at least $5,000; some contemporary estimates were as high as $20,000.[19]

Thornton now pursued a variant tactic to justify his removal of the sheriff; he accused Conklin of being too friendly with Francisco Gonzales y Borrego. Thornton, however, later admitted — in fact boasted — to Catron that he had no real reason for removing Conklin, a Republican, but wanted a sheriff of his own politics and temperament.[20]

Conklin unsuccessfully contested his removal as sheriff in the courts; even before the case was settled, Cunningham was in turn accused of not paying over collected funds. An attempt was made to replace Cunningham with Harry C. Kinsell, but Cunningham successfully defended his position in court and was retained as sheriff[21] until the next election, when Kinsell was voted into office with a $2,000 campaign contribution by Catron. It is ironic that in this election Catron was elected delegate to Congress but lost the vote of Santa Fe County in the process.

Up to this time the *Santa Fe New Mexican* was a Republican newspaper owned and edited by Max Frost. The slaying of Francisco Chavez had been duly reported, though given no sensational treatment. The situation, however, was soon to change. During the last weeks of 1893 there were repeated reports that the *New Mexican* was going into Democratic hands — rumors consistently denied by editor Frost. Nevertheless, negotiations had been under way for some time for the purchase of the paper by a syndicate headed by William T. Thornton. During the first Cleveland administration the *New Mexican* had almost gone bankrupt when it lost the Territorial printing it had monopolized and suffered competition from Democratic newspapers in Santa Fe. When Cleveland was reelected in 1892, Frost had reason to avoid again facing this stringent competition.

The January 4 issue of the *New Mexican Review* broke the news of the purchase. Concurrently it was announced that the *Santa Fe Weekly Sun,* owned and edited by Jacob H. Crist, would be combined with the *New Mexican,* although Crist, it was declared was not to control the editorial policy of the new management. George H. Cross was to be general news editor. Frost, it seems, had decided to retire from the newspaper field to devote full time to the practice of law.[22]

It is a singular fact that the newspaper was, a few years later, again owned and edited by Frost. While there was possible economic reason for the interregnum ownership, in the light of events that soon transpired, an unsatisfied curiosity might cause an interested person to wonder if the *New*

Mexican was loaned to Thornton and his associates for the deliberate purpose of reaping the rich harvest of political hay that was at the time just ready for the harvest. The *Santa Fe New Mexican* was the most influential and powerful newspaper in the Territory. Jacob Crist's *Weekly Sun* was relatively unimportant, so for the Democrats to gain control of the *New Mexican* and at the same time deny the voice of this organ to the Republicans was a real coup. There seems little doubt that the purchase was politically oriented to work against the Republican party and particularly against Catron, the leader of that party.

A serious squabble had been brewing in New Mexico political circles for some time. Democrats accused Republicans, under former Governor L. Bradford Prince, of harboring criminals, particularly the murderers of Francisco Chavez, a Democrat. Republicans contended that the slaying of Faustin Ortiz, a Republican, had likewise gone unpunished, and that the atmosphere of revenge and reprisal in which these murders were carried out caused possible witnesses to be close mouthed, and made securing of evidence and indictments a time-consuming process.

It is possible, even probable, that the Republican administration did not act with full energy and resourcefulness. Conversely, Democrats acted reprehensibly by making solution of crimes secondary to political advantage to be gained.

This was a no-holds-barred political fight and, for the Democrats, Governor Thornton led the attack with able lieutenants in Judge Napoleon B. Laughlin, District Attorney Jacob H. Crist, and Sheriff William P. Cunningham — with other Democrats playing lesser roles. For the Republicans, Catron assumed a relatively large share of the leadership. The opening blow was struck when the *New Mexican* came out under Democratic management. Thomas Hughes, editor of the *Albuquerque Citizen,* asked: "What is the *New Mexican* going to do with Tom Catron?" The answer was: "Treat him as it treats every other citizen of New Mexico — fairly!"[23]

The *New Mexican* added the somewhat defensive explanation:

> As a rule we do not feel that it is incumbent upon us to take heed of and answer such interrogatories as this, inspired, apparently, by a desire to create mischief, but in this instance the answer is frankly made in order that Editor Hughes and all other particularly inquisitive Republicans may know just where the *New Mexican* stands under its new management.[24]

The Francisco Chavez murder case had been simmering for months and, with this issue of the *New Mexican Review*, it came to a boil. Announcement was made of the arrest of Francisco Gonzales y Borrego, Antonio Gonzales y Borrego, Lauriano Alarid, and Patricio Valencia for the murder of Chavez. Hipolito Vigil had been killed while resisting arrest. Significantly, the article presenting this startling information was prefaced by a long resume of the Chavez murder. It also contained a statement concerning the manner in which Sheriff Cunningham was able to learn of the identity of the alleged slayers and the difficulties he had to overcome in pursuing his quest. Only then was the anxious reader of the day acquainted with the identity of the apprehended men.[25]

Two days before the arrest, on January 8, 1894, Francisco Rivera made an affidavit in Catron's office stating that he was being intimidated by Sheriff Cunningham. As chief prosecution witness at the trial, he was to claim that this affidavit had been forced upon him. Catron maintained that Rivera had come to his office voluntarily.[26]

Former Governor Prince rushed impetuously into the fray with an interview carried by the *Albuquerque Democrat* in which he claimed that Hipolito Vigil had not been killed because he resisted arrest but that he was treacherously and wantonly shot down with a Winchester rifle in the hands of Deputy Sheriff T. H. Tucker even while the warrant for Vigil's arrest was being read. Prince chirped bravely on that there would yet be serious trouble over the incident.

Prince was promptly roasted over the now roaring political fire. It was gleefully pointed out that he was mixed up in his facts — that when Vigil had been ordered to give himself up he had, instead, sought the slim sanctuary of a light post and commenced blazing away with a 45 Colt revolver. His first shot had been so hasty that it struck the sidewalk six feet in front of him. Another bullet was delivered so that it barely missed the protective post, and telltale powder burns remained as mute testimony of his homicidal intent. Vigil had evidently emptied his weapon before he fell dead.*

The newly Democratic *Santa Fe New Mexican* didn't let the slaying of Hipolito Vigil rest with pointing out the facts involved in his killing. The report insinuated that Vigil, a member of the city police force, got what was coming to him. It was pointed out that Vigil, a justice of the peace at the time Francisco Chavez was killed, had subsequently been well supplied with official positions. Furthermore, it alleged that the conspiracy to murder Chavez was concocted in Vigil's office.

L. Bradford Prince was also further singled out for not having brought the murderers of Francisco Chavez to justice while he was governor.[27]

The preliminary hearing before Judge Edward P. Seeds of the accused slayers of Francisco Chavez commenced on January 14, 1894, and continued for the next three weeks. Napoleon B. Laughlin assisted District Attorney Jacob H. Crist in the prosecution, while the firm of Catron and Spiess represented the defendants. Some forty witnesses were called and 1,500 pages of testimony set down. Throughout the hearing the *Santa Fe New Mexican* covered the case in great detail, and with constant emphasis on political involvements. Trial

---

* *Santa Fe Weekly New Mexican Review,* January 25, 1894. It was later revealed that one of the bullets fired by Vigil had come so close to striking Francisco Gonzales y Borrego that it left two bullet holes in his coat. Borrego had been apprehended earlier and was standing nearby in the custody of a deputy.

by newspaper was not uncommon in those days, but this was a particularly frenzied effort to influence the public against the accused before any legal decision could be rendered. Typical of the headlines was that in the account of January 25:

DAMNABLE!
A FORMER MEMBER OF
THE "ALLIANCE LEAGUE"
DETAILS AN AWFUL
CONSPIRACY

Ex-Sheriff Chavez Assassinated Because of His Po-
litical Influence

A Letter of Warning — Juan
Gallegos Urged to Do
the Job

Another Day of Sensations in
the District Court

The Prosecution Closes — a General
Denial Entered by the
Defense

WILL TRY AND PROVE AN ALIBI

The coverage of the *New Mexican* was in marked contrast to that of earlier days. When it is remembered that this newspaper came under Democratic control only three weeks before the start of the hearing, it is not difficult to conclude that the interests of the accused were secondary to red hot political antagonisms. Be it also recalled that the newspaper was acquired by a syndicate headed by the Democratic governor of the Territory. Do not forget that the respective attorneys for the prosecution and the defense were divided by animosities aggravated by a decade of bitter economic and political strife. Recall also that the prosecuting attorney had but lately headed the *Santa Fe Sun,* which was now amalgamated with the *New Mexican.* Consider that the *Sun* had carried on a vituperative personal attack against the head of the legal firm for the defense, but that this acrimony had been largely ineffective because of the relative unimportance of that newspaper. Now remember that T. B. Catron was the leading Republican in the Territory, both politically and economically. Admit that Catron was a mighty antagonist who used his power with guile and who would run roughshod over opponents to fight fire with fire. It is not difficult to conclude that Tom Catron, while attorney for the defense, was himself on trial.

Considering the unpunished attempt on his life and the obvious lawlessness rampant at the time, it might have been possible, by the use of enough propaganda, to induce the public to believe Catron had taken matters into his own hands and fought back in kind. This is just what the prosecution, under the guise of the trial at hand, was evidently trying to prove. And so it was in the process of the hearing that Juan Gallegos testified that late in 1891 Hipolito Vigil first spoke to him about killing Francisco Chavez. Later the other defendants, who with himself were all members of the Alliance League, spoke to Gallegos about doing away with Chavez. Gallegos was told that Catron would give him $700 for killing Chavez and that, if any trouble followed, he need have no fear because Catron would defend him. It was pointed out that Francisco Gonzales y Borrego had killed Sylvestre Gallegos and that Catron had been the attorney in his defense. Gallegos admitted that he had neither talked to Catron about the matter nor had he seen any money. Furthermore, Gallegos stated that these conversations had never been brought up in a meeting of the Alliance League. He had, though, believed the defendants because they had sworn to their assertions.

The newspaper devoted nearly a full page to this testimony, saying that it was of "so startling and damnable a character, and given by a witness who was evidently so earnest in detailing the inside history of the conspiracy, that the *New Mexican* herewith prints it in full. . . ."[28]

Judge Seeds, after hearing the lengthy testimony, remanded the accused over for trial at a subsequent term of the district court. The Judge, in his summation, gave the testimony of Juan Gallegos as a reason for his decision. He did not believe that Mr. Catron had ever offered $700 for the killing of Francisco Chavez, but he did believe that Juan Gallegos had told the truth when he testified that the defendants had told him so. Judge Seeds stated his belief that the testimony of Gallegos, together with that of Francisco Rivera, was all that need be considered. Rivera testified that he had seen the defendants at the location of the murder. The judge chose to believe Rivera and not to believe the testimony of the defendants that they had been playing cards at the time when Chavez was gunned down. The judge stated his conviction that the alibi of the defendants fell to pieces, that they had testified falsely, and hence the witnesses, Francisco Rivera and Juan Gallegos, must be believed.[29]

Three weeks after the hearing, Catron received a typewritten letter from Juliana V. Chavez, a portion of which follows:

Mr. Catron, you are not above suspicion of knowing more about the assassination of my son than you have ever found it convenient to reveal, this suspicion is a natural one, the murderers as far as discovered are political partisans of yours, they frequented your office, were members of the same society, sworn with you to mutually protect each other, you have always defended them in their commissions of crimes, you have gone on their bail bonds and thus turned them loose on the community to commit other murders, and now in order to justify your conduct and the assassinations, you attempt to slander the memory of my dead son.[30]

Strangely enough, this letter was printed in full in the March 8, 1894, issue of the *Santa Fe Weekly New Mexican Review*. Did Catron send a copy of the letter that he received through the mail to the *New Mexican* for publication? Hardly.

Did Mrs. Chavez have a typewriter with which to prepare the letter to Catron? It is not likely that she did. Did Mrs. Chavez compose the letter? Probably not, although there is little doubt that she did sign it. Who then did prepare the letter? There seems little doubt that the letter was the production of newspaper officials or of persons close to those officials. The hearing of the men accused of killing Francisco Chavez had been completed, and the trial was pending. Was this further trial by newspaper? It probably was, though of Tom Catron rather than any person accused of a crime.

The trial was delayed for more than a year; meanwhile, Catron was elected delegate to Congress. Napoleon B. Laughlin became judge of the first judicial district and would normally have tried the case, but he had assisted with the prosecution in the preliminary hearing so was disqualified. Humphrey B. Hamilton, judge of the fifth district, was prevailed upon by Laughlin, Crist, and Catron to try the case. Catron thought that it could be tried in a week and, by holding nights, within three days;[31] however, it lasted thirty-seven days.

The trial commenced on April 23, 1895, and even while it was in progress Catron received an ominous letter from Richard Hudson concerning the defendants. Hudson, in conversation with a Santa Fe man, mentioned that he thought the accused would be acquitted. The answer was the report of a rumor that if they were acquitted they would be mobbed and murdered the very night they were let out of jail, and that Sheriff William P. Cunningham would be the leader with his deputies to back him.[32] They were not acquitted, though. The trial testimony did not differ materially from that of the preliminary hearing. On May 29, 1895, just three years after the murder of Francisco Chavez, the jury returned a verdict of murder in the first degree, and the accused were sentenced to hang.

The *Santa Fe New Mexican* had grown bolder in its personal attack on Catron as the trial progressed. Finally, by the sly stratagem of quoting other Territorial newspapers, it openly accused him of hiring assassins to kill honest men.[33] Catron wrote to his wife: "I had to fight the court and every public official in the whole democratic party. The people generally do not approve the verdict. I hope never to have to work in another one as I have in this one. It has left me more prostrated than any case I have ever had."[34]

The trial had been so vexing that Catron urgently called upon John H. Knaebel in Denver to assist in preparing an appeal for a new trial. Knaebel complied, and the appeal was presented to the court on June 15, 1895. Catron did not speak; the appeal was presented by Knaebel and Charles A. Spiess.[35]

The appeal set forth some fifty reasons why a new trial should be granted and concluded with an affidavit by William E. Myers, one of the jurors. Myers contended that Sheriff Cunningham had, on at least six different evenings, presented himself to the jurors and conversed with them in Spanish, a language that Myers did not understand. Cunningham's action was in violation of instructions given to the jury by Judge Hamilton, who had instructed that neither bailiffs nor the sheriff were to talk to the jurors. On April 29 Cunningham played cards with the jurors, one of whom was Myers. When Cunningham left he said, "I will bring you boys some cigars next time I come down." Myers further contended that Bailiff Juan Delgado frequently told the jurors that all witnesses for the defendants were sons of bitches, and that the evidence of the defendants was untrustworthy and unreliable. One morning the jury members met an uncle of the Borrego brothers on the street, and Bailiff Delgado said, referring to the uncle and his nephews: "They are all killers." Myers also reported that Severiano Rivera, another bailiff, conversed with jury members in Spanish. At one time the jurors were taken to the race track to see Sheriff Cunningham's horses run. On the way back they passed the house of Patricio Valencia, and Juan Delgado said to Myers: "Here is the place we arrested one of those sons of bitches."[36] James F. Williams, who had been drawn on the jury but was excused, presented an affidavit which confirmed that of juror Myers.[37]

Sheriff Cunningham and bailiffs Delgado and Rivera each made an affidavit denying the truth of the assertions made by Myers. Upon the conclusion of the evidence, Judge Hamilton denied the motion for a new trial and again sentenced the accused to be hanged. John H. Knaebel, in later years, always contended that he had made the right to a new trial perfectly clear but that Judge Hamilton had lacked the moral courage to grant it.[38]

In July, Lauriano Alarid and Patricio Valencia made detailed confessions, implicating themselves as well as the other defendants in the slaying of Francisco Chavez. It became the contention of the defense attorneys, as well as some newspapers of the Territory, that these confessions were made on promise that the confessors would be pardoned, or at least that their sentence would be commuted to life imprisonment, and that efforts had been made to divide mutual loyalties of the accused toward one another. The confessors claimed that they had not fired shots. Lauriano Alarid stated that he was in town acting as a lookout. Patricio Valencia maintained that he was near the scene of the murder and heard shots but that by the time he arrived Chavez was already dead and there was no need for further shooting.[39]

Various appeals would continue to make this a demanding case for Catron, but even more sensational immediate developments were at hand. On the morning of August 20, 1895, District Attorney Jacob H. Crist filed charges with the Supreme Court asking that Catron be disbarred. Thomas Benton Catron was to enter one of the most critical periods of his career.

13
Disbarment Crisis

The attempt to disbar Thomas Benton Catron from the legal profession in New Mexico was the culmination of a long series of enmities and intrigues. The trouble started about 1884, when Catron accepted stock in the Monero Coal and Coke Company in settlement of a bad debt. As the largest stockholder, he was elected a member of the board of directors and became president of the company. When the manager of the mine left, he placed his brother-in-law, Edgar A. Walz, in charge of the business. The other directors, from Boston, became dissatisfied with the management and authorized Thomas L. Rogers to come to New Mexico and find a replacement for Walz. Rogers did not consult with Catron when he employed Jacob H. Crist as superintendent; he departed, leaving Crist to take possession of the mine.[1]

Crist, fifteen years Catron's junior, was born in Louisville, Pennsylvania, and came to New Mexico in 1884. He settled in Rio Arriba County and within a few years had established a reputation as a seeker of office for the purpose of making money out of men who bought and sold legislation.[2]

Crist believed, probably with some justification, that Walz would not readily give up possession of the mine. There was contemporary presumption that Crist arranged the mur-

der that followed. Late one night an employee of the company
was shot, and the assailant ran away in the darkness. Great
indignation followed, and the next morning most of the company employees joined in a search for the assassin. Crist, with
some persons employed by him, immediately took possession
of the mine, barricaded it, and threatened death to any person
who might approach. Walz now telegraphed Catron for instructions and was ordered to take back the mine if possible
but to avoid bloodshed. Walz did not see how he could comply
without a probable fatal fight, so withdrew, leaving Crist to
take over the operation of the company as superintendent.[3]

At the next annual election of directors Catron secured
a board friendly to him and turned out the former officers of
the company. Thomas Nickerson, the second largest stockholder, in the interest of harmony, requested that Crist be
retained as superintendent. Catron consented, but in the fall
of 1887 Nickerson became disenchanted with Crist as superintendent and suggested his removal.

Under Crist's management the mine had become de-
plorably run down; the Denver and Rio Grande Railroad
Company, principal customer, complained that not enough
coal was furnished. Also, the mine was losing money, which
Catron had to offset with advances from his own pocket.
Accordingly he needed no urging, and on February 1, 1888,
he replaced Crist with Alex Bowie, a trained coal expert.[4]
Crist became bitterly hostile to the company and, early the
following year, sought appointment as a mine inspector with
a view to causing Catron trouble. Catron blocked the appointment, although it is probable that his interference would not
have been necessary because Crist's lack of qualification for
the job was well known.[5] Within a month the enraged Crist
was holding meetings with the people of Tierra Amarilla for
the purpose of having suit commenced to set aside the patent
of the Tierra Amarilla Grant, Catron's largest land holding.
To this end Crist enlisted the aid of a local priest who raised
money from the pulpit to further the movement.[6] Catron

ignored this mischievous demeanor for some three months until Crist hired a certain Tomlins to get possession of the mine by a spurious prior filing. He not only furnished the money for Tomlins, an impecunious man, but also acted as witness and attorney in the case.[7] Crist was forestalled in this intrigue; nevertheless, he continued his scheming for several years.

Meanwhile, Catron sold the Monero Coal and Coke Company to Wilmot E. Broad and Pascal Craig in a deal that did not include mine machinery located on the right-of-way of the Denver and Rio Grande Railroad Company.[8] Broad and Craig allowed too much time to pass without proving up and paying for the land. David Rae filed on the land and was the winner in a contest that ensued. He then tried to claim the machinery as part of the mine; Catron filed replevin action; Rae intervened by proposing to give bond and retain the property. Behind Rae in this movement were Jacob H. Crist and Charles H. Gildersleeve.[9]

A number of persons were involved in the long and bitter suit that followed, and all agreed that the case was probably hopeless as long as Napoleon Bonaparte Laughlin, Crist's business partner and fellow Democrat, was on the bench of the first judicial district.[10] Laughlin, four years younger than Catron, was born a native of Illinois, graduated from the University of Missouri, removed to Texas where he practiced law, and then came to New Mexico in 1879 to continue his law practice.

It happened that T. B. Catron was an admirer of the life of Napoleon Bonaparte, after whom Laughlin was named. A section of Catron's library was devoted to the life of Bonaparte, and a bust and pictures of the general were prominently displayed in his law office. While Catron had no similar degree of admiration for Laughlin, he had thought enough of him to support his unsuccessful candidacy for district judge as early as 1888.[11]

At the time of Laughlin's appointment as judge of the first judicial district in 1894, he was strongly supported by Jacob H. Crist. Catron, though, had changed his opinion of Laughlin and opposed his appointment on the grounds that he was no lawyer; that he was a man of extraordinary political prejudices; that he was controlled by the smallest kind of men; that he would not administer law according to precedent and principle; that he would administer law according to favor and the desires of his friends; and that, since Laughlin's practice was in the first judicial district, he would be called upon to preside over cases in which he had a personal interest.[12]

Over the years the Denver and Rio Grande Railroad Company was the principal purchaser of coal from the Monero Coal and Coke Company. This gave them leverage, and they refused to pay more for coal than barely enough to keep the company solvent. The main cunning fellow in this tactic was T. C. Jones, who concurrently, was acting in concert with Crist in trying to induce the people on the Tierra Amarilla Grant not to recognize Catron's title. They also collaborated in the Monero litigation and by 1898 were in possession of the mine and running it to suit themselves.

A factor in the victory of Crist and Jones seems to have been that Crist committed deliberate perjury in his affidavit to set aside a judgment. He stated that Catron was the attorney for Wilmot E. Broad and Pascal Craig in their hearing in the case against David Rae in the land office. As a matter of fact, Alexander L. Morrison was that attorney, and Catron was not even at the hearing because he was sick with shingles. Also, Laughlin had been Rae's attorney at the time of the land office hearing and therefore agreed with Catron that under no condition would he try the case at hand; indeed, he agreed to change the venue. At the time, Laughlin was soon to be replaced; Catron, supposing the venue had been changed, asked for a continuance so the case could be tried before the new judge, John R. McFie. Laughlin, however, did not change the venue and tried the case.*

As a result of this decade of contention between Crist and Catron, it is evident that Crist decided on a bold move. On August 20, 1895, he filed charges with the Supreme Court asking that Catron be disbarred. Catron immediately indicated that he had barely commenced to fight. He wrote: "This fellow has been hounding me; while I care but little about him, he is simply annoying. I do not wish to be on the defensive and with such a dog as he is I wish to be somewhat aggressive." [13]

Heretofore Crist's harrying had been annoying; now it was downright dangerous. That afternoon Catron wrote to Charles A. Johnson of Durango, Colorado, inquiring about indictments pending against Crist at Lake City, Colorado. He had known of these indictments, found in 1883, but had not acted concerning them until Crist pressed him beyond endurance. Catron also realized that, because of the lapse of time involved, it might be difficult to revive the indictments. He was determined to try, though, and inquired of Johnson for full details in the matter. [14]

Johnson's reply was enlightening. There were two indictments against Crist originally found in San Juan County (Silverton) for larceny of household furniture. A change of venue had been requested and granted to Hinsdale County (Lake City), but through stupidity — or more probably cupid-

---

* Catron to Gortner, November 23, 1899 (C.P. 105, Vol. 17). Several years later T. B. Spence recalled to Catron a similar involvement with Laughlin and Crist. Spence had written a strong letter to Laughlin trying to induce him to bring suit. In describing this letter to Catron, Spence said: "I would rather than five dollars I had taken a copy of the last letter that I wrote to him so that I could send it to you just to show you what I forced him to swallow. I did not curse him or use obscene language for I knew that was unlawful, but I felt like doing the former. I almost exhausted the English language. I used every word to express corruption, stagnation and condemnation that I could think of besides using every figure of low character in both divine and profane history that I could think of from Balaam to Judas and from Judas to Arnold and old Crist came in for a share of it." Spence to Catron, March 17, 1904 (C.P. 103, Box 19).

ity — the cases were never properly transferred and it was claimed that the indictments had been entirely lost. Catron, however, knew that his friend H. L. Pickett of Silver City had somehow managed to obtain copies of the indictments against Crist. He now requested that Pickett send him certified copies so they could be used in place of the originals. Pickett promptly sent the requested copies; however, by October 3 Catron received information that the original indictments had been found. It also developed that he would have to guarantee about $100 in costs for making Crist's arrest. This was not a normal procedure, but these cases were old and complicated by the change of venue. He was not anxious to make this guarantee but agreed to do so providing further investigation revealed there was a good chance of making the indictments stand up in court.[15]

When word got around that Catron was planning action against Crist, two persons who apparently thought they had been unjustly incarcerated at Crist's instigation wrote to Catron providing information. At the same time, they requested aid in their respective dilemmas. The first, Andrew P. Morris, a Negro in jail at Tierra Amarilla, sent three letters. Morris was evidently a rather bright young man with little formal education, though with some ability to communicate his thoughts in redundant writing. Let him tell his story as he might have, had he more carefully organized the contents of his three letters.

Jail, Tierra Amarilla, New Mexico

Hon. Mr. Thos. B. Catron
Dear Sir:
    I came to New Mexico in July 1890 and found employment with A. T. Sullenberger as a night watchman at Amargo. In August of that year I took out a homestead and, almost immediately, Thomas Carr, deputy U.S. Marshal Ernest Kutz, and Jacob Crist wanted the land. They threatened to kill me if I did not give them the property. In spite of their threats I did not give up my homestead. In 1892 Carr again quarreled with me about the land, but we made up and he got me work around his railroad section boardinghouse at Amargo.

Thomas Carr had a sister, Nora, who worked as a waitress in the boardinghouse.

In the fall of 1893 Miss Carr found herself in a delicate situation and implored me to marry her to cover up. When her pregnancy began to affect her, Thomas Carr also urged me to marry his sister. I was not responsible for her condition, but I might have married her because she is a good woman and I pitied her. I would have married her, but deputy U. S. Marshal Ernest Kutz, not knowing how things were, thought I was to blame for her pregnancy and got jealous even though he really did not care for her. Finally she got very sick with pregnancy and begged me the harder to marry her. I would have done so, but Ernest Kutz paid a young girl dishwasher to watch us and report to him. He then took steps to break up our — as he thought — intimacy, and Nora had to flee up to Cresco, Colorado, above Chama, where she had a sister. But they sent her to Durango, Colorado, to her uncle, Timothy Carr, where she was made to take medicine to take it away.

There was a rich Englishman named Cope who boarded at the section house, and I am pretty sure he was responsible for Nora's condition. It lies, though, between him and a former roadmaster named Nelson. It may have been Nelson because he left the country about the time she began to be sick. It may also have been George W. Kutz, Emmet K. Wurt, or a host of others including George H. Tice. I think, though, she was gotten in that state by the rich Englishman. Nora was often with him at the house of Mrs. M. J. Voorhees whose business in the past had been that of a procuress.

The last thing Nora said before she left for Cresco was for me to come up and marry her. She was twenty years old then, but she had been abused by her brother nearly all her life and she wanted me to go with her some place where we could live in peace. I did not meet Nora because, right after she left, Thomas Carr and others hatched a plot to kill me and get my land. Carr begun by whispering about that I had insulted his wife. Then he got a cousin, Helen Carr, to spread about that I had called her names. The idea was for Mike Carr, Helen's brother, to make a fuss about it and all get excited and try to get me killed.

Mrs. M. J. Voorhees wanted my ranch very badly, especially as I owed her fifty dollars, with interest, to be let run until I got ready to pay it all. Also helping in this scheme all they could were George H. Tice, T. C. Jones, David Rae, Ernest Kutz, Jacob H. Crist, and other members of the Carr family. Special Agent C. C. Coleman was also implicated. I have two good witnesses; Mr. and Mrs. Stephen Nolan of Amargo. Mrs. Nolan, especially knows all about the scheme. She worked for the Carrs at the section house and knows all the secrets.

In January 1894 I heard that Ernest Kutz was hiring men to kill me. Three weeks later I was ambushed near Cope's saloon, at Amargo, by Ernest Kutz and E. Webb. The next night, near the postoffice at Amargo, another attempt was made on my life by George W. Kutz and Emmet K. Wurt. That same night the gang threatened to kill Mr. and Mrs. Nolan — and to blow up their house with dynamite — when they were hunting me to kill me. Jacob H. Crist and George H. Tice were also in on the deal to have me killed.

A short while later I was arrested for alleged illegal cutting of timber. I was really to be killed at the time of the service of the warrant by Constable David Rae, but a friend of mine came up and they were afraid to kill me in his presence. I have been imprisoned since. Shortly after I went to prison the timber was cut off my land by the Biggs Lumber Company of Chama.

This gang has done all in their power to induce me to go under the act of habeaus corpus and then run away. They've even promised me money, but I laughed at them for their pains. I'm staying here until I get this matter settled. Now I hear that Ernest Kutz and Emmet K. Wurt propose to turn state's evidence when my case comes to trial. They think that Mr. Crist will help them out by their doing so, but remember Sir, if you please, that Mr. Crist paid Bill Moore, in fact sent after him to come, and Moore, along with Kutz and Wurt, and one C. F. Thompson, are the ones who killed Justice of the Peace Manzanares at Cañon Largo. In Colorado I don't know all that Crist done, but he and Ernest Kutz were in that Porter Lumber Company rascality a few years ago.

Governor William T. Thornton wrote me a letter saying that he could not look after my case himself, and suggested that Mr. Crist represent me. I replied that I had had enough of Crist, and also of Thornton upholding Crist in his dirty work.

Now Mr. Catron, I hope that you will take my case. If you do I will prove up my homestead and give it to you under a mortgage. Also, I should not wonder if you get a letter from parties at Chicago about me. If you will write to the editors of the Colored Press at Chicago, you will find out whether or not you will be paid for taking my case. It is a society affair and I am pretty sure they will secure the payment. I hope you will answer this, if you please, as early as is convenient.

I remain respectfully at your service
                    Andrew P. Morris
                    Tierra Amarilla, Rio Arriba Co.
                    New Mexico[16]

Morris's first letter and one from Perfecto Padia were both dated September 12, 1895, so it is probable that they had contact regarding their respective missives. Padia's letter was in Spanish, and the essence follows.

Hon. Mr. Thomas B. Catron

Dear Sir, I am Perfecto Padia, the prisoner they took in the case of the Borregos — who are accused of the death of Francisco Chavez — which was judged in Santa Fe in June past. I was not presented in the court as a witness by Mr. Crist because I did not choose to agree with Attorney Crist nor with Sheriff Cunningham. They wanted me to declare in the court that I had pretended to be asleep in the cell next to the Borregos and that I had overheard them saying secretly that they had killed the deceased Chavez; furthermore, Crist and Cunningham wanted me to say that I had witnessed the killing. Crist and Cunningham promised to give me my liberty if I would declare this in court, and also that they would help me with money.

Crist had me in his office on the day that I arrived in Santa Fe before the trial, and kept me there almost three hours making me these promises. The next morning Cunningham promised me the same. Mr. Crist came to the penitentiary, after Sheriff Cunningham had been there, on the same business.

Now I have learned that they are accusing you of buying witnesses. I thought it best to inform you what has happened, and I am ready to help you with my sworn testimony whenever necessary. I have learned from a Dutchman in the jail that they tried to make him swear that he had seen the cripple — whom you have seen in the jail — carry files and a handsaw to the Borregos. They threatened him with pistols, one in the chest and the other in the mouth, to try and make him swear in this manner. I did not see with my own eyes these abuses to convict men with false testimony by force of threats, but the Dutchman told me what happened when he returned to his cell.

Since I know your capabilities I am making this known to you to see if you can get them to sing. This is what I know: I can help you with my sworn statement and with this letter that I send to you by my wife who came to see me. I gave her the letter so she could put it in the post office at Nacimiento. Postmaster Kinderman is very friendly with Attorney Crist so I was afraid that if they saw your name on the envelope they would open the letter and see the contents.

If you can help me with your influence in my case, I will give you my gratitude and good wishes. I am a poor man with a large family and can offer you no money because I have none. If I had money it would not pain me to give it to you, but I offer you what I can. If I can serve you, do me the favor to answer this letter, if it pleases you, promptly. I remain your humble servant

Perfecto Padia

Rio Arriba County jail

New Mexico Territory[17]

Catron wrote to Alex Read at Park View concerning the letters from Morris and Padia, requesting factual and precise information in the form of affidavits.[18] He had further minor correspondence with Morris, but details of their relationship are not available. Padia, who continued to deny his guilt of any crime, was executed at Tierra Amarilla on September 24, 1896, for the murder of John Vipond. His final statement on the gallows affirmed his assertion that Crist and Cunningham had tried to bribe him, by promises of freedom, to become a false witness against Catron.

Like numerous other Catron sympathizers at the time, W. L. Stevens provided him with information that, hopefully, might be useful in the fight against Crist. According to Stevens, three years earlier Crist had represented Francisco Abeytia in the sale of an interest in the Tierra Amarilla Grant to Catron. The negotiated sales price was $1,100, but Crist advised Abeytia to take $600, and keep the difference. Abeytia later learned of this duplicity and was not willing to make an affidavit as to the facts.[19]

Catron's main concern was the arrest of Crist on the old indictments, so he followed through with vigor and determination. He realized the risk involved in having Crist incarcerated and then not sustaining a conviction. He was willing to gamble thus, but he did not want a dead sure thing against himself. The determining factor was rounding up witnesses, and this Charles A. Johnson was making every effort to accomplish.

By the middle of October Catron was involved in the disbarment case against him. While he was satisfied that the finding of the Supreme Court would be in his favor, he still pressed for Crist's apprehension. The matter of witnesses was not settled, but a trap was being set for Crist's seizure if and when the witnesses were located. Catron learned that Crist and Judge Napoleon B. Laughlin planned a trip to Tierra Amarilla and would spend the night of November 1, 1895, in Antonito, Colorado. The significance here is that to reach Tierra Amarilla on the Denver and Rio Grande Railroad, they would have to go through Antonito. Catron now gave orders to Johnson, providing witnesses were located, to have the sheriff of Hinsdale County meet Crist at Antonito and take him into custody before he reached Tierra Amarilla.[20]

By October 25 the Supreme Court had rendered a verdict in favor of Catron. The protection motive in securing Crist's arrest was removed, and punitive impulse was the remaining factor. By this time the desire to punish Crist was sufficiently strong for Catron to continue to press for the capture of his tormentor.

As it turned out, witnesses against Crist were in Utah, and there was no reasonable certainty that they could be brought to Colorado to testify. Accordingly, Johnson thought it inexpedient to have Crist detained at Antonito as planned. Despite Catron's desire to see Crist brought to justice, the difficulty of gathering witnesses precluded further efforts to see him placed behind bars.

What were the charges made by Crist against Catron? They were five in number, and Catron spoke of them frankly in a letter to Stephen B. Elkins, in Washington, in which he mentioned the part played by a contemptible scalawag named Crist.

The first specification charged Catron with obtaining an interview with Ike Nowell, a material witness for the prosecution at the Borrego trial, and trying to induce Nowell to give entirely different testimony at the trial than he had given at the preliminary hearing. It was further alleged he had attempted to induce the witness not to testify during the trial at all.

He explained to Elkins that prior to the preliminary examination Nowell had given his partner, Charles A. Spiess, an entirely different account than he did at that examination. His purpose in visiting Nowell at the penitentiary, Catron explained, was to ascertain whether Nowell would not tell the truth at the trial, as he had earlier stated it to Spiess, rather than what he had sworn to at the preliminary hearing. "This man," said Catron, "who was serving a term in the penitentiary, was pardoned and went on the stand and told a deliberate lie about my conversation. I took the stand and contradicted him flatly, and it is now sought to have the supreme court give more credit to him than to me."[21]

The second imputation was based on an affidavit of Bernardino Baca, son of Santiago Baca, that Catron offered to lend him $175 if he would agree to get information from Crist's office and from the sheriff as to what they were doing to prevent a new trial for the Borregos.

This allegation Catron flatly denied; he claimed that his partner, Spiess, had heard Baca offer to get this information if Catron would make him the loan. Catron claimed that he had refused to have anything to do with Baca's proposition.[22]

This charge was later dropped, possibly because the affidavit on its face did not present a strong case. There was presumption at the time that somehow it had leaked out that Catron had something against Baca, and against Crist, that could be effectively used at the trial and that, consequently, Crist had induced the committee to whom the charges were presented to drop the Bernardino Baca specification. Eventually substituted was the accusation that Catron had influenced Porfilia Martinez de Strong, who was a witness for the defendants in both the hearing and the trial, to give false testimony.

The third complaint was with reference to the testimony of one Max Knodt who changed his evidence materially at the trial from what it had been at the preliminary hearing. The allegation was that Catron, by means of a pass to Fort Wingate, induced the witness to change his testimony.

Catron explained to Elkins that he had indeed secured a pass for Knodt, but it was for the purpose of seeing a woman who had formerly been his cook. Knodt had stated on cross-examination at the trial that the pass had nothing to do with his testimony, and Catron alleged the same.

The fourth charge, Catron stated, was based on the affidavit of an old vagrant named Rosa Gonzales y Baca, who said she came into his office at his request and that he offered to pay money if she would induce her two sons, witnesses in the Borrego case, to testify in favor of the defendants and not for the Territory.

This, Catron claimed, was absolutely false and that, furthermore, she was a woman of the worst repute whose blackness of character was probably exceeded only by that of her sons.

The fifth and last charge was that Catron had offered money to Mauricio Gonzales, son of Rosa, to make an affidavit swearing he was not at a certain place at the time Francisco Chavez was killed.

The truth was, Catron informed Elkins, that Gonzales had made an affidavit to Catron to this same effect four months prior to the time it was alleged he attempted to secure the affidavit by payment of money. He labeled Gonzalez' entire evidence a fabrication.[23]

More effort was being spent by the prosecution, including the entire Democratic party in the Territory, in trying to link him with the murder than in attempting to convict the defendants. He reminded Elkins that the killing was on July 29, 1892, the identical date on which he had been in Washington City. The prosecution was unable to do more than throw mud on him during the trial because all of the people from whom they had obtained affidavits were "penitentiary convicts, jailbirds and disreputable characters, unworthy of credit or belief, and would not be sufficient to convict a sheep-killing dog with."[24]

Catron's partner, Charles A. Spiess, was included in the charges brought by District Attorney Jacob H. Crist. It was alleged that Francisco Gonzales y Borrego had made a confession to his mistress, Dominga Apodaca, and that Crist had referred to this confession in his opening remarks at the Borrego trial. It was claimed that Spiess, armed with this information, hurried to Las Vegas and offered Dominga money, his protection as a lawyer, and the protection of his firm, if she would not testify against the Borregos. It was also imputed that Spiess had offered ten dollars to Luis Gonzales if he would make an affidavit that Governor William T. Thornton had offered him money to testify against the Borregos.[25]

Despite his confidence that the charges against him and Spiess were politically motivated, and without foundation of fact, Catron feared that some members of the Supreme Court might think this an excellent opportunity to destroy his influence in Washington so that statehood could not be accomplished, and to put him in bad repute so that he could not effectively speak out against them in the future.

On August 24 the Supreme Court, on petition of District Attorney Jacob H. Crist, appointed a committee of five members of the bar to consider the accusations against Catron and to file formal specifications in regard to such of the charges as they might deem proper. The members of the committee, instructed to act in conjunction with Solicitor General John P. Victory, were S. B. Newcomb, Andreius A. Jones, Bernard S. Rodey, William Burr Childers, and Eugene A. Fiske. Catron considered Childers and Fiske his personal enemies, so anticipated little consideration from them, but he thought himself on sufficiently good terms with Newcomb, Jones, and Rodey to write each a polite and formal request that they consider the case on its merits. He suggested that it was the duty of each to prepare such charges as the majority deemed proper, but reminded them that it was their privilege to decline presenting any charges if that course seemed proper. Above all, he requested immediate action.[26]

While it was not part of his request, he secretly feared that it was the purpose of his antagonists to conduct a protracted investigation that would keep his name constantly in the public attention and thus hamper his effectiveness as a public leader in the Territory.

Catron also considered another precautionary step as expedient in case the committee should present charges to the Supreme Court. He knew that Gideon D. Bantz, who had recently replaced Albert Bacon Fall as a member of the court, was a first cousin of Mrs. Elkins. Catron's letter of August 24 informed Elkins that Bantz appeared to be straightforward but that he seemed to be siding with the group that was attempting to hamstring him. Catron believed that Bantz would act in a fair and impartial manner toward him if he were acquainted with the facts of the case. He requested that Elkins, if he had any way of properly communicating with Bantz, use his influence to see that Bantz was informed of Catron's position in the controversy.[27]

Despite sometimes personal differences, Elkins always came to Catron's aid in a real emergency, and this was no exception. He promptly sent Judge Bantz a superbly polished and appealing letter setting forth the facts. He pointed out that Catron's leadership and positive character had aroused antagonisms from certain quarters; that there was no doubt that many people in the Territory would like to break him down and that this cut some figure in the proceedings to disbar him; that Catron stood almost alone as the survivor of lawyers in the Territory of twenty-five years earlier; that it could safely be said Catron was the leading lawyer of the Territory; that Catron had lately been elected to Congress by a flattering majority and therefore enjoyed the endorsement of the greater part of the people; and that with his expertness and acknowledged ability it was hardly possible that Catron would do anything that would justify the action proposed. Elkins further stated that he wrote without Mr. Catron's knowledge — which was true in the sense that he mailed the letter prior to informing Catron that he was doing so — and as an act of simple justice to him. The letter concluded: "I find it difficult to express myself on a question so delicate, but hope you will believe that I am influenced by the best motives in attempting to set Mr. Catron right before you, and to prevent injustice to him."[28]

There is no certainty that Elkins' letter was significant in Catron's ultimate vindication; nevertheless, it is a matter of fact that the letter aroused the sympathy and championship of an unexpected ally. Bantz first reacted with caution; he was noncommittal and careful to acknowledge that Catron's high position maintained over so many years before the bar should count for something. Later, though, Bantz was more positive in his appraisal. Elkins reported to Catron: "Sam tells me that his wife talked to him very favorably, so much so that I thought he would stand by you."[29]

When it was confirmed that charges against Catron and Spiess were to be investigated by an official committee, almost the entire legal profession in New Mexico became emotionally involved. Catron received numerous letters from his fellow attorneys offering their services. Positions were drawn on anything but political alignments, and sentiment was overwhelmingly in favor of Catron among members of the legal profession. One of the three lawyers retained to represent Catron and Spiess, Neill B. Field of Albuquerque, was a Democrat. Frank W. Clancy of Albuquerque and Frank Springer of Cimarron were Republicans. While Springer had earlier bitterly opposed Catron in Colfax County troubles, this was apparently a matter of simple justice that called for past differences to be forgotten.

Standing by in the wings ready to help Catron in any way possible was Albert B. Fall, wheelhorse of the Democratic party. In 1893 Catron had bitterly opposed Fall's appointment as judge of the third judicial district, even going so far as to characterize Fall as "the most offensive man in the whole Territory and the most venal."[30] It is characteristic of Catron that this sentiment was expressed so unguardedly that it came to the attention of Mr. Fall, who was not pleased. Catron's opposition continued throughout Fall's tenure on the bench, and he was, in part, responsible for Fall's hasty resignation on January 7, 1895. Fall had received word that if he did not resign he would immediately be removed. But now, only months later, Tom Catron was in big trouble so he swallowed his pride and called on Fall for aid. Fall replied: "I will leave at once. In this matter, I am not only an attorney but your *friend,* and this I say to no man unless I mean it. I want you to understand that if, as today, I have to get out of a sick bed to go to Santa Fe, then will have no hesitation."[31]

Characteristic of other offers of legal aid was that of T. A. Finical who wrote:

> I have never offered to do anything in this case for the reason that legal talent of unquestioned ability had so freely proffered assistance that it would have been presumptuous in me to even suggest anything of the kind. However, my gizzard has always been with you, and permit me to say that if there is any skirmishing around the suburbs to be done, or anything else that you think I might be useful in, you will confer a favor by commanding me.[32]

In due time the committee of five filed its recommended charges with the Supreme Court, and on October 9 the court set October 14 as the date for the trial. But October 9 also witnessed one of the most sensational aspects of the whole case. A long article appeared in the *Albuquerque Daily Citizen* entitled "Is it honesty or partisanship?"[33] The article censured the Supreme Court for its conduct of the Catron-Spiess case, and was especially vehement toward Chief Justice Thomas J. Smith. Smith was charged with going to Albuquerque from Santa Fe on the evening of October 6 to confer at length with William Burr Childers, at the latter's residence, concerning the case against Catron. By this action, the article maintained, Smith had cast himself in the role of a prosecutor and, therefore, disqualified himself from judging the case.

Smith was also accused of selecting members of the investigating committee so that it would be hostile to Catron, yet have the appearance of being nonpartisan. As a matter of fact, it was deemed improper that a special committee was appointed at all, rather than have the matter referred to the regular grievance committee of the bar association.

How valid was the judgment of the *Citizen* article concerning the nonpartisanship of the investigating committee? It was a foregone conclusion that Childers and Fiske would stand against Catron. He knew, though, that he could count on Rodey and Newcomb. The crucial vote would be that of Andreius A. Jones. Newcomb was able to secure a promise from Jones to vote favorably; regardless, when the opposition brought pressure to bear, Jones went back on his word and voted to retain all of the charges.[34]

Who wrote the *Citizen* article and delivered it for publication? Thomas Benton Catron was the author, as a letter from him testifies.

Dear Hughes:

The editorial in your paper came to hand today and the democrats and members of the supreme court are very indignant. Some people think that it may cause them to be vindictive against me. I have just wired you that I would meet you to-night in your office, but on reflection, I have concluded that the best thing would be to have some one else see you, so I have requested Mr. Fort to go down. It may be that the firey and untamed chief justice may wish to take out a writ of contempt against you, so I have reflected on the matter and should they get a contempt on you, you must absolutely stand pat and not give away any information that will injure me. If you should have to undergo any punishment I will undertake to make up the difference in any event. What I was thinking was that it might be well, if you do not desire to be brought up for contempt, for you to take a short trip to Arizona on some business which you have there, and go at once, as they may issue their warrant secretly. However, if you are willing to stand the proceeding, it might be a good thing as it will advertise your paper all over the territory and probably do more to bring the united Republican Party to your assistance than anything else. I wish you would not however in any manner connect me with the article. Simply say that it was based on information gathered by you from various sources and the public. Tell McCreight to say nothing about it, as I mentioned that I left it with the merchant next door to be handed to you and told McCreight to say nothing. If they take steps against you, it will be the best thing on earth for your paper. It will do you no good to have me implicated with you. If you should go to Arizona for a few days, we can stave off any proceedings for contempt till the July term, and by that time I expect to have a new supreme court for the three territories. I shall bend every effort to that end.

Any little thing which they could connect me with now might turn the entire court against me and cause them to believe thieves, whores and convicts. I think everything is all right however.

This will be handed to you by Mr. Fort; do not let it get into anyone else's hands. Better destroy it at once.

Very truly yours,
T. B. Catron

Hon. Thos. Hughes,
Albuquerque.[35]

On the same day Catron wrote Hughes another letter that evidently was intended for publication.

Santa Fe, N. M. Oct. 10, 1895.

Editor of Citizen:

I have noticed an article in the Citizen of the 9th inst., which seems to reflect on Chief Justice Smith, and have learned that it is claimed by some of my political and personal enemies that I inspired the article or wrote it. As you are aware I had nothing to do with it. I cannot believe that a gentleman occupying the high and responsible position of Chief Justice of this Territory has been guilty of the great impropriety of counselling in regard to the conduct or merit of any cause to come before him. I suggest that you make this communication public, as an attempt is being made, as I understand, to prejudice me in the case pending against me in the supreme court. I am informed that Chief Justice Smith did not go to Albuquerque to consult in my case and has not consulted at any time about it, and I think he should be set right in that regard.

Respectfully, T. B. Catron

We publish the foregoing as requested and state that our information came from other sources than that of Mr. Catron. He is not in any manner responsible for that article and we gladly print what Mr. Catron says, so as to put him right, as also the Chief Justice, to whom we desire to do no wrong.

The editorial in this paper of the 9th inst., entitled: "Is it honesty or partisanship" was published on what we deemed reliable authority, gathered from various sources. We are now informed that Mr. Childers and Judge Smith disclaim any idea that they were in consultation at any time Sunday night in that matter against Catron, but Mr. Childers says that Judge Smith's visit was on other matters. Of course Judge Smith and Mr. Childers know best and we are willing to give them the benefit of a denial and all reasonable doubts. We are glad to be informed that the statements made by us as to the visit of Judge Smith last Sunday was not for the purpose and object we had been informed it was made for, and we are glad to have the public so understand, and on this make the amende honorable, as we have heretofore had great confidence in the integrity of the Chief Justice. We hope hereafter to be able to entertain the same confidence.[36]

Evidently William T. McCreight, Hughes's partner, showed these letters to Frank W. Clancy, one of Catron's attorneys in the disbarment proceedings. Clancy promptly wired Catron: "McCreight shows me card. Publication will be ruinous. Countermand immediately."[37] It is plain that Clancy saw what Catron failed to perceive — that this letter did not apologize at all; instead, it simply cleverly reiterated what had already been said.

Why did Catron write the article and deliver it to Thomas Hughes for publication? The trial of Catron and Spiess in disbarment proceedings was scheduled for only four days away. With so little time before the trial, he must have known that the article would have repercussions. It is not likely that he wrote it in a fit of uncontrollable pique; it is probable he had information indicating that members of the Supreme Court were in a mood to go against him and that he staked all on an effort to establish a climate of public sentiment which members of the court would dare not ignore. Chief Justice Smith, he knew, was very tender in regard to newspaper articles. He had once fought a duel with an editor from Richmond Virginia, for writing an article about him. Catron observed: "His skin is so thin that the slightest attack punctures him. I think the papers now should puncture him so much that his skin will be too open for a first class sieve."[38]

While Catron was author of the *Citizen* article, he did not act alone in the general planning and strategy of that time. Word was throughout New Mexico that this was now a fight against Catron in which all Democrats were expected to join. Republicans rallied to Catron's cause, and a resounding battle was fought in the collective press of the Territory. It became like a whirlpool with Catron in the vortex struggling to keep his head above water, and he proved to be a champion swimmer. He cooly directed the Republicans' press assault attacking Chief Justice Thomas J. Smith, defending editors Hughes and McCreight and guarding freedom of the press. A few good editorials, he believed, would bring his opponents to their senses if they had any. In the campaign he advocated that Eastern papers also take up the cudgel.[39]

Catron's opponents, at the time, suspected he was author of the *Citizen* article and made every effort to determine his authorship, but details of the secret were well kept. William Burr Childers, particularly, attempted to learn what had happened. All he could find out was that a lawyer had left the article in the *Citizen* office.[40]

The investigating committee concurrently called the court's attention to the article and suggested that it was libelous, calculated to impede and embarrass, and that it tended to scandalize the court and overawe its deliberations. Bernard S. Rodey, for one, denied his connection with the recommendation of the committee and requested that his name be stricken. While he did not countenance publication of the article, he was not satisfied it was the duty of the committee to call the court's attention to it.[41]

The Catron-Spiess trial was postponed. Catron's opponents evidently wanted time for the first flush of public excitement to abate. Catron may not have forseen this contingency. He may have suspected that inertia would prevail and that the court would render its decision on schedule.

Thomas Hughes decided to take Catron's advice as regards a trip to Arizona; he left on the morning of October 11 to solicit business for his paper. Word was around that he had probably been warned from Santa Fe — although not necessarily because warrants for his arrest and that of William T. McCreight were already out — and a search was being made in Albuquerque for a marshal to make the arrests.[42] Hughes was subsequently taken into custody by a United States marshal at Winslow, Arizona.

Following up his plan to embarrass Thomas J. Smith at every turn, Catron sought further information to be used against the chief justice. He knew of a legal case between Stephen W. Dorsey and the father of William H. Alley of

Boston. The amount involved in the cause was in excess of $150,000, and the original verdict, rendered by Chief Justice James O'Brien, was in favor of Alley. An appeal was made, and Chief Justice Smith reversed the decision. Shortly thereafter Dorsey came down from Denver with his wife and accompanied Judge Smith and his wife on a two weeks' trip to Mexico City. Catron was reliably informed that Dorsey paid the transportation from El Paso to Mexico City, and Mrs. Smith herself had advised him that their bills were paid for them. She did not specify by whom, but Catron had information that it was Dorsey. Also, Mrs. Smith revealed that a large number of gifts had been presented to them — in fact everything that Mrs. Smith expressed admiration for — and that the only thing she and the judge had paid for was a lady's hat. Mrs. Smith was no doubt indiscreet; it is not likely that the people of Mexico City had been so carried away by the small amount of pomp displayed by this vacation party that they presented these gifts without charge. The presumption was that Dorsey also paid for these donations. Catron commenced proceedings to secure affidavits concerning these transactions.[43] He was too busy, though, to implement details of the investigation and nothing was accomplished.

Catron believed that newspapers from one end of the country to the other should "open up like a line of sharpshooters against Smith, Crist and Thornton."[44] To provide information for this barrage, he wrote a memorandum to W. S. Williams, publisher of the *Socorro Chieftain,* which contained denunciations far more scathing than those in the *Citizen* article. Evidently cooler heads, or less hardy souls, counseled against the use of this additional publicity blast. The more virulent passages follow.

Tom Smith, son of "Extra Billy" Smith, brother of . . . the embezzler, who fled from justice in Arizona, and brother of the other Smith who took a prominent part in the murder of Dave Broderick by Terry in California, says he washes his hands of the Catron & Spiess case.

If he does he ought to do so near the mouth of the Rio Grande, as the filth he has personally injected into it from his own hands would pollute the waters of that stream to such an extent that it would cause an epidemic along the whole course of that river.

Why has neither Tom Smith nor "Affidavit Friday," Childers, dared to deny the truth of the Citizen article? Friday made the affidavit on which the editors of the newspaper were arrested for exercising the right of free speech. Yet he did not dare, with all his facility for swearing, when occasion offers, to say that all of said publication, so far as it related to his connection with Smith in the case, was untrue in the least.

Gov. Thornton not only pardoned Davis without any recommendation from the pardoning board and at the request of district attorney Crist, who never saw the evidence or heard officially the facts of the case, but contrary to his oath received a fee from Davis to secure the pardon, but our Governor has pardoned others on promise of political help to be given just before the last election, and although he knew Crist opened an election-corruption office in front of the voting stand at Plaza del Alcalde in Rio Arriba county, and bought and paid for votes all day long with the moneys furnished him as chairman of the Democratic Central Committee, still supported him and appointed him to the office of district attorney.

Crist and Thornton would like to switch public sentiment off the track as to that bribery of Crist by convict Davis to get him pardoned, by howling about the "wounded honoh" of Tom Smith and prosecuting and damning of Tom Hughes.

If Tom Smith attempts to rebuild his fence in the east, he had better do it with posts a foot thick and two feet apart with fifty double barbed wires, or some of the cattle on the outside will scent some of his iniquity and break in. Keep them out, Thomas, keep them out for God's sake.

Who is Tom Smith anyhow? Is it the same man who claims to be a "Virginian, be God, sah!", — who insisted he was a resident of Virginia when he wished to be appointed a member of the court of private land claims, and immediately thereafter, when he could not get it, claimed to be a resident of New Mexico, without returning to the territory, in order to be appointed a judge of the supreme court of this territory. Is he the same Tom Smith who has frequently been found drunk in Las Vegas and after having befouled himself been carried home by his companions to avoid scandal? Is he the same doubting Thomas, who was drunk on the bench at Vegas and was kindly advised to adjourn court because he was sick and go to his room?

The Citizen article surely had some effect. It knocked the saw-dust out of Smith five times in five minutes and then gave him a congestive chill, by which he was confined to his bed a whole week. Thomas, keep cool, or you will lose all your saw-dust and have another chill.

Some hard things are said about Tom Smith, and his moral character, but it is whispered that his physical manhood is even more a myth than his morality, for instance: he wears a bouquet, he makes men doff their hats at meeting him, he insists upon an imposing courtesy from members of the bar, he smothers his poor rotting physique with musk and perfume. Is it true that in reality the chief justice is physically that which his lady-like manners indicate? We might cite his "domestic bliss" as another proof, but that isn't necessary.

The chief justice of New Mexico wears a cape over-coat. The cape has a delicate white silk lining. No matter whether the wind blows or blows not — whether there be a hurricane or a storm, this "man" keeps his pretty little silk cape folded neatly back, so as to expose the captivating lining. How proud we ought to be of our lady-like chief justice? Everyone will anxiously await the appearance of the "manly" creature with his new spring bonnet next Easter.[45]

When the disbarment trial of Catron and Spiess got under way, Judge Napoleon B. Laughlin requested a continuance so he could further examine the evidence. He had not yet received any of that for the defense, and probably not all presented by the investigating committee; yet Catron was informed that as early as October 24 and 25 he was busily writing an opinion. Since he had not received the defense testimony, it is entirely reasonable to assume that the opinion was against the defendants.

Catron wrote to his friend, W. S. Williams, expressing concern that Laughlin seemed exceedingly weak, and of his fear that Laughlin would allow his judgment to be warped by Crist, Cunningham, Thornton, and Fiske. Accordingly, Catron requested that Williams confer with Judge Humphrey B. Hamilton at once and see that, if Laughlin filed a dissenting opinion, the court prepare a finding absolutely vindicating himself and Spiess. He wanted no smirching or smoothing over but a clean vindication with which he could go before the world. It was simply a question of whether he was to be believed or the witnesses who had been arrayed against him. He wanted no halfway opinion stating that his conduct had not been exactly proper but not bad enough to disbar him. He desired an opinion stating that there was absolutely nothing to militate against him and that he had done nothing wrong. He wished Hamilton to prepare a brief, pointed, and positive opinion in the case that would take the guts out of anything that Laughlin might write.

Catron pointed out that the whole matter had been not only aggravating but expensive. His business had suffered greatly, not only from want of his attention but also because people would not send him business when charges were preferred against him. He wrote:

> I have been suspended like Mahomet's coffin, for the last two months, unnecessarily.... Hamilton should certainly consider these matters and see that the decision is an absolute, complete, unconditional vindication. This is what I ask him. He can afford to give it.[46]

By the middle of October the trial was under way, and the contempt proceedings against Thomas Hughes were also considered. On October 16 Hughes printed an apology to Chief Justice Smith and the Supreme Court. In it he avowed that the article was published through gross carelessness and without malicious intent. Catron opposed the retraction because it would lead people to believe that contempt had been committed.[47]

As it turned out, the apology did not reduce Hughes' sentence, and it did, to an extent, humiliate him. William T. McCreight published a card in the same paper explaining that he had no personal knowledge concerning publication of the article and that he was more closely connected with the business end of the concern than with the editorial department. McCreight was not primarily responsible for editorial policy and, on the basis of his disclaimer, was discharged upon payment of a $25 fine and costs.

Hughes' punishment was more severe. On October 23, 1895, the court rendered a verdict of guilty in his case and sentenced him to a fine of $1.00 and costs and imprisonment for sixty days. The guilty verdict was unanimous, but justices Bantz and Hamilton dissented as to imprisonment. The prison sentence was originally to have been served in Santa Fe; however, Edward L. Bartlett, who represented Hughes, secured a modification so he was permitted to serve his time in the Bernalillo County jail where he would be closer to the operation of his paper. Bartlett also requested that Hughes be given a few days to arrange his affairs. The court denied this privilege, and Hughes was ordered locked up the following morning.

In explanation to the court Hughes had maintained that he found the offensive article upon his desk typewritten and unsigned. He claimed to have read the item only hurriedly and that, because of shortage of copy, sent it to the printer without a more careful perusal of its contents. He asserted that he did not read the entire article until it was printed. The court, though, believed he had guilty knowledge of its contents. Judge Laughlin wrote the opinion claiming that Hughes only aggravated his case by professing ignorance of the purpose, effect, and authorship of the article. To the contrary, the court felt that his flight from the Territory could only have been to avoid the consequence of the court order for his apprehension.

The day following Hughes' sentencing, Charles A. Flinn filed an affidavit with the Supreme Court stating that Hughes had confided to him that Neill B. Field wrote the contentious article. On the strength of this affidavit, and other information, the court swore out a warrant against Hughes charging perjury.[48]

Catron and his friends soon had cause for concern because Hughes displayed uneasiness at the charge of perjury. Catron assured him that the facts on which the perjury warrant was issued constituted nothing like perjury — that Childers' affidavit was not sufficient to convict a sheep-killing dog. He advised Hughes to give bond, thus releasing subpoenas for telegrams (which had been issued to the Western Union Telegraph Company in an effort to link Catron with the *Citizen* article) and allowing them to be removed from the Territory. He warned that Hughes must keep his mouth sealed because, if he were prudent, there was no possible danger of his being convicted of perjury or even indicted. There were no funds for a grand jury meeting in December which would throw it over into May. Catron explained:

> By May the times of these roosters will be so far towards their close that they will have the eternal saw-dust scared out of them. So keep quiet and do not have any fears whatever. In the first place, they can prove no perjury against you in any event; in the second place, do not help them to get up even a suspicion. Third, do not enable them to throw out their drag net and get hold of all the correspondence of your friends.*

The court now issued another dragnet subpoena, even broader than the first for all telegrams bearing in any manner on the Hughes contempt case. The subpoena ordered that all telegrams be produced by November 20, on which date there was to be a preliminary hearing against Hughes for perjury. Hughes had waived examination, and the court directed him to give bond in the sum of a thousand dollars to answer any indictment which might be found by the next grand jury.

Catron informed J. J. Dickey, superintendent of the Western Union Telegraph Company at Omaha that, since Hughes had waived examination and been admitted to bail, the subpoenas were *functus officio* (no longer valid). He insisted that the whole scheme was nothing more than an attempt to injure him personally, and that it was the duty of the telegraph company to protect the public against this outrageous procedure. He therefore requested that, under some pretext, all originals and copies of pertinent telegrams emanating from Santa Fe and Albuquerque be sent east and kept in some safe location. This would, he claimed, cut off almost the entire source of information of these people who were trying to improperly secure copies of telegrams. Since Hughes had waived examination and given bond, the current subpoenas

---

* Catron to Thomas Hughes, October 30, 1895 (C.P. 105, Vol. 13). This letter was evidently written by Catron, but signed by Robert Gortner.

were not in order; nevertheless, Catron feared that new subpoenas might be issued early the following year when there
might be a session of the grand jury. He reminded Dickey that
Western Union had competition from the Postal Telegraph
Company and, if his company were to surrender the communications of its patrons, it would soon have no business.[49]

By October 25 the Supreme Court finished examination of
the evidence in the Catron-Spiess disbarment case and rendered its decision vindicating the two lawyers. Chief Justice
Smith was not in attendance — reportedly he was ill — and
Justice Needham C. Collier pronounced the verdict. He stated
that Justice Laughlin dissented from the majority and would
give his reasons for doing so in an opinion to be handed down
later. Justice Hamilton subsequently wrote the majority
opinion.

Laughlin, in dissenting, held that to claim testimony unworthy of belief, simply because the moral character and standing for truth of some of the witnesses was impeachable, was
to "destroy the most fruitful source of testimony for the detec-
tion and supression of crime."[50] The majority, as expressed
by Justice Hamilton, felt that the low moral character and
poor reputation for veracity of the prosecution witnesses rendered their testimony beyond belief.[51]

Catron now received numerous letters congratulating
him on his vindication. One is typical:

> I note with pleasure the favorable termination of your matter
> before the supreme court, but did not doubt that the termination
> would be favorable to yourself in the beginning, but was very much
> disgusted that Laughlin intended to file a dissenting opinion censori-
> ous of yourself, but if he does so he would only give an exhibition of
> what an ass can do. In Colorado, among all informed people, it is well
> understood that this whole matter is a manifestation of political spite
> of the lowest and smallest order.[52]

Despite the decision of the court, the case raged on in the
newspapers of the Territory. Democrats held that, since the
opinion had not been unanimous, it was a victory for their

side; newspapers sympathetic to Republicans claimed that the verdict was complete vindication for Catron and Spiess.

Judge Laughlin was not content merely to dissent. Catron reported his conduct in a letter to William J. Mills:

> This man Laughlin is trying to hamstring all of us here. He tried to disbar me and when he could not do it he wrote a filthy, dirty, dissenting opinion, had it published and caused his clerk to send a copy to every member of Congress and every head of Department in Washington, with the idea of breaking down my influence.[53]

Immediately after the court announced its decision in favor of Catron and Spiess, a partial canvas of members of the bar association revealed that the election of Catron as president of the association would be a certainty. At the formal election on October 28, he was elected with twenty-four votes for Catron and one for George W. Knaebel. The election was an important matter for Catron, and he felt more vindicated by the faith of his fellow lawyers than by the favorable decision of the court in the disbarment proceedings just finished. Even while the case was under consideration, he had lobbied strongly for his own candidacy. While he was confident of victory, still he felt that a vote of confidence by his fellow lawyers would cause some members of the court to call a halt before taking extraordinary measures against him. Furthermore, he felt he was entitled to the position. He had helped organize the bar association but had never served as president. He wrote:

> I am the oldest member of the bar; I am in good standing; have done nothing wrong; am not ashamed of myself, nor am I willing to take a back seat. I have made up my mind that from this time on my course shall be aggressive against the hounds who are attempting to dog me out of the bar.[54]

Actually, the election had been scheduled for October 3 at a meeting of the bar association in Albuquerque before the case against Catron was tried. At this time at least three-fourths of the members would have voted for Catron. However, a justice of the Supreme Court suggested that to elect him president before the disbarment case against him was settled would tend to show disrespect to the court. As a consequence the election was postponed. Catron's opponents used the time afforded by the postponement to work against his election as president.[55] In accordance with regular routine the president would be from Santa Fe. Solicitor General John P. Victory, chairman of the committee investigating charges against Catron, and District Attorney Jacob H. Crist, who had preferred the charges, now became candidates in opposition to him. His virtually unanimous election over two of his most persistent harassers provided Catron with much satisfaction.

Within a few days Catron wrote a number of letters to his friends thanking them for their support. He was elated, of course, by his vindication. But he seemed even more pleased that he had bested Chief Justice Smith. He said:

While I never had any doubt of the result, still there are two members of the bench who would have emasculated me if possible. One of them, thank heaven, took the diarrhoea from the article published by the "Citizen" and was soon afterward thrown into a congestive chill, from which doubtless under the interposition of divine providence he was not allowed to recover in time to take part in the nefarious transaction.[56]

Against Judge Laughlin, though, Catron seemed to feel a degree of pity and was saddened by his dissenting opinion. He wrote to Judge Humphrey B. Hamilton thanking him for his clear and exhaustive analysis of the case. He went on:

The only regret that I have is that Judge Laughlin could not see the force of your statements. I fear some malicious individuals have been carrying to him a series of lies in regard to myself and Spiess, and that he has become prejudiced, violently, and is not strong enough to rise above the prejudice. Laughlin has known me many years. He has practiced with me at the bar. He has never known me to do a dishonorable or improper thing. I may have made mistakes and errors — that we all do. Laughlin, however, knew all these witnesses who are pitted against me. He knew Nowell to be a prostitute's pimp, a convicted felon, and next thing to a perjurer. He knew the character of all the other witnesses and how he could ever make up his mind to believe

them in preference to me I am at a loss to comprehend. I hope before
you get through with your opinion officially he may yet join in it. I
know he is not a strong man — that he is capable of being influenced
and prejudiced in matters and that he allows his prejudices to carry
him away. I fear that he has allowed a lot of disreputable characters
such as Crist and Cunningham to get to his ear and that he has gone
so far with them that he cannot get away from them. If my fears are
well grounded I hope he will be able to, through the influence of
yourself and the other judges, break loose from them, be independent
and allow his best judgment to control him. I believe his impulses are
good and that he would not, if left to his own calm judgment, go
wrong, but I am afraid he has not been influenced by his judgment
in this case.[57]

On the evening of December 23, 1895, Thomas Hughes
completed his sixty days in jail and was released. His Republican friends had decided earlier that his release should be
accompanied by a gala celebration, and they engaged the
opera house and a brass band. Upon his release a procession
headed by the First Regimental Band carried Hughes from
the county jail to the opera house in New Albuquerque.
Hughes, riding in state in a hack drawn by two white horses,
puffed contentedly at a cigar as he waved to friends and well-
wishers along the way. At the opera house he was treated to a
display of Republican eloquence, with Charles A. Spiess in
the forefront of the assembled speakers substituting for Catron
who was in Washington.[58]

And Tom Catron did not forget his promise to "make up
the difference" for Thomas Hughes' forbearance in accepting
quietly the jail sentence in behalf of Catron and the Republican party in New Mexico. The *Citizen* was run with a small
staff and scant fiscal support. Even while Hughes was in prison,
William T. McCreight informed Catron that the newspaper
was pinched for funds, and Catron responded with financial
aid.[59]

Out of the severe tensions attending the disbarment proceedings grew a rift between Catron and his partner Charles
A. Spiess. Spiess had become a member of the firm on November 3, 1893, and remained until August 14, 1897. Soon after

the termination of their partnership there was a dispute, the immediate cause of which was suspicion on the part of Spiess that Catron had conspired with their common enemies, Jacob H.Crist and Napoleon B. Laughlin, to deny him appointment to the office of district attorney. Spiess later wrote to Catron explaining that he had mistakenly entertained this supposition. Catron answered with brutal frankness:

> I do not desire to become your enemy, nor to engage in hostilities to you, but I would advise you to be a little more prudent, before you fall into traps which evidently must have been laid for you by men whom you seem to have been more willing to trust than me....I write this letter in this way because your letter does not seem to me to be manly. It seems to be a labored effort to make an excuse for an action on your part which you know, so far as I am concerned, is inexcusable. I hope that you will no farther indulge in such escapades as this and that hereafter we may be the same as heretofore.[60]

Needless to say, relations between the two men were not again as they had been before. A few years later there was an even more serious misunderstanding between them brought on by Ralph E. Twitchell. Catron and Twitchell had long been on less than cordial terms. This bad feeling dated back as early as 1892, when Catron appointed Twitchell to a certain local Republican committee. Twitchell did not perform as Catron expected; in a letter of chastisement, Catron said, in part:

> I also am informed that during the last week you attended the fair in Albuquerque; that at that place you were under the influence of whiskey and frequenting a very low dive, and "shooting craps," and that you were carrying arms, also, at that place; that you were searched by a policeman, but that just a minute before you were searched you had warning, and removed your pistol and gave it to another man.... Unless you are willing to swear off drinking, absolutely, and from gambling and frequenting such dives, and unless you agree to tell me absolutely the truth in every instance in this campaign, I think you had better resign.[61]

In January 1900 Twitchell distorted and widely spread a statement made to him by Frank Springer, one of the counsel who defended Catron and Spiess in the disbarment proceedings. Springer had, he later stated, told Twitchell of Catron's avowal, in connection with the Borrego case, that he was not responsible for Spiess' action in relation to certain witnesses at Las Vegas. As reported by Twitchell, Springer's words took on the connotation that Catron had looked to the defense attorneys for protecting his own interests only and was willing to ignore those of Spiess.[62]

Frank W. Clancy, Neill B. Field, and Albert B. Fall, the other defense attorneys, categorically denied there had been any implication that, on Catron's behalf, Spiess' interests should be sacrificed or in any way neglected.[63]

Catron's relations with another former partner, Governor William T. Thornton, also remained at odds, especially at the time final efforts were being made to hang Catron's clients in the Borrego case. In September 1896 a copy of an unsigned letter addressed to Thornton appeared in the *Albuquerque Citizen* which said, in part:

> "Poker Bill" is now engaged in playing a game in which the lives of four men are at stake. He wants to have the Borrego brothers hung, and he will see that Lauriano Alarid and Patricio Valencia are sentenced to the penitentiary for life, provided they will make a confession which will hurt Hon. T. B. Catron in the campaign [for delegate to Congress] this fall.[64]

Thornton answered with a letter to Catron, a copy of which appeared in the *Santa Fe Daily New Mexican* on the same day he delivered the letter:

> This communication to the *Citizen* was prepared in your office, and at your dictation. In keeping with your well known character, you were too much of a poltroon to assume the responsibility thereof by affixing your name thereto. . . . Your accusations against me are on a par with the slanderous charges which you prepared and caused to be published against the Chief Justice of this Territory last year, when you permitted the Editor of the *Albuquerque Citizen,* in whose paper you had it published, to go to prison and suffer your act. Then, as now, you sent out your slanderous shaft under a nom de plum. Now, as then, you will show yourself to be too much of a poltroon and

coward to assume personal responsibility for a communication which you know, and knew when you sent it, to be false and slanderous, but will attempt to throw the responsibility upon some of your willing tools that you keep around you.[65]

Thornton's letter provoked Catron mightily; in fact, it appears to have been one of the few times in his political life that he considered using bodily violence. On consideration, he concluded that nothing was to be gained "by actual physical warfare."[66] Instead, he wrote to Thornton:

I am this morning in possession of your letter of the 10th inst., written from the "office of the Executive," — having just returned from Colorado, where I was looking after some mining interests. . . . It has the appearance of being designed to provoke me to some act of violence, which might give your adherents an opportunity to injure me physically; but I am unwilling to attribute to you such a design. I prefer to consider your act that of one smarting under some fancied injury, to such a degree as to render you temporarily insane. I shall try to avoid your example. As I left Santa Fe on the same day of your publication, and did not receive your communication until this morning, your delay in writing it is to be regretted. The coincidence of time in my going and of your publication, was of course purely fortuitous; but some may not so believe.[67]

As a result of Thornton's letter to Catron — published in his own newspaper — Thornton was tried by the Masonic Order and acquitted by a vote of twenty to seven. The intention of the Grand Lodge in ordering the charges against Thornton was to discourage Masons from abusing one another in the public press.*

The cause of Catron's stringent troubles — The Borrego case — continued in September 1896 with an appeal to the Territorial Supreme Court. A motion was entered to set aside the existing judgment on the grounds that the defendants

---

* Max Frost to Catron, February 18, 1897 (C.P. 106, Box 2). In his fight against Catron, Thornton strongly backed an attempt to have the capital city changed from Santa Fe to Albuquerque. This was, at the time, the latest of several efforts in that direction. It was currently felt by many that a strong reason for Thornton's support of the measure was personal spite brought on by Catron's determined effort to prevent the Borregos from being hanged.

had never been properly arraigned. Judge Napoleon B. Laughlin set aside the motion declaring that the omission was merely a clerical error, and October 15, 1896, was set as the time for execution.

Growing out of this situation was yet another attempt to disbar Catron and Spiess in a move pushed by Eugene A. Fiske and Jacob H. Crist, the grounds being that they had made improper affidavits that their clients had not been arraigned. The movement was shortlived, though, because of intervention by Judge Humphrey B. Hamilton.[68]

The next move by Catron in behalf of his clients was an appeal to the United States Supreme Court, which was granted by Mr. Justice David J. Brewer one week before the date of execution. The appeal was denied, and February 28, 1897, was set as the new date for execution. An appeal of January 20 was also denied. Catron, who was in Washington as delegate to Congress, informed his associates in Santa Fe that nothing further could be done. The prisoners should be told that there was no further hope from judicial proceedings, and they must, from then on, act for themselves. The Borrego brothers were reported to have made determined efforts to escape, and, despite statutes forbidding the move, the prisoners had been removed from the county prison to the Territorial penitentiary. Catron urged that they be returned to the prison and insisted that in this Sheriff Harry C. Kinsell should cooperate. It was their legal right, Catron insisted, that the prisoners be returned to the prison.[69]

As a final resort Catron made a personal and impassioned plea to President Grover Cleveland requesting a reprieve for his clients. He brilliantly reviewed the entire case, concluding that the evidence upon which they were convicted was entirely circumstantial and given by alleged accomplices, ex-convicts, petty thieves, and prostitutes.[70]

Mrs. Catron tried to help by calling on President Cleveland's wife, but she was notified that the latter refused to interfere with such matters coming before the president. At the

White House she learned that an appeal would have to be made through channels and in writing, so had her husband prepare a proper petition which she submitted to the president. She also traveled to Baltimore and received a letter from Cardinal Gibbons to the president requesting his favorable consideration of the petition.[71]

Concurrently, a petition requesting that the sentences be commuted to life imprisonment was signed by nearly three thousand residents of the Territory and submitted to Governor Thornton. Included among the petitioners were leading members of both political parties, the Archbishop, and a majority of both houses of the legislative assembly.[72]

Governor Thornton declined to concede a commutation, but President Cleveland granted a respite until March 23, 1897. Immediately Catron received numerous telegrams from Santa Fe telling him that Thornton, urged on by Childers, Laughlin, and others, was seriously entertaining open rebellion against the president by insisting that the prisoners be executed as scheduled. President Cleveland, though, had doubted his authority to act in the matter and, thinking his order might be ignored, instructed Governor Thornton to duplicate the directive for a thirty-day respite. The governor complied and issued a similar order over his own signature.

William McKinley was to be inaugurated as the new president on March 4, so Governor Thornton left for Washington to plead with McKinley that the respite be revoked. Also, Thornton desired to be in Washington to have his say in regard to new Territorial appointments.

The purpose of Catron's plea for a respite had been to gain time until McKinley was inaugurated in hopes that a new governor might be obtained before his clients were executed. Now he drove himself through the whole wearying process of preparing a new case to present to President McKinley. New affidavits would be helpful showing the conduct of Sheriff Cunningham and his deputies in playing cards with the jurors and influencing them in other ways. New affidavits were needed from primary prosecution witnesses as well as from as many jurors as possible. Catron wanted a statement from Governor Thornton as to why he had removed Sheriff Conklin, as well as a statement from the county treasurer showing that Conklin was not a cent in default when removed by Thornton. It would be helpful, Catron thought, to secure affidavits supporting all possible charges against the governor, showing his private conduct in attending saloons and gambling constantly while governor. Finally, he thought it advisable to have an affidavit from each condemned prisoner, particularly those who had made confessions, stating that whatever confessions they had made were under promise of pardon or commutation of sentence.[73]

Catron's partners in Santa Fe worked valiantly in the face of disheartening obstacles. Time was short. Relatives of the condemned men were apathetic. Even the prisoners seemed weary of waiting. Francisco Gonzales y Borrego, when requested by his brother to prepare a new affidavit, wrote:

> [The sheriff] told me about the papers that you want; and it is true what he told you that I had destroyed them. The reason that I destroyed them is that I promised with all my heart to my God and Redeemer Jesus Christ, that I will not say a single word if unfortunately we are executed — that I will die like a lamb, as he taught us how to die; I also promised him that I would not leave a single letter behind me, and for this reason I do not write again those papers for you which you desire; anyway, you know all the record of the case, and in the matter you can do as you please, after I am dead. . . .[74]

The story of the monumental struggle for governor at this time will be related later. Suffice it to say here that Governor Thornton's presence in Washington, and other circumstances, was sufficient to block the timely appointment of a new governor.

President McKinley gave himself ten days to review the case. At the end of this time he refused to interfere further. The execution was carried out on April 2, 1897, by Harry C. Kinsell, sheriff of Santa Fe County. William T. Thornton had

prevailed, and the following day he telegraphed President Mc-
Kinley his resignation as governor of New Mexico.

Why had Catron so staunchly defended his clients even
though his involvement threatened to jeopardize his legal
career in New Mexico? In assessing the complexities involved,
one consideration stands out: his extensive correspondence
indicates that he believed them to be innocent. Having reached
that conclusion, his nature seemingly demanded that he
defend them with the fullest measure of his ability, energy,
and acumen. Will Keleher — who knew Catron personally —
sagaciously wrote concerning this facet of his character:

> Thomas Benton Catron figuratively painted on a big canvas with
> a large brush, using plenty of paint and many colors. Fearless, able and
> resourceful, when he attached himself to a cause for a client, Tom
> Catron's loyalty and devotion knew no limits.[75]

Involved were antecedents of such long standing and so
many conflicts of personality that, once he became enmeshed,
there was no way to extricate himself except to simply walk
away. His character was such that he could not bow to expediency by walking away from a fight the cause of which he
believed was just.

Possibly a bit more in the realm of conjecture, his clients
were loyal to the Republican party, and this demanded personal loyalty from Catron in return. He had for so long been
the party leader that, perhaps unconsciously, he came to
equate party loyalty with personal fidelity. Linked with this
anomaly is the tradition that he habitually placed persons
politically in his debt by loaning them money and then making no effort to collect when the loan came due. This general-
ization is not valid in all or, perhaps, even a majority of
instances. There is, nevertheless, substantiation that this was
his practice at times. Moreover, there is evidence that his
clients had worked actively with him in this type of recruitment for loyal Republicans. A letter from Francisco Ganzales
y Borrego is a typical indication:

Honorable T. B. Catron

    dear Sir I have the honor to report to you that I have two men that they have agreed to come to the Republican party but know that they allways want some money they want $10.00 each they say that they will sign you a promisory note for a sertian time for to pay it to you. I will tell you that each one of them is worth 2 votes and I am sure that they will be onest with us and to our party now if you want to come and talk to them your self you must do it by coming up to my house this afternoon and you wil see them but if you do not want to come and you want to believe me send me the money and send me some note Blanks and I will make them sign the notes for you give me an answer Respectfully
Yours
Francisco Gonzales y Borrego[76]

    The whole impact of the disbarment proceedings on Catron's life resists definitive analysis. That it required his expenditure of large sums of money there is no doubt. The defendants had no financial resources of their own. What is more, the notoriety surrounding the case, and the adverse hammering of the Territorial press, particularly that of the *New Mexican,* cost him heavily in political leadership. Likewise, especially virulent in the following years was the widely disseminated printed dissenting opinion of Napoleon B. Laughlin.

    In a final analysis, there may be justification to believe that the tribulations he encountered brought him the fame that helped overcome adversities carrying over the next several years and which aided him to close out a long and eventful career with the United States senatorship; probably his most cherished goal of all.

14
Catron Fights Otero

There was some confidence among leading Republicans that Governor Thornton could be removed before the Borrego brothers were executed and that a replacement might be instrumental in securing clemency for them. This feeling was bolstered by his vindictive efforts to see that the hanging took place, his disgraceful conduct in his answer to the "Poker Bill" letter, his consequent censure by the Masonic Order, and his general deportment demeaning the office of Governor.

The move for Thornton's removal was headed by Catron, although he by no means acted alone. On September 16, 1896, while Democratic President Cleveland was still in office, Catron wrote urging this action:

The letter of Gov. Thornton is regarded here by all good citizens as being unwise, in bad taste, and calculated to bring about a state of unrest and possible blood-shed. It is calculated to lower the character of our territory and bring it into disrepute. He is insane in his desire to hold office and to exercise power. Today he is a blatant free-silver advocate, abusive of everybody who favors the republican nominee or the Indianapolis democratic nominee. He expects the election of Bryan and that he and his henchmen will be continued in power. New Mexico is fast approaching statehood, and he believes, together with his friends, that if Bryan is elected and I am put out of the way, they will have easy sailing in capturing the new State of New Mexico. I have no doubt

[269]

that Thornton's letter to me was written with the design of getting me into some kind of broil and having me killed. . . .*

Catron admitted that his own indignation was a factor in his urging the governor's removal; more particularly, he expressed the opinion of the good people of the Territory that Thornton had lost his usefulness as governor. He recommended the appointment of John W. Poe, president of a Roswell bank. Poe, Catron pointed out, was a Democrat who favored the nominee of his party for president, was sound on the money question, a law-abiding citizen of good judgment and sense, and a courageous person.[1] He must have suspected that his urging the removal of a Democratic governor by a Democratic president near the end of the respective term of each would probably be to no avail; nevertheless, his determination to see Thornton removed prompted him to the effort.

The impending inauguration of President McKinley on March 4, 1897, brought new expectation that Governor Thornton might be replaced and resulted in a rush of applicants for the position. Catron, from the beginning, favored his good friend, Pedro Perea; nevertheless, his objective, as well as that of other Republicans in the Territory, was to secure a replacement for Thornton before the Borrego brothers were hanged. He made it plain to Perea that he would stand for him as governor as far as possible but that if another candidate had greater assurance of being appointed he would have to go along with that appointment. As he wrote:

I would not believe that you would be willing to have the lives of four persons sacrificed simply to secure the office for yourself. As I say, I am for you first and all the time until I see that it will endanger the lives of these four men; then I will take anyone else with whom I can succeed. I hope that you will agree with this.[2]

---

*Catron to President Cleveland, September 16, 1896 (C.P. 801, Box 1). Catron informed S. B. Elkins of his letter to the president and requested that Elkins cooperate in the effort to have Thornton removed.

Among the earliest candidates were Alexander L. Morrison and former Governor L. Bradford Prince. Another possible candidate was T. W. Collier. Regarding candidates, Melvin W. Mills, Catron's most respected political adviser, wrote: "If I could make a compromise on Perea I would jump the first train that comes along for Washington."[3] Mills thought, though, that Prince would have the surest probability of being appointed governor before the Borregos were hanged. He suggested, however, that Morrison might be an alternative for Prince. Perea, Mills felt, would be satisfied with such a compromise under the circumstances, particularly since it would then be planned to have Perea appointed Territorial auditor.

Pedro Perea did not take kindly to the possibility of being sidetracked in favor of Morrison. He wrote to Catron:

I was born in 1852 and my father was a citizen of the United States at the time. I think he was a member of the New Mexico legislature the year I was born. Hence I think I ought to be an American citizen by this time.[4]

Morrison, on the other hand, was born in Ireland. Perea asked Catron to consider where the Republican party in New Mexico would be if it were not for the so-called Mexican vote. He likewise pointed out that Morrison would be a candidate of Max Frost and that Frost would control him completely if he were appointed governor. Frost was not Catron's friend, and Perea's argument carried considerable weight.

Catron acknowledged Mills' recommendations. He agreed that Morrison would be a better candidate than Collier. He did not, however, approve of Prince, whom he felt could not be trusted and who had been false to every man who had helped him. Despite Mills' assertion to the contrary, he still thought Perea would be the most likely candidate but agreed to go along with Morrison if it became necessary to do so.

Prince, knowing that Catron favored Perea, wrote that while he was a candidate he was not at all in opposition to Mr. Perea and recognized Perea's qualifications for the position.

He would though, he insisted, stand on his record of a previous term as governor, accompanied by endorsements of persons interested in business enterprises in the Territory.[5]

Catron acknowledged Prince's letter with his usual blunt frankness. He stated that he stood for Perea, and he continued:

> I do not think that you ought to be a candidate. You came to the Territory with an office in your pocket. You afterwards left the Territory and became a resident of New York, and came back again only when you could get another office. Your canvassing of the Territory for the last two years in behalf of free and unlimited coinage of silver contributed, in my judgment, very materially to the defeat of the Republican party in the Territory at the last election. . . .[6]

He admitted that Prince probably had not tried deliberately to injure the Republican party and that it was a matter of mistaken judgment, but he insisted that it certainly was bad judgment. If Catron thought he could dissuade Prince from pursuing his own candidacy, he was mistaken.

Until the Borregos were hanged on April 2, 1897, there was at least some conviction among possible Republican candidates for governor that each would step aside if another appeared to have an inside track for appointment. Some present-day Catron detractors — of which this author knows there are many — may believe that this was an inconsequential cause for united sentiment among possible candidates; nevertheless, the complex record of the time speaks for itself.

When this reason for united restraint among Republican candidates was removed, it became a case of every man for himself. Perhaps with the political power that Catron wielded in earlier days, he might have been able to keep the candidates in line. However, he had met with political adversity and no longer had the effective control over his followers that he had enjoyed in former times. Unbeknown to all concerned, this became a factor in the eventual appointment of Miguel A. Otero as governor of New Mexico.

In rapid succession other candidates now came to the fore. Catron considered Hugh H. Price a good man if an

American were to be appointed, but he firmly believed that the Mexican-American element had been long enough ignored. Thus, he staunchly adhered to his advocacy of Pedro Perea. Gib Prey of Webster City, Iowa, was also a candidate, but Catron was convinced that as a nonresident he should not be considered. He favored Francis Tracy Tobin, of Philadelphia, if a nonresident were appointed.* George H. Wallace, he felt, had slight recommendation from any county except San Miguel, where he was temporarily domiciled. E. F. Hobart announced his candidacy late but claimed he had considerable backing, which is doubtful. William H. H. Llewellyn was an aspirant whom Catron did not believe would be appointed because he had done everything in his power to defeat McKinley in his nomination.†

On May 2, 1897, there occurred an important meeting in Washington attended by Henry L. Waldo, Jefferson Raynolds, Edward L. Bartlett, Miguel A. Otero, William H. H. Llewellyn, John H. Riley, Richard Hudson, Holm O. Bursum, and Ira M. Bond. It was acknowledged by all attending that President McKinley was anxious for an agreement to be reached if possible regarding a candidate so as to relieve him of the embarrassment of making a selection from so many candidates. Bursum still advocated Price but said his man would step aside if an agreement could be made on Perea. Prince stated that he was getting disgusted and out of heart at the long delay in making an appointment. Waldo reported that he had to leave for New York the following day. Raynolds, who backed Wallace, was also anxious to leave. No agreement was reached, and the meeting was postponed.[7]

Successive meetings were held. Bond reported to Catron that Wallace feared he was out of the race and, if so, would

* Catron to President McKinley, April 14, 1897 (C.P. 103, Box 2). Catron unabashedly used the term "Mexican" where today the usage would probably be something such as "native New Mexican" to gloss over racial reflections not then felt.

† Ira M. Bond to Catron, May 1, 1897 (C.P. 103, Box 2); Catron to S. B. Newcomb, May 14, 1897 (C.P. 105, Vol. 13). Other candidates presented their names for consideration, but probably not the nineteen or twenty suggested by Miguel A. Otero, *Nine Years as Governor*, p. 1.

support Miguel A. Otero. Bond felt that Otero would be acceptable to Perea if the latter were denied the appointment.[8]

On May 19 Llewellyn claimed he was no longer a candidate and told Otero, in strict confidence, that he would have Senators William B. Allison and John Henry Gear urge the president that Otero be appointed. He likewise told Wallace and Price each the same thing in regard to their candidacy. Each quickly sought the others to get them to withdraw, thinking they had a sure thing. Their feelings can be imagined when they compared notes.

Prince was feeling less disheartened than he had earlier because William M. Berger was pressing for his appointment. Bursum, who had returned to New Mexico, promised to meet the others more than halfway if they would unite on Perea, or any other on whom all could agree. But none would remove their candidacy. Elkins, at Catron's constant insistence, steadily urged that Perea be appointed. President McKinley informed Elkins that he could have everything just as he wanted it in West Virginia, but would promise nothing else. Miguel A. Otero's name was being more frequently mentioned as a compromise candidate.*

The account of Otero's appointment as governor has never been adequately related. Otero leaves the impression that Jefferson Raynolds was responsible for his designation to office. Catron, at the time, also believed that Raynolds — or Wallace — made the recommendation to McKinley that resulted in Otero's selection, and he so informed Elkins.[9] The fact seems to be that Elkins, while a staunch supporter of Pedro Perea, was in the final analysis responsible for Otero's appointment.

Perea had earlier entered into correspondence with Prince about the governorship — for which Catron scolded

---

* Bond to Catron, May 19, 1897. This is at variance with Otero's claim that his subsequent appointment came to him most unexpectedly. Otero, *Nine Years as Governor*, p. 1.

him gently — and as a result wavered in his own candidacy and withdrew or recommended Prince. Elkins, while informed of Perea's indecision, made one last bid with President McKinley for Perea's appointment. He told the president that a native New Mexican should be named, but McKinley was reluctant to choose a man he had never seen and favored Wallace. Elkins knew that Wallace would not do, and seeing that Perea was out, he advocated Miguel A. Otero for governor and suggested that Wallace be named Territorial secretary. Under the circumstances, Elkins felt this was the very best he could do in behalf of the Territory and of Catron's wishes.[10]

Catron, upon learning of Otero's appointment, characterized him as "a very nice, gentlemanly young man of fair ability"; however, he did not feel that Otero had done anything politically entitling him to the office and that Perea would have made a better governor. Still, there was no immediate indication of the rift between them that was destined to run a virulent course throughout Otero's administration. To comprehend how this breakdown of cordial relations came about, it is helpful to understand basic alterations taking place in New Mexico at the time.

As Howard Roberts Lamar has ably pointed out, the last twenty years of the nineteenth century, starting with the impetus provided by railroad transportation, brought fundamental changes in New Mexico which "modified her economy, affected her native culture, modernized her government and laid the basis for her admission to the Union in 1912."[11]

Miguel A. Otero came on the scene in New Mexico at a time when the Territory had for two decades resisted political changes that inevitably must follow economic and cultural pressures. Gone was the day when it took weeks and even months to communicate with the United States. New Mexico was bursting forth from her tight little ring of isolation, and Otero was the perfect symbol for this transition. Born in St. Louis in 1859, he was raised on the frontier but educated in

Missouri and New York. In the aggregate, he was a product more of cosmopolitan United States than provincial New Mexico. By following his destiny in New Mexico he became the symbol of transition from the old to the new order. It was Catron's fate to represent the old in this transition, and conflict between him and Otero was indubitable. Otero put this antagonism on a personal basis when he wrote:

> It was inevitable that we should come to conflict. He was dictatorial and absolutely ruthless in his methods. . . . Never a good judge of character, he was blind and egotistical enough to think that he could get my support.[12]

The truth is that the quarrel, as it evolved, had a more fundamental basis than personal differences. It was a struggle between the old and the new order. Though each would not admit it later, both tried hard to contain their animosities and act in accord. That they both failed to do so is a topic requiring more careful analysis than has previously been accorded the subject.

In later years Otero compensatorily defended his governorship and tried to give the impression that he was entirely sure of himself in all regards from the start. He was, however, beset by the usual political cares accompanying the beginning of any term in office, particularly in the matter of selecting officials. On July 22, 1897, he was in Washington to confer with President McKinley about federal appointments. He followed pressures already established when he concurred with the President in the appointment of George H. Wallace for Territorial secretary. Both Jefferson Raynolds and Elkins had earlier urged that Wallace be so named. Catron did not believe that Wallace was entitled to the office because he was a nonresident of the Territory and owned no property there.[13]

Catron strongly urged that Solomon Luna be appointed United States marshal. It was his opinion that Luna was the strongest Mexican politically in New Mexico and would do more than any other person to help the Republican party in the Territory.[14] Then, as always, he was undividedly loyal to the Republican party in New Mexico. His advocacy of "home rule" was constant. Nevertheless, there was insistency for Senator Joseph B. Foraker's brother, Creighton, and he was appointed United States marshal.

In the matter of surveyor general, Catron was consistent with his ideals of party loyalty when he recommended Philip H. Harroun of Santa Fe. Quinby Vance of Sierra County, formerly receiver of the United States land office at Las Cruces, was also a candidate. Catron pointed out that Vance had not been in harmony with the policies of the Republican party and that, during the election of 1896, he had been a free silver advocate of the most extreme type. Furthermore, he abused everyone who endorsed the Republican platform at St. Louis. He admitted that Vance was backed by substantial men and good Republicans from Ohio, but he felt that this was not sufficient recommendation for holding office in New Mexico. Vance, however, was named.

While Catron did not concur with Otero's early appointments, he conceded that the governor was responsible for them and should be free to make his choices in keeping with that responsibility. The split between them grew gradually, and no single incident was solely responsible. The opening wedge occurred in November 1897 when Pedro Perea, Solomon Luna, and Catron agreed to pay Otero's expenses for a trip to Washington. Otero intimated that it would take at least $500 for himself and his wife and child. Catron thought it best to make no objection and gave Otero a check for the requested amount. He then called on Perea and Luna for their proportionate share.[15] Catron was willing to advance his part of this money because an important reason for Otero's trip was supposedly to press for Catron's candidacy as United States attorney, as well as the candidacy of judges and other political appointees advocated by him.

Early in 1898 Catron learned that Luna had paid Otero an additional $232 when it had been Catron's distinct understanding that anything over the original $500 would be paid by Otero. Even worse, Catron later learned that W. N. Coler & Co., bankers in New York, paid Otero several hundred dollars for the same trip because Otero "had gone East partly to assist them in getting some action through Congress which would aid them in securing their interest in the territory of New Mexico. . . ."[16] This maneuver on the part of Otero was probably not illegal but was certainly unethical deception and deceit. The incident was immediately an irritant to Catron, but it was only later, when it seemed to him that Otero had not put forth adequate effort in behalf of his candidacy for United States attorney, that it became a major issue.*

Years later Otero wrote that Elkins told Catron: "McKinley will only appoint judges in New Mexico who are endorsed by Governor Otero. I suggest that you see Otero."[17] There is no intimation of this statement in Elkins' correspondence to Catron. The fact is that before Otero left for Washington to secure appointment of judges, he and Catron were already in agreement concerning who the new judges should be. Otero told Catron — who agreed — that he intended to recommend William J. Mills for chief justice, Frank W. Parker for the third district, and John R. McFie for the first district. It was also understood that, if he succeeded in naming other judges, he would be partial to Luis Sulzbacher and George W. Prichard. As it turned out, Otero agreed to name three judges while President McKinley selected the other two. Otero did name Mills, Parker, and McFie; McKinley's selections were J. W. Crumpacker and Charles A. Leland.[18]

---

* There is a sidelight on this issue. In 1888 Otero had been a candidate for county clerk from San Miguel County. In the interest of party harmony, an agreement was made to give Epifanio Baca $500 to withdraw from the race. Catron agreed to pay half of this amount if Otero and his friends would pay the remainder, and did so the same day. Later, Otero asked Catron to pay the other half also and Catron refused. He said: "I see that when one expends his money voluntarily, and attempts to help others, he gets no thanks, but generally makes enemies." Catron to Otero, October 28, 1888 (C.P. 105, Vol. 2); Miguel A. Otero, *My Life on the Frontier, 1882–1897*, pp. 223, 230.

Otero is unfair in implying that Catron disagreed with his selection of judges. Not only did they agree on selections but they concurred that Democratic judges then in office should be removed as soon as possible. It was particularly desirable that Thomas J. Smith, Gideon D. Bantz, and Napoleon B. Laughlin be displaced at once.[19] As a matter of fact, Otero used the urgency of appointing new judges as an excuse for delaying efforts to have Catron appointed United States attorney. Catron agreed to the delay but made it perfectly clear that the position was of great importance to him and that he expected Otero's eventual aid.

Catron's name had been suggested by interested persons for various offices, including governor and chief justice of the Supreme Court,[20] but he was interested only in the position of United States attorney. He sought to replace the incumbent, William Burr Childers. Childers, a native of Tennessee, had moved to Albuquerque to practice law. He served as chairman of the New Mexico Democratic Central Committee and was a supporter of the party's gold wing. His reward had been appointment as United States attorney by President Cleveland. Childers had been a leading spirit in the move to disbar Catron and was not forgiven. While Catron felt hostility toward Childers, he also considered the district attorneyship significant politically and that the office would place him in a position to materially strengthen the Republican party in the Territory.*

Catron enlisted the aid of Elkins, who submitted his name to the United States attorney general. When it became known that Catron sought to become United States attorney, there arose in the Territory immediate and vigorous opposition to his candidacy. In the forefront of this resistance were former

---

* Catron to Elkins, August 23, 1898 (C.P. 105, Vol. 15). Catron, at various times, intimated to Elkins that the salary as United States attorney would be useful to him. As an alternative, for the same reason, he wanted to become attorney for the Pueblo Indians, but did not receive either office.

Governor Lew Wallace and Eugene A. Fiske. Wallace sent a protest to President McKinley that reportedly was a "scorcher."[21]

Fiske, who also fancied the United States attorneyship had long been feuding with Catron. Fiske had been chief of the land claims division at Washington and was permitted to resign on account of questionable transactions with land claimants in that office. In New Mexico, Catron blocked Fiske's confirmation in the legislature as attorney general during the administration of Governor Wallace. Catron had opposed Fiske in a suit over ownership of the Juana Lopez Grant and ruthlessly exposed Fiske's shady tactics in certain land matters. For example, John H. Riley and James J. Dolan desired the survey of a certain township in Lincoln County, and Fiske represented that he could secure the survey if Riley and Dolan would pay him $500, one-half of which he claimed he must pay to Surveyor General Henry M. Atkinson. The money was given to Fiske, who reported that he paid Atkinson. Later the story came out, and Atkinson made Fiske deny, in Riley's presence, that the transaction had been made as claimed by Fiske.[22]

In October 1897 Elkins sent information that Catron's enemies were making a prejudicial fight against him with the president. They were making effective use of the widely distributed dissenting opinion of Laughlin made by him in the earlier disbarment proceedings against Catron. Elkins did not think that Fiske would be named but thought they might defeat Catron's appointment. At first both the president and attorney general had been favorable to Catron, but now they did not seem so.[23] It seems clear that Elkins was warning Catron to prepare for the worst, but Catron still expected Elkins to somehow overcome all problems and make everything right.

Catron was also looking to Governor Otero for aid. It was substantially understood that Otero would help Catron after the judges were appointed. In December, Otero wired Catron that he was devoting every effort to settlement of the judiciary problem. He thought that the attorneyship would not be up for some time; meanwhile, he had heard nothing against Catron.[24] This could hardly have been exactly the case, because it was general knowledge that Catron's opponents were trying to block his appointment.

In January 1898 Otero returned from Washington and gave Catron a rather gloomy account of his prospects. Up to this time Catron seemed confident that Otero was working in his behalf. As far as the general public was concerned, in the interest of party unity, he continued to voice this optimism, but now commenced to use Elkins as a sounding board for private misgivings that Otero might not be on the level with him. He wrote Elkins informing of the $500 that had been advanced to pay expenses for Otero's recent trip to Washington. He complained that Otero had gone to Washington to make a display of himself, and believed that Otero had not acted sincerely in his best interests.[25]

By April, Catron's bitterness was even more evident. He wrote to Elkins:

> The fact is that Otero is an ingrate and when he left here I raised the money to pay his expenses, on a positive promise that he would support me. I learn now that he has told others that if he supports me or recommends me he is afraid that he will lose his influence with McKinley. That is all bosh. . . . He tells all my friends that he has no objection to my appointment and would rather see me appointed than anyone else, but is afraid to recommend me.[26]

Miguel A. Otero, in the parlance of the times, was caught between a rock and a hard spot in regard to the appointment of Catron for United States attorney. The new order was taking over, and Otero was reluctant to buck the tide. The situation was clear to Elkins, Catron's staunchest supporter for the position. Catron had been prejudiced by his enemies in Washington, and Otero knew it. Elkins reported: Miguel Otero was afraid, although I think he wanted to do so, to push you vigorously. . . .[27]

Otero was willing to say that he had no objection to Catron's appointment but would not give him an unqualified endorsement. He was feeling his way over rocky shoals in unfamiliar waters and would go no further than he deemed prudent. Catron could not — or would not — see that his was a hopeless cause. He had devoted more of his time, fortune, and undivided loyalty to the Republican party in New Mexico than any other person of that time, and apparently he felt that his efforts should be rewarded regardless of the consequences to political aspirations of others — including Miguel A. Otero. Catron was insistent; Otero was adamant. The rift between them was complete. Efforts by others at conciliation were to no avail, and there developed between them one of the bitterest feuds in New Mexico history.

In later years Otero asserted that he had been reluctant to support Catron because the latter had, in the spring of 1897, advocated Solomon Luna for United States marshal over him. Otero claimed he had supported Catron for delegate to Congress in 1894, and Catron had promised to repay the political debt.[28] This may have been Otero's recollection in later years when the falling-out had gone beyond all reconciliation, but there is little doubt that, at the time, he endeavored to help Catron within limitations that he considered well advised.

Catron enlisted the aid of Pedro Perea, delegate to Congress, and Perea's successor in 1901, Bernard S. Rodey. Both did what they were able, but each found, as had Elkins and Otero, that Catron's enemies had made it an impossible task. Rodey, in a recommendation to Attorney General John W. Griggs, credited Catron with being "one of the ablest men in the nation, let alone in the territory."[29] It is true that, at the time, Rodey was under personal obligation to Catron who had loaned him money to save his home from foreclosure; nevertheless, Rodey's compliment seemed entirely sincere.

All along there was some reluctance on the part of President McKinley to remove Childers as United States attorney in favor of Catron, or any other candidate, because he saw an opportunity to pay a political debt to the Gold Democrats by retaining Childers in office. As time passed it became evident that Childers would be held over until the end of the normal four-year term. When the end of the term drew near, Childers changed his party affiliation and became a Republican. Catron's humiliation was complete when Childers was appointed for a subsequent four-year term. He accused Childers, probably with justification, of becoming a Republican merely to hold office, but the matter was finished; Catron finally gave up the hopeless quest. Four years later, when Childers' term expired, he recommended W. H. H. Llewellyn for United States attorney.*

As friction between Catron and Otero increased, their fight was carried on in the legislative assemblies of Otero's administration. Catron was a member of the Council from Santa Fe in 1899 and opposed Otero's fiscal policies. Otero spent money with a lavish hand and made the Palace of the Governors a center of social and political activities in New Mexico affairs. Catron accused Otero of extravagance; Otero deplored that Catron devoted "his brains and energy to crushing opposition to himself with no thought of public welfare."[30]

Under his leadership, with the patronage of his office as a potent weapon, Otero led the Republican party into organization of a political machine so powerful that the appointment of a notary public was considered an important political favor. Otero perfected an efficient political machine, controlled the press, was largely instrumental in selecting delegates, and ran the Territorial government like a growing business. He became so powerful that he "acknowledged no equal and brooked no rivalry to his leadership."[31] In order to gain favor in the inner circle, some of his followers, knowing of his quarrel with Catron, worked diligently to destroy Catron's public character in an effort to remove him from control of Santa Fe's Republican party. Their zealousness was not always encouraged by, or even known to, Otero. An example is the

---

*Catron to the Attorney General of the United States, July 16, 1904 (C.P. 105, Vol. 23). Catron had accurately predicted Childers' party switch.

infamous penitentiary poison plot early in 1899. Following is an account, in part, from the *Los Angeles Times*; it is a pungent commentary not only of the event but of New Mexico politics at the time as viewed from outside the Territory.

Santa Fe, the ancient capital of New Mexico, is in the throes of one of its annual political sensations. That is, one political faction is accusing the other of conspiring to assassinate somebody. A political contest in New Mexico that does not develop a conspiracy to murder is a tame affair, and not worthy of record, and a genuine political fight that does not result in the assassination of a few prominent citizens is a popular failure and a false alarm. . . .

The row that occupies the immediate attention of the patriots of Santa Fe takes the form of the prosecution of a number of prominent citizens on the charge of conspiring to destroy what purports to be the reputation and character of another prominent citizen by accusing him of putting up a job to poison a job-lot of his political enemies. The accusations on both sides are based on the sworn statements of a mangy scoundrel who has just served a term in the penitentiary.

This aforesaid mangy scoundrel is one Garner, who was sent up from Albuquerque for petty swindling. While a prisoner he made an affidavit that he was hired to break into the penitentiary for the purpose of poisoning a choice assortment of Democrats, including the governor, district attorney, prison warden, mayor of Santa Fe and a few others. All of these notables were to be invited to a banquet in the prison, and Garner was to put strychnine into their grub, and make a general clean-up of politicians obnoxious to one Tom Catron. . . .

When Garner swore that Catron had hired him to poison all the leading Democrats of Santa Fe, he found ready credence. All the men named as victims believed him as a matter of course. Some of them were prominent, others imagined themselves to be prominent, all were secretly tickled to be considered important enough to be removed from Catron's path with rough on rats. Garner's story would put shame to the productions of a nickel novelist or a New York Journal reporter. In his first affidavit he swore that he had been employed by Catron and Marshal Fornoff of Albuquerque to go to the penitentiary and poison the Santa Fe politicians. A part of his affidavit is as follows:

"It was explained to me that I could ascertain from the cooks when these parties that were to be killed would visit the penitentiary and dine there, and then I was to poison the food and in that way kill them. . . . I met Mr. Catron once in Albuquerque, out some distance from town, near a creek or ditch, and I talked with him and he with me fully about the killing of these men. I saw Fornoff and talked with him at the same time, but at a different place. Catron told me on that occasion that 'he did not want me to make an ass of myself as the

Borrego boys had done, so it would cost him more to get out of it than it did to do the job.' . . .

Among the alleged conspirators [against Catron] are ex-Governor, Thornton alias "Poker Bill," a [l]obby politician addicted to petty deception but probably not New Mexican enough to promote murder, notwithstanding his long association with Catron as a law partner; J. H. Crist, a small caliber lawyer and jobber, who imagines himself to be of as much importance as a yellow dog with a tin can on his tail; Col. Bergman, an old Prussian martinet, who was warden of the prison; Dr. J. H. Sloan, a leading physician and ardent politician, who would punch Catron's head at the drop of a hat, but wouldn't conspire to hurt a fly; an ex-sheriff and a few others of lesser note.

That these men gave a moment's consideration to Garner's clumsy tale is in itself an illuminant of Santa Fe politics. Catron, a lawyer and admitted to be a shrewd schemer and a man of some sense, signing a contract with a felon for the slaughter of half a dozen men at so much per head, is too fantastic a figure to be seriously considered. It is equally preposterous to suppose that half a dozen men having the sense attributed to domestic geese would conspire to induce a convict to tell such a fool tale. That the felon concocted the whole thing to gain favor with prison officials, and then worked Catron at the other end of the string is a rational conclusion that seems to have kept itself out of the minds of the entire outfit. . . .

The whole affair is characteristically New Mexican, and would be impossible anywhere except Santa Fe.[32]

Miguel A. Otero implied that he worked closely with Catron to establish the latter's innocence in the poison case.[33] This was true on the surface, but there was a matter behind the scenes that rankled Catron. The report of the grand jury investigating the matter thoroughly vindicated Catron but failed to bring an indictment against W. H. Garner — alias Schultz — because it was considered that he was of unsound mind. The part of the report dealing with the failure to indict Schultz, and the reason for it, was suppressed in the *Santa Fe New Mexican*.[34]

The *New Mexican* was controlled by Max Frost, an Otero supporter, and Catron looked upon this omission as an effort to cloud the issue and cast doubt in the reader's mind. Although the report vindicated Catron, apparently no indictment was found, so people would wonder if Catron's vindication were actually complete. The Otero faction had to admit publicly that Catron was in no way responsible for the plot; still, by implication, they created doubt that this was actually the full truth. Otero claims to have hoped that the hatchet was buried between him and Catron,[35] but this bit of duplicity seems to indicate that there was not full faith on the part of Otero and his adherents.

Concurrent with the poison plot occurred the trial of Oliver Lee and James Gilliland for the alleged murder of Albert J. Fountain and his son. The trial was to commence on May 25, and William Burr Childers, one of the prosecution attorneys, requested the benefit of Catron's counsel even if it was only for a day or two.[36] This request was an unusual recognition of Catron's ability, because Childers was aware of his efforts to displace him as United States attorney. Childers was also aware that Wilson Waddingham had died on May 16 and that Catron was involved in a desperate struggle to learn how badly he had been hurt by Waddingham's manipulations, the nefarious facets of which had only then been revealed by the untimely death. Despite the seriousness of Catron's personal problems, he complied with Childers' request.

The next major eruption of the feud between Catron and Otero occurred in connection with the Territorial Convention for the purpose of electing six delegates to represent New Mexico at the Republican National Convention to be held in June 1900. Otero accused Catron of causing a bolt by arranging a fusion ticket made up of Democrats and Catron Republicans.[37]

Catron's version was different. He claimed to have been nominated chairman of the convention and that the governor's doorkeeper, Antonio Alarid, was nominated against him. When the roll of the sixty-seven delegates was called, Catron was assured of victory; therefore fifteen of those favorable to Otero withdrew and named a committee to put up a ticket of local officials for the coming election. They named David M. White as candidate for the Council. The straight Republican Convention continued with the remaining fifty-two delegates, elected Catron chairman, and nominated him for the Council.[38]

In the election that followed, Charles Easley, the Democratic candidate, was elected with 1,300 votes. Catron received 1,283, while White — the Otero faction candidate — received 291 votes. There is justification in Catron's contention that if he was a factionist he was quite strong and the other candidate quite weak. He maintained that the whole bolt was initiated by Otero who attended the meeting when it put up the bolting ticket, and by Max Frost, editor of the *New Mexican*.* Furthermore, Catron claimed that the governor had promised J. Francisco Chavez, president of the Council, appointment as superintendent of public schools if Chavez would fix a rule requiring a two-thirds vote of all Council members before Catron could get a hearing in the Council, or before a report from the committee on privileges and election could be made. To cinch the matter, Charles A. Spiess was made chairman of the committee of five members, three of whom were hostile to Catron.[39] Spiess, who had been appointed district attorney by Otero, was a bitter enemy of Catron, although he had formerly been his partner.

The circumstances of Catron's defeat increased his determination to fight Otero with every means at his command. Catron's wide correspondence caused him to believe there was much discontent with Otero's growing power in the Territory. He was convinced that if the governor's remaining in office could be determined by a mandate of the people, he would be removed. Of course Otero served at the discretion of President McKinley, so Catron determined to work through him. Along with others, he decided to present charges against Otero to the president. Otero's term expired on June 7,

---

*Catron to Elkins, January 13, 1901 (C.P. 105, Vol. 18). Otero, *Nine Years as Governor*, p. 132, contradicts himself. He blames Catron for the bolt and, on page 196, admits that Catron encouraged David M. White to run on an independent ticket, thus causing the election of Charles F. Easley. Furthermore, he admits advising some members of the Council to defeat any contest Catron might file.

1901, and by that date numerous protests against the reappointment of Otero were on file with the president and attorney general. Eugene A. Fiske had earlier competed against Catron for appointment as United States attorney but now worked with him in a cause each considered more important than personal differences. Both enlisted the aid of Frederick (Fritz) Muller, a former Rough Rider. It was thought that Muller would be a useful contact to work through Vice President Theodore Roosevelt.

To replace Otero, Catron suggested Quinby Vance, a former surveyor general, but he was not as interested in any particular appointee as he was in ousting Otero. Because of dissension between the Catron and Otero factions of the Republican party, other persons presented themselves as candidates thinking they might gain preferment. Among these was Charles H. Elmendorf, formerly of Nebraska, who was then engaged as manager of Catron's American Valley enterprise. Another was Francis Tracy Tobin, Philadelphia lawyer and Catron friend.[40] Others mentioned at the time were Joshua S. Raynolds and Rufus J. Palen.

On June 1, 1901, Otero left for Washington to answer charges filed against him. He later maintained that he experienced no particular difficulty and believed that his friendship with McKinley assured his reappointment.[41] Charles H. Elmendorf, an on-the-scene reporter, thought that Otero and his friends had been hopeful but not at all confident. Nevertheless, Otero prevailed when, on June 15, President McKinley presented him with his commission. Catron believed that Jefferson Raynolds, who had access to McKinley through relations to his wife, was largely influential in the matter.

In Catron's disappointment he was moved to remark:

"This appointment . . . is going to injure the Territory very much and hold it down. If the ring rule which now prevails here is to continue, I am of the opinion that many of our best people will pull out. If I could get 50¢ on the dollar for my property I would go."[42]

Otero was confident of security in his position for another four years; however, the assassination of President Mc-

Kinley in September of 1901 reopened the issue of governorship in New Mexico. Catron and Fiske, through a New Mexico Reform League, made a new move to have Otero dismissed and replaced, this time, by Frederick Muller. In October Catron submitted a long and detailed memorandum to President Theodore Roosevelt. This letter, as well as answers made by Otero in later years, may be studied by an interested reader.*

Catron and his associates believed that Muller, because of his former association with Roosevelt as a Rough Rider, would be a likely candidate in the move to replace Otero. W. H. H. Llewellyn, however, was Roosevelt's chief source of information concerning the Rough Riders in New Mexico, and Llewellyn supported Otero.

To weaken Llewellyn's influence, Catron sought to expose a skeleton in his closet. In November 1901 Catron wrote to Joseph Reed of Council Bluffs, Iowa, asking for information concerning some crime Llewellyn had been tried for in Iowa. Reed answered that Llewellyn had been accused of assault to commit murder but had been acquitted by the jury on the grounds of self-defense. He was only a boy at the time, and the man he shot was unpopular. The scrap was about a woman, and perhaps the jurors felt that the victim, being a family man, ought to have had more sense than to become involved with a boy about a petticoat.[43]

Former Governor L. Bradford Prince, who was generally no friend of Catron and himself aspired to the governorship, submerged his own feelings and lined up with the move to oust Otero. Mrs. Prince was a daughter of Colonel Sam Beardsley who was influential with Senator John T. Morgan of Alabama. Morgan promised assistance. Another former governor of New Mexico, General Lew Wallace, likewise no

---

* Otero, *Nine Years as Governor,* pp. 188–98, 373–84. Otero answered, in a general way, most of the charges made by Catron. There was, nevertheless, one significant omission — that of any reference to General W. H. Whiteman, Otero's adjutant general who later figured in more significant charges made by Catron in an effort to prevent a third term for Otero.

friend of Catron, was also in the fight against Otero. Wallace, like Roosevelt, was a man of letters and was a friend of the president, so his influence was important.

In the next move against Otero, Eugene A. Fiske was accorded an interview with President Roosevelt, who referred him to the secretary of the interior for more detailed discussion. In Fiske's talk with the latter, it developed that both the president and the secretary were displeased with the men Otero had selected for office in New Mexico when he had been appointed by President McKinley earlier in June. Otero had promised to get rid of these appointees; on the strength of this promise, both Secretary Ethan Allen Hitchcock and his chief were inclined to retain Otero in office even though it was revealed that he had not answered a single charge against himself except by typewritten memorandum, not signed and of course not sworn to. His answer had consisted, for the most part, of calling the men who had made the charges liars. Furthermore, his supporters reportedly spent more than $5,000 in behalf of retaining him in office.

It may have been that Otero's antagonists relied too heavily on Frederick Muller as a candidate to supplant him. President Roosevelt told Fiske that he liked "Fritz" and would do almost anything for him but did not believe that he sized up for governor. Further conversation revealed that General Lew Wallace had made Fiske "quite solid" with the president and, in their discussion, Roosevelt asked if he would accept the governorship. Fiske replied that he "did not want it and could not afford to take it."[44] With no acceptable alternate in view, it appears that Roosevelt had no choice but to continue with Otero.

The fight for control of the Republican party in New Mexico continued throughout Otero's administration. Numerous letters were received by Catron indicating widespread opposition to Otero throughout New Mexico, and Catron was repeatedly called upon to head up this opposition. In 1902 the

Oteroites spread the word that Catron had "withdrawn from all contests and fights." Catron set the record straight when he wrote:

> I wish to tell you plainly that I withdraw from nothing; I propose to be in at the finish and all through the game. You can count on that from top to bottom.[45]

He further stated:

> They have made a very villianous, mean and ugly fight against me in this place by means of lying, by the expenditure of money, by threatening individuals, by using all the employees in every way, threatening to discharge them and threatening to prosecute them and everything that could be imagined, or thought of, and they have intimidated, scared and worked a great many people to change them over, but there is no change I think. They may beat me in this county, but I think they will not.[46]

Otero, in his recollections of later years, stated that at the Santa Fe County Convention that year the Catron faction bolted and named a contesting delegation.[47] Newspapers favorable to Otero at the time reported the same thing. Catron on the scene, told the full story in an immediate report to Frank Hubbell, chairman of the Republican Central Committee. Sixty-three delegates, authorized by that committee, met to elect two delegates to the Territorial Convention to be held at Raton. Catron called the convention to order and received nominations for temporary chairman. E. C. Abbott was nominated on behalf of the Otero-Frost adherents, and R. L. Baca for those sympathetic to the opposition headed by Catron. A call of the roll, carefully tallied by Catron, resulted in 32 votes for Baca and 31 for Abbott. The vote, nevertheless, was announced as 30 for Abbott and 28 only for Baca — five short of the total voting. In the resulting furor two meetings were held in the same room with 32 participants in the Catron camp and 31 siding with the Otero opposition. The former, having the majority, were later recognized and their delegates certified to the Raton Convention.[48]

In 1904 Catron was elected to represent Santa Fe County in the Council despite determined opposition by Otero adherents and difficulty in carrying on his campaign because he was badly injured in a fall from a buggy.[49] That year he again supported Bernard S. Rodey for election as delegate to Congress. Rodey had been elected in 1900 and reelected in 1902. Catron prophetically warned him that Otero was no friend of his and was not in favor of his nomination. Shortly before the convention Governor Otero informed Rodey that he would not support him for renomination unless he agreed not to appoint Frank Hubbell as chairman of the Republican Central Committee. Rodey refused to agree to this stipulation, so Otero prevailed upon William H. Andrews to become a candidate for delegate. Andrews, who had only recently moved to New Mexico, reluctantly agreed and was nominated. Catron and Hubbell promptly formed an independent Republican party and nominated Rodey to head the ticket.

Rodey was defeated in the following election. Andrews received 22,305 votes to Rodey's 3,149. The Democratic candidate, G. P. Money, was out of the running with 17,125 votes. Catron and his followers were widely blamed for fusing with the Democrats. He must have known that an independent ticket would not have much chance of success and that defeat would hurt him politically, but he had promised Rodey his support and refused to follow Otero's lead in dumping him.*

Catron's major political effort now was to see that Otero was not appointed for a third term. Despite Otero's sly infer-

---

* Otero, *Nine Years as Governor,* pp. 232–33, states that another reason for withdrawing his support from Rodey was the latter's advocacy of joint statehood with Arizona (see also chapter 16). This author cannot agree with Howard Roberts Lamar, *The Far Southwest, 1846–1912,* p. 495, that Catron backed Andrews or that the election was close. Catron opposed Andrews on the grounds that he was not a good candidate and that he would not be good for statehood. He said of Andrews: "I am decidedly opposed to his election because he obtained [the nomination] by very unfair means and because he is dishonest and disreputable." Catron to Pedro Perea, October 29, 1904 (C.P. 105, Vol. 23). It is true that Catron later worked with Andrews in attaining statehood, but he was unquestionably opposed to him at this time.

ence that he was not a candidate for renomination because he deserved a vacation,[50] the last months of his administration were attended by considerable behind-the-scenes maneuvering over whether or not he would be a candidate. Typical is the following statement:

> I received your letter of November 3rd just previous to the election and four or five days after I made an agreement with Andrews and Bursum to support Andrews, based on assurance from Otero, guaranteed by Andrews and Bursum, that Otero would not be a candidate for reappointment as Governor, and that if he should be such he would not receive the support of the Republican organization. This was a very formal verbal agreement . . . .[51]

Throughout much of his administration Otero won most of the battles in his war with Catron, but a reversal of form came with dramatic suddenness near the end of Otero's tenure in office. For eight years Catron had been warning that there was corruption in Otero's administration. Twice he had been instrumental in submitting formal charges to Washington, and both times was confounded when the charges were overlooked and Otero was returned as governor. But his lifelong habit of persistent attention to detail finally paid off. He had been quietly adding details to a considerable body of charges against the governor; only months before the end of Otero's administration, an event occurred that gave him positive proof of skullduggery in high places.

As early as 1901 Catron had warned President Roosevelt that:

Governor Otero has appointed as his adjutant-general at a salary of one thousand dollars per annum, W. H. Whiteman, who was appointed by President Harrison, associate justice of the supreme court of New Mexico, and failed of confirmation in the senate because he embezzled money he had collected for some Swiss clients as their attorney in this territory. The Swiss minister or consul-general at New York preferred charges against Whiteman when he was appointed, for embezzlement. The matter was investigated, found true, and Whiteman was either rejected or his name withdrawn. Governor Otero knew of these facts, yet thereafter appointed him to said office.[52]

Early in February 1905 Whiteman became involved in a scandal for which, regardless of anything he may have done in the past, he was not to blame. A signed affidavit by Nelson N. Newell revealed that about three years earlier Page B. Otero, the governor's brother, had, upon at least three occasions, procured a quantity of military stores that were in the custody of Adjutant General Whiteman — including rifles, ammunition, blankets, and camping equipment — by means of shaping a blank key to fit the lock. A comic opera touch was added by the fact that Otero broke the key off in the lock and had the devil's own time extricating it.[53] These stores found their way to a ranch owned jointly by Governor Otero and his secretary of state.

Whiteman, being responsible for the military stores, had no recourse but to report the matter to the War Department. A perfunctory investigation was made, and Governor Otero brought back from his ranch a part of the supplies, thus admitting to that extent the correctness of the charges made by Whiteman. Governor Otero, to punish Whiteman, now procured eight indictments against him from the grand jury charging him with obtaining warrants of the Territory upon false pretenses. The fact is the warrants were for a perfectly legitimate use in connection with the proper distribution of militia stores and were obtained in a manner suggested by the governor himself. Moreover, one indictment would have legally sufficed, had Otero really believed that Whiteman was guilty of any criminal intent in violating the law.

At the suggestion of the court, he was tried on the strongest indictment, with the understanding that if there was no conviction the other indictments would be dismissed. The case was tried and the jury instructed to find for the defendant. The other indictments were not dismissed but were held over to the next term of court. With the indictments still held over his head, Whiteman was prevented from securing other employment he sought in the East. Backed to the wall, he saw no other recourse than to file formal charges against Otero with the Justice Department in Washington.*

Catron now quietly secured an audience with President Roosevelt. Armed with numerous items reflecting on the Otero administration, including the Newell and Whiteman affidavits, he saw the president on June 14, 1905. Exactly what Roosevelt said to him is not known, but he probably stated that Otero would not be reappointed, and may well have advanced a plea for party unity. Whatever the conversation, it was sufficiently important that Catron decided to withdraw the charges against Otero.†

Catron's appointment with the president had been a carefully kept secret. That very evening there was held in Santa Fe a "smoker" to celebrate the eighth anniversary of the governor's term in office. Those who attended the affair came away confident that Otero would be able to succeed himself. Catron's informant stated:

> This information is obtained by me upon positive declaration on my part of no knowledge of the politicial situation. It seems to me they are quite hopeful and wholly in the dark as to what opposition is being made.

Not knowing that Catron had succeeded in that opposition, he added:

---

* W. H. Whiteman affidavit, March 25, 1905 (C.P. 402, Box 1). The Newell and Whiteman affidavits were notarized by Catron's secretary, W. A. Barney, and were undoubtedly prepared in Catron's office. There is also evidence that Otero sought to vent his spleen on Catron at this time. In February and March 1905 Otero had corresponded with George W. Hall, stock inspector for Montana, at Havre, concerning the whereabouts of W. C. Moore, who was still wanted in connection with the murder of Alexis Grossetete and Robert Elsinger in the American Valley two decades earlier. (Otero Papers, State Records Center, Santa Fe.) Malicious rumors were still rife (as they are today) that Catron played some nefarious part in these murders. The timing of this correspondence was such as to indicate Otero may have wished to use any information gained against Catron.

† Catron to William Loeb, Private Secretary to the President, June 20, 1905 (C.P. 105, Vol. 23). Catron withdrew the charges against Otero on the day following his visit with President Roosevelt by means of a telegram sent while on the train to Chicago en route to Santa Fe.

God forbid that we should have another four years' reign of the present little Czar and that the rascals should go unpunished.[54]

Otero maintains that in October 1905 he called on Roosevelt and told the president that he was not a candidate for reappointment but that the best people in New Mexico wanted him to continue and he would serve if the president saw fit to reappoint him. Roosevelt is said to have replied that he wished he had known of Otero's attitude earlier because he would not have considered appointing anyone else if he had known that Otero would accept.* If this is true it would seem that, in view of Roosevelt's conversation with Catron earlier, he must have been speaking with tongue in cheek.

In October 1905 James J. Hagerman inquired of Catron how much money was paid out under Joint Resolution no. 7, approved February 22, 1905, and if there were proper vouchers with the auditor or treasurer showing how the money was spent. He had heard that the money had been disbursed without any detailed accounting for expenditures.[55]

Catron, after exhaustive examination into the matter, reported that $12,000 had been appropriated for payment of contingent expenses of the legislative assembly. He was unable to ascertain how, when, where, to whom, or for what purpose these monies were paid, although he inquired at the office of the auditor, the governor, and presidents of the Council and House. He then added a detailed analysis of where some of the money might have gone. Public printing was done by the *New Mexican* printing office, managed by Max Frost, in the name of Duncan and McNair, public printers. Catron learned by astute questioning of Frost and others that the governor's message printed in Spanish consisted of about 900 pages, yet payment was made for 3,000 pages.[56]

Hagerman's answer to Catron was a fitting tribute to his perseverance in fighting an administration that he understood to be corrupt and selfish. Hagerman said:

---

* Otero, *Nine Years as Governor,* p. 336. Otero states that the president gave him advance information of his intention to appoint Herbert J. Hagerman as governor.

I am much obliged for your full and illuminating letter of Oct. 24. It is worse than I thought. When honest men in charge of public (or any other) business want to do what is fair and square they do not first have to create a big blanket to hide under. If we should have four years more of that way of doing things, where would we land? You have one satisfactory thing to look back to, and that is that you stood up like a lone rock and protested vigorously.[57]

Interestingly enough, three months later, on January 22, 1906, the elder Hagerman's son, Herbert J. Hagerman, was installed as governor of the Territory of New Mexico.

15
Retrocession

In a number of respects the period from 1906 through 1911 was a low period in the life and fortunes of Thomas Benton Catron. He was plagued by ever increasing financial problems and business reverses, and his political fortunes were at a low ebb. He had been countered politically at nearly every turn during the administration of Miguel A. Otero as Territorial governor. His voice in the political affairs of the Republican party in New Mexico was still heard but only in a relative whisper from his stronghold in Santa Fe. Here on April 6, 1906, he was elected mayor,[1] but this office consumed little of his restless energy.

Late the previous year there had been a rumor that President Roosevelt intended to appoint Herbert J. Hagerman to succeed Otero. In view of Catron's feud of several years standing with Otero, any replacement was welcome; nevertheless, Catron took an early and sincere interest in the appointment.

Hagerman, the son of James J. Hagerman, the enterprising developer of railroad and irrigation facilities in the Pecos Valley, had graduated with honors from Cornell University. He entered the State Department with plans to become a career diplomat, a position for which he was admirably suited by temperament, education, and personality. Ethan Allen

Hitchcock was appointed ambassador to Russia and took young Hagerman with him as second secretary of the embassy. Hitchcock, who later became secretary of the interior, was pleased with Hagerman, and, when President Roosevelt sought a successor for Governor Otero,* recommended his appointment.

When word came to Catron of the probable appointment, he wrote to the father, James J. Hagerman, expressing his pleasure and offering advice. This counsel was not unsolicited, for the elder Hagerman had earlier sought information from him concerning facets of corruption in the Otero administration. Catron wrote concerning the rumor:

> If such is the case and he is to be appointed, I shall be very much pleased, especially if he will take immediate steps to have the "Aegean stables" cleaned and they ought to be cleaned in one day, as Hercules was required to clean the ancient ones. . . .[2]

Catron suggested that to do this, new Territorial officials should be appointed all along the line and especially the attorney general, district attorney for the Santa Fe district, and superintendent of the penitentiary. He urged that criminal prosecution should be carried on against the plunderers of public funds and rendered assurance that the grossest rottenness would be found everywhere.

In his letter to Hagerman, Catron expressed a desire to be appointed attorney general and requested the father to speak to his son with reference to his appointment if it could be done with propriety. Catron said he did not want the position for the salary; indeed, that was related to one of the matters he wished to see corrected. He maintained that, in one way or another, all Territorial officials were drawing more salary than they were entitled to by law. Catron's object was to reduce expenses and compel officials to live upon legitimate salaries.

---

* George Curry, *Autobiography,* p. 192, states that Otero was charged with disrupting the Republican party in New Mexico and that President Roosevelt requested his resignation in the interest of party harmony.

If appointed, he promised that he would use the courts to take the place of the river which Hercules had used to remove rapidly the uncleanliness which had accumulated.[3]

A few days later Catron wrote to President Theodore Roosevelt stating his belief that Hagerman would be a competent governor and that, since he had not participated in factional controversy, his appointment would accomplish the healing of differences within the Republican party. He urged that new appointments would be necessary if the prospective governor were to accomplish this purpose.[4]

Hagerman was appointed and, on January 22, 1906, was installed as governor. Despite Catron's urging, and that of numerous other New Mexico Republicans, several Territorial and district offices continued to be occupied by Otero appointees. This was one factor in the ultimate failure of Hagerman's administration, but there were others. When he took office he furnished his residence luxuriously and installed a staff of servants, including a Negro butler. This was an innovation for the politicians with whom the new governor had to deal, and one about which they were inclined to joke. While this was a small matter, it pointed to a fundamental reason for Hagerman's failure. His qualifications for a foreign diplomatic career were excellent, but he lacked experience in the rough-and-ready practical politics prevalent in New Mexico. He was completely honest and sincere but lacked tact to carry out his high-minded reforms.*

Governor Hagerman let it be known that he had been sent to New Mexico to clean house and to restore harmony in the Republican party. The president had been fully advised of contentions over leadership in that party; moreover, many reports had reached the White House of alleged graft and mismanagement of official business in the Otero administration. President Roosevelt wanted malfeasance corrected, if it existed, and desired that party harmony be restored. The new

---

* George Curry believed that Hagerman was ill advised early in his administration and laid much of the blame for inferior counsel on Neill B. Field. *Autobiography*, p. 194.

governor struck out blindly without adequate investigation
and soon found most of the Republican leadership against
him. The result was a movement to "get" Hagerman. One
potent tool in this campaign was the charge that he created
more disunity among Republicans than existed before his
arrival in New Mexico.

Catron was not then among the top leaders of the Republican party and did not seek Hagerman's removal. Dominating the leadership were Holm O. Bursum, chairman of the
Republican Central Committee, national committeeman Solomon Luna, and Territorial secretary Jefferson Raynolds.[5]
When Hagerman took office, Bursum was superintendent of
the penitentiary, having been appointed by Governor Otero.
Hagerman, hearing persistent rumors of irregularities in
prison finance and administration, employed an independent
auditor to check the records. The result was a report of an
alleged shortage of $7,500.

The matter was placed before the grand jury by District
Attorney Robert C. Gortner who was, at the time, Catron's
partner. By a close vote there was failure to return an indictment, so no criminal prosecution followed. However, the
prison records indicated that money had been received and not
accounted for, so Gortner recommended that civil action be
instituted to recover the money in question.[6]

Hagerman removed Bursum and formally demanded that
he pay the alleged shortage. This Bursum did, but under protest. The case was tried in district court, and Bursum was
ultimately exonerated.*

Bursum now vengefully declared open war on the new

---

* Bursum's alleged misconduct was later used against him and was instrumental
in his failure to be elected the first governor of New Mexico as a state. A special
referee was appointed to again examine the books. District Attorney Gortner
inspected the referee's report and concluded that "If the referee's totals are correct,
then Mr. Bursum did not owe the Territory of New Mexico the items which were
presented before the Grand Jury as evidence of shortage against him." Gortner to
Frank W. Parker, July 11, 1907 (C.P. 109, Vol. 9). It is evident that Bursum bore no
personal ill feeling against Gortner or, if he did, concealed it well. He later endorsed
Gortner for attorney general under Governor Curry, but Curry selected James M.
Hervey for the position. Bursum to Gortner, November 29, 1907 (C.P. 103, Box 30).

governor, and many Republican leaders supported him, but the party was split wide open. Democratic leaders seized gleefully upon the discomfiture of their opponents. Word of the disharmony soon reached President Roosevelt. Other irritations followed in close enough order to convince the president that he had made a mistake in appointing Hagerman, so the president called the governor to the White House for an explanation. Hagerman tried to explain the many complications of the difficulty, but Roosevelt was not impressed. He called for Governor Hagerman's resignation, which was tendered on April 20, 1907.*

Meanwhile, Catron was having political problems of his own. In the election of 1906, he ran for a seat in the legislative council. The governor had reapportioned the counties, adding Sandoval County to Santa Fe County, which had previously been a council district by itself. Epimenio Miera, from Sandoval County, was also a candidate. Prior to the election Miera induced the probate clerk to have only his name printed on the ballots and to delete Catron's name. This required that Catron's name be inserted by pasters, a procedure that over the years resulted in a great deal of fraud. It was possible, by unscrupulous manipulation, to provide ballots at the polls without the pasters properly fixed thereon. Then too, Catron maintained that the apportionment had been illegal, and he cited Territorial law to support his contention. For these reasons he expressed his intention of contesting the election which had resulted in a majority for Miera in the combined counties, although Catron received a majority in Santa Fe County. Mindful of the schism in the Republican party, he explained that his action would not affect other districts.[7]

Before initiating the contest, he learned that Governor Hagerman had consulted with Miera before making the apportionment, so reasoned that the divisions were probably made on Miera's advice. Subsequently, Catron did not contest the

---

*Curry, *Autobiography,* pp. 192–99, is an excellent summary of the controversy.

election, probably because he did not wish to add further to the factional splits in the Republican party at that time.

To heal the wounds of that party, President Roosevelt had in mind George Curry as a successor to Governor Hagerman. Curry had been a captain in Roosevelt's Rough Rider regiment and later served in the Philippine Islands in the army as chief of police of the city of Manila. He was governor of Samar when the President called on him to serve as governor of New Mexico. By August 1907 Curry finished his interim duties and was inaugurated as governor of New Mexico on the eighth of that month.*

Catron approved of George Curry as governor and showed his approval in a tangible way. Congress was not in session when Curry took office. In January 1908 his appointment was up for confirmation before the United States Senate. There seemed to be some delay, so Catron asked Stephen B. Elkins to look into the matter. On behalf of Curry, he explained:

I think that Curry is the best man who has ever been appointed for Governor of New Mexico; he seems to be entirely satisfactory to the entire people of the Territory and we all want him confirmed. . . . I do not believe that any reasonable or tangible objection can be made to Governor Curry and believe that our people all want him, regardless of politics.†

In 1908 Catron replaced Epimenio Miera for the seat in the legislative council that Miera had won over him in the disputed election of 1906. At the district nominating convention Miera had threatened to bolt and swing Sandoval County to the Democrats if he were not nominated. Governor Curry and other Republican leaders interceded with offers of a compro-

---

* Twitchell, *Leading Facts of New Mexican History,* Vol. 2, pp. 550–51, indicates that Roosevelt requested Hagerman to find a suitable position in his administration for Curry, who desired to return to New Mexico. All that Hagerman offered was the position of game warden. Twitchell ventures the opinion that had Hagerman replaced Raynolds with Curry as territorial secretary, it would have reacted favorably to his administration.

† Catron to S. B. Elkins, January 8, 1908 (C.P. 105, Vol. 26). Curry, *Autobiography,* is somewhat more reserved in his general estimate of Catron.

mise, by which Miera withdrew from the senatorial race and ran for the House of Representatives. In turn Governor Curry, Holm O. Bursum, and Solomon Luna used their influence to have Miera elected speaker of the house.[8]

During this session of the legislature Governor Curry presented a list of his appointees to the Senate for confirmation and was accorded approval of all appointments except that of former Governor Miguel A. Otero for treasurer. Otero was opposed by Senators Catron and L. Bradford Prince. Curry knew that Catron's leadership could block Otero's confirmation. He called on Catron at his home to explain that he was under obligation to Otero for having appointed him an officer in the Rough Rider regiment. Without that appointment he could not have won the friendship of Colonel Roosevelt and would not have been appointed governor. While Catron did not like Otero, when appealed to in this manner, he unhesitatingly promised to make the motion for his confirmation. This he did, but Prince was not as generous. He voted with a few others against Otero's acceptance.

In December 1908 occurred an event that saddened Catron as did few other things in his life. His partner, Robert C. Gortner decided to move permanently to California. Gortner had come to New Mexico early in 1891 from Goshen, Indiana, and was soon employed by Catron as his secretary. He was an extraordinarily capable young man in typing and shorthand; moreover, his intelligence was matched by his wit and charm.* Physically impressive and handsome at six feet in height and 170 pounds in weight, he was athletically inclined, having been a champion bicycle rider in his youth. Light hearted and gay, he offered a marked contrast to the stern exterior of his employer. But the older man saw something in the youngster that he found in few others — a permanent friend. He tutored

---

* Robert Gortner's early letters to people in his home town are preserved (C.P. 109, Vol. 1).

young Gortner in the law and, when he was ready in 1896, made him his partner.*

It is notable that his unhappiness at the loss of his partner was followed the next year by his greatest bereavement; his wife, Julia, died on November 8, 1909. Of the four sons, Thom was in the Philippine Islands and Fletcher was in attendance at the University of Chicago. Catron wrote to Fletcher, his youngest son:

> She was your best friend, and now I am left as your best friend. I ask you to constantly think of her, remember what she wished you to be. She wanted you to be a bright, intelligent, well educated, honest and industrious man; She wanted you to aid me along with the aids which Charlie is giving me; she often spoke of what she and I might do by way of travel and seeking comfort when I could safely leave all my business affairs in the hands of yourself and Charlie.[9]

But even as he wrote to his son, the father's thoughts were also with Bob Gortner, his former partner. In his letter to Fletcher he wrote:

> I had hoped that Mr. Gortner would remain with me and that would enable me to retire and look after my health, and more particularly that of your mother.[10]

He had already written to Gortner:

> I want you back. I am not feeling well, but will brace up and be all right in a short time, but my private business demands all of my time and I need your help in it also. Charlie is doing splendidly, he is a good lawyer and will improve. Some day I hope to have Fletcher in the office, but I am 69 years old and want to get out of the law practice as soon as I can do so safely, so come back. I think you can do better here than there; you and your wife have many friends.[11]

Gortner answered promptly:

> It has just reached the point with me where I know I can succeed here, and now comes your letter which makes me blue all through. . . . There was never a stronger attachment between men than I had for

---

* See Appendix 1. Gortner left the partnership from March 1899 to April 1901 to devote his full time as district attorney of the first judicial district.

you — and still have. It grieves me deeply to feel that I can't, simply can't go back and live there. The damned little dirty town, made rotten enough by the mere presence there of that despicable little Renehan, and filled for the rest with jealous gossiping women, would be a hell on earth for Zip and me.... This old world is a kind of an angular ball, sometimes, isn't it?*

At the same time Gortner wrote to Charles Catron:

I almost feel at times that I will throw up everything here, and go back there, and take hold of his work, and help him, and let the damned gossips and dogs that live in that town yelp and howl as much as they want to. I love your Father, devotedly; he is, I believe, the best friend I ever had, and now when he says, after nearly a year, that he wants me, I don't know how I can refuse.[12]

Charles Catron answered Gortner with an illuminating observation about his father. Catron had talked to his son about retiring so he could enjoy the rest of his life. Charles was afraid, though, that if he had no work to do he might go under. He was satisfied that his father would work as long as he lived simply for the pleasure of it.[13]

Throughout the summer that had just passed Governor Curry had been having differences of opinion with his immediate superior in Washington, Secretary of the Interior R. A. Ballinger.† As a result, on October 25, 1909, Curry sent his resignation to President Taft to be effective February 8, 1910. Less than two weeks after his wife's death, Catron wrote to President Taft asking that he try to induce Governor Curry to withdraw his resignation:

It is my desire in writing this to state to you that I have known every Governor of New Mexico who has served as such since I have been in the territory quite intimately, and that George Curry is the

---

* Gortner to Catron, November 14, 1909 (C.P. 103, Box 34). Zip was a nickname for Gortner's wife, Zepora. The Renehan referred to was A. B. Renehan. Precisely what Renehan did to cause this uncharacteristic outburst from Gortner is not known. Some time later Gortner wrote to Catron: "as you know, Renehan stole a number of my letters from Charlie's desk...." Gortner to Catron, March 25, 1910 (C.P. 103, Box 35).

† Curry, *Autobiography*, pp. 242–49, presents this controversy fairly and dispassionately.

only one of them who has seemed to take hold of the matters as Governor in the right way and identified himself with the interest and welfare of the Territory. All others have been schemers for their own political advancement. I would suggest that if you could induce Governor Curry to withdraw his resignation and remain in office until we shall acquire statehood, it would be of great benefit to the Republican Party in making New Mexico beyond question a Republican State. . . .[14]

It is a little saddening to realize that George Curry in no appreciable measure reciprocated Catron's wholehearted endorsement; but then, Curry was only one of many who failed to return Catron's honest praise.

As it developed, President Taft had already accepted Governor Curry's resignation when Catron wrote to him. It is probable that Curry could not have been dissuaded in any case. Taft chose Chief Justice William J. Mills to succeed Curry. While Catron had recommended Nathan Jaffa he was equally pleased with the selection of Mills; in fact, he had not thought that Mills would accept, but was delighted when he had. Mills, an able lawyer and excellent judge, had not been an active candidate but was of the conservative type in politics that appealed to President Taft. Catron was convinced that his appointment would do much to assure that New Mexico would join the Union as a Republican state.[15]

Catron had now lived a full and eventful life. Most men of the age of sixty-nine years would have ceased to strive for new goals, but Catron's drive and energy had not yet run their course. Ahead was another decade of new adventures and mastery of unusual challenges.

16
Statehood

The history of New Mexico has been unique in many ways, and its unparalleled quest for statehood stands out as one of the most unusual features of that history. No other state strove as valiantly for admission or was rebuked as many times when on the threshold of success. Some fifty Congressional acts were introduced between 1849 and 1910 calling for New Mexico statehood. The forces of national politics consistently played a role in the statehood movement. Opening of the slavery issue in 1850 became an insurmountable obstacle prior to the Civil War. After the Civil War

the many bills for New Mexico's statehood were blocked because of bitter antagonism over Reconstruction, the intense rivalry between the two major parties, and the East's fear of Western domination in the Senate. Unfortunately, more potent forces working against statehood were religious bigotry, racial discrimination, and general ignorance concerning conditions in the Southwest. Even the free-silver issue and the Populist crusade were factors.[1]

Much of the failure to achieve statehood, however, must be attributed to conditions within New Mexico; many residents there preferred Territorial status. For the most part mining interests, substantial merchants, railroads, and some large land owners opposed statehood because they feared an increase in taxes. Politicians in the Territory wanted statehood when their party was in power but were fearful of the initial advantage to the opposition when it was not; consequently, there was usually political resistance at any given time. In general, Republicans favored and Democrats impugned statehood, but there were responsible exceptions on both sides.

By the treaty of Guadalupe Hidalgo, ratified May 30, 1848, "New Mexico became a part of the United States with a guarantee that her people should be admitted into the Union at the proper time on an equal footing with the other states."[2] President James K. Polk urged that early statehood advocates in New Mexico take no action until Congress had provided them with a civil government. Despite this advice, in October 1848 a faction in the area, acting upon a suggestion made by Thomas Hart Benton, drew up a memorial to Congress requesting a Territorial form of government. One clause requested protection from the introduction of slavery.

When this memorial was read to Congress, Southern senators attacked New Mexico vigorously. Antislavery advocates of the North then deluged Congress with petitions urging that slavery be abolished from the territory newly acquired from Mexico. The status of any new government in New Mexico thus became linked with the national political issue of the extension of slavery. This identification was to plague New Mexico in many ways in the years to come.

In 1849 the new president, Zachary Taylor, expressed hope that Congress would soon admit New Mexico into the Union as a state. As a practical aid toward this goal, in the spring of 1849 Taylor sent James S. Calhoun, an Indian agent, with unofficial authorization to promote a drive for state government. Another new arrival, Colonel George A. McCall, had instructions from the secretary of war to promote statehood. McCall insisted that a Territorial form of government would not be granted, so in the spring of 1850 a convention was elected and assembled at Santa Fe to adopt a state constitution.*

---

* In the fall of 1849 another convention had drafted a plan for Territorial government and elected Hugh N. Smith as delegate to Congress. In July 1859 the House refused to admit Smith as Territorial delegate.

A governor, legislature, and congressman were elected. Catron further tells the story:

> The legislature assembled and elected two United States Senators. The Senators and Representative were sent to Washington to present the Constitution and recommend our admission. President Taylor, who was at the time the chief executive, laid the Constitution before Congress and recommended our admission. A lengthy debate was had upon the proposition to admit us, the democratic party very generally opposing us, and the Whig party very generally supporting us. The act failed, it is believed, because the constitution which was presented absolutely abolished slavery, and in lieu thereof the present organic act under which we now exist was enacted.*

In 1869 and 1870 efforts were made to admit New Mexico into the Union as the state of Lincoln. The Territorial legislature adopted a proposed constitution, but Congress did not pass an enabling act. Governor William A. Pile was accused of bargaining with Democrats to split state officials with them in return for a promise of their support to help him gain a seat in the United States Senate if New Mexico were granted statehood. Catron, who was appointed attorney general in 1869, was charged with entering into a conspiracy by conniving with political leaders at a recent Republican Territorial Convention. Thus, almost from the start of his public life in New Mexico, Catron was involved in one way or another with efforts to achieve statehood for the Territory. Moreover, more often than not, it was unjustly imputed that his interest to that end was motivated by acquisitive instincts and attended with conniving procedures.

Why did Catron desire statehood? It was commonly supposed that statehood would increase taxes, but Catron believed that achievement of statehood would reduce taxes relative to property values. In 1890 he pointed out that Territorial expenses were $165,000 a year; he estimated that $65,000 more

---

* Catron to Joseph M. Carey, January 15, 1893 (C.P. 105, Vol. 6). An attempt was made to put the new government into immediate operation. Presumably it was assumed that approval would follow, and it might have had it not been for the untimely death of President Taylor.

would be needed to cover added expenses of government as a state.[3] It was his contention that the value of taxable property in the Territory was $47,000,000 and that it would require only a small increase in the taxable rate on this amount to make up the small difference of increased cost of government. The important consideration, to his way of thinking, was that the value of property would more than double under statehood so that the taxable rate could actually be lowered and still derive the required revenue. To support this contention he pointed out that, in other Territories that had lately become states, property values had so doubled within less than twelve months after time of admission.[4]

He firmly believed that New Mexico as a state would more readily attract outside capital which would foster economic growth and thereby increase the value of real estate. His correspondence reveals that he steadfastly adhered to this belief for three decades before statehood was achieved. Because statehood was so long deferred, other factors entered strongly into his financial matters and caused the loss of much property, so it can only be conjectured what result statehood at an earlier date might have brought to his fortunes.

Another factor in his desire for statehood that cannot be overlooked is hope that he would one day become a United States senator from the new state. This consideration is so extensively indicated in his correspondence as to give credence to the tradition that he and Elkins first mutually agreed to aspire to this lofty station when traveling to New Mexico by wagon train in 1866. It is apparent that at times he tried to delude himself into the belief that economic factors were all important in his desire for statehood and that the glitter of United States senatorship meant little to him.[5] Still, there is little question that a great deal of his thinking during his long lifetime in New Mexico was geared to the hope of one day proudly bearing the title of United States Senator. This was particularly true after 1895, when Elkins went to the Senate from West Virginia.

The Territory of New Mexico, as well as the United States, was predominately Republican during most of Catron's political career, and he worked constantly to keep it that way in the Territory because statehood would increase representation of the party in Congress. He strove ceaselessly to assure party leaders that New Mexico was "sound upon all of the national issues,"[6] because he thought it foolish to expect that a Republican administration would admit a Democratic Territory. Conversely, he had no expectation that a Democratic administration would admit a Republican New Mexico. While the possibility of Democratic control seemed almost too revolting for him to contemplate, he wanted statehood at all costs. He expressed his reason: "If I can get New Mexico as a State, be it Democratic or Republican, my property will be doubled in value. . . . I would gladly let the Democrats take and keep the State, if I can double the value of my property."[7] A less tangible reason why he desired New Mexico statehood was sheer idealism; he was attached to his adopted land and wished for it to be on a par in every way with its neighbors.

One vexing delay involved a handshake that caused a postponement of thirty-seven years. Elkins, Territorial delegate to Congress in 1875, delivered a speech on the floor of the House that won many adherents to the cause of statehood. A New Mexico statehood bill passed with decisive majorities in both House and Senate, but it became necessary to return it to the House to act upon minor Senate amendments. While awaiting action there, a Northerner made an impassioned speech condemning the South for starting the Civil War. Elkins, who had been absent from the floor, returned in time to see others congratulating the speaker. Not knowing what had transpired, and seeking to be cordial, he joined others in shaking hands with the Northerner. Southern Congressmen mistook the handshake for an endorsement of the speech and proceeded to kill the bill for New Mexico statehood.

Elkins was able to get a bill through the next session of

the Senate, but the drama of the handshake that had defeated the earlier effort attracted wide attention to New Mexico, and the bill was not passed by the House. There were numerous unfavorable comments on New Mexico in several newspapers, typically:

> If any geographical division of this country were to be selected for the final jumping off place for the American citizen, it would surely be New Mexico. A man could pass into the mysteries and doubts of his future existence in that region with perfect equanimity. The change could hardly be for the worse. It comprises the tag end of all that is objectionable in an imperfect civilization. The scum and dregs of the American, Spanish, Mexican, and Indian people are there concentrated. . . .[8]

Colorado was admitted to the Union in 1876, and its Republican vote cost the Democrats the presidential election; consequently, leaders of both parties began to use expediency as a criteria for admission of new states. By 1888 Democrats realized they could no longer keep out Dakota Territory. The result was an omnibus bill, in December 1887, introduced by Daniel W. Voorhees of Indiana, Democratic leader of the Senate. In January 1888 a similar bill was presented in the House by his son, Charles Stewart Voorhees, delegate to Congress from Washington Territory. Both called for admission of South Dakota, North Dakota, Washington, Montana, and New Mexico. Details of the House bill were objected to, and a substitute was introduced by William M. Springer of Illinois. The House committee on Territories reported the bill favorably, but New Mexico had been the subject of a great deal of vituperative and unjust reporting by the press of the Nation, so five Republican members presented a minority report in March 1888 recommending that New Mexico be stricken from the bill.

This minority report charged that many people of New Mexico were not only uneducated but unfamiliar with the language, customs, and system of government of the United States. Authority for much of the report was W. W. H. Davis'

El Gringo, or New Mexico and Her People, which had been published in 1856 and, even at that date, was prejudiced against the inhabitants of the Territory.[9]

Early in 1889 this report again became a subject of discussion in Congress; to counteract it, Elkins suggested to Catron that he and friends write to Senator O. H. Platt, chairman of the committee on Territories, presenting the claims of New Mexico for statehood and suggesting any amendments that might be deemed prudent.[10] Catron immediately complied, pointing out that the popular vote in the Territory was largely Republican, as reflected in both houses of the legislature. He warned, however, that a feature of the Springer bill could defeat the Republican majority and permit Democrats to control a state convention. The bill allowed the governor, United States marshal, and United States attorney, immediately upon passage of the bill, to redistrict the Territory according to the best information available. These three officers — respectively, Edmund G. Ross, Romulo Martinez, and Thomas J. Smith — were all Democratic politicians.

Catron pointed out that:

> The best information they would obtain, would be what any irresponsible person might tell them, that is, that every democratic precinct possessed twice the amount of its actual population, and every republican precinct not half of its actual population, and thereupon, they would so group the precincts together, that they would elect at least two-thirds of the delegates to the convention from the democratic party.[11]

Catron suggested that either the redistricting provision of the bill be changed or the time for redistricting be delayed until the newly elected President Harrison was afforded time to appoint new officials to the posts in question. But Senator Platt thought that it would be impossible to get his colleagues to consider New Mexico along with the other Territories listed in the Springer bill, and that New Mexico would have to take her chances along with Wyoming, Idaho, and Arizona. In view of the circumstance, it is probable that he chose to read more implication of postponement into Catron's letter than was therein expressed. Platt said:

All of my information from New Mexico — and I have a good deal of it — bears out Mr. Catron's letter; and I think with him that the only way to make a Republican State of it to postpone the question of admission until Republican judges, governor, and other officers, have been in the Territory long enough so that the Mexican population can realize that it is a Republican administration we are to live under.*

As it turned out, South Dakota, North Dakota, Montana, and Washington were admitted as states in 1889, but New Mexico's bid was turned down.

Catron learned of the rejection from William J. Mills who informed him from New York that there was no prospect for statehood. Mills was satisfied that this condition was at least five years off.[12] From Senator William M. Stewart of Nevada, Catron learned that the adverse reports that had been made with regard to the character of the people of New Mexico had found a strong lodgment in the minds of many senators. Stewart concluded with a personal note that does much to explain the importance of Catron's role in the statehood movement.

I wish you were here to explain in person the exact condition of New Mexico, because I know it is greatly misunderstood. I believe that if New Mexico were to become a State it would rapidly increase in population and be one of the best States in the West. I am aware that the great difficulty under which you have labored has been the uncertainty of land titles. You need representatives in Congress. If you were in the Senate to assist in the formation of laws for settlement of land titles and also for the purpose of remonetizing silver, you could not only help New Mexico, but all the West. I hope we may bring New Mexico in and that you may become her first Senator.[13]

There had been suggestions from Washington that New Mexico's chances for statehood would be better if a constitu-

---

* O. H. Platt to Elkins, February 5, 1889 (C.P. 102, Box 2). Platt, probably deliberately, misinterpreted Catron's warning. It was not a preponderance of Mexican population that might have caused the situation Catron feared.

tion were available to present to Congress for inspection; accordingly on February 28, 1889, the Territorial Council authorized a convention to draw up a constitution. The bill was introduced by George W. Prichard, a Republican from San Miguel County. Governor Ross allowed passage of the bill without his signature, but other Democratic leaders contended that the apportionment was unfair to their party. Efforts to achieve a compromise were unsuccessful; Democrats, acting upon instructions from Democratic Central Committee chairman William Burr Childers, refused to participate in the election. As a result, only one Democrat was elected; nevertheless, the convention wrote a constitution. Copies of the document in English and Spanish were widely distributed throughout New Mexico, but it was not immediately voted upon by the people.[14] The Democratic reaction was one of opposition to statehood as promulgated by such Republican party bosses as Perea, Catron, Chavez, and Prichard.

In the spring of 1890 Congress was considering a bill for the admission of Idaho and Wyoming into the sisterhood of states. Friends of New Mexico who were in Washington alerted the Territory that it was an opportune time for New Mexico to be included in the bill. Among these friends were William L. Rynerson and William H. H. Llewellyn. Rynerson was in Washington in connection with political matters, including an effort to block the appointment of Eugene A. Fiske as United States attorney. He was, at the time, in the process of incorporating the Tularosa Land and Cattle Company with himself, Catron, and John H. Riley. Fiske had made himself obnoxious to these incorporators, and Rynerson's trip followed. Meanwhile, Catron made strenuous efforts to have Frank Springer appointed instead of Fiske.* Fiske, however, was appointed.

While in Washington, Rynerson noted the statehood sit-

---

* Catron to W. M. Stewart, December 27, 1889 (C.P. 105, Vol. 2). Catron wrote letters to numerous other persons, including several to Elkins, advocating Springer over Fiske.

uation and informed Catron that a delegation ought at once to come there and present New Mexico's claim. He also sent a letter to the *Santa Fe New Mexican* with the same information.[15] In these letters he urged that the delegation should include such persons as Mariano S. Otero, J. Francisco Chavez, Judge L. S. Trimble, John H. Riley, Governor Prince, Frank Springer, Elias S. Stover, and William H. H. Llewellyn. Llewellyn was also then in Washington and, the following day, also wrote to Catron on the same subject.

Llewellyn believed that, if the proper efforts were made, there would not be the least trouble getting an enabling act passed by Congress. He maintained, though, that if New Mexico failed of admission at that time, it might be years before there was another such golden opportunity. He advocated, as had Rynerson, that a delegation of New Mexicans come at once to Washington, and he named the same persons as desirable members.

Llewellyn had been privileged to discuss the matter with I. S. Strubble of Iowa, chairman of the House committee on Territories, and had secured his favorable reaction. There were, though, he indicated, two objections that would have to be overcome. Republicans in Congress were fearful that New Mexico would be a Democratic state. Another objection centered around Senator Glen E. Plumb of Kansas, who had supported Eugene A. Fiske in his bid for United States attorney Plumb was aware that Rynerson and Catron had tried to block Fiske, and he opposed statehood for New Mexico on the supposition that Catron would be one of the senators. Llewellyn believed, though, that he had a man who would induce Plumb to remove his objection to Catron. He concluded:

> The question is simply this: have we life, spirit and energy enough to put this proposition through, or will we quietly submit to continued Territorial form of Government, with all of its attending embarrassments and disgrace, and remain in the same list as Utah.[16]

Urged by Catron and Max Frost, editor of the *Santa Fe New Mexican,* Governor Prince, himself thoroughly in accord with the idea, appointed a committee of fifty-four members headed by himself. While only twenty-nine actually went to Washington, the group was a representative one and hardly deserved the slur voiced by Senator George F. Edmunds of Vermont: "Since having seen the delegation from New Mexico I am more than ever convinced of necessity of public schools in that territory."[17]

While this lobby for statehood was quickly gotten together, there was no difficulty in assigning to it additional purposes. Settlement of Spanish and Mexican land grants in New Mexico had long been a vexing problem, as had the need for Territorial land to support schools, and additional associate justices of the Supreme Court. It was along these lines that the delegation was most successful. A Court of Private Land Claims was established the following year, and donation of land for educational purposes followed some years later.

The reaction among members of the committee was mixed as to the desirability of statehood for New Mexico at that time, as well as was the extent of their individual efforts to that end. Henry L. Waldo, general solicitor of the Atchison, Topeka, and Santa Fe Railroad in New Mexico, seemed more interested in the land grant problem than the statehood movement. On the other hand, William C. Hazeldine, general counsel for the Atlantic and Pacific Railroad, worked with particular fervor for statehood. In the aggregate, the committee was poorly organized, and each member followed his own inclination as to procedure.

Members of the committee remaining in New Mexico were mostly members of the bar association, and Catron was asked to carry the heaviest load on the home front. Hazeldine left for Washington on March 7, 1890; before leaving, he requested that Catron prepare for him an address to be presented before Congress and, if possible, another for the public in general. He requested that Catron send these documents to him in Washington. It is evident that he was aware of the lack of organization. He said:

Try and find a few moments to look into this and if you can get only three or four of the committee together or even if you do it yourself, let us have something that will appear to be by authority of the Convention. You are authorized to count me as present if necessary.[18]

He also requested that Catron try to have the committee designate the fifteenth to the twenty-fifth of March as a time when all citizens of New Mexico who could possibly spare the time be urged to repair to Washington and there make a joint effort for admission as a state.

Later in March Hazeldine reported his progress to Catron and to Catron's law partner, Frank W. Clancy:

I have been privately requested by the Republican majority of the committee on Territories to prepare an enabling act, authorizing our people to vote upon the constitution already prepared by us. I do not say that this will even be adopted or approved by the committee; but it is a step in the right direction, and shows quite a change of sentiment to that entertained when I arrived here. I should be pleased to have you get up a rough draft making it as short as possible, of what you think such an act should contain and send it to me at your earliest possible convenience, telegraphing me when you do so. I should have this, if possible, next week. It would be well, also, I think, to get up an official address, and have the same printed for me to present to each Member of Congress together with a copy of the Constitution. Will some of you please see to this? I believe if there had been a united effort, and if proper attention had been paid to the matter, and the Territory represented by men who knew what they were talking about, we could have had a favorable report on our admission under the new constitution by this time. I am working day and night, and have certainly been able to change the predominant feeling so that it is now favorable to us. Still, it is very hard for one man to do much with such a large body to deal with.[19]

The same day Hazeldine found to his surprise that it was alleged no official presentation was ever made to Congress of the constitution adopted earlier and that members claimed they had no knowledge — except through newspaper rumors — that any constitutional convention had ever been held in New Mexico. Something had to be done quickly, so Hazeldine prepared a memorial presenting a copy of the constitution to Congress.[20]

Numerous other problems were present. Particularly perplexing was the opposition of the senators from Kansas. Senator Plumb, especially, used all of his enormous force and great ability in opposition. One additional purpose of the delegation from New Mexico was to press for favorable irrigation legislation. New Mexico consumed much of the surplus grain produced in Kansas, and it was feared that legislation favorable to New Mexico would enable that Territory to produce its own supply of grain.[21]

As time passed Hazeldine became convinced that if New Mexico did not then obtain admission, it would be long postponed. He felt that every pressure should be brought to bear; still, he had exhausted his own supply of time. He wrote:

> I think I have done my share, and want somebody else to take hold now. Without any egotism on my part, I feel confident that if I could spare the time to devote three or four months to this matter I could certainly pass the enabling act.[22]

But no one else stepped forth to lend a helping hand. It is evident that Governor Prince had merely appointed the delegation and then simply turned the members loose to do the best they could. By contrast, the delegates to Congress from Idaho and Wyoming had devoted almost all of their time during the four years just passed to gaining admission for their respective Territories.[23] They were successful; New Mexico failed.

Their labor was in marked contrast to that of the Democratic delegate to Congress from New Mexico, Antonio Joseph, who was first elected in 1884 and became so well entrenched that he continued to win elections even after the inauguration of President Harrison in 1889. He was indifferent to the cause of statehood during his early years in Congress and gave it only mild support at any time. In 1890 he appeared to be working in harmony with the delegation to Washington until he received unfavorable replies to his inquiry, addressed to several prominent Democrats in the Territory, as to the acceptability of the constitution drawn up by the Santa Fe convention. He then withdrew his support from the movement, although he had personally been willing to see statehood achieved. Without his blessing all hope of admission at that time vanished.[24]

The constitutional convention, noting that Wyoming and Idaho had adopted constitutions by popular vote prior to admission, reassembled for two days in August and made a few changes in their document. The Republican Central Committee carried on a campaign throughout the Territory urging voters to support the constitution. As was usual in such instances, Catron was called upon to largely underwrite expenses of the campaign and to personally prepare necessary literature.[25]

The balloting was scheduled for October 7, 1890; meanwhile, in September, Catron requested that his friend, Senator William M. Stewart from Nevada, introduce a bill in Congress requiring that jurors in the Territories be able to read and write. He felt that if the Associated Press sent out prompt word of this proposed law, it would furnish a practical argument for education and aid approval of the constitution by the voters. Stewart introduced the bill as requested, on the last day of the session, and it was referred to the committee on Territories.

The Democrats, who were fighting the proposed constitution with every available means, learned of the bill and guessed that Catron had requested its presentation. Democratic newspapers now condemned the measure as a mere trick to deceive the voters and voiced suspicion that Catron was responsible for its introduction. Catron wrote to Stewart:

> The bill you introduced has raised considerable "fuss." I fear it was introduced too late to do us much good as our election comes off tomorrow.
>
> The Democrats & Catholic Church are opposing statehood & they charge now that as you introduced the bill by "Request" it was I who requested it.
>
> If it should be known that I requested it, it might hurt me very seriously politically as the whole Catholic Church would jump on me,

and all the Mexicans who cannot read & write also. I hope you will keep my name *entirely secret.*[26]

The constitution was defeated by a vote of more than two to one, but only partially because of opposition to statehood itself. Newspapers published during the campaign gave little hint of such opposition. The vote was, to a large extent, a protest against the constitution, particularly because it was mostly a unilateral Republican production. Democrats felt that apportionment to the convention was unfair to their party. Many voters who owned little property assumed that the constitution favored large land owners and that the weight of taxation would be thrown on the majority. The Catholic Church opposed the constitution because it provided for non-sectarian public schools. There was some contemporary presumption that these facets of resistance were decisive, but a fair analysis indicates that political and economic objections were also important. Another factor was explained by Catron:

> The great opposition amongst many is, that they are afraid of the Mexican people, and that they would control the State to the injury of the Americans.[27]

Persons with this type of prejudice would be inclined to not voice it and yet go to the polls and express it. Catron, for one, felt that such bias was unwarranted. He continued:

> This you and I know is not true. The Mexicans have always divided up the offices fair with Americans, and as they are divided in politics just the same as the Americans, it would be impossible for them to get control of the State exclusively in their own interests and against the interests of the Americans. Besides, they have no disposition to do so.[28]

During the next twelve years, some twenty bills for admission of New Mexico to statehood were introduced in Congress. Only three passed the House and were considered by a Senate committee. For six of these years Catron was related to the office of delegate to Congress by either defeat or victory — he was a candidate three times and was defeated twice. He tells of the beginning of this period in 1892:

There seems to be a disposition among a great many of my friends here to insist that I shall become a candidate for delegate this year in this Territory. They do not seem to take well to the lies that the Republicans might decline to put any one in nomination. There is some little disagreement and dissension in our party, no more, however, than there is in the Democratic party; barely as much. If I came to the conclusion that it was absolutely necessary in order to secure statehood for New Mexico for me to make this race, I will probably do it, on condition, however, that all Republicans in the Territory get together, stop ill feeling and dissension, and unite upon one single ticket and one single line of political policy.... I believe that if I should become a candidate I could carry the Territory, but it would take a hard fight and maybe considerable money. I have not yet determined what to do. I do not desire to run; I desire to avoid it, but if I come to the conclusion that it is essential in order to obtain statehood for New Mexico, I feel that I should attempt to do it.*

Catron was now fifty-one years of age and had made up his mind that he did not intend to work hard for more than ten years longer if he could get himself financially in condition to avoid it.[29] This meant resolving numerous problems in connection with his business affairs. Since he had reached the zenith of his adventure in empire building about 1890, he may have seen the change for the worse in his personal fortune and felt that he should concentrate on his business. There is no question that he was reluctant nor any doubt that his final decision to run was based on his desire for statehood. It was a sacrifice for him at this crucial time in his life, possibly more of a sacrifice than he realized.

When he announced his final decision, his friends recognized that he was honestly a reluctant candidate for office. Richard C. Kerens, a member of the executive committee of the Republican National Committee, wrote:

It seems to me it would be a great sacrifice on your part to be the parties candidate; at the same time it may be necessary to demonstrate the fact that the Territory is Republican and can be carried. This it seems to me would be all the evidence the Senate would require to immediately pass the statehood bill....[30]

---

* Catron to R. C. Kerens, August 10, 1892 (C.P. 105, Vol. 5). Catron also wrote similar letters to a few other friends.

R. B. Thomas, of Deming, had this to say: "Your determination to sacrifice your own inclination and interests to aid the cause of statehood is certainly laudable."[31] E. R. Chapman, of New York, expressed it this way: "It seems to me that this would be the best and easiest way of making the passage of the Admission Bill an absolute certainty."[32] W. H. Newcomb, of Silver City, was particularly complimentary: "more is at stake than even you can estimate, *it in my opinion means the admission of New Mexico as a state which must interest every person within her borders.* Later it will be Senator Catron."[33] P. R. Smith of Deming was opposed to Catron's party but admired him and his statehood efforts.[34]

Catron was unsuccessful in his bid to unseat the Democratic incumbent, Antonio Joseph. The majority for Joseph was about 600 votes, a reduction of about 1,500 from two years earlier. Charges of fraudulent Democratic voting were widespread, and there was talk of contesting the election. Catron, however, was satisfied with his relatively good showing and did not insist on a contest. Considering the calumny heaped upon him by his political enemies at the time, it is a wonder he succeeded as well as he did. Two happenings in Catron's life about which he was particularly sensitive were dragged into the gutter of political mudslinging.

John P. Casey prepared an unsubstantiated statement to the effect that Catron had been implicated in the murder of Alexis Grossetete and Robert Elsinger in the American Valley a decade earlier. The plan was to release this statement to the public just prior to the election, but Catron learned of the scheme and forestalled it by threat of a suit. It was not possible, however to stop the concurrent whispering campaign.[35]

The second Democratic stratagem was to secure a copy of the report made by Frank Warner Angel in 1878, following his investigation of troubles in Lincoln and Colfax counties. It was rumored that this report contained specific charges against Catron which, it was hoped, could be used against him in the campaign. Catron learned of the plot and enlisted the aid of Elkins to assure that a copy of any charges against him would not be released from Washington.[36] As was true of the Casey statement, the full impact of political advantage was not realized; nevertheless, so vicious was the word-of-mouth canard that even today, in the 1970s, whispers can be heard by attuning one's ear to the grapevine of oral transmission.

In 1894 Catron was again reluctant to run. He gives his reasons, as well as the cause of his final decision, to make the race:

> It was not my desire to be nominated and I had absolutely declined. The convention had already taken two ballots before my name was called, when someone in the convention nominated me while the ballot was being taken, and before the roll was completed every delegate in the convention changed his vote to me. Of course, under such circumstances as these, I could not refuse. I look upon this election as preparatory to statehood; and if I were to get anything under statehood, I could not in the face of such a situation refuse to accept. I would much have preferred not running for the reason that, owing to the exceedingly depressed condition of matters financially in this Territory, I have not money to spare nor have any of my friends. The great consolation I have is that the other side have no money either. It is true that they have all the federal officials who will contribute a small amount. That will put into their coffers as much as probably a couple of thousand dollars. It really looks to me as if my election is absolutely certain. Last election I made the best campaign that has ever been made in this territory and spent considerable money. The result of that campaign now is very apparent. I am recognized as being the logical candidate throughout the territory, both by Republicans and Democrats and many Democrats have notified me that they intend to support us. The best part of that is that those who have so assured us of their support go farther and say that they intend to support the Republican party henceforth and permanently.[37]

Catron defeated Joseph by 2,762 votes, largely because of Joseph's lack of endeavor to have New Mexico brought into statehood. Catron's goal above all others in the two years he served as delegate to Congress was achievement of statehood. His own explanation of why he was unable to achieve more in endeavors toward that end is valid. He served during the Democratic Cleveland administration, which was supported by a Democratic Senate. All that he succeeded in doing in the

House was blocked in the Senate, and much that he might have achieved in the House was nullified because of opposition from the administration.[38]

In 1896 Catron, as the incumbent, had but little practical choice than to seek reelection. His reluctance to do so, however, was apparent. In the final analysis it was only his desire for statehood that caused him again to make the race. His business affairs continued to be pressing; related to his statehood desire was optimism that if New Mexico became a state the economic outlook would improve and relieve him of his financial stringency. Throughout the decade his correspondence in behalf of statehood was enormous, and much of it was related to economic factors.

There are a number of possible reasons for Catron's defeat by Harvey B. Fergusson in 1896. Ralph E. Twitchell's judgment that the year 1896 marked a decline in Catron's political power cannot be questioned.[39] In addition to his defeat by Fergusson, he also failed to be reappointed as national committeeman. Catron attributed his defeat to the Anglo population in the Territory going wild on the free-silver platform. It is probable, however, that Republican losses to the free-silver heresy were offset by the vote of old line Democrats who refused to support William Jennings Bryan.

The most important reasons for his defeat undoubtedly centered around the Borrego case and the attempt to disbar him from the legal profession in New Mexico. Judge Napoleon B. Laughlin's widely disseminated dissenting opinion was the climactic factor thereto. There are reasons relating to Catron's personality why he became vulnerable to the machinations of his political foes as a result of adverse publicity from this front. Melvin W. Mills, his good friend and most astute political adviser, pointed out as early as 1892 that Catron should make peace with all the people he was fighting and quit his foolish resentment and ugly demeanor. Catron, Mills felt, should imitate Elkins a little in flattery. He admitted that Catron was not born with this quality but felt that he could rake up a little deceit and cultivate it. When the election was over and Catron defeated, Mills concluded that Catron could run for senator where he could manage the few necessary persons — Mills seems to have forseen that the first U. S. senators would be selected by the Territorial legislature — but that he had not the natural-born deception for the rabble of the whole country necessary to get down on his knees before people he did not like and beg them for office.[40]

The Spanish-American War indirectly increased chances for statehood. More of Theodore Roosevelt's famed Rough Riders came from New Mexico and Arizona than other areas, and many hoped that this connection would favorably influence New Mexico's fight to become a state. After the war, Roosevelt maintained close contact with his former soldiers. The first Rough Rider reunion was held at Las Vegas in June 1899. While in attendance, Roosevelt promised that New Mexicans could count on him and that he would return to Washington to speak on their behalf. President McKinley, who stopped in Deming in May 1901, was more careful not to commit himself on the statehood issue; however, his death by an assassin's bullet made Roosevelt's pledge more meaningful to New Mexicans. As Warren D. Beck notes in *New Mexico*, "Unfortunately, they failed to realize that Roosevelt the Rough Rider and Roosevelt the politician who became President were not always in agreement.[41]

In May 1902, Congressman Rodey raised hopes that the long quest for statehood might soon be ended when he succeeded in getting the House to pass an omnibus bill providing for the admission of New Mexico, Arizona, and Oklahoma. Rodey informed Catron that the big problem was to get Senator Albert Beveridge of Indiana, chairman of the committee on territories, to consider the bill at all.[42]

The measure was championed by Senator Matthew S. Quay of Pennsylvania, but Beveridge made an obsessive crusade to keep New Mexico out of the Union. In November 1902 he assembled a subcommittee of his committee on Territories at Chicago for the purpose of investigating conditions in the Territories. This subcommittee held sessions in New Mexico at Las Vegas, Santa Fe, Albuquerque, Las Cruces, and Carlsbad. Most of the testimony was taken from professional people or politicians, and the committee's report, made in December, dealt largely with the use of Spanish in the courts and schools and in daily life. Little attention was paid to resources and institutions or the ability of the Territory to bear the expense of statehood.

It is evident that the committee was interested in solidifying preconceived notions rather than in objectively gathering facts. The report stressed that the majority of New Mexicans spoke only Spanish; that it was impossible to conduct courts without an interpreter; that dockets of nearly all the justices of the peace were kept largely in Spanish; that Spanish was taught exclusively in some schools; that many communities had no communication with the outside world; that part of the population had no understanding of the institutions of government; that jurors signed their names by mark; and that, aside from the large towns, the people lived in mud huts as they had for a century past. The committee urged that statehood be withheld from New Mexico until a majority of the people there became identical in language and customs with the rest of the nation.[43]

While Beveridge belittled the people of New Mexico, he also had reasons with national implications for opposing the addition of new states. In the past, states had been rushed into the Union merely to increase representation of the party in power in Congress. He referred to these as "rotten borough" states and deplored such shoddy tactics as a means for remaining in political power. Another important reason for his opposition to New Mexico statehood was his belief that powerful special interests had the most to gain by the move. This was just another of his many encounters with the "malfactors of great wealth."[44]

The associations of William H. "Bull" Andrews, who arrived in New Mexico in 1902, did much to confirm Beveridge's suspicions. Andrews was a friend of Senators Quay and Penrose, who were also from Pennsylvania. Andrews, a big man with a barrel chest and a face that looked like a painting of J. Pierpont Morgan, was a skillful politician and loyal to his masters. He did what Quay told him; he was the satchel carrier. An article in the *Detroit Journal,* October 30, 1905, describes Andrews: "He carried conventions for him (Quay), got delegates, took all sorts of risks and went to any extreme." [45]

This is the program which, it was said, Andrews and his ring plotted:

First — The building of the Santa Fe Central railroad from Santa Fe south through the rich mining lands to the town of Torrance, the ultimate construction of a branch to Albuquerque, and the sale of the property to the Atchison, Topeka & Santa Fe road.

Second — The organization of the Pennsylvania Development Co. to develop the mining lands along the road.

Third — The admission of New Mexico to the Union as a state.

Fourth — The control of the legislature of the new state to legalize the bonds of the Santa Fe Central road.

Fifth —The election of "Bull" Andrews as United States senator from New Mexico.

Sixth — The election of complaisant state officials.[46]

Throughout the short session of 1902–03, Senator Quay and other supporters of New Mexico statehood had the votes necessary to pass an enabling act, but Beveridge used the power of his chairmanship of the committee on Territories to block all efforts to bring the matter to a vote. President Roosevelt, when confronted with the Beveridge report, lost his enthusiasm for the Quay bill and withdrew his support. The result was a measure supported by the administration to combine Arizona and New Mexico in one state. It was argued that the predominately Anglo population of Arizona would balance the Spanish-American population of New Mexico and invalidate the recommendations of the Beveridge committee.

Catron was unalterably opposed to joint statehood from the beginning. It was alleged that he had selfish reasons for this stand, including the fact that it might be more difficult for him to become a senator from that combination of Territories. His reasons, however, as presented to Senator Quay, were cogent and persuasive. New Mexico had been under its system of laws for more than fifty years, as opposed to about thirty years in the case of Arizona, and laws of these Territories differed radically in many respects, especially in regard to water rights, irrigation, and grazing. Laws on the subject of taxation and property assessments were different in the two Territories. There were radical differences in the school laws as well as laws of inheritance and ownership of real estate. In fact, he pointed out, the entire system of laws of one or both would have to be revised. Furthermore, to a great extent, the general interests of the people of Arizona were affiliated with those of the Pacific Coast people; those of New Mexico's inhabitants with the population of the Mississippi Valley and the Atlantic Coast. Thus, in their usual way of handling business and matters of general interest, these Territories had been drawn apart rather than brought together. To a great degree, Catron believed, they had grown to be strangers to each other, and to be thrown together in one state would result in an undesirable fight and scramble for political control. Catron added:

> Our people, and myself among them, have the greatest regard in the world for the activity, energy, intelligence, high standing and enterprise of the people of the Territory of Arizona. I know them to be thoroughly and fully equipped in every regard to take up and support a State government alone, without the assistance of New Mexico, and I know the same facts to be true in regard to New Mexico....[47]

Catron then presented Senator Quay with an analysis (see Apendix 3) of the reasons why the people of New Mexico wanted statehood; why they felt they were entitled to become a state; and why截 they should be supported by the Republican party nationally to that end.[48]

In March 1904 Congressman Rodey was working on a bill that he hoped could be so framed as to be accepted by both Territories. He tried to convince Catron that this was a workable solution.

> Mr. Catron, before this fight is over, everybody in both the territories will understand that separate statehood is absolutely dead and buried and has ten tons of rock over it. There is no hope for it at all. The nation wont stand for it. It is joint statehood or nothing, that is all there is about it.[49]

But Catron was adamant; he believed that Rodey had only hurt himself politically by advocating jointure and so informed him. There is no question that he considered himself Rodey's friend and staunchly supported him. As it turned out, Catron was correct in his analysis. Governor Otero, angered by Rodey's position, supported William H. Andrews in the election for delegate to Congress later that year. Rodey ran on an independent Republican ticket and was badly beaten.*

Catron continued to press his case for single statehood, as did others in the Territory, but it can be convincingly argued that he spent more time, energy, and brains for a longer period of time in the quest than any contemporary. He was, to a certain extent, a loner in his approach, yet he was more cooperative and less bellicose in this endeavor than in most that touched closer to his own affairs and personal life. He was sympathetic to those who failed, because he also had failed, but his own failure did not deter him from constant striving. At home he never ceased trying to convince those who wavered that statehood was important in their lives; abroad, in neighboring states, in the nation's capital, from coast to coast, he carried on an unremitting campaign extolling the virtues of his neighbors and his Territory. Only in

---

*Catron to B. S. Rodey, April 20, 1904 (C.P. 105, Vol. 23). See also chapter 14 herein. In 1906 Rodey accepted a judgeship of the district court of the United States for Puerto Rico. He continued his friendly endeavor to dissuade Catron from taking the stump against joint statehood. He wrote, with something less than accurate insight into the future: "You will never live long enough to see New Mexico a State if you fight it and beat it this time." Rodey to Catron, July 3, 1906 (C.P. 103, Box 26).

defense of persons of Mexican origin did he tend to belliger-
ence, yet even in this area he was mostly positive in his presentation, informing others of their virtues rather than defending their faults. In this crusade he spoke personally whenever
possible, but it was by writing letters that he presented his
case most forcefully. Busy as he was, he repeatedly found time
to compose penetrating essays in the form of personal letters
that showed his wide acquaintance with every facet of life in
New Mexico.

On the issue of joint statehood with Arizona, however,
he would not bend; his arguments were numerous and cogent.
One involved the debts of the respective Territories. The
jointure bill provided that all of the debts of Arizona and New
Mexico would be assumed by the new state. New Mexico's
debt was approximately one million dollars while that of Arizona was four times larger. New Mexico, with nearly double
the taxable property of Arizona, would be compelled to
assume a debt four times as large with no compensation. And
he always came back to the point of protecting the people of
New Mexico. The Mexican people, he claimed, would be prac-
tically disenfranchised, for in Arizona they were not allowed
on juries and were only rarely awarded any office, even the
most insignificant.[50]

For his own welfare it would have been expedient to
accept statehood in any form, but he would not, could not,
it would seem, bow to expediency. He explained his position:

capital has no confidence in the territorial government and will not
invest here. You cannot secure a loan of $1000 on $50,000 of property in this Territory in the East. You cannot get people to come
here and invest in view of the fact that it is a Territory. For that reason,
there are many people who are willing at any cost or sacrifice to accept
this joint Statehood proposition, but 9/10 of the people are decidedly
and distinctly opposed to it, I amongst the number, although probably no one in the entire State would be as much benefited by Statehood as I would. I have immense property, as you know, all of which
would be within six months after the State became organized doubled
in value; yet I am willing to make that sacrifice to avoid it.[51]

In April 1904 Rodey's joint statehood bill passed the House, but there was no chance, Elkins explained to Catron, to secure its passage in the Senate at that session.[52] The following year Senator Albert Beveridge, realizing that his filibustering tactics could not prevail indefinitely, proposed that Oklahoma Territory and Indian Territory come in as one state with Arizona and New Mexico admitted as another. Beveridge supported the measure as eloquently as he had condemned those in the past. The bill was passed by Congress and signed by the president. Jointure was accepted by the inhabitants of Oklahoma and Indian Territory, but the assumption that Arizona and New Mexico would do likewise proved to be invalid.

Delegate William H. Andrews had joined former Delegate Bernard S. Rodey in favor of jointure and they were supported by others including Holm O. Bursum, Solomon Luna, and Max Frost. They argued that:

accepting the administration policy would strengthen the party position in national councils, Arizonians would probably not accept and the onus for defeat would lay with them; but if they did accept jointure a division could later be made, either by political separation or a tacit recognition that each portion of the State would enjoy local autonomy.[53]

But some would not go along with this temporizing attitude. These included T. B. Catron, Miguel Otero, and Napoleon B. Laughlin.It is strange to see Catron in this alignment, for Otero and Laughlin were in the very forefront of his implacable political enemies. Each, however, agreed in his own way that the practical difficulties of statehood jointly with Arizona were so great that values received would be negated.

It happened that Senator Joseph Foraker of Ohio insisted upon an amendment calling for ratification by a majority of voters in both Territories.[54] Most New Mexicans preferred single statehood. This was especially the case since the new entity would be known as Arizona; still, they felt that self-government was more important than surrendering the long existing Territorial name, and they accepted the measure by a substantial margin. The people of Arizona preferred to wait for single statehood rather than join the dominant Spanish-speaking element of New Mexico; they voted just as overwhelmingly against the measure and thus defeated it for both Territories.

In its national platform of 1908, The Republican party endorsed statehood for Arizona and New Mexico. Influenced by the stand of his party, and perhaps because of his personal friendship for Governor George Curry, President Roosevelt changed his mind; in his last annual message to Congress he recommended the admission of Arizona and New Mexico as separate states. But Senator Beveridge continued his opposition to single statehood, so Governor Curry journeyed to Washington to speak personally for the cause. He reported his reception to Catron:

we found it impossible to get a bill out of the Senate Committee on Territories during this session. Senator Beveridge had a majority of the committee with him, and although some of them were for Statehood, they had agreed with him not to report the bill during this session.[55]

Catron, in his answer to Curry, remonstrated mildly:

They complain that we are backward and behindhand and yet at the same time they will do nothing to enable us to get out of the behindhand or backward condition, as they claim it to exist; of course their claim is not true. They ought to be willing to help us as they have helped other people. We have ample people to sustain a State government; we have enough for two representatives in Congress. I noticed one of the letters that was published in the New Mexican, which was published as coming from a Member of Congress to Mr. [W. S.] Hopewell, in which he said he thought we ought to remain out until we had enough population to entitle us to one representative in Congress. If the gentleman in question had looked at the last census, he would have seen that our population exceeded the amount that was required to entitle one district or state to a member of Congress at that time, and since then a man with his eyes shut ought to know that we have been progressing very rapidly.[56]

Governor Curry, though, was not discouraged. He believed that in case of the nomination and election of William H. Taft, who was very friendly toward New Mexico, Beveridge and the other opposition senators would fall in line. During the period when the nomination of Taft remained uncertain, Catron let it be known that he personally, as well as other leading men of the party, were decidedly in favor of him.[57]

Catron also, in a thoughtfully conceived letter to Senator Beveridge, tried to break down the long-standing opposition of that stern antagonist. He wrote:

My object in writing to you is because the people of New Mexico, whose population has doubled since you made a flying trip through the Territory, two or three years ago, are extremely anxious for admission to Statehood. We feel that an in justice has been done us for a long time.[58]

He then followed with a carefully reasoned resume of the qualifications of New Mexicans for statehood with facts dating back to 1849. He concluded:

I have just read an Associated Press dispatch, which says that you have declared yourself opposed to admission of New Mexico to statehood at the present term, giving, as a reason, that you do not favor Andrews, or have no use for him. My dear Senator, as far as your opinion of Andrews is concerned, nineteen-twentieths of the Republicans here agree with you. Mr. Andrews can never be elected a United States Senator of this Territory. The great mass of Republicans are unalterably opposed to him. It was felt at the last election, after he was nominated, that it would be better to elect him than a Democrat, so we did it. The office of delegate is a thankless job. He has no vote; he is only a licensed and paid beggar. . . . From my observation of your course in Congress, I believe you are too great to allow such a small factor as Andrews to influence your action against us. I wish to assure you that when New Mexico shall be admitted, there will be two senators and two representatives sent to Congress who will not be Socialists, Democrats or of any other off-colored condition, but that they will be true, staunch Republicans, that believe in the protection of the individual, the betterment of his condition, the preservation of all property rights, and the general advancement of this portion of the country.[59]

A few days later Catron again wrote to Beveridge stating additional qualifications for New Mexico statehood. He estimated that in excess of three-fifths of New Mexico's inhabitants were of Anglo-Saxon origin, and he pointed out that in the past three years over forty thousand homesteads had been filed by people mostly from the East. Many newcomers were engaged in successfully growing cotton, an entire new industry that had sprung up in the past four years. Every occupation and profession was receiving its proportion of increase in number. One hundred fifty thousand immigrants were expected from the East that year, and New Mexicans believed they would have a total population of close to seven hundred fifty thousand by census time in 1910. Entire sections of the Territory were filling up. New towns were being created, and older ones were increasing rapidly in population. But Beveridge continued immovable in his opposition. There was only one indication of his relenting; he said that he would waive his opposition after the census was taken in 1910.[60]

In February 1909 Andrews informed Catron that a statehood bill would pass the House on the fifteenth of that month. Catron answered by reporting a rumor that Andrews had tried to make combinations to elect himself senator. If he had succeeded, he would have pushed the bill through sooner. Having failed, the rumor went, he had the bill held up so that it would not pass the term of Congress in session in order that he might hold the position of delegate to Congress for two more years.[61] As a matter of fact, in view of the opposition of Beveridge and others, the bill probably would have failed in the Senate even though it had passed in the House sooner.

In October an event occurred that probably had little bearing on the statehood issue, despite its dramatic implications. President Taft visited New Mexico and stopped at Albuquerque, where he was entertained by a banquet at the Alvarado Hotel. During the afternoon the president spoke briefly to an audience assembled on the lawn of the hotel, and his remarks seemed to express little enthusiasm for New Mexico's cause. Governor Curry, who had earlier received an unqualified commitment from Taft, understood his seeming lack of zeal to be only his conservative nature. Others, though, were not as assured.

That evening Catron, Holm O. Bursum, Owen N. Marron, and a few others made brief speeches. Each presented reasons why New Mexico was ready for statehood, and all were complimentary to the president. The last speaker was Albert B. Fall. To the consternation of all present, he reviewed the long history of broken promises of statehood. He stated that past presidents were notable for making promises while touring the country only to forget them later on, and he sarcastically concluded that their distinguished guest for the evening was no exception.

The president, who had requested that he not be called upon to speak, did not let this rudeness go unchallenged. He promptly rose and told a story about a young lawyer who engaged in a long argument with a judge. The judge patiently told the verbose youngster that he agreed with him on the law and was with him in spite of the reasons advanced. President Taft concluded: "Judge Fall, I have heard your argument and am for your cause in spite of it." [62]

Fall later confided to Governor Curry that he had spoken with deliberate intent of causing the president to go on record publicly in favor of statehood. President Taft, for his part, later told Curry that Fall's speech had irritated him but had no effect on his attitude toward statehood for New Mexico.

On January 14, 1910, Edward L. Hamilton of the House Committee on Territories introduced an enabling act for Arizona and New Mexico. The bill was referred to Senator Beveridge's Committee on Territories. True to his word to Elkins that he would relent after 1910, and undoubtedly resigned to the inevitable, Beveridge now concerned himself with writing a bill that would be in the public interest. The House accepted his suggested revisions by a unanimous vote and, on June 20, 1910, President Taft signed the bill. Catron, who had traveled to Washington in May and remained there to lend his assistance in the final effort, was present at the signing.

News of the enabling act flashed to New Mexico, and there was understandable jubilation there. In a newspaper a few days later, "pretty well down to the bottom of the first column. . . ."[63] was mention of Catron's role in the achievement. Andrews, who had worked hard for statehood and was in a position to know what had transpired in the last weeks of the struggle, noticed the scant attention paid to Catron and promised to set the record straight. He wrote:

> When I come out I will make a speech one at Albuquerque and one at Santa Fe and I will give the true history of the statehood bill, that is I will see you get proper credit because you were a strong factor in securing the bill.[64]

Andrews did write the speech but did not have occasion for its delivery. A portion dealing with Catron is here presented for the first time:

> About two months before the adjournment of Congress, President Taft made a speech in Patterson, N. J., in the course of which it was reported in the public press that, after enumerating the various measures, which he was urging before Congress with reasonable expectation of their passage in fullfillment of the pledges of the Republican party as contained in the Chicago platform, he said in substance, that he was afraid that he might not be able to secure the passage of the enabling act creating the two new states of New Mexico and Arizona, because there was a general feeling throughout the East, that these States would either send Democratic Senators and members of Congress or Republicans opposed to the general policies of the administration and the republican party. This speech struck consternation to the friends of Statehood everywhere and there could hardly be found in either House of Congress a man who expressed confidence in the passage of the Statehood bill during that session of Congress; while it was generally believed that the act for which we had striven for so many, many years would be delayed until another presidential election. Those were gloomy hours for us! Just at that time there appeared in Washington, on private business, your fellow townsman, the Hon. Thomas Benton Catron. For forty years it had been the dream of this man's life to secure Statehood for New Mexico. I urged him to join our

shattered forces and lend the weight of his great name to our desperate cause. Without any commission from the people, without any compensation and without any hope of personal reward or recognition, he abandoned his private undertakings to remain in the heat of the city for seven weary weeks, struggling for Statehood for New Mexico, — and it was a struggle, a conflict, a battle! Men matched their wits against one another and forces and motives were marshalled through all the influence that could be brought to bear. Early and late, without a word of complaint, full of faith and courage, this old time fighter struggled for New Mexico's cause, and the true story of our triumph cannot be written without giving to him a large measure of credit for our final victory. I have heretofore, in public and in private, and shall hereafter, repeatedly accord to Pres. Taft, General Hitchcock, Chairman Hamilton and to various other members of both houses of Congress, the full measure of praise and credit to which they are entitled for their work for New Mexico; but at this time and in this county and city, I want to take occasion to lay special stress upon the fact that it is my genuine belief, that, regardless of all other forces which were in operation, there was one influence without which Statehood might not have been secured for New Mexico and Arizona, and that was exercised by your heroic old Roman Thomas Benton Catron.[65]

While Andrews gave much credit to Catron, the latter, in turn, passed on a great deal to Elkins. In a letter to Mrs. Elkins after the death of her husband, he wrote:

New Mexico will always remember that almost the last official act of his life in Congress was to go with me into the House of Representatives after the New Mexico bill had passed the Senate and insist upon the House concurring in the amendments which had been made in the Senate, he assuring me that if we did not do that the bill would never pass a conference committee and we would be deferred indefinitely in getting statehood. I told our people that, and they feel grateful to him, and I assure you that I feel more grateful, probably, than anyone else because I believed he advised us right and worked for our best interests.[66]

Under the enabling act the chief justice of the Supreme Court, the governor, and the secretary of the Territory were authorized to apportion the one hundred delegates which the act provided should meet at Santa Fe and write the constitution. This apportionment was made and, nine days later President Taft signed the act, Governor William J. Mills issued his proclamation calling an election for September 6,

1910, to select delegates to a constitutional convention to commence in Santa Fe on October 3, with authorization to sit for no more than sixty days. Seventy-one of the hundred delegates were Republicans, and twenty-eight were Democrats. There was one Socialist, Green B. Patterson of Chavez County, who challenged the distinction, usually claimed by Democrats, of speaking for the common man. He exulted that no one was closer to the poor man and grass roots than he since he was the only man who came to the convention "directly from a dug-out." *

Of the one hundred delegates, thirty-two were Spanish-Americans. There was some objection to this representation. An article in the *New York Sun* of September 24, 1910, contemporarily supposed to have been authored by Edward D. Tittman, a Democratic delegate from Sierra County, said:

> The above is not a list of those present at some bull fight in a Mexican village, but of thirty-two . . . delegates elected to the constitutional convention which is to meet at Santa Fe on October 3, to form a constitution for the American State of New Mexico.[67]

The convention, however, convened as scheduled. Catron, with the aid of his Spanish-American friends, was selected temporary chairman. Charles A. Spiess was nominated and elected president of the convention. The Republican majority kept control of the convention by a resolution calling for a committee of twenty-one members to select all committees. The committee of twenty-one, with Solomon Luna its chairman, had for its members men who, more than the others, performed the work of the convention. Catron, besides being a member of this basic steering committee, was on six of the twenty-seven other committees. Always thorough in preparation, he provided himself with copies of all the states' constitutions for guidance.

---

* Thomas J. Mabry, "New Mexico's Constitution in the Making," *New Mexico Historical Review*, 19; 170. This article was an address made by Mabry, then a justice of the Supreme Court, at the annual meeting of the State Bar Association of New Mexico, in Santa Fe, October 22 and 23, 1943.

Thomas J. Mabry, in an article that is as interesting and readable as it is informative, explains that

The document, as finally written, was largely the handiwork of such able delegates of the majority as T. B. Catron, thereafter U. S. senator; Charles A. Spiess, president of the convention and an outstanding attorney; Charles Springer of Raton, also an able lawyer and representing as well as possessing, large property interest; H. O. Bursum, an able man though not a lawyer, a ceaseless worker and the party's first candidate for governor; A. B. Fall of Three Rivers, an able lawyer, then in the prime of life and in his best fighting condition; Clarence J. Roberts; Frank W. Parker, and Solomon Luna, of Valencia. Luna never made a speech in the convention, but it is said, that he needed only to lift a finger or his eyebrows, to stop any proposal which he deemed against the best interest of his people, his party, or the proposed new state. I omit mention of many able democrats, since these, after all, were in a hopeless minority, and, as I have often said, were there to get into the document what they could, of our program, but whose principal function seemed to be to vote "no." [68]

The convention was a rough-and-tumble political fight throughout. There was much objection to the constitution because women were not given full suffrage; prohibition was not provided directly; Spanish-speaking people were thoroughly — some thought too thoroughly — provided for in their rights; there was no provision for direct legislation; and it was made extremely difficult to amend. On the other hand, both parties were united in ending the pernicious and extravagant fee system for county officers. An overwhelming majority of all delegates favored electing judges, disagreeing only as to the length of term and salaries to be paid.

Perhaps the bitterest controversy was over districting the state for judicial and legislative purposes. Charges of gerrymandering were much heard then and for at least twenty years after the state's first election. It was over this point that the refined amenities of statecraft were sometimes forgotten. But the gerrymandering continued despite loud wailing from the minority. That the Republicans were in the majority and were well united seemed proof enough to them of the justice of their course. Perhaps, after all, there was some validity to their contention that the Democrats were against them anyway and were there to raise hell with whatever the majority did. Years later the complaint against the gerrymander subsided when Democrats gained control of the Senate, the House, and most of the district judges. There was then "no occasion to kick about the tight shoes that had theretofore pinched the political foot."[69]

There is evidence that a successful gerrymander as to legislative districts *was* carried out. The Democrats elected their governor, approximately half of the state officers, and one representative to Congress. The Republicans, though, controlled the new state Senate and House by two-thirds majority in each.

Despite the bitter controversy prevailing through most of the deliberations, personal differences were mostly forgotten at the end when there was much forgiving on both sides. Three barrels of beer supplied by an unknown well-wisher may have helped to calm belligerent spirits. The convention adjourned about four A. M. on the morning of November 21, without using the entire sixty days allowed. Something over $7,000 of the $100,000 appropriated by Congress for holding the convention was left over and returned to the United States treasury — a precedent that was rarely continued. In the final analysis, most of the selfish motives that may have existed were circumscribed or thwarted, and tribute may be paid to the patience, skill, and patriotism of the delegates as a whole.

Catron said of the proceedings:

We had our constitutional Convention. I was a member of it. We have formed a fairly good constitution. There are some things about it which I do not like, but our convention was composed of a very fine party of men, many of them good strong thinkers, and no one man could dictate what should go into the constitution. We had to agree that the State Officers and Judges should be elected. I wanted the judges appointed, particularly those of the Supreme Court, and we so prepared the bill in the Committee of Judiciary, but when we reported it to our republican caucus, while we had a good majority in the caucus for it, we found that there were enough republicans in the caucus who would not be bound by it to join with the democrats and make a majority of two against us. We had 71 republicans and 29 democrats, so we were compelled to agree to elect the judges, in doing so we secured an agreement that the Initiative, Recall and primary elections should be left out and only a modified referendum, very limited in scope, was put in.[70]

The election for ratification or rejection of the constitution as formed was held January 21, 1911, with a total of 45,141 votes cast. There was a majority of 18,343 votes in favor of the constitution. While there had been considerable opposition to numerous features of the document, there was also an overwhelming desire for statehood at any price. Those who would have favored a more liberal instrument were well aware of substantial opposition to statehood existing in the populous states of the East. There was little inclination on the part of a majority of voters to risk the possibility of another long postponement by rejecting the constitution. It was well realized that affirmative legislation by Congress would be required to have another chance.

During the next several trying months while Delegate Andrews sought to secure approval of the constitution by Congress, he corresponded regularly with Catron as regards procedure. On February 24, 1911, President Taft recommended approval, but Congress did not concur because Arizona's acceptance of her constitution was made a condition for approval of that of New Mexico. Unfortunately for the advocates of statehood, in the month preceding — on January 4, 1911 — they had lost a staunch supporter with the death of Stephen B. Elkins. Delegate Andrews lamented to Catron: "I think that if you had been here and poor old Steve was alive, that we could have gotten in in the session just closed."[71]

Die-hard Democrats now hoped that Congress might be induced to provide amendments that would either defeat the constitution or provide more liberal terms. A delegation composed of Andreius A. Jones, Summers Burkhart, Harvey B.

344   *Statehood*

Fergusson, P. F. McCanna, Felix Martinez, J. D. Hand, W. R. McGill, and Thomas J. Mabry was sent to Washington to lobby in behalf of Democratic wishes, and the fate of the constitution hung in the balance. Andrews requested that, if possible, Catron join him in Washington. Catron regretted that he was unable to comply; his legal affairs were so demanding right then that he had been dragged from pillar to post all over the Territory and had not been able to spend even as much as three days at a time in his office.[72]

Early in August a resolution was adopted by Congress requiring Arizona to vote again on the article of her constitution providing for recall of the judiciary, and that an amendment clause, providing for a method of amending the constitution, be resubmitted in New Mexico. On August 15, President Taft vetoed the resolution because of Arizona's liberal acceptance of direct legislation. A compromise was then worked out in Congress whereby Arizona would be required by a vote of her citizens to remove the feature obnoxious to the president, and New Mexico would be bound, at its first state election, to modify the method of amending its constitution. Arizona complied with this directive long enough to become a state; the offending clause was replaced at the next election after statehood. New Mexico voted for, and retained, a modified amendment clause and found that, even then, it was difficult enough to secure desired amendments even when there was agreement as to their need by both major parties.

On August 21, 1911, President Taft signed the resolution admitting New Mexico and Arizona as states in the Union. Enthusiasm throughout New Mexico was rampant. Bonfires blazed in every town as citizens celebrated in joy and relief. The struggle for self-government of more than half a century had finally ended.

Catron wrote to Delegate Andrews:

> I think you have done your whole duty and done it well. The people of New Mexico owe you much gratitude, and I think they should and will look upon your claim for preferment with the greatest

consideration. You certainly shall have my support, even if I have to take a back seat.[73]

There remained only the election of state officers and the final admission to statehood. November 7 was set as election day, and party machinery started preparing. Republicans planned their convention for Las Vegas on September 28; Democrats chose October 2 at Santa Fe. Particularly significant to aspirants to the United States Senate was the initial choice of legislators, because they would elect the first senators.

The Republican convention was organized in the interest of Holm O. Bursum for governor. Bursum's laxity of methods in conducting public business while superintendent of the penitentiary had caused lack of confidence in his capacity as an executive. There was strong opposition within the party to his candidacy by those who thought that selecting him would jeopardize the success of the party at the polls, even though the remainder of the ticket largely represented party strength. Despite this opposition, he was selected by a commanding majority over Secundino Romero of San Miguel County. Most Republican delegates assumed that the substantial majority of that party would prevail despite opposition to Bursum.

The Democratic convention placed in nomination a ticket generally considered to be, for the most part, somewhat weak except for William C. McDonald, their candidate for governor. McDonald was a businessman whose sound conservative judgment appealed to business interests in the new state. The Democrats conducted an effective campaign under the leadership of their chairman, Andreius A. Jones. A segment of the business element, who were nonpartisan and heavy taxpayers, had questioned the benefits of statehood. They now felt that the conduct of the new government was not safe in the hands of Bursum and cast their vote for McDonald. Herbert J. Hagerman was a prominent leader of this group. Then too, Prohibitionists felt they had not been fairly represented in drawing up the new constitution and rebelled against the Republican majority.

The Republican convention had urged that voters defeat the measure calling for modification of the amending clause of the constitution that Congress had required be submitted for vote. The Democratic convention urged the change. Thousands of Republicans and Democrats alike had been willing to sacrifice almost anything for statehood and had approved the constitution even with the original amending clause. Now that statehood was assured and they could safely express their true sentiments, they voted in favor of the so-called "blue ballot" amendment, as well as in favor of candidates of the party that had urged its approval. McDonald, a particularly strong candidate, was especially favored in this way.

The Republican Progressive League had been organized in Santa Fe on October 4, 1911, and endorsed McDonald because they would not accept Bursum. Thus aided, the Democrats won five administrative positions and elected Harvey B. Fergusson to the National House of Representatives. Republicans won six administrative offices, control of the new state legislature, and elected former Governor George Curry to join Fergusson in Congress.

The Republican split was confirmed when the Progressive League resolved into the Progressive party of New Mexico. Bronson Cutting was destined to become the leader of this new entity and solidified his power by courting the goodwill of New Mexicans of Mexican ancestry, assisting them with money, political jobs, and assurance of stature in the affairs of the new state. He became their champion in the first decades of statehood government, as Thomas Benton Catron had for so long been in the Territorial period.

Catron had been fearful that the nomination of Bursum as the Republican candidate for governor would be a mistake. While he personally esteemed Bursum highly, he knew that the opposition of former Governor Hagerman would count heavily against him. Catron believed that the logical candidate for Governor was Solomon Luna. He questioned the wisdom of starting with an uphill pull when a downhill pull was available. Possibly Catron realized that Luna, by becoming governor, would be removed from the senatorial race since Luna was recognized as a likely winner in that contest should he choose to run. On the other hand, Catron always believed that nothing should be done to discourage Mexican fellow citizens. While Catron feared a division of the Republican party with the nomination of Bursum, it is characteristic of his political philosophy that his support of the nominee of the Republican party was never in doubt.[74]

Upon completion of the first state election, in accordance with provision by Congress, a canvassing board met to examine the returns of the election. This board, consisting of the governor, secretary, and chief justice, was engaged for nearly five weeks in the performance of its duty. Republicans to assist the board were represented by Catron and Albert B. Fall; Democrats by Neill B. Field; and Progressive Republicans by C. D. Cleveland. The certificates of the canvassing board were sent to Washington. Then, on January 6, 1912, President Taft signed the proclamation admitting New Mexico as the forty-seventh state of the Union.

17
Senator Catron

Even before President Taft's statehood proclamation, there had been maneuvering over who would become the first senators from New Mexico. Resulting from close cooperation of W. H. Andrews and T. B. Catron in the statehood movement during May and June 1910, there grew persistent rumors that they were also scheming to divide the senatorships between them. There was talk that this was true because Catron gave Andrews full credit for the final passage of the enabling act, while Andrews acknowledged that it would have been difficult, if not impossible, without Catron's aid. When it became established that these rumors were rife, and that they were aimed at hurting the political image of each, they mutually affirmed that the stories were untrue and that they would, by public denials, combine their efforts to refute the·supposition. The truth is that Catron had, nearly a year earlier, warned Andrews of similar whispering to the point that Andrews was trying to make combinations with others which would assure him a seat in the Senate.[1]

When statehood was assured, Catron showed his appreciation for Andrews' unceasing efforts to attain that goal by promising to support Andrews for a seat in the U.S. Senate. This promise was the first indication in their extensive correspondence of either supporting the other, or of cooperation between them in regard to the Senate. While Catron had agreed with Andrews to deny that they were combining their efforts in order to become senators together, Catron had opposed Andrews for the position before the promise was made. It is a measure of Catron's extraordinary desire for statehood that he changed his attitude toward Andrews as a result of the latter's efforts in the statehood movement. He kept Andrews informed of political developments in New Mexico, even in such minor matters as a dinner given for justices of the Supreme Court. Charles A. Spiess, it seems, responded to a toast claiming much of the credit for final statehood approval and belittled Andrews' role. Catron advised Andrews:

> I think you ought to get back here as soon as possible and look after your fences you know that republics are ungrateful, and people of republics are much more ungrateful. When you do things for them they are very apt to say you only did your duty and are entitled to no credit. There are some of the aspirants for preferment in the new State who are talking that way about you, and of course if you remain away it will have its effect. I have told and shall continue to tell everyone with whom I talk that they cannot afford to overlook what you have done and that I am satisfied without your efforts the statehood resolution never would have passed.[2]

At the same time that he was encouraging Andrews, Catron received numerous letters urging that he pursue his own candidacy. It can safely be assumed that he never lost sight of this possibility. He later confided to a friend that after Elkins died he lost a great deal of ambition "but did not lose it all."[3] While he backed Andrews strongly, it was evidently with at least the hope that he also would be named.

Catron's first communication, in September 1911, in regards to his own candidacy for senator was, fittingly enough, with Melvin W. Mills of Springer. Over the years Mills had been his confidant in crucial political matters. It was believed that Charles Springer would be a candidate, and Catron knew that Mills might be called upon to back Springer because of geographic proximity of their residence. It developed, though, that Mills' allegiance was only to one man over Catron —

Judge Henry L. Waldo. Since Mills understood that Waldo would not be a candidate, he considered his first obligation was to help Catron in every way possible. Catron, in assessing his own chances, wrote concerning rumors (which he personally did not believe) of combinations being made variously between Charles Springer and Albert B. Fall, and Springer and William J. Mills. Catron pointed out that Andrews was a strong candidate, but he had not heard of anyone combining with him. As for himself, Catron stated that he had not combined with anyone else; nevertheless, he believed that he had considerable strength.[4]

Mills' reply to Catron gave insight into the practical aspects of politics in New Mexico at that time. He wrote:

> There are a few men who are candidates that I guess have some money. It may be that Springer, [William J.] Mills, Fall and some others have got some of this filthy stuff to scatter about. If so, they will likely be able to work up a combination that will lay us one side; notwithstanding all our service in behalf of New Mexico these many years.*

Catron's disbelief of rumors to the point that Albert B. Fall was entering into schemes with others which would lead him to a senatorship was well founded. Fall officially took the position that he was not a candidate at all; in fact, he regretted that others were openly seeking preferment. He believed that the Republican convention to be held on Septembr 28 should be free to pledge support to senatorial candidates without any previous political pressure brought to bear on delegates. If he were to be chosen by the convention as one to whom Republican support would be given, he would then feel more like becoming a candidate. He considered it unlikely, however, that the convention would give preference to senatorial candidacy. In that case, if he should be chosen by the legislature after the election, his appreciation of the honor might overpower his disinclination to accept public office.[5]

---

*M. W. Mills to Catron, September 12, 1911 (C.P. 103, Box 37). By "us" Mills was undoubtedly referring more particularly to Catron than to himself. It would seem, also, that Mills recognized Catron's financial difficulties at this time.

Thomas Benton Catron, United States Senator, 1912–17.

This reluctant candidate gambit is probably as old as politics. If Fall sought to increase his own chances in this way, his ploy was successful, because he later became the strongest candidate when senators were chosen.

Actually, aside from discussing the matter with Melvin W. Mills and a few other close friends, it appears that Catron did little in behalf of his own candidacy prior to the September 28 Republican convention. Frank Lavan, a Catron law partner and nephew, candidly assessed the senatorial situation soon after that convention:

> As the result of the convention held in Las Vegas last week, T. B. is, in my opinion, a much stronger candidate for the U. S. Senate than he was before that time. He is the strongest man in the territory today, but it is a well known fact that the machine is against him. There are a number of candidates for the U. S. Senate, and they all fear him so out of a spirit of self-protection they have apparently organized to defeat him. If Sol Luna chooses to run for the U.S. Senate, there is nobody that can beat him, but he declines to declare himself and nobody seems qualified to speak for him. The other candidates are Charles Springer, A. B. Fall, W. H. Andrews and Mills, the present governor, but he can apparently be eliminated from serious consideration.[6]

Despite much talk that Catron and Andrews were working toward seats in the Senate together, Andrews refrained from even discussing the matter formally with Catron prior to the convention. When he did, his letters were merely brief formal announcements that he was a candidate and would appreciate such assistance as Catron deemed proper to extend.[7]

As for Catron, even after the convention, he quietly bided his time, with but little urging on his part that others support him for senator. The November 7 election passed; for Catron its chief importance was the election of his son, Charles, to the legislature. As the year drew to a close, Melvin W. Mills again summed up Catron's chances, and his assessment was not encouraging. He expressed a personal hope that his friend might wind up his life in New Mexico affairs as one of the first senators, but he did not believe that Catron could count on a dozen members of the legislature. It was Mills' opinion that Albert B. Fall was in the lead. He could not see that Andrews or Governor Mills had much following. Aside from Fall, he believed that some native New Mexican stood to win, probably O. A. Larrazolo or Felix Martinez.

In forty-five years Melvin W. Mills had not seen as much sentiment among the Mexicans that they must stand by themselves or else surrender all chances for public place. Mills urged that Catron pitch his pipe with either Martinez or Larrazolo and do so promptly. He concluded: "I see that you are so much more alone, all by yourself as it were, more than you used to be; in fact, I see that the coming . . . of these new people has the effect of supplanting the old fellows." *

On March 12, 1912, Governor William C. McDonald called for the legislature to meet, and eight days later voting began for New Mexico's first United States senators. Republican candidates besides Catron were Albert B. Fall, William H. Andrews, L. Bradford Prince, O. A. Larrazolo, Eugenio Romero, William J. Mills, and Jose D. Sena. Charles Springer had given up his own candidacy and transferred his support to Fall. Democrats were represented by Felix Martinez and Andreius A. Jones, while Herbert J. Hagerman and W. H. Gillenwater were the Progressive Republicans.[8]

There seemed little doubt that Fall would be elected unless there was a compromise resulting from the contest between Catron and Andrews for the other senatorship. Republican leaders were divided in their allegiance, although there was more support for Fall than the others. Holm O. Bursum supported Fall and Andrews. Solomon Luna, who usually backed winners, gave quiet but effective support to Fall and Catron. Charles Spiess had promised to back Catron but worked

---

* Mills to Catron, December 25, 1911 (C.P. 103, Box 37). Larrazolo was a Republican and Martinez a Democrat. There is no indication that Catron went out of his way to secure the favor of either. He did, however, continue to pledge his support to New Mexicans of Mexican origin. It was their assistance, in turn, that ultimately won him the senatorship.

actively for Fall and Mills. Catron feared that Spiess' promise might have been lightly given; their old partnership quarrel evidently still rankled. Catron knew that, despite Spiess' promise, he might lean toward Mills. At worst, though, he thought that Spiess would become lukewarm and not help. He did not anticipate that Spiess would go over to Fall.[9]

As the time for voting approached, there was a strong underground movement for Fall and Martinez, which subsided when Fall refused to deal with the Democrats. Despite early balloting, which did not show well for Catron, he never lost confidence. During the voting he wrote:

> I have reason to believe that there is a larger number of members who favor me, but did not vote for me. And that while I am really the first choice of a great many of them, on account of local and peculiarly personal reasons, they are at present favoring someone else. I am inclined to believe that the choice will fall upon A. B. Fall and myself in the end.[10]

Through seven successive ballots there was much shifting of votes, but no candidate received a sufficient number for election. There were guarded newspaper accounts of money being spent by one candidate or another, most of them connected with Andrews and his supporters. Most, if not all, of these stories were probably false.[11] As the balloting progressed it became evident that Mills had no chance, so Charles Spiess and John H. Clark induced him to withdraw. Andrews, also, when it became evident that his continued resistance might only create party disharmony, listened to the advice of Holm O. Bursum and withdrew.

At this juncture there was a factor that shaped the actions of Catron and Andrews toward each other unknown to the assembled delegates. As stated, Catron had earlier promised to back Andrews even to the extent of himself stepping into the background.[12] Did Catron honestly mean that he would take a back seat? Was he truly willing to give up the dream of a lifetime? It is possible that he was. He had cooperated fully with Andrews in the struggle to achieve statehood, but early

in March 1911 a determining circumstance entered their relationship that had plagued his rapport with the other men for
much of his adult life. Andrews asked Catron to sign notes
with him in the amount of three thousand dollars. This was at
a time when Catron absolutely could not afford to do so. His
son, Charles, who was managing his business and financial
affairs, had repeatedly chided him for the practice. But he
signed the notes. He wrote Andrews that he did not much
like to do so and warned him sternly that he must be absolutely
protected in the matter.[13]

Catron admonished Andrews several times against allowing the notes to bother him, even while encouraging Andrews
in his senatorial aspirations.[14]

Over the years Catron had often loaned money, or signed
notes, with just such a warning. Repeatedly, no effort was
made by the borrower to repay the loan. Understandably,
Catron grew increasingly disillusioned by such evidences of
feeble fidelity to promises and, for time after time, all that he
gained for his trust was an enemy. Characteristically, he was
very patient when the money was not paid on time, and then
grew bitterly antagonistic when payment continued to be deferred beyond reason. This was to prove no exception in the
case of the loan to Andrews.

Even as touchy as Catron was at this stage of his life about
loans that were not repaid, he had been, up to the time Andrews withdrew, himself ready to withdraw at any time that
it appeared Andrews would be elected.[15] As it was, Andrews
was the one who made this concession, but Catron continued
to favor him in other political matters whenever possible even
though basic understanding between the two was to remain at
odds.

When the roll was called for the eighth ballot, Catron
lacked four votes of election. Before the result was announced,
however, enough legislators changed their vote to assure that
he would join Fall in the winner's circle. The Spanish-Americans on the Republican side switched to Catron at the critical

time. When the result of the voting was announced, Fall had thirty-nine votes and Catron thirty-eight; thirty-five were necessary for election.*

Catron received numerous letters of congratulations, among them one from Melvin W. Mills who summed up the feelings of many Catron well-wishers when he wrote:

> I have said and wished thousands of times that your life struggle in New Mexico should be rounded up with the highest office within the gift of the people.[16]

In answer to a telegram from the wife of the late Senator Elkins, Catron replied:

> The great regret that I encounter in connection with it will be in not meeting your late husband and my classmate there. I have always desired, ever since he went to the Senate, to go there as a senator and be with him in that body; I know that he wished the same also, but fate has decided otherwise.[17]

Other correspondence also indicates his regret that Elkins died before they could realize their ambition of serving together in the United States Senate.[18]

On April 2, 1912, the new senators from New Mexico and Arizona were sworn into office, making the United States Senate a body of ninety-six members. Prior to the ceremony a lottery was held to determine the length of term of the new members. Senator Catron drew the five-year term ending March 4, 1917, and Senator Fall drew the term ending March 4, 1913.

Catron was assigned chairmanship of the committee on expenditures in the department of the interior, and was made a member of the committees on coast defense, conservation of natural resources, Cuban relations, industrial expositions and Pacific railroads. Later he was assigned to the committee on military affairs.[19]

Rio Grande Republican, March 12, 1912. The final vote was: Republicans — A. B. Fall 39, T. B. Catron 38, L. Bradford Prince 3, O. A. Larrazolo 2, Eugenio Romero 1, William J. Mills 1, Jose D. Sena 1; Democrats — Felix Martinez 25, A. A. Jones 23; Progressive Republicans — Herbert J. Hagerman 3, W. H. Gillenwater 2.

As Thomas Benton Catron entered the Senate, he bore a striking physical resemblance to the late President Grover Cleveland. The outstanding characteristic of this resemblance was the physical dimensions of each. In Catron's case they were chest, 44 inches; waist, 46½ inches; and hips 49½ inches. He was 5 feet 9¼ inches tall. His weight varied somewhat from time to time but reached as much as 240 pounds. He had weighed over 200 pounds since the age of thirty-three. He bore his weight cheerfully enough but did make some effort to attain a slimmer figure. To this end he made occasional visits to the Battle Creek Sanitarium at Battle Creek, Michigan. Here he would lose ten or twenty pounds in two or three weeks only to see it slowly return. Between visits he tried various obesity cures. One was from the Tremont Medical Company of Boston. He inquired: "How many bottles will I have to use and how long will it take to reduce me to about 190 pounds? I do not care about being reduced lower than that or 180." [20]

Over the years his desire to lose weight seems to have been from practical considerations as much as concern about his personal appearance. His size made it difficult to secure properly fitted clothing; it was necessary that his suits be tailored. In this regard, he wrote to his wife: "They now say the suit was a 'ready-made' suit, but that of course is ridiculous. No ready made suit could be found which would come anyways near fitting me." [21] He had no special source for purchasing suits, trying one tailor and another from time to time, always looking for conservative cut and quality material at a reasonable price. He once, at the suggestion of his wife, ordered a suit from Brooks Brothers in New York but after a troublesome delay in delivery found that it didn't fit. Then, too, it was his candid opinion that fifty dollars for a coat and vest made almost too high priced a suit. One reporter, searching for Senator Catron in a crowd, was instructed to look for a "large man, slightly stooped, not caring much for his personal appearance and whose clothes don't fit." [22] If allowed to follow his personal inclination, he was just as happy ordering clothing from Montgomery Ward as Brooks Brothers.

His troubles with securing a proper fit sometimes ran into amusing incidents, although he generally did not consider them in that light at the time. On one occasion he purchased a pair of trousers, obviously of inferior material, and had worn them only two days when the "entire seat bursted to pieces." [23] He was away from home at the time and was forced to bed while he got a tailor to come and fix them. A more clothes-conscious man might have had an extra pair along for emergencies.

In that connection a story is told about a trip he was to take to Mexico City. He started down the walk from his home, carrying nothing; then he returned, as though he had forgotten something. When he departed the second time he waved a red bandanna handkerchief to indicate that he had corrected the oversight and was now thoroughly prepared. In his later years he required a hearing aid. His granddaughter, Mrs. Sue Catron Bergere, tells the story of Catron's being summoned unwillingly to court as a witness. Since he didn't want to testify, he turned off his hearing aid, and when the judge asked him a question Catron kept asking him to repeat a little louder, that he couldn't hear. Finally the judge gave in and said, "Oh, forget it, you're excused." [24]

As he grew older and stouter, his weight caused a bothersome asthmatic condition. Senator Catron liked good food, which he realized was the cause of his stoutness; his favorite breakfast was a stack of pancakes with scrambled eggs on top. Generally, however, his health was excellent and his habits moderate. He did not use tobacco in any form, took an infrequent drink of whiskey, and occasionally drank wine with meals. He had suffered pneumonia when he was ten years old, and malaria while a soldier in the Civil War. He started wearing spectacles for reading in his middle years, but sometimes forgot and left them behind in his travels. During his life he was involved in three serious falls from runaway buggies, with resultant injuries including a broken collar bone and arm. The newspapers reported that as the result of one accident in 1904, he sustained injuries to his head which might prove fatal.

As Catron entered the Senate, it was noticeable that his vigor and activity belied his years. In the realm of intellect, especially, he stood out. One contemporary account describes him:

> As an orator, Mr. Catron possesses an eloquence which is wonderful. In the first place his voice is one of a particularly pleasing quality, and in the second, while never committing the crime of "talking down" to his audience he has the happy faculty of making his remarks understandable to all, and of putting matters before his hearers in such a logical, clear, simple way that they cannot fail to grasp his meaning and see the reasonableness of the issue which he is advocating. Coupled with his distinguished appearance, these points make him a great favorite with audiences.[25]

This author asked three persons who knew Senator Catron to describe their recollections of him as a public speaker. Will Keleher, author and attorney, had this to say:

> It is my recollection that Thomas B. Catron was an excellent public speaker. He had a voice suited to his big burly physique, crowned by a massive, leonine head. Mr. Catron was capable of appraising the capacity and attitude of his hearers, whether delivering the keynote speech at a Republican Convention, which he did on many occasions, or addressing a political rally, a jury, or district or supreme court judges.
> Catron's voice was boomlike when he turned on the stops, soft and persuasive when making telling points. I would classify Mr. Catron not so much a silver tongued orator, which he was not, but as an outstanding, effective speaker, who was master of the English language, and who achieved desired results.[26]

General Thomas B. Catron II, Senator Catron's son, recalled this about his father:

> As I recall, the pitch of his voice was medium, tending to high. He spoke neither slowly nor very rapidly. In his public addresses he spoke very much as usual unless and until he intended an "oratorical effect." His mode of speech was compelling; he did not speak too loudly except that the volume would raise when he was stirred or angry.

His talk reflected education, wide reading and knowledge, and was very logical. His vocabulary was extensive and he certainly could be, and often was, a colorful speaker.[27]

Frank F. Catron, Lexington, Missouri attorney and second cousin of Senator Catron, wrote:

In conversation the pitch of his voice was low but his articulation was very clear; more on the deliberate side than otherwise. He did not speak quickly; but he did speak without noticeable pause and used few gestures.

Commenting further, I would say that the speech of T. B. Catron was rythmic and smooth flowing. He never seemed to be at loss for the proper word in the proper place, indicative of a considerable vocabulary. Within my limited observation, however, I would not say that he was a colorful speaker, but rather that his vocal effectiveness was due to some other quality. Perhaps, to his positive assertiveness, which carried conviction in the court room, or before a deliberating body, but definitely not to the less putative exuberance of the average political audience.[28]

It is not surprising that the three did not remember Senator Catron in exactly the same way. It is noteworthy, though, that each recalled his persuasiveness as being attributable to his intelligence, extensive vocabulary, and logical presentation.

Senator Fall was assured of only a one-year term. A provision of the constitution placed the responsibility of reelecting Fall, or electing his successor, on the legislature that had just elected him. There was no specification indicating whether this was to be done at the session then in progress or at the second session to begin January 14, 1913. There was some disposition in the Republican-dominated legislature to immediately reelect him, thus assuring that he would have a full term in office. This inclination was, nevertheless, by no means unanimous.

Frank Lavan explained the situation in a letter to Catron soon after he was sworn in as senator:

We are all tickled over your drawing the long term. Kind of feel a little apprehensive for Fall though, as the impression seems to be general that he is going to have considerable trouble in getting a reelection, at least during the present session. I have talked with a couple of the members who seem to be of the opinion that by withholding any action until the session in January, 1913, they will at least have a check on Fall until after the coming Presidential election.[29]

Fall was aware that at least a portion of the legislature was disinclined to immediately reelect him, so took up the matter with Solomon Luna. Fall's choice of a person to champion his cause was an indication of his political wisdom, and his procedure in the matter confirmed that sagacity. He pointed out to Luna that he and Senator Catron were already busily at work looking after New Mexico's interests, and continued:

> We are in excellent shape and an immediate election of Senator at the present time for the long term, would simply show the people that we are united and with the assurance to them that I would have a 7 year term in the Senate there is nothing which New Mexico wanted that she will not get. I appreciate the conditions there and understand just what fight is being made. If I were entirely out of the race, however, or even if I were to die, it would be the greatest mistake in the world for the legislature ever to elect Andrews to the Senate. Many of the old line Senators have expressed their feeling in this matter very plainly.[30]

Fall continued, informing Luna of hearsay then current in Washington that an agent of Andrews had fixed up the drawing, through Senator Boise Penrose of Pennsylvania, so that Fall secured the short term. The reported plan was for Penrose then to bring such pressure to bear on Luna that he would be compelled to support Andrews. Fall preferred to believe that the whole story was utter nonsense from beginning to end, and he only repeated it as it had been stated.

Catron was torn between Fall and Andrews in the controversy. He continued to acknowledge the importance of Andrews' role in achieving statehood, and appreciated his manliness in withdrawing from the Senate race in the interest of party harmony as soon as it was apparent that he could not be elected. Catron realized that this action had done much to assure his own election. On the other hand, he appreciated

Fall's position and desired to do nothing to injure him; in fact, he declared that had he drawn the short term he would have expected the legislature to reelect him. Catron wrote to his son, Charles (a member of the legislature) concerning the problem. He impressed upon Charles the importance of the legislature then in session electing the successor to Senator Fall, whether it be Fall or anyone else. He urged his son to use his own best judgment, and suggested: "If Mr. Andrews cannot be elected and Judge Fall can be with your help, . . . elect him."[31]

Catron, right then, imperceptibly but clearly favored Andrews, but primarily because of gratitude for his role in securing statehood and his own seat in the Senate. The personal animosity that had earlier induced Catron to describe Fall as "the most offensive man in the whole Territory and the most venal,"[32] had long since been replaced by grudging respect, if not open admiration and sincere friendliness. Within the month all indecision was removed and Catron switched his allegiance openly and frankly to Fall. Why? The loans which Catron had signed with Andrews remained unpaid, and he could not afford to remain as guarantor. Fully as important, Andrews commenced to take advantage of Fall's absence in Washington by bringing devious pressure to bear on New Mexico legislators with the view of promoting his own election to the Senate. Catron wrote to his son in the legislature and urged him to do what he could to break up the combination started by Andrews and to secure the reelection of Senator Fall.[33]

The legislature delayed in the matter of senatorial selection, and Catron wrote to Solomon Luna on behalf of his colleague. It had come out in a conversation between Catron and Senator Penrose of Pennsylvania that Penrose had no idea Andrews could be elected to the Senate; furthermore, Penrose understood that Andrews banked on raising money in the East to promote his candidacy. It would not be possible, as far as Penrose was aware, for Andrews to raise money in this way, and it would be useless for him to rely on any such proposition.

While concluding that Andrews should not be elected, Catron was strongly convinced that the matter of electing a senator should not be deferred until the following year. The revolt of the Republican Progressives (insurgents) was already underway. This was to result in the struggle of Theodore Roosevelt to unseat President Taft under the symbol of the bull moose, and the consequent election of Woodrow Wilson. Catron foresaw this possibility and pointed out to Luna that, if the legislature put off electing a senator until January 1913, and a Democrat were elected President in the interim, a Democrat might be returned instead of Fall. In behalf of Senator Fall, he wrote:

> The members of the Senate here very generally think the legislature ought to get together and reelect Fall. He has got much standing with all Republicans, both standpatters and Progressives, and they are all anxious to see him return.[34]

Early in June the legislature had still postponed the election of a senator for the term starting in 1913. Senator Catron encouraged his son to do whatever he could to hurry the matter along:

> Judge Fall will be there when you get this. He is going out to see if he cannot get matters together for his reelection, and I wish you would help him all you possibly can; he stands well here and will make a good Senator and be of immense benefit, I believe, to the State, and he deserves to be reelected. He and I are working together in absolute harmony in every respect.[35]

In further support of Fall, Catron expressed his opinion of William H. Andrews' tactics:

> I hope you will allow no junketing committee to go around through the State. I understand Mr. Andrews' way of doing business and know he would jeopardize every interest we have in that State to further his own interests."[36]

Finally, on June 4, 1912, the state Senate adopted a resolution inviting a joint session of that body and the House to vote on the United States senatorial matter. The following day the House passed a resolution stating that it would not ballot for a senator during that session. In this voting, a dissident element, stirred up by William H. Andrews, combined with the Democrats to pass the resolution. There then immediately followed a political maneuver, engineered by Charles C. Catron, that would have been a credit to Catron in the heyday of his political power.

Charles C. Catron and other members of the House informed the Senate that if they would take another ballot at ten o'clock that evening, seventeen of them would be present and vote in joint session. At the appointed hour there were twenty-three senators present and the seventeen members of the House, as well as one stray Democrat from the House who got into the room and could not get out. The Senate roll was called; fifteen members voted for Fall, two voted for Andrews, and six Democratic senators (as well as the stray Democrat from the House) refused to vote. Combined with the vote from the House, this gave thirty-two votes for Fall as against two for Andrews, with seven refusing to vote.[37]

On June 6 it dawned on the Democrats, and the Andrews-inspired recusant Republicans, that they had lost the election for United States senator. William H. H. Llewellyn and R. L. Baca, acting on behalf of said Republicans, now introduced a resolution rescinding the former resolution and providing that the House should proceed to take a ballot for United States senator. This resolution caused a split between the Andrews Republicans and the Democrats. Pandemonium reigned supreme in the House for about three hours during which the "solid seventeen" were silent spectators and took no part in the fistic and verbal combat.

When order was restored and the resolution carried, the House voted, with twenty-five votes for Fall and two for R. L. Baca — the remaining members of the House refused to vote.

Senate and House journals were immediately compared; the lieutenant governor, as presiding officer of the joint session, announced that, inasmuch as A. B. Fall had received a majority of votes in the separate ballots of both Senate and House, he had been duly elected senator to succeed himself on March 4, 1913, for a period of six years.*

This broke up the combination between the Andrews Republicans and the Democrats. Although only two days remained in the session, the House was able to pass various Senate bills that had been bottled up by that combination; William H. "Bull" Andrews was finished in New Mexico. While he remained in the state for a few more years, he eventually returned to Pennsylvania from whence he had come a dozen years earlier, apparently hoping to buy himself a seat in the United States Senate. He spent a fortune in this endeavor and died on January 16, 1919, almost penniless.

As far as can be learned he never repaid the loans that Catron co-signed with him, although Catron repeatedly, and with increasing firmness, demanded that he do so until as late as September 1914.[38] Catron, however, always insisted that Andrews was more important than any other person in the final acquisition of statehood. He should not be forgotten for the service he rendered, regardless of what his motive may have been.

In January 1913 the legality of Senator Fall's election was questioned when Summers Burkhart, special legal adviser for Governor McDonald, prepared an exhaustive brief claiming that the election had been irregular. The case was widely discussed with considerable vehemence in the press of the new state. Variously named as a possible successor to Fall were former Territorial Governor Miguel A. Otero, Felix Martinez, Andreius A. Jones, and national Republican Commit-

---

* C. C. Catron to T. B. Catron, June 10, 1912 (C.P. 110, Vol. 2). T. B. Catron was trying to obtain repayment of a loan from Llewellyn at this time.

teeman Charles A. Spiess. Fall, however, was confirmed in his election by the state legislature.*

In 1921, when Charles C. Catron's herculean task of settling his father's estate caused his own business to suffer, he called upon Senator Fall for aid in securing the attorneyship for the Pueblo Indians in New Mexico. He pointed out that for the past eight years he had done a great deal of work for them without remuneration because, during those years of Democratic administration, United States attorneys had been appointed who did not understand the Indians and had immediately started to destroy the customs and internal management of the pueblos. This resulted in the Indians going to Charles C. Catron for aid, which he gave them.

He was unable to contact Fall directly, so left a reminder with the senator's secretary concerning his leadership of the "solid seventeen" which had secured Fall's election as senator in 1912.[39] Soon thereafter Fall was appoined secretary of the interior, and Charles Catron again wrote to him about the position. He also secured a number of recommendations which were sent to Fall. Charles Catron never received an answer but later learned that Secretary Fall had someone else in mind for the attorneyship. He was saddened rather than angered by the slight; he explained: "It does grieve me to feel that one man for whom I did so much at a time when it was vital to him should think so lightly of past favors."[40]

The change that came over Thomas Benton Catron when he became a senator from New Mexico was so remarkable that it is difficult to comprehend. Albert B. Fall, during the first

---

Albuquerque Morning Journal, January 24, 1913; C. C. Catron to T. B. Catron, January 3, 1913 (C.P. 110, Vol. 2) January 27, 1913 (C.P. 101, Vol. 16); T. B. Catron to W. H. Andrews, February 10, 1913 (C.P. 501, Box 36). This seems to be the only basis for Otero's contention (*Nine Years as Governor*, p. 193) that he and Catron were both candidates for the United States Senate and that one of Otero's friends had deserted him, thus causing Catron's election. Tenuous at best, this claim is further invalidated by the fact that the opposition in question was Fall, not Catron. One of Otero's numerous inconsistencies is expressed (*ibid.*, p. 201) when he writes that he didn't care to become senator — that he liked his job as Territorial governor so well that he wished to become the first governor of New Mexico elected by the people.

weeks he served in the Senate with Catron, was prompted repeatedly to comment about the transformation of his colleague. Fall marveled:

> I do not know what Mr. Catron is privately writing or telegraphing to New Mexico. Here he is doing exactly what I want him to do in every matter. He does not go to the departments unless I will go with him; he does not call at the White House unless I will make the appointment; he does not pay any attention to what is going on in the Senate unless I call his attention to it; he is in a state of perfect happiness and spends from one to two hours every morning in the luxurious baths provided for the Senators in our Office Building. I think I could say nothing more to add strength to my statement that he is the most completely changed man whom I have ever known.[41]

It is easy to understand that Senator Fall was amazed. It is readily possible to delineate, with too bold a stroke, the domineering side of Catron through much of his life; nevertheless, that side of his character was present. His contemporaries spoke and wrote of it; his own letters demand that it be recognized. As Will Keleher astutely noted:

> No man ever crossed swords with Tom Catron in New Mexico in a lawsuit, in a political row, or in a business transaction, who was not willing to admit that Catron was an expert swordsman, an aggressive and powerful adversary.[42]

It is true that Thomas Benton Catron become a senator as he was approaching his seventy-second birthday. Fall, two decades younger, noted this in passing but attached no significance to it as an explanation for the change in Catron's personality. Catron's forthright attitude toward others over the years was called into play mostly when he observed in them weakness when strength was called for, laziness when energy would carry the day, or incompetence when ability was the better aid to accomplishment. He was, however, no stranger to the Washington scene and association with possibly abler men than he found at home, so this basic tenet of his relations with others does not account for the change when he became senator. Catron himself said of the Senate and of senators as a class:

I have been sworn in and am now acting as a Senator of the United States. It is a great distinction to occupy the place, yet I feel that it is not so very great after all, as I have grown up to understand it and mixed with them a great deal until they look to me like ordinary mortals, although men of somewhat superior ability.[43]

Two factors can be pointed out as influencing the modification of his outlook on life and his reactions to persons around him. For much of his life he had been faced with incredibly complex and difficult business problems. When he entered the Senate, his son Charles (and the younger brothers to a lesser extent) largely took over these matters. The other factor is less tangible, more difficult to express, and far more difficult to assess. Others had for so long pointed out that a place in the United States Senate would be a fitting climax for his long and productive life that it came to mean more to him than had the acquisition of his goal been an idea nurtured only in his own mind. When that height of his ambition was at last reached, it became as a soothing ointment applied to a long-suffering spot of soreness. Simply put, consciously or otherwise, he evidently decided to enjoy himself, to cease unremitting toil, and to allow others to carry a larger share of the drudgery without crimination on his part, even though their performance might not meet his exacting standards. Who can say exactly why a man grows weary of fighting and accepts conditions as they are rather than as it seems to him they ought to be? That it came in Tom Catron's life at all is the marvel rather than that it came so late.

But the change in Catron was one of honest cooperation and contentment, not of surrender or willingness to be pushed around. The latter might seem to be indicated by such expressions of Fall's as:

Catron and myself will have no trouble agreeing on these matters as he does not want to fight me at all and every indication is that after I have talked with him he will agree on anything.[44]

Still, Fall was not gloating or giving the impression that he was dominating Catron. In fact, he must have experienced

some difficulty in expressing his relationship with his colleague
in view of the new Catron image. Considering Catron's former
forcefulness, Fall may have secretly wondered how long the
honeymoon would last. While in his early days in the Senate
Catron almost seemed to revel in wholehearted cooperative-
ness as if he were scourging himself with the newly found joy
of it, he did moderate more to his norm as time passed. There
is no question, though, that he had an image of the proper
senator. When he embarked on that career, it would seem
that he went through a period of self-examination to mold
himself in that image, and probably the process was studied
and deliberate, for Catron was not above taking stock of himself.

Cordial relations between him and Fall did last. They
were both individuals of strong temperament, and they did
not always completely agree, but their differences were not
the volcanic eruptions of earlier days. In this fresh rapport,
Catron acted with newly found consideration, and Fall had
sense enough not to abuse the relationship. It is unfortunate
that Fall's political opportunism was to cause further friction
when Catron sought reelection as senator. In the main, though,
as for Catron, the magically rapid mellowing brought about
by a seat in the United States Senate lasted, within bounds
that could be at all reasonably expected, until the day he died.

As senators Catron and Fall entered upon their tenure
in office, a problem they faced was how to relate to the growing
feud between President Taft and former President Roosevelt.
The Progressive movement had been gaining strength in the
United States from the days following the Civil War, accompanied with a demand by the people for a larger popular
voice in government. This movement gained new impetus
upon the emergence of the nation into the twentieth century
and became strong enough to be widely heard as the election
of 1912 approached. The leader of the new movement was
Senator "Fighting Bob" La Follette of Wisconsin. Theodore

Roosevelt had been preaching Progressive policies, but he did not seem to be a candidate for the presidency, so the Progressives chose La Follette as their standard bearer. But eastern Progressives distrusted La Follette and hoped to persuade Roosevelt to enter the race. Their opportunity came in February 1912, when La Follette suffered a temporary nervous breakdown, and many declared that he was too ill to continue the Progressive battle.

By chance, at this time Roosevelt became incensed at a speech made by President Taft in which he branded the leaders of the Progressive movement as emotionalists and neurotics. Despite his former friendship for Taft, Roosevelt now declared that "his hat was in the ring." La Follette, embittered, remained in the fight. The result was a lively but unseemly scramble for delegates to the Republican convention.

Senator Fall, while a professed friend of Roosevelt, assured President Taft that he would support whoever was nominated.[45] Senator Catron believed that the delegates from New Mexico should stand by Taft. He was afraid, though, that the acrimonious fight then going on between Taft and Roosevelt had so embittered the two factions that it would be impossible for either to be elected. The Roosevelt people claimed that their candidate was so strong that he would attract enough Democrats to more than offset the Republicans who would not vote for him.

Catron did not believe that this was true, especially when there was such a radical division in the Republican party. He hoped that the Republican convention would see the situation as he saw it and nominate a third person who was not embroiled in the factional fight. He summed up his feeling in a manner somewhat extraordinary for the redoubtable leader of the so-called Santa Fe Ring of earlier days:

> There are certain clicks and kinks and rings who get hold of things and try to run them and do run them without reference to any sense of decency, at times — that is what is the trouble just at the present time.[46]

As the struggle for power developed, Senator Fall changed his mind about Roosevelt, declaring that he did not approve of his course or his platform, particularly his conservation policies, although he thought them no worse than those of the Taft administration. He was not in accord with the so-called Progressives in the Senate, nor would he "follow blindly the beliefs of the machine Republicans in that body."[47] He could not see that Taft had any positive policy on any subject and felt that he had come to be regarded as impossible by many who had insisted on nominating him, or rather using him to defeat Roosevelt, at the Republican convention in Chicago. Fall claimed to have adopted a policy of strict neutrality while trying to do what he could for New Mexico. He came to be known in the Senate as an independent Republican with no entangling alliances with Democrats or either Republican faction.

Senator Catron continued to be straight Republican in his policies and, therefore, was regarded in the Senate as a reactionary standpat Republican.[48] While he had secret misgivings that Taft could not be elected, he bravely urged his fellow Republicans in New Mexico to carry on a good fight for the sake of their party and state.

Catron's fear that the Republican split would cause the election of Woodrow Wilson was realized, as was his expectation that a Democratic administration would call for a lowering of the tariff. On April 7, 1913, President Wilson called a special meeting of Congress to consider the tariff, currency, and other related matters. The following day he appeared in person before Congress in joint session in violation of a tradition of one hundred and thirteen years' standing. As part of his attack on special interests, Wilson claimed that American energy, inventiveness, and industry need fear competition from no nation on earth. With the object of production of revenue, he urged Congress to reduce tariff schedules so that national competition might be restored and so that no industries might enjoy monopolistic privileges at the expense of the rest of the country. He maintained that a tariff which limits our commerce with the world violates just principles of taxation, and makes the government a tool in the hands of private interests.

Oscar W. Underwood of Alabama championed passage of the bill in the House. There was more serious opposition in the Senate. In the face of persistent lobbying from protectionists, the president took the issue directly to the people of the country. The resulting Underwood-Simmons Act of October 1913 was never tested under normal conditions of production and trade. Within ten months of the enactment, World War I broke out and created an artificial prosperity, under which tariff duties sank to relative insignificance.

Catron had opposed the bill strongly. It is ironic that a high-tariff man of his firm convictions came to the Senate at a time when the rates were effectively reduced for the first time since the Civil War. He thought that the proposed rates would be ruinous and made an able speech in the Senate against passage of the act. He centered his comments on the proposal for free wool and reduction of rates on woolen manufactures. From the standpoint of the United States, and especially New Mexico, he maintained that free, raw wool would drive small producers out of business and that flocks would be consolidated in monopolies. He did not concur with the Democrats that such measures as free wool would lower the cost of living. To the contrary, he believed that the measure would enable foreign manufacturers to undersell American fabric producers.[49]

Even earlier he had urged that the Republican stand on the tariff was important to New Mexico by pointing out that the principal products which brought money into the state from outside were wool, lead, zinc, and copper. It was his opinion that these industries should not be allowed to be broken down and that they would be broken down if tariff duties protecting them from cheap products and cheap labor

of foreign countries should be reduced to the amount proposed by the Democratic party. He acknowledged that the
Progressive party proposed to keep more protection than the
Democrats, but not enough, in his opinion, to justify the wool
grower, or lead, zinc, or copper miner, to continue in the business in which he was engaged.[50]

Related to the question of wool production was the problem of land for grazing purposes. In much of the semiarid
West, a great deal of land was required to graze any considerable number of animals. It was normally possible to acquire
no more than 320 acres from the public domain and, in some
localities, no more than 160 acres. In areas of scarce running
water and low precipitation, it was frequently necessary to sink
a well to water stock. It was too expensive to develop water
facilities on the small tract available from the public domain;
furthermore, it was required by law that homesteaders reside
on the land they claimed and provide evidence of cultivation.
The three-year Homestead Act of 1912, supported by Senator
Catron, provided some modifications. Residence was required
for only seven months of the year. One-sixteenth of the land
was required to be cultivated the second year, and one-eighth
of the area the third year.

Senator Catron was praised for his support of this measure, but he did not believe that its provisions were liberal
enough. He added his name to the growing list of legislators
who tried to attain further modification when he introduced
a bill in the Senate eliminating the residence requirement
entirely on land having insufficient water for domestic purposes, and specifying that improvements other than cultivation
be allowed as a requirement for final proof.[51] Like so many
others throughout the history of public domain disposal, his
measure was not passed.

From the start of his term in office Catron favored the
640-acre grazing homestead,[52] but this was not enacted into
law until December 29, 1916, when Congress passed the Stock-
Raising Homestead Act providing for 640 acres in reasonably

compact form. It was required that the land be classified as grazing land or forage crop land and could not contain merchantable timber or be suitable for irrigation.

Throughout his senatorial career Catron was a firm advocate of military preparedness. Early in 1913 he was a guest speaker at a banquet celebrating the birthday of General Robert E. Lee and took this occasion to go on record as favoring a greater American navy, declaring that "upon this question, if upon no other, he and Colonel Roosevelt were agreed."[53] Although an inland man, he also suggested that the nation build up her merchant marine.[54]

He spoke out even more strongly for expansion of the army and marine corps. His position as a member of the committee on military affairs lent weight to his opinion, but there was another distinction that was unique. He was the only Republican Confederate soldier in the United States Senate. As a matter of fact, with the exception of William Mahone of Virginia, he was probably the only Confederate Republican who had ever sat in the Senate, "and it may be said that Mahone's Republicanism was not deep enough to cause him pain, while Catron [was] such a Republican as gladdens the hearts of the standpatters."[55]

At the time, the most that the military dared hope for was five additional regiments of infantry and a regiment of field artillery. Senator Catron made the startling proposal of doubling the number of infantry and cavalry regiments and increasing the field artillery. Senator Catron declared that the army was entirely inadequate to meet present necessities. Before the war with Spain, there were twenty-five regiments of infantry and ten of cavalry, all stationed within the continental United States. As Catron spoke fifteen years later, there was a large increase in population, and it was required to station troops in the Philippines, Hawaii, Panama, and Alaska. Still, there had been an increase of only five regiments in each of infantry and cavalry. Senator Catron favored thirty additional regiments of infantry, fifteen of cavalry and such increase in the field artillery as would round out the organization of an adequate army. He maintained that a larger army was needed for training officers and men and to meet emergencies. The marine corps he considered to be well prepared for emergency action and could, within a few hours notice, be made ready to embark for any place where it was needed.[56]

Senator Catron's reasons for strengthening the military were based, in no small measure, on the tension then existing between the United States and Mexico. In February 1913 Victoriano Huerta had seized power in Mexico, and President Wilson refused to recognize the government at Mexico City because, in his opinion, it was founded on violence. When Senator Catron first heard of the revolt, he considered it a blessing in disguise because it would bring about intervention by the United States.

Catron, as a considerable land owner in Mexico, had long been familiar with the country. He was convinced that sooner or later it would be necessary for troops to be sent across the border to stop rioting and anarchy. With the coming of the Huerta revolt, he contended that all pretense of stable government in Mexico had likely come to an end. The Mexicans, he maintained, were perfectly equal to starting five new revolutions in five days, all with loss of American property if not also American lives. He was convinced that intervention was inevitable and should have been carried out earlier.*

Late in 1913 Francisco "Pancho" Villa, leader of a faction in northern Mexico, captured Juarez. Senator Catron, in an unofficial capacity, took it upon himself to visit the lion in his den. He called on Villa in Juarez and cautioned him against the wholesale execution of prisoners that had been his practice following the surrender of the city. People outside of Mexico, he warned Villa, did not look with favor on a fiesta

*Washington Times, February 10, 1913. Catron had, as early as May 1911, urged intervention in Mexico. T. B. Catron to Thom Catron, May 11, 1911 (C.P. 105, Vol. 31). With the chaotic conditions there, he did not consider that a thousand dollars worth of property was worth more than fifty dollars. *Albuquerque Morning Journal,* September 7, 1912.

of butchery that witnessed celebration of a victory by standing helpless prisoners of war on the edge of a grave and then shooting them down.

Villa did not promise to desist from the executions but showed concern about possible intervention. Senator Catron reminded him that his visit was that of a private citizen and that he did not speak officially; however, the policy of the United States obviously was to avoid intervention if possible but intervention would follow if it became necessary. Villa declared that this would cost the United States a great deal of money. Senator Catron assured him that this would not prevent intervention if the need arose.[57]

Senator Catron returned from his visit with Villa more than ever convinced that the armed forces should be strengthened and that a firm stand should be assumed in relations with Mexico. He declared that conditions there were worse than they were in Cuba when we intervened in that island "in behalf of humanity." There was more loss of life as well as greater destruction of property, and most of the property belonged to citizens of the United States.*

Senator Catron's advice, as well as that of others, was not heeded. Finally, on March 9, 1916, Villa led a band of several hundred desperadoes across the border, and raided Columbus, New Mexico, killing seventeen Americans. By this time Venustiano Carranza had replaced Huerta as the leader in Mexico. The next day President Wilson secured Carranza's grudging approval of an American punitive expedition to pursue Villa. Catron did not approve of seeking permission to make this move. He said:

Why should the Government ask permission of Carranza or anybody else to cross the boundary in pursuit of men who have committed such a dastardly crime as this [?] When Mexican bandits or whatever they may be, cross the border, enter the United States, burn our towns

---

*Washington Post, January 9, 1914. More specifically, Catron urged that the military be strengthened at El Paso. Catron to Secretaries of War and Navy, April 24, 1914 (C.P. 501, Box 32).

and murder American men, women and children, it certainly is time for action of the most aggressive sort.

It is no time for parleying and standing upon ceremony. The United States should have sent troops into Mexico to capture the first band that injured an American. If we had done this two or three years ago the attack on Columbus would never have occurred.*

Even earlier Senator Catron's urging of preparedness came into focus when Archduke Francis Ferdinand and his wife were murdered in the streets of Sarajevo, Bosnia, on June 28, 1914. Most Americans did not dream that this would be the signal for a general European war. Catron, when asked to comment, avoided stating his own views but reported the general feeling in Washington that the war would be over in six months and possibly in three months.[58] As a member of the committee on military affairs, he had, however, for nearly a year been advocating drastic expansion of the army, navy, and merchant marine, and he now preached that doctrine even more forcefully. President Wilson, nevertheless, proceeded only guardedly in this direction. As late as December 1914 Wilson rejoiced that the United States was not ready, and never would be ready, to put in the field a nation of men trained to arms. He resented the attack against his administration of the National Defense Society formed in August of 1915, and it was not until December of that year that he recommended to Congress any substantial increase in the army and navy.

While Senator Catron spoke out clear and loud in opposition to administration policies when he was convinced that to oppose was in the best interest of the nation, when he thought that Wilson was right he backed the president as unreservedly as he spoke against him on measures that he thought were

---

New York American, March 10, 1916. The Villa raid resulted in a significant and scholarly speech by Catron in the Senate. His subject was "Mexico, Its People and Their Customs." Some time later Senator Catron again visited Villa in Juarez, this time at the request of the State Department, and officially explained the attitude of the United States in its relations with Mexico. William A. Keleher, *Fabulous Frontier,* p. 136.

wrong. Thus, early in 1916, the *New York World* queried the senators regarding their attitudes toward Wilson's foreign policy. Senator Catron said:

> I heartily indorse the president's foreign policy and his attitude toward the belligerents and other nations. To discontinue the shipment of arms now would be absolutely unneutral. We must continue to let our citizens go wherever they please on the high seas and must protect them.*

Typical of Senator Catron's utterances in behalf of preparedness throughout the war were answers to questions propounded to him by the *Brooklyn Daily Eagle* early in 1915. He said, in part:

> The European war now going on has shown to the United States, that any government and particularly this Government must be prepared to defend its citizens and their property at any moment. War, as it is shown by this one comes on apparently without warning and any country which has not a considerable degree of preparedness in the shape of army and navy, not only for defence but for aggressive action, must find itself laboring under difficulties and embarrassments.... The present army is ridiculously inadequate for hostilities with any European Government. The navy is comparatively stronger and better prepared for conditions of war than the army, but it needs much strengthening.[59]

Senator Catron also repeatedly reaffirmed his conviction in behalf of building up the United States merchant marine. The question had been related to the Panama Canal tolls controversy of 1914. Some two years before the August 1914 opening of the canal, Congress passed a law exempting American coastwise shipping from the payment of tolls. Great Britain immediately protested on the grounds the law violated the clause of the Hay-Pauncefote Treaty which opened the canal to vessels of all nations on terms of entire equality. Senator Catron, in an able speech before the Senate on June 1, 1914, brought out the opposite argument to the point that the same treaty conferred upon the United States absolute authority to

---

*Albuquerque Morning Journal, January 11, 1916. The same article chided Senator Fall for his grudging endorsement of the administration's policy.

regulate the tolls so that they were just and equitable. Some senators argued that the bill should be repealed because it in reality amounted to a subsidy.*

Catron failed to see why the United States should refrain from subsidizing a merchant marine when other countries did just that. He explained his position:

Listen to a single amazing illustration. We give the owners of foreign vessels the sum of $150,000,000 annually for transporting our products to the markets of Europe. The money is in gold. I would like to hear King Solomon, said to be the wisest man who ever lived, give an offhand opinion of the American people in this connection. One hundred and fifty million dollars would build 100 ocean carriers.

The freights of one year, in other words, would construct a fleet of 100 vessels, made of American materials by American workmen. Is the farmer interested? He is. The farmer pays for having his wheat or cotton taken to Europe. The freights are subtracted from the price he receives, and the freights go into foreign pockets. Is the farmer an ass? No; he cannot help himself. Is the manufacturer an ass? My reply answers both questions.

Foreign ships are cheaply built and cheaply operated. Then foreign nations subsidize their vessels. Their ships go through the Suez Canal, pay tolls, and the tolls so paid are returned to the owners of the ships. Moreover, foreign nations will give back the money their ships pay in passing through the Panama Canal. Also, the United States is paying many millions of dollars yearly for having mails — letters written in this country, you understand — carried to Europe by European vessels.[60]

Despite the arguments of Senator Catron and a few others, in June 1914 President Wilson successfully insisted on the repeal of the provision relating to American coastwise shipping. He stated no other reason for his demand than that it involved diplomatic negotiations of a very delicate nature. It later came out that this was the price he paid to obtain British support for his policy in Mexico.

To assess Catron's role in the Senate, it should be remembered that he was a Republican serving during the time of

---

* Actually, Britain did not object to such a subsidy — she used the practice in connection with the Suez Canal — but feared that the rates would be set so that foreign shipping would be forced to bear the entire cost of upkeep of the canal.

Wilson's Democratic administration. Coincidentally, that situation had also prevailed when he served as Territorial delegate to Congress during the Democratic administration of Grover Cleveland. It came to be chiefly the function of faithful Republican senators to largely oppose the measures of Wilson's administration. This he did as ably as any colleague, particularly with his speeches on the tariff and Panama Canal toll controversies. His voice on the matters of intervention in Mexico and military preparedness was as important as that of any other person during his term as senator. But it was the uniqueness of his position in the nation's capital that made him stand out, just as uniqueness was a key characteristic of much of his life. It is altogether unusual that the son of a slave owner and a combatant for the rebel cause in the Civil War should go to the highest tribunal of our land as the staunchest of the staunch in the political party that had put down that rebellion.

In February 1916 Senator Catron was nearing his seventy-sixth birthday, but he confidently announced that he was a candidate for reelection. It is significant that the Machiavellian touch of Albert Bacon Fall lurked in the background of this last political endeavor of Thomas Benton Catron. A prelude of renewed misunderstanding between Fall and Catron started in 1914 when William H. Andrews, in a last bid for political preferment in New Mexico, sought election as representative to Congress. Fall told Catron that Andrews' friends were reporting that he, Catron, was backing Andrews for the nomination. Catron denied this allegation, stating that he had informed Andrews he would not pledge himself to support his nomination. Fall, unconvinced, wrote to Charles Springer:

> Mr. Catron is not always frank with me, however, and I do not feel as though I could always speak confidentially to him.[61]

The fact is that Catron *had* communicated with Andrews. He wrote:

If you are the nominee, I shall give you my unqualified support, but as to whether I will support you to be the nominee is another question. I am beginning to doubt as to whether a man who pays no regard to his debts as you do and compels his friends to pay his notes and makes no effort toward protecting him, is really a good man for Congress. . . .*

Early in 1916 Fall warned Catron not to count on his support for renomination. He gave the vague explanation that the people of the North should elect a candidate acceptable to those of the South, who at the same time could be elected; that the people of the South were entitled to this consideration and an equal counsel in the selection; but that the nominee should come from the North.[62]

As far as Catron was concerned, what he said was that if he, Catron, were nominated, Felix Martinez would run against him on the Democratic ticket and probably beat him. On the other hand, Fall believed that Frank Hubbell could probably beat Martinez. Still, in a mercurial effort to be all things to all issues, Fall admitted that Hubbell was not senatorial caliber in many respects. Hubbell, though, was a half-breed who could get out the Mexican vote, and he was "one of the wealthiest men in the State with possibly more available cash in reach than any other man in politics, or likely to get into the game in New Mexico."[63]

More to the point, however, National Committeeman Charles A. Spiess favored Catron, and Fall resented their mutual opposition to his Progressive ideas as well as their refusal to look favorably upon Roosevelt as a candidate for president against Woodrow Wilson.

Fall continued to drop subtle seeds of inference that he opposed Catron's nomination because he thought Catron

---

*Catron to Andrews, July 6, 1914 (C.P. 501, Box 26). Catron also questioned whether Andrews would be elected if nominated. This was only one of half a dozen similar letters written by Catron to Andrews in the seven months that had just passed. It has been widely mistaken that Catron backed Andrews during these years. For example, see Keleher, *Fabulous Frontier,* p. 125. This is not surprising because Catron's political enemies certainly did their best to leave this impression.

could not be elected. Finally, however, he exposed his real vindictive reason. He harped back to the 1912 Republican convention:

> His [Catron's] action in opposing me in every way possible at Chicago, when I considered that New Mexico had been honored by my selection to make the nominating speech for Roosevelt, left such a bitter taste in my mouth that although I have from time to time forgiven Catron for worse things, I shall have nothing to do with him in the future.*

What were the "worse things" that Fall referred to? Had he really forgiven them? One can conjecture that Catron's characterization of him as "the most offensive man in the whole Territory and the most venal,"[64] may not have been forgotten. Surely there is not in the English language a more galling condemnation encompassed in so few words.

Senator Catron was not renominated; Frank Hubbell was. It is not possible to definitely analyze the factors that motivated the delegates at the 1916 Republican convention in New Mexico in their rejection of Catron. Would he have been nominated in 1916 if Fall had backed him as he had been backed by Catron in 1912? Even a computerized analysis would be only an opinion — but it is the conviction of this writer that he would have been. In that case, history would have been only a little different. Barring the possibility that renomination would have increased the remaining years of life for Catron, the main difference, perhaps, would have been that a weary old man would have fulfilled his life span serving in an office that he had striven for mightily, and that he had, in large measure, made possible by unswerving devotion to the cause of statehood for New Mexico.

As for Senator Fall, he continued playing both ends against the middle until the ignominious ramifications of the

---

*A. B. Fall to W. A. Hawkins, August 3, 1916 (Stratton). On the other hand, Catron unquestionably was backing Fall at this time in his bid to be elected by the New Mexico legislature for a second term in the United States Senate.

Teapot Dome scandal obliterated that middle. As it developed, Fall's candidate, Hubbell, was not elected. Fall lamely admitted his error: "I realized of course, our mistake in the nomination of Hubbell long before the campaign was over, and very much feared its result before we made the nomination."*

Catron and his friends held Senator Fall personally responsible for his failure to be renominated and for the election of a Democrat to the Senate. Fall excused himself: "Of course my conscience is clear upon this matter, as Mr. Catron's defeat was largely due to his own actions in seeking the nomination."[65] Fall probably meant to emphasize the word "actions." With that word deleted, it would have meant that Fall blamed Catron for opposing his will and seeking the nomination at all — which was probably closest to the truth.

Nevertheless, Catron had served the nation well. His service as United States senator also permitted him, at the end of his days, an interlude of relative tranquility for which he, in return, sought to give in full measure the benefit of his experience for that nation as he had always given. As Confederate, as Unionist, and as an American, he had faith in the land and its people and gave unstintingly of his time, his fortune, and his energy in a personal demonstration of that faith.

---

* Fall to H. O. Bursum, January 17, 1917 (Stratton). Hubbell was defeated by A. A. Jones.

18
Declining Fortune

The growth and decline of T. B. Catron's empire can be measured in decades. Starting with the initial Mora Grant purchases in 1870 and some other land acquisitions, including minor interests in the Tierra Amarilla Grant, the first two decades were periods of gathering momentum. The larger and more costly interests in the latter were purchased in 1881 and 1882. By 1890 Catron reached the zenith of his business career, and the balance of that decade witnesses a slow deceleration. The first year of the twentieth century marked a rush toward the nadir of his fortunes. Wilson Waddingham had died a year earlier, and during wretched 1900 Catron learned that the manipulations of his supposed friend had done irreparable damage to his financial structure. In 1900, also, he became unfortunately involved with Charles H. Elmendorf in the American Valley Company. The next decade brought substantial losses culminating with the forced sale of the Tierra Amarilla Grant in 1909 at a sacrifice, and the sale or loss of other property along the way. During the last decade of T. B. Catron's life, his eldest son, Charles C. Catron, strove to save what he could of his father's dwindling empire.

On January 2, 1904, Charles had joined the firm of Catron and Gortner. In 1912, when T. B. Catron became a United States senator, Frank Lavan was associated with the firm, and Charles assumed active leadership. There then remained but fourteen grants,* and Charles' first effort was to save the Mora Grant. He was unsuccessful; it was sold in 1913 for taxes.

Despite Charles' strenuous efforts and careful economy, only seven grants remained at the time of his father's death in 1921, and these were heavily encumbered.† He wrote:

> As you are aware, prior to the death of my father I was compelled to assume a vast amount of his personal indebtedness at the First National Bank and other banks, all of which, however, is amply secured by collateral security or mortgage. . . .[1]

Charles described his position:

> I am head over heals in a mix-up in connection with T. B.'s affairs trying to get them straightened out and have had no time to sit down and write you fully of my plans.[2]

Again he wrote:

> I have managed to clear matters up and have gotten everything in good shape, although it has left me badly pinched.[3]

In 1914 Fletcher Catron became a junior partner. During the last two years of Fletcher's education at the University of Chicago, Charles had been largely responsible for his conduct. Fletcher's father had tried to be firm, especially in money matters, but had not been entirely successful. Charles, though, put his brother on a limited budget and made it stick. He wrote:

> Now cut out this nonsense and bullshitting and adhere strictly to the truth and to hell with your accounts, we do not want to see them, but limit yourself within the scope of this letter or beat your old man out of whatever you want.[4]

----

* These were the Anton Chico, Bosque del Apache, Caja del Rio, Eaton, Espiritu Santo, Juan de Gabaldon, Juana Lopez, Los Luceros, La Majada, Mora, Ortiz, Pacheco, Piedra Lumbre, and Santa Teresa.

† The Anton Chico, Bosque del Apache, Eaton, Espiritu Santo, Juan de Gabaldon, Juana Lopez, and Santa Teresa. There were also other properties including the Catron office building and residence in Santa Fe, a brick plant at Grants, New Mexico, timber land in Oregon, and the Gibraltar Building in Kansas City, Missouri.

As the summer of 1914 approached, Charles wrote to Fletcher:

Enclosed please find check for $50.00 which is to purchase your transportation home this summer. It has been arranged that you are to work in the office this summer, working in the mornings and afternoons two hours each, for which the firm will pay you $50.00 a month if you are any good; otherwise you will be fired.[5]

In 1914, also, Charles decided to expand the firm to a fifth member with the addition of Reed Holloman. His purpose was to free himself from details of law practice so he could devote more time to his father's business. He made up his mind to sell some grants in order to stop the large payment of interest and make his father easy before the next senatorial election. He informed T. B. Catron:

It will do you no good to find fault with this program for I have positively made up my mind to do this in order to sell a grant for you and get you out of debt.... Of course I would appreciate your approval, but whether you will it or not, a grant will be sold and everything will be cleared up.[6]

Charles C. Catron had touched on a fundamental facet of the relationship between himself and his father. T. B. Catron looked upon land as empire; his son viewed that commodity in the more modern business sense as a source of cash income which would provide greater freedom of action in commercial endeavors.

Furthermore, their personalities clashed. In 1894 Charles had been at school in New Haven, Connecticut, under his mother's care. Julia informed her husband that their son had been dismissed for improper conduct. The incident provoked T. B. Catron to the first of only two threats to use physical chastisement recorded during his entire adult lifetime. He informed his wife:

I wish to say to him that if I ever hear anything more of this kind, I shall turn him out into the streets and I will never speak to him again and he shall never come into the house. He can go to the dogs or wherever he pleases, but I will never recognize or acknowledge him or have anything to do with him, neither will I consent for you to. I want to treat him well, but I cannot afford to have a son of mine insulting people and neglecting his studies and acting in such an outrageous manner. But before I turn him out into the streets, I will take good caution to give him the most unmitigated whipping he ever had in his life.[7]

But even in the same paragraph the father tempered his resentment and added:

If he wants to act decently and like a good boy — and when he wishes he can be one of the best boys in the world — I will be happy to have him do so. But he must stay at home and devote himself to his studies.[8]

Charles C. Catron admitted that relations with his father were "like two pieces of flint meeting. . . ."[9] The father was also aware of the irrepressible conflict between them and suspected that the unhappy condition was caused because they were too much alike. In the autumn of his father's years, Charles wrote to him:

I believe that you have hit the nail on the head when you say that we are too much alike. I do not blame you for getting aggravated at times, but my nature unfortunately causes me to flare up when you get aggravated. I will do all that I can to be more considerate in the future and I feel that if you would take me a little more into your confidence and feel and act as if I really had some interest in your affairs that we would get along wonderfully. Let's try talking things over a little bit hereafter. This would be much better than trying to bark each other down.[10]

Charles C. Catron always deplored the extravagant amount of money that his father spent on politics. He explained his feelings in the matter with the memory of his father's death fresh in his mind.

I hardly think that I will carry forward the political career which my father followed. For the last twenty years I have found that politics was not a very remunerative occupation. My father probably spent over a million dollars in following up this hobby. I in turn have learned to detest it and have confined my efforts strictly to the practice of law and have conducted all of my father's business in this branch for the last ten years.[11]

T. B. Catron's lifelong unproductive and disconcerting habit of indiscriminately signing notes for, or making loans to, people was a particular irritant to Charles. The elder Catron realized that this proclivity, for the most part, only made him enemies; nevertheless, he was unable, or unwilling, to very often say no when approached with a plea to sign a note or make a loan. It was not at all unusual for him to borrow money in order to loan it to someone else. It is reported that, at the time of his death, he held notes for unpaid amounts totaling about two hundred and fifty thousand dollars.*

Charles C. Catron wrote to his father: "You have a very unfortunate habit of signing notes for every one that presents them to you."[12] Again, he communicated his displeasure to his brother, Thom: "there are . . . incomes from various sources, all of which the Honorable Tomas Benton converts to his own use and amuses himself in supporting some blackmailing son-of-a-bitch."[13] In a somewhat more kindly but nonetheless serious vein, he informed his father: "I understood you to say you had already been stung enough without signing more notes."[14]

Typical of loans that Catron made and had difficulty collecting was one to Patrick F. Garrett made in May 1899, while both were attending the trial of Oliver Lee at Hillsboro. Garrett promised to repay the money within two weeks. In July

---

*William A. Keleher, *Fabulous Frontier,* p. 140. Among those to whom T. B. Catron loaned or gave money, were Edgar A. Walz, Charles C. McComas, W. H. Nesbitt, Louisa A. Walton, W. A. Glassford, Ada Atkinson, P. R. Puckett, Roman A. Baca, J. Francisco Chavez, August Kirchner, Mrs. Derwent H. Smith, William Breeden, Eugenio Yrissari, J. W. Scofield, J. G. Albright, M. S. Hart, John P. Casey, J. D. Warner, Ralph E. Twitchell, Bernard S. Rodey, S. D. Lasier, Patrick Higgins, William H. Whiteman, Mrs. Andres Sena, Margarita Johnson, Mrs. W. C. Hazeldine, Mrs. Irene Catron, Patrick F. Garrett, Burt J. Forbes, Neill B. Field, James S. Fielder, W. E. Griffin, Dr. M. A. Bartleson, Pascal Craig, Wilmot E. Broad, A. L. Morrison, A. M. Bergere, G. W. Hickox, Gus O'Brien, George Sena, Albert B. Fall, George Curry, Robert E. Morrison, Elfego Baca, G. L. Selignac, F. D. O'Brien, Miguel A. Otero, William Dalton, W. S. Strickler, Charles H. Elmendorf, W. H. H. Llewellyn, Nicolas Galles, Felix Garcia, W. H. Andrews, Eugenio Romero, O. B. Crum, Carlos Ortiz, and Manuel Baca y Delgado.

he informed Catron that he was experiencing difficulty in securing the amount, but rendered assurance that he would do so in a short while. Three years later the loan remained unpaid; Catron, needing the money badly, requested repayment.* Garrett was now collector of customs at El Paso, Texas. A year later Garrett answered but made no mention of the loan; instead, he requested that Catron secure a railroad pass for a friend.

Catron remained patient but did not refrain from scolding Garrett:

> You surely do not owe much money and you ought to try to pay what you owe, especially as you hold a responsible position as you do, the time will come around when there will have to be a re-appointment and then all those businessmen will turn loose against you and you may find it somewhat difficult to get a party to stand by you.[15]

Garrett evidently did not like to be reminded of the debt; he wrote:

> Now the only thing I know that you can do (other than wait until I get the money) is to take judgment which will not increase the value of your claim. I hope you will not write any more such scorching letters as you have written. . . .[16]

Garrett continued to ignore further correspondence concerning his debt. Catron's letters became increasingly insistent; early in 1906 he wrote:

> I am still without answer to any of my letters; it seems that you regard gambling debts superior to a debt of money loaned to accomodate you. . . . I am awfully sorry you were not re-appointed Collector, but I am forced to believe one of the principal reasons why you failed of appointment was because the people of El Paso protested against your re-appointment on account of your neglect of your obligations. . . .[17]

---

* Catron to P. F. Garrett, July 9, 1903 (C.P. 105, Vol. 22). Catron addressed Garrett as My good friend; later, My dear Pat, My dear Sir, My dear Garrett, and Dear Garrett.

Catron wrote one more letter to Garrett in June 1906. No record is available that the loan was repaid, or even further acknowledged.

A loan made by Catron to Ralph E. Twitchell also caused friction. Catron finally demanded payment of a long-overdue promissory note. He insisted on immediate payment, explaining:

> You will remember that the money for which this note was given was loaned to you to enable you to pay up money which you told me you had collected while District Attorney of this District and had used and not turned in. You stated at the time that you were in a bad fix; that they were threatening to file an information against you and have you arrested and that if I did not furnish you with the money at that time, or the greater part of it, you would be arrested and put in jail and you wanted to avoid that as it would ruin you.[18]

Twitchell replied:

> Your highly esteemed favor of yesterday is before me. I have read the statements therein contained and take this occasion to say that outside of the main fact of my alleged indebtedness to you of the amount you claim, the balance is an unmitigated falsehood from beginning to end, and you know it. . . . Go ahead and crack your whip; you will probably find out that the lash is not quite as long or as effective as you think, and you will also ascertain that there are others who can do a little on their own account.*

While Catron was often shrewd and tough in business details, he would make remarkable concessions in other matters; for example, his customary practice in lending money.

> He always went through the same routine with the borrower, first gruffly refusing to make a loan, cussing out everything and everybody; then reluctantly consenting to lend the money; then quibbling about the rate of interest and time of maturity. The borrower always signed a mortgage and note, admonished by Catron of the strict obligation to pay on the due date, under penalty of foreclosure.[19]

But he often failed to file a mortgage deed for record, and he seldom foreclosed.

---

* Twitchell to Catron, January 23, 1901 (C.P. 103, Box 11). Bad as Twitchell's relations were with Catron, they mutually shared even less esteem for Max Frost, editor of the *Santa Fe New Mexican*. When informed of a purported conversation between Catron and Frost, Twitchell wrote: "I don't believe Catron would speak to Frost. It took me a good many years to find out what a lying scoundrel he [Frost] is." Twitchell to Robert Gortner, December 23, 1903 (C.P. 103, Box 19).

At least a few of Catron's kindnesses were appreciated. Silas D. Lasier was a veteran of the Civil War. Starting about 1880, he faithfully and capably served as a clerk in Catron's law office. By 1898 he had grown too old and feeble to work, but Catron continued to help him with money. Lasier's gratefulness was touching:

> First let me thank you from the bottom of my heart for your good kindness in helping me so often, and you can rest assured that whether I live or die I shall always hold you in grateful remembrance as the kindest friend I ever had. God Bless you.[20]

Catron continued to support him. Two years later Lasier wrote with a handwriting enfeebled by infirmity that contrasted pitifully with his earlier vigorous style:

> I have been sick for nearly a month troubled with my kidneys. The doctor has prescribed for me, but I cannot get the medicine because I have no money to buy it. Won't you kindly let me have a little money so that I can send for it. I do not know what to do unless you help me for I am getting steadily worse, and I will try not to trouble you again.[21]

The letter was prophetic. There was no need for him to trouble his only benefactor another time; the blessed peace of death soon relieved him of the need for a further helping hand.

T. B. Catron had led a full life. While he had lost most of his land, he had accomplished his lifelong ambition of United States senatorship. This goal accomplished, there was little left for him to strive for. He was ill with cirrhosis of the liver and bronchitis for the last two years of his life and was confined to his bed for the final six months. Still, with the iron will, rugged constitution, and optimism that had served him well, he would not admit that he was growing feeble.

> It was said of Senator Catron that like William Jennings Bryan he never appeared to grow tired from speech making, or travel, or other business. His strength was prodigious and his endurance marvelous despite the sedentary life he was compelled to lead as a lawyer.[22]

But the old gladiator had met his match in the ring of advanced years. A month before the end Charles reported his condition:

It is my personal belief that T. B. will not last much longer. His mind is clear and his will power is something wonderful, but I see his strength failing daily.... He keeps saying that he is going to get well and has gone so far as to get recommendations for his appointment as Ambassador to Chile, well knowing he cannot take the position, but he says it makes no difference; that they will give him a year's leave of absence after appointment.*

Sentaor Thomas B. Catron quietly passed away at his residence in Santa Fe at eight o'clock on the morning of May 15, 1921, at the age of eighty years, seven months, and nine days. In accordance with his wishes, funeral services were held under auspices of Montezuma Lodge No. 1, A.F.&A.M. The services were held on the afternoon of May 17, 1921, at the Scottish Rite cathedral from which place the remains were escorted to the Catron mausoleum at Fairview cemetery. Three of his four sons, John, Charles, and Fletcher, were active pallbearers, along with Judge Colin Neblett, William A. Bayer, and George W. Armijo. The other son, Thom, had been with his father for several days in his illness but had been called away by a telegram announcing the sickness of one of his children. The list of honorary pallbearers — friends, foes, admirers, and detractors — read almost like a roll call of those who shaped the history and destiny of New Mexico during the half-century just passed.†

George W. Prichard presented the eulogy at Senator Catron's funeral. He reviewed the senator's career as a student,

---

*C. C. Catron to John W. Catron, March 14, 1921 (C.P. 101, Vol. 29). A few months before his death, T. B. Catron divided his possessions among his sons and named Fletcher Catron executor of his estate. Because his property was legally divided before his death, his will was never probated.

† *Santa Fe New Mexican*, May 16, 1921. Those listed were A. M. Bergere, E. C. Best, C. A. Bishop, Summers Burkhart, Holm O. Bursum, Clark Carr, Frank W. Clancy, Charles Conklin, George Curry, E. P. Davies, E. W. Dobson, Albert B. Fall, Neill B. Field, Thomas P. Gable, Martin Gardesky, Julius Gerdes, B. C. Hernandez, Levi Hughes, A. A. Jones, N. B. Laughlin, David Leahy, Jerry Leahy, Jose Amado Lucero, Malaquias Martinez, John R. McFie, Merritt C. Mechem, Nestor Montoya, Fritz Muller, Victor Ortega, Marcelino Ortiz, Juan Ortiz, Frank W. Parker, John Pflueger, George W. Prichard, L. Bradford Prince, R. E. Putney, Benjamin Read, A. B. Renehan, James A. Rolls, Clarence J. Roberts, Ramon Sanchez, Jose D. Sena, A. Spiegelberg, James Seligman, S. Spitz, Howard Vaughan, and Prof. J. A. Wood.

soldier, lawyer, husband, parent, businessman, public servant, and political practioneer, then continued:

But it is of the qualities of his mind and his characteristics as a man that I wish more particularly to speak, for these are the things that should be preserved in our memories and never be forgotten.

First his frankness — frankness was a part of his nature. No one ever doubted where he stood on any public question, nor any other question in which he was interested, he simulated nothing. Hypocrisy was never laid at his door. His convictions were his own. He would swerve neither to the right nor to the left from opinions honestly formed. He never sought the cheap applause of anyone. I have seen him stand alone against the views of others like the rooted oak against the storm, when by yielding he could have gained an advantage to himself, but he was too big to sacrifice a conviction for either a temporary or permanent gain.

As the unpolished diamond reveals not its beauty, nor value within, so this great man with a more or less rugged exterior, was not always understood. His outward sternness deceived the stranger, but not those who knew him.

No man had a bigger, or kinder heart than he — no man in our State contributed more to charity — no man more cheerfully gave his money for the benefit of his community and his State — no man helped the poor more than he. We get this from those whom he helped not from him. He spoke not of his kindly deeds. He did no charitable act for personal effect. He courted no applause and feared no censure. His mind was too big for the one, and his heart was too brave for the other.

Thomas Benton Catron had his faults. Who has not? But they were the faults of the gladiator. He punished his enemies while the combat was on, but like the true fighter, he laid aside his weapon when the battle was over. He did not cherish animosity toward an enemy. Sometimes he tried to make himself think so, but his friends knew better. He never had an enemy he would not take by the hand and help when appealed to. His enemies were usually self-constituted enemies, either from jealousy or fancied wrongs. Those who had the hardest things to say of him knew the least about him.

It was sheer intellectual force that gave him ascendancy over other men, that made him a political leader. It was his imposing presence and deep knowledge of public affairs that won men to him. He had none of the blarney and graces of the ordinary politician. He despised shams. He was as sincerely earnest in politics as he was in matters of business.

His great mind was like a magnet — it drew to itself everything within reach. Every cell of his big brain was a storehouse of unforgotten events. Names, dates, facts came to him like winged servants to obey his will. Who of you that knew him well have not been charmed and fascinated by the range of his knowledge? Who of you that knew him have not drunk deeply at the fountain of his wisdom?

The impress of his great personality left on this State is ineffaceable. The last half-century of history of the State would be incomplete with the work of his life left out. As a soldier, citizen, lawyer, political leader, statesman, parent, he has passed away, but his memory will cling with us. Not only those of this generation, but those that will follow us will share knowledge of the life and fame of this great man.[23]

E. Dana Johnson, the brilliant and scholarly editor of the *Santa Fe New Mexican,* ably assessed the role of Thomas Benton Catron in his era:

Fifty years of most picturesque and strenuous history in New Mexico passed in review in the period spanned by the career in this state of Thomas Benton Catron, who passed away at the age of fourscore years at his home in Santa Fe Sunday morning.

"Uncle Tom" Catron was actively identified for half a century with that history; he was one of the most picturesque figures of an era; the story of his life is the story of an epoch, and any historical work which correctly depicts that period must give Mr. Catron a prominent place in it.

The New Mexican under the decade of its present ownership was consistently and continuously opposed to the Catron political activities and influence. For that reason we are perhaps not qualified to give an impartial estimate of his political status in the history of his party and his state. But as a rarely interesting personality who made his mark indelibly on his period; a man of commanding intellectual ability and personal force; a man whose homely and picturesque personal eccentricities lent a touch of humor to even the bitterest political fights in which he was engaged and often endeared him to his enemies; as a man who made and lived history in New Mexico from the Civil War to the treaty of Versailles, from Grant to Harding; a contemporary of Indian massacres who lived to see airplanes circling over his home city, and whose time ran from stage coach days to those of the high-powered automobile; the New Mexican feels that the death of Senator Catron is an outstanding mile post along the way of history of the southwest; and that his passing breaks another connecting link between Nowadays and New Mexico's historic past. He was an integral part of Santa Fe for fifty years and loved the old capital profoundly; his connection with Santa Fe's professional life, her schools, her politics, her public life, was one of his ruling passions; he was wrapped up in her past, present and future and his greatest pride was his prominence in the affairs of his home town. It is superfluous to state that every soul in Santa Fe, whatever his politics or whatever his attitude toward the

Catron political activities, will miss this bold and familiar figure keenly from the life of the capital.

It was characteristic of Mr. Catron that he made no effort to see that a detailed story of his career was available for those who were to announce his death to the world. It was difficult to get him to yield up his photograph and furnish material for complimentary sketches in biographical works. Printed pages furnish only meager details of his life. It is extremely unfortunate that his tardily begun autobiography was unfinished; it goes without saying that the completed part will be of absorbing interest; and had it been finished it would have been one of the greatest human documents of the century.

Mr. Catron was a powerful leader of his time; blunt, outspoken, uncompromising, at times he ruled with a rod of iron in the days of his greatest political ascendancy. He was frankly a "practical politician;" the appellation "boss" complimented instead of offending him; political power was meat and drink to him and those who went to the political mat with "Uncle Tom" always knew they had been in a fight. The New Mexican can testify to this whole-heartedly. Nor would Mr. Catron himself expect this newspaper to bestow effusive encomiums on a political record which it had so often honestly attacked. Politics aside, we shall miss him, miss his occasional visits to the office, miss his personality on the street and at political gatherings, as will the rest of his community. The all-round caliber of a citizen is shown by the gap he leaves in his home town; and Senator Catron, needless to say, leaves a big one.[24]

E. Dana Johnson, on the grounds that he might be prejudiced, declined to give a specific estimate of Catron's stature in the history of his party and his state.

Thomas Benton Catron was a product of his evironment, yet, to a degree, he shaped that environment. He arrived in New Mexico at a time when building empires was a possibility for those who aspired to power and wealth. Catron did so aspire and acquired a vast expanse of land which, however, became a heavy burden until the day he died. A major factor of his life was managing his affairs to protect title to his property, complicated by his almost psychotic aversion to selling. He consistently priced his holdings beyond the prevailing market until placed in a position of having to sell at a sacrifice. Furthermore, he contributed large sums to political causes, and it was well known that he would make loans even when obliged to borrow. Many of these advances were never repaid.

As a total result, he was pressed into constant and heavy borrowing. His life was a never-ending struggle to earn as much as he spent. He lived well and supplied his family with every reasonable want, yet these expenditures were minor in the aggregate. His overall financial involvements were the central feature of his life.

His personality defies clear analysis, but he was a remarkable man. He was an aristocrat and a genuine mental giant. He could be the personification of gentle kindness and tactful consideration. Unhappily, while naturally reserved and patrician, he also possessed an ability seldom rivaled in his era to put together words of sarcasm and invective that could easily antagonize persons toward whom they were directed. This outspokenness made Catron many enemies who rarely saw his good qualities. His friends admired him and reluctantly admitted his failings. In a sense each was right. Some of the good things he did were admirable and some of the bad were deplorable.

He was a hard worker who unreservedly backed causes he espoused, and he abided by the consequences of his decisions. He accepted freely the heavy burden of onerous responsibility; his iron will enabled him to suffer in silence great pressures of adversity. It is a credit to his ability that he came many times from the brink of financial or political ruin. Conversely, it is a reflection upon his judgment and tact that he found himself so often in nearly untenable situations. It is evidence of the strength of his character that he turned deficiency and opportunity alike to his purpose and made his will the strongest influence in his Territory during his era.

A secret of his power was adjustment to the time and place in which he lived. He came to a realm of new opportunity and grasped that moment firmly. His goal was possession of land and political power. The native people could best help him to gain his objectives, so he counted many of them among his best friends and staunchest partisans. The predominate language of his adopted homeland was Spanish, so he acquired proficiency in that language.

He deplored weakness and lack of ability in those who should be strong and able, but he was magnanimous toward those whom equal opportunity had not blessed. He might lend money as a tool of political power, but he also freely made loans that were tantamount to a gift. Recipients of his bounty frequently became his bitterest critics when it came time to repay a loan. This he deplored; nevertheless, he never ceased to spread his favors widely, and he welcomed the infrequent occasions when they were sincerely appreciated.

Measured with total impact as a standard of comparison, no New Mexican was his equal in the combined legal, cultural, commercial, financial and political affairs of the last forty years of Territorial New Mexico and the formative years of statehood. Likewise, no New Mexican of that period was as well known throughout the Territory, state, nation or world.

Measured by the yardstick of national accomplishment, only two New Mexico residents of his time can be considered his peers. One, Albert Bacon Fall, reached his fruition of accomplishment in a later period; the other, Stephen Benton Elkins, was only a transitory resident of New Mexico.

Catron's political life in New Mexico spanned half a century. He enjoyed politics, but the larger cause of his political activity was his land. His most demanding political consideration was statehood for New Mexico, for he was ardently loyal to the advancement of his revered Territory. True he would have prospered through advancement of his properties' values, but he was not wholly self-centered in this. He did far more to further the development and affluence of the Territory than was needed to increase his assets, either real estate or power.

One well-wisher, Bernard S. Rodey, wrote frankly and penetratingly about Catron's character as he approached the duties of United States senator:

> For goodness sake, now that the opportunity has arisen, now that you have the highest office you will probably ever hold, let the REAL

THOMAS BENTON CATRON'S principles have full sway and not
[let] the New Mexico Santa Fe county Catron's actions govern him. I
have for years been of the belief that there were two characters to T. B.
Catron. One a very high type of statesman, and the other a precinct
politician wholly foreign to the first character. I need not say more,
you know how I think along these lines, for I have often told you of it.
Then Mr. Catron be true to yourself, avoid and repudiate scrubs and
scoundrels, and for the rest of your life live up to your real innate
character.[25]

It is a credit to Catron's adaptability that, in his larger
role, he rose to the challenge implied in Rodey's charge to him.

Even with his last and biggest challenge behind him, he
continued in the more gracious mold.

Friends of Senator Catron remarked . . . that the last two years
revealed the best side of the man's character; he never uttered a complaint in his long and painful illness; he was cheerful and sweet-
tempered day and night . . . and everyone around him found the senator a kind hearted and genial man. Unlike most patients suffering
from a painful, deadly malady, he never showed a peevish moment.
He was a jolly good fellow in sickness as he had been rather stern and
severe many times in health.[26]

Senator Catron had started to dictate his memoirs to his
son, Fletcher, during the last two weeks of his life, but he
grew too weak to continue after he had described his early
life in Missouri. George W. Prichard, in his funeral eulogy,
predicted that more of the life of this notable man would be
written. E. Dana Johnson regretted that his tardily begun
autobiography was not finished because it would have been
one of the greatest human documents of the century.

Thomas Benton Catron and His Era is an attempt to fulfill Col. Prichard's prophecy and to tell the tantalizing story
of this unusual person in a manner that, in some small measure, realizes Mr. Johnson's illuminating analysis.

Partners of Thomas B. Catron

Stephen B. Elkins*	1874 (January):	1876 (May)	
Charles H. Gildersleeve	1876 (May):	1877 (June)	
William T. Thornton	1877 (June):	1883	
Charles C. McComas	1882 :	1883	
Frank W. Clancy	1882 :	1890 (December)	
John J. Cockerel	1886 (January):	1887 (August)	
John H. Knaebel	1888 (June):	1890 (December)	
William J. Mills	1888 (August):	1890 (April)	
W. E. Coons	1891 (July):	1893 (November)	
Charles A. Spiess	1893 (November):	1896 (August)	
Robert C. Gortner	1896 (March):	1899 (March)	
	1901 (April):	1908 (December)	
Charles C. Catron	1904 (January):	1921 (May)	
Ira L. Grimshaw	1908 :	1910 (November)	
Frank J. Lavan	1912 (December):	1918 (October)	
Fletcher A. Catron	1914 (June):	1921 (May)	
Reed Holloman	1914 (July):	1919 (August)	

* Elkins selected Henry L. Waldo to handle cases in which Catron was adversely employed.

Deposition of Frank Springer[*]

My name is Frank Springer, and I am, by profession, an attorney at law.

I came to Colfax County in Feb., 1873, and have no personal knowledge of affairs in New Mexico previous to that time; there had been some troubles in Colfax County before that, I learned, growing out of controversies between the Maxwell Land Grant and Railway Company, and settlers, in regard to title and possession of portions of a large Mexican grant, claimed by the company. I heard a great deal of talk at that time and afterwards about a so-called "Ring" which it was alleged, controlled to a large extent the courts in New Mexico.

---

[*] This affidavit, dated August 9, 1878, consists of thirty-two handwritten pages of questions and answers. The questions are substantially stated in the answers and are, therefore, deleted in the transcription of the first six pages (to which are confined any mention of T. B. Catron). The remaining twenty-eight pages deal largely with the murder of Rev. Thomas J. Tolby as a leading cause for troubles in Colfax County, condemnation of Governor S. B. Axtell for removal of Colfax County courts to Taos County, and a brief statement concerning the indictment of Mrs. W. R. Morley (covered in the text). The original affidavit is to be found in the report and testimony in the matter of charges against Samuel B. Axtell, Governor of New Mexico, by Frank Warner Angel (N.A.R.G. 48).

The names of Judge Palen, Mr. Elkins, [and] Mr. Catron were mentioned most frequently in this connection and in regard to Colfax County the name of Dr. R. H. Longwill was often spoken of as being connected with, or in some way representing the so-called "Ring." He was probate judge of the county when I came here, an office which combined the powers of Probate Court and County Supervisors, at that time. It was a frequent subject of comment and complaint that through the persons above mentioned, the powers of the courts were unfairly used to advance the interests of the said Maxwell Land Grant and Railway Company.

Certain articles have appeared in the *News & Press* newspapers of Cimarron of June 20, 27, and July 4th purporting to give a history of some events in the past history of the county, previous to my arrival here. They contained in substance, what I have heard on a great many different occasions and from a great many different persons, what, indeed, has been common and current report among those who lived in the county during the times mentioned. I have no personal knowledge of them, as facts, except that I have seen the originals of the letters published in the three articles above mentioned and know that those signed by Mr. Elkins are in his handwriting, with which I am well acquainted, also that those signed by Longwill and McBride are in their handwriting, and I have every reason to believe that those signed by Jones and Hogan are genuine, and were addressed and mailed to Dr. R. H. Longwill through the usual channels.

The facts upon which the existence [of a Ring] was predicated were not generally within my personal knowledge, except as to facts connected with subsequent troubles in Colfax County which impressed me with the belief that a few men had almost absolute control of affairs in the territory. In 1873, Mr. M. W. Mills, who had been a prominent opponent of the Maxwell Company, and of men who controlled it, was elected a member of the territorial legislature. Very soon after this he became very intimate with Dr. Longwill, whom he had before strongly opposed, and after he went to Santa Fe, to attend the session of the legislature, he wrote to Longwill, in which he informed him that "by a little sharp figuring," he had "got in with the big side." A copy of the letter is hereto attached as Exhibit A. From that time on Mills became and continued very intimate with Longwill as well as with Messrs. Elkins and Catron, and represented them in business and political matters in the county to a very large extent, at least their intimacy and harmony of interests was very apparent to outside observers, and in 1875, when Mills was again a candidate for the legislature, and Longwill for Probate Judge, all their powers were exerted to promote his election. A circumstance came under my observation during that election campaign which impressed this strongly on my mind. In June 1975, a man by the name of Francisco Griego murdered two soldiers in Cimarron, in a gaming table quarrel, shooting and stabbing them in the back. He fled and was a fugitive for some time, when at last he came in and gave himself up. He was at once taken before the Justice of the Peace who was a clerk in Mills office and examined, and bound over to await the action of the Grand Jury, in $1,000.00 bail, this action of the justice being taken after an hour recess, and a conversation with Longwill and Mills, as I was credibly informed at the time by several persons.

The political campaign was then opening, and some weeks afterward, I heard a conversation with one C. Lara, an especial friend of Griego, who was then actively working in the interest of the Longwill and Mills ticket, as was Griego, himself. Lara had previously been on the other side, and on my asking him the reason for his change of attitude, he told me that his friend was in danger of prosecution for the killing of the soldiers, and that he — Lara — had been to Santa Fe, and had talked with the gentlemen, and that they had promised him that if he and Griego would use all their influence with the Mexicans in favor of the ticket of Elkins and Longwill, his friend Griego should not suffer, and that for this reason he was obliged to work on the side that he had always before opposed.. Upon my asking him who the gentlemen were who had promised this, he mentioned with much reluctance, Messers. Breeden and Catron. Whether his statement was true or not, I do not know, but I observed that both Lara and Griego labored earnestly in the direction indicated, and that when the District Court came on in September, Lara was appointed interpreter for the Grand Jury, and although the most positive and abundant evidence was produced against him, Griego was discharged, without being indicted for anything, nor were any further proceedings taken against him in the matter.

Statement by T. B. Catron

STATEMENT BY T. B. CATRON
ON WHY THE PEOPLE OF NEW MEXICO
WERE ENTITLED TO STATEHOOD

Catron to Matthew Quay, January 6, 1903 (C.P. 105, Vol. 20).

Our people are in favor of prosperity; even in the high tide of free silver in the year 1896, by the union of the Democrats, Populists and every other organization outside of the Republican party, they were able to beat the Republican candidate [Catron] by eighteen hundred only out of thirty-six thousand votes; the Republican Candidate went upon the platform endorsing the National Platform enunciated at St. Louis in that year. Two years thereafter that majority disappeared and the Republican candidate [Perea] was elected by over two thousand on the same platform; two years thereafter, that is, in 1900, the Republican candidate [Rodey] had over thirty eight hundred majority and now he has nearly ten thousand; five thousand of which in any event is pure, straight, unqualified Republican majority. The present legislature of New Mexico is solid Republican in the Council and only three Democrats out of twenty-four in the House; our people are favorable to the tariff which now exists; they want protection for their industries; they are prospering everywhere; there are no beggars amongst us; our schools are healthy, in good condition, well attended and are all taught in the English language; all of our people over eight years of age and under twenty five years or thirty years, almost to a man can read and write; among the older ones, who lived here before any school system was first established, there are some who cannot read and write; they are not so very numerous, one reason why more of the people, who are under [over?] forty years of age cannot read and write, is that when our school system was first established, there was a prejudice among the people of Mexican origin against mixed schools and they refrained from sending their daughters to schools for several years until they became educated to the propriety of doing so and as a consequence some of the girls did not receive as much education as the boys; this prejudice, however, has disappeared and our people are now advancing along the line of prosperity, wealth and education and intelligence equal to that of any Territory which has ever existed in the United States. No Territory can prosper unless capital can be induced to go into it; it is true labor may build it up to a certain extent, but without capital, labor is always crippled and can advance but slowly by way of development and prosperity. Capitalists in the East, as well as the extreme West, do not have confidence in a Territorial Government where a change in every National Administration, makes a change in officials, and a great change in the local laws being always brought about by the influence of a changed administration, besides the local laws are subject to change and modification at the will of Congress; Capitalists do not think they can count upon the stability, certainty and the best ability which might under a State government be brought to bear to sustain the public welfare and protect the property interests and lives of the individuals. Many people are unwilling to locate in a Territory because there is want of a great amount of self government therein: they have no right to elect their officers, either Territorial or Federal or the Judges who administer their laws; the Acts of their Legislature are subject to a veto power by a Government not of their own choosing; people who have been educated in any one of the States, are attached to the form of government where they were educated; they feel that a Territorial Government is not a free government; that it is a Government of tutelage; that it is a government for minors, one which is only preparatory to a State government; the American people do not like to go backward, they are progressive in every regard, they wish the greatest amount of freedom in enacting their laws and in the execution of them by their servants selected by themselves alone.

We want State government for these reasons and because we believe we would be still more prosperous under such government; we do not wish a State government, however, where the local laws would have to be radically changed, where the rights of individuals would be interfered with and altered from their existing conditions and where a portion of the State might possibly be arrayed into hostility against the other portion in a sectional fight for preferment or to secure government.

Notes to Chapters

NOTES FOR CHAPTER ONE
Pages 1 to 8

1. Thomas Catron to Judge Joseph Reid, May 15, 1911 (C.P. 105, Vol. 31).
2. Frank F. Catron to the author, September 3, 1964.
3. Oscar Doane Lambert, *Stephen Benton Elkins*, p. 5.

NOTES FOR CHAPTER TWO
Pages 9 to 19

1. E. S. Adams, adjutant general, War Department, Washington, D.C., to Vioalle Hefferan, March 20, 1939.
2. Hiram Bledsoe to Catron, June 25, 1893 (C.P. 102, Box 19).
3. John C. Moore, *Confederate Military History*, Vol. 9 (Missouri), pp. 47, 48.
4. *Ibid.*, p. 62.
5. *Ibid.*, pp. 91, 92.
6. Edwin C. Bearss, research historian, Vicksburg National Military Park, to the author, February 15, 1966.
7. Ed W. Strode to Catron, October 29, 1904 (C.P. 103, Box 21).
8. Moore, Vol. 9, p. 198.
9. *Parole* (C.P. 801, Box 1).
10. Catron to S. W. Hudson, June 1, 1895 (C.P. 105, Vol. 12).

NOTES FOR CHAPTER THREE
Pages 20 to 32

1. Frank F. Catron to the author, January 12, 1965.
2. *Ibid.*, September 3, 1964.
3. *Washington Herald*, September 6, 1914, Catron scrapbook.
4. William A. Keleher, *Fabulous Frontier*, p. 120.
5. *Washington Herald*, September 6, 1914, Catron scrapbook.
6. Thomas B. Catron to Joseph M. Carey, January 15, 1893 (C.P. 105, Vol. 6).
7. *Santa Fe Weekly New Mexican Review and Livestock Journal*, July 31, 1884.
8. Edgar A. Walz to Catron, June 8, 1897 (C.P. 103, Box 3).
9. *Santa Fe Weekly New Mexican*, December 22, 1866.
10. Interviews, Adlai Feather, June 29 and October 12, 1964.

11. Catron to W. C. Gordon, April 4, 1912 (C.P. 501, Box 6).
12. Keleher, *Violence in Lincoln County*, p. 117; *Kearny Code*.
13. *Santa Fe Weekly New Mexican*, May 18, 1869.

NOTES FOR CHAPTER FOUR
Pages 33 to 73

1. Lena Paulus, *Problem of the Private Land Grant*, p. 49.
2. Victor Westphall, *The Public Domain in New Mexico*, p. 49.
3. *G.N.M.* 9/15/1903, 58 Cong., 2 Sess., *H.E.D.* No. 1, pp. 383–4 (4649).
4. *Ibid.*, p. 384.
5. Westphall, p. 51.
6. *G.N.M.* 9/15/1903, 58 Cong., 2 sess. *H.E.D.* No. 1, p. 383 (4649).
7. William Brayer, *Blackmore*, p. 167; Frank L. Washburn to Catron, May 15, 1894 (C.P. 102, Box 21); Catron to Washburn, May 26, 1894 (C.P. 105, Vol. 10).
8. Catron to Adelbart Ames, July 26, 1893 (C.P. 105, Vol. 7).
9. Catron to Franklin H. Mackey, March 25, 1889 (C.P. 105, Vol. 2); Catron to Ames, July 26, 1893 (C.P. 105, Vol. 7).
10. Marcelino Martinez to S. B. Elkins, December 16, 1903 (C.P. 103, Box 19).
11. *Deed* (C.P. 206, Box 2).
12. Catron to Adelbart Ames, July 26, 1893 (C.P. 105, Vol. 7).
13. Catron to S. B. Elkins, November 18, 1893 (C.P. 105, Vol. 8).
14. Catron to R. G. Head, November 12, 1895 (C.P. 105, Vol. 13); Catron to M. S. Baldwin, December 3, 1897 (C.P. 105, Vol. 13); Baldwin to Catron, December 11, 1897 (C.P. 103, Box 4); Ames to Catron, December 24, 1900 (C.P. 103, Box 11); Baldwin to Catron, February 23, 1901 (C.P. 103, Box 12).
15. Frank Lavan to A. C. Voorhees, February 3, 1911 (C.P. 111, Vol. 1).
16. C. C. Catron to Howard Vaughn, September 25, 1912 (C.P. 101, Vol. 15); C. C. Catron to Severino Martinez, March 11, 1913 (C.P. 111, Vol. 1).
17. *Deed* (C.P. 305, Box 1).
18. Thomas B. Catron to S. B. Elkins, November 8, 1888 (C.P. 105, Vol. 2); *Deed* (C.P. 305, Box 1).
19. *Agreement*, July 22, 1882 (C.P. 305, Box 1).
20. *Santa Fe Weekly New Mexican*, July 4 and August 1, 1876.
21. *Deeds* (C.P. 305, Box 1); *Santa Fe Weekly New Mexican*, April 24, 1877.
22. *Deed* (C.P. 305, Box 1).
23. Catron to Wilmot E. Broad, April 27, 1905 (C.P. 105, Vol. 23); Catron to Broad, January 29, 1901 (C.P. 105, Vol. 18); Broad to Catron, July 30, 1901 (C.P. 103, Box 11).
24. Catron to Frank W. Broad, December 6, 1907 (C.P. 103, Box 30).
25. *Ibid.*, August 11, 1908 (C.P. 105, Vol. 28).
26. Charles C. Catron to A. B. Renehan, August 12, 1921 (C.P. 101, Vol. 29).
27. *Docket 3458* (C.P. 305, Box 1); George W. Julian to William A. J. Sparks, March 28, 1887 (C.P. 305, Box 1).
28. Julian to Jacob H. Crist, December 19, 1888 (F.R.C.).
29. *Agreement*, November 21, 1885 (C.P. 305, Box 1).
30. Julian to Sparks, March 28, 1887 (C.P. 305, Box 1); *Docket 3458* (C.P. 305, Box 1).
31. James M. Freeman to Catron, April 15, 1889 (C.P. 102, Box 3).
32. S. B. Elkins to Catron, April 16, 1889 (C.P. 102, Box 3); Catron to Elkins, April 24, 1889 (C.P. 105, Vol. 2).
33. Catron to John W. Noble, March 20, 1889 (C.P. 105, Vol. 2).
34. Noble to Catron, March 26, 1889 (C.P. 801, Box 1).
35. Catron to S. B. Elkins, November 18, 1889 (C.P. 105, Vol. 2).
36. John H. Knaebel, James M. Freeman, and C. C Clements to Attorney General, March 18, 1893 (CP. 305, Box 1); Freeman to Catron, April 20, 1894 (C.P. 102, Box 21).

37. Catron to Richard C. Kerens, August 10, 1892 (C.P. 105, Vol. 5).
38. Knaebel to Catron, April 10, 1894 (C.P. 102, Box 21).
39. Catron to Freeman, May 16, 1894 (C.P. 105, Vol. 10).
40. *Agreement*, February 13, 1883 (C.P. 305, Box 1); Catron to Nicolas Galles, December 7, 1890 (C.P. 105, Vol. 3).
41. Catron to Eugene H. Wilson, September 26, 1903 (C.P. 105, Vol. 22).
42. Miguel A. Otero to G. T. Kessler, February 6, 1895 (C.P. 305, Box 1).
43. T. B. Catron to Charles C. Catron, May 29, 1909 (C.P. 104, Box 1); William C. Van Gilder to T. B. Catron, September 24, 1909 (C.P. 103, Box 34); Charles C. Catron to Robert Gortner, June 7, 1909 (C.P. 110, Vol. 1).
44. Catron memorandum, April 12, 1901 (C.P. 103, Box 12).
45. Catron to Waddingham, January 6, 1893 (C.P. 105, Vol. 5); Catron to Stoddard, August 19, 1899 (C.P. 105, Vol. 6).
46. Catron to Waddingham, January 6, 1893 (C.P. 105, Vol. 5).
47. Catron to Waddingham, February 9, 1893 (C.P. 105, Vol. 6).
48. Catron to E. G. Stoddard, June 29, 1899 (C.P. 105, Vol. 16).
49. Catron to Waddingham, June 8, 1898 (C.P. 109, Vol. 2).
50. Stoddard to Catron, May 16, 1899 (C.P. 103, Box 7); Catron to Stoddard, June 29, 1899 (C.P. 105, Vol. 16).
51. Knaebel to Catron, September 2, 1900 (C.P. 103, Box 11).
52. Catron to C. K. Bush, June 17, 1904 (C.P. 105, Vol. 23).
53. William J. Mills to Catron, June 12, 1907 (C.P. 103, Box 29).
54. Bush to Catron, October 26, 1904 (C.P. 103, Box 21).
55. Catron to Stoddard, August 3, 1899 (C.P. 105, Vol. 16); Catron to Sister Angelica Ortiz, August 6, 1902 (C.P. 105, Vol. 20).
56. Knaebel to Catron, September 9, 1909 (C.P. 103, Box 8).
57. Catron to Charles M. Gilbert, March 30, 1901 (C.P. 105, Vol. 18); Catron to W. Howard Ramsey, February 26, 1912 (C.P. 105, Vol. 31).
58. Catron to Fred Robertson, United States Attorney, May 10, 1914 (C.P. 108, Box 1).
59. Catron to Don A. MounDay, November 29, 1910 (C.P. 105, Vol. 30).
60. *Ibid.*, September 29, 1910.
61. William C. Van Gilder to Catron, August 20, 1910 (C.P. 103, Box 36).
62. *Las Vegas Optic*, July 28, 1913.
63. *Santa Fe Weekly New Mexican*, January 31, 1871.
64. *Records*, First National Bank of Santa Fe. *Santa Fe Weekly New Mexican*, May 23, 1871.
65. Catron to J. S. Sniffen, February 8, 1893 (C.P. 105, Vol. 6).
66. Adlai Feather to the author, April 26, 1966; John H. Riley to Catron, December 22, 1889 (C.P. 102, Box 5).
67. *Santa Fe Weekly New Mexican Review*, November 1, 1894.
68. T. A. Finical to Catron, January 13, 1898 (C.P. 103, Box 4).
69. Smith H. Simpson to Catron, April 30, 1889 (C.P. 103, Box 7).
70. *Santa Fe Weekly New Mexican Review*, November 1, 1894; and numerous other sources.

NOTES FOR CHAPTER FIVE
Pages 74 to 96

1. Adlai Feather to the author, August 8, 1964; *Receipts*, November 11, 1868 (C.P. 803, Box 1).
2. Victor Westphall, *Public Domain in New Mexico*, p. 16.
3. Colonel August V. Kautz to Captain J. M. Goniglo, July 20, 1871 (C.P. 803, Box 1).
4. Interview, Adlai Feather, July 5, 1966.
5. *Santa Fe Weekly New Mexican*, September 28, 1875.
6. Frank Warner Angel, *Report on Charges Against Axtell*, October 3, 1878 (N.A.R.G. 48); *Santa Fe Weekly New Mexican*, May 30 and August 22, 1876.

7. *Santa Fe Weekly New Mexican,* April 20, 1878; Interview, Adlai Feather, July 5, 1966.
8. William F. Keleher, *Violence in Lincoln County,* p. 103; Frederick W. Nolan, *John Henry Tunstall,* p. 275.
9. *Santa Fe Weekly New Mexican,* April 4 and 27, 1878.
10. Frederick W. Nolan, *Tunstall,* pp. 261, 262; *Ibid.,* pp. 278, 279.
11. *Ibid.,* p. 267.
12. Catron to Wilson Waddingham, September 2, 1897 (C.P. 105, Vol. 14).
13. Keleher, *Violence in Lincoln County,* p. 81.
14. *Ibid.,* p. 90; Angel, *Report on Charges Against Axtell,* October 3, 1878 (N.A.R.G. 48).
15. *Santa Fe Weekly New Mexican,* March 16, 1878.
16. Col. Edward Hatch (by Loud) to Assistant Adjutant General, April 23, 1878 (N.A.R.G. 94).
17. Robert W. Beckwith et al., to Gen. N. A. M. Dudley, May 1, 1878 (N.A.R.G. 94).
18. Dudley to Acting Assistant Adjutant General, May 25, 1878 (N.A.R.G. 94).
19. Dudley to Frederick C. Godfroy, May 28, 29, 1878 (N.A.R.G. 94); Edgar A. Walz, *Retrospections,* p. 3.
20. Catron to S. B. Axtell, May 30, 1878 (N.A.R.G. 94).
21. *Ibid.*
22. Interview, Adlai Feather, July 5, 1966; *Santa Fe Weekly New Mexican,* April 5, 1879.
23. Angel, *Report on Charges Against Axtell* (N.A.R.G. 48).
24. "Regulator" to Edgar A. Walz, July 13, 1878 (N.A.R.G. 94).
25. *Santa Fe Weekly New Mexican,* September 7, 1878; Walz, *Retrospections,* p. 3.
26. Keleher, *Violence in Lincoln County,* p. 137.
27. Nolan, *Tunstall,* pp. 380, 385; Dudley to Acting Assistant Adjutant General, July 23, 1878 (N.A.R.G. 94).
28. *Ibid.,* Dudley, August 24, September 7, 1878.
29. Nolan, *Tunstall,* p. 402.
30. United States Judge Advocate to Judge Advocate Department of Missouri, September 23, 1879 (N.A.R.G. 94).
31. Lt. M. F. Goodwin to Capt. Thomas Blair, July 23, 1878 (N.A.R.G. 94).
32. Keleher, *Fabulous Frontier,* p 124.
33. Dudley to United States Attorney General Devens, September 16, 1879 (N.A.R.G. 94).
34. *Ibid.*
35. *Santa Fe Weekly New Mexican,* April 12, 1879.
36. *Ibid.,* December 6, 1879.
37. Nolan, *Tunstall,* p. 463; Walz, *Retrospections,* p. 5.
38. Robert W. Larson, *New Mexico's Quest for Statehood, 1846–1912,* p. 139; Maurice G. Fulton, *History of the Lincoln County War,* pp. 27, 53.

NOTES FOR CHAPTER SIX
Pages 97 to 121

1. Bronson Cutting to James Roger Addison, December 11, 1911 (L.C. Manuscripts Division, Box 12, courtesy of David Stratton).
2. It seems best that the writer of this letter remain anonymous.
3. Jim Berry Pearson, *The Maxwell Land Grant,* pp. 49, 50, *passim.*
4. J. Francisco Chavez to A. T. Ackerman, September 18, 1870 (N.A.R.G. 60).
5. Alexander P. Sullivan et al., to Attorney General, September 26, 1870 (N.A.R.G. 60).
6. *Temporary Attorney's Commissions* (N.A.R.G. 59).
7. Governor Marsh Giddings et al., to President of the United States, January 13, 1872 (N.A.R.G. 60).

8. *Denver Rocky Mountain News,* quoted in *Santa Fe Weekly New Mexican,* January 23, 1872; August Kirchner, *Affidavit* (N.A.R.G. 60).
9. William A. Keleher, *Violence in Lincoln County,* p. 12.
10. Catron, *Affidavit,* February 16, 1872 (N.A.R.G. 60).
11. Governor Giddings and Chief Justice Palen to United States Attorney General Williams, February 17, 1872 (N.A.R.G. 60). S. B. Elkins sent a similar telegram.
12. W. W. McFarland to Attorney General Williams, February 19, 1872 (N.A.R.G. 60).
13. *Santa Fe Weekly New Mexican,* February 20, 1872. Catron's commission was dated March 8, 1872. *Attorney's Commissions — Permanent,* Vol. 4, p. 35, General Records of the Department of State (N.A.R.G. 59).
14. *U.S. Attorney Reports — New Mexico* (N.A.R.G. 206).
15. Governor Giddings to United States Attorney General, March 3, 1873 (N.A.R.G. 60).
16. Pearson, *Maxwell Land Grant,* p. 59; *Santa Fe Weekly New Mexican,* November 12, 1872.
17. Frank Warner Angel, *Report on Charges Against Axtell,* October 3, 1878 (N.A.R.G. 48); *Santa Fe Weekly New Mexican,* April 14, 1873.
18. *Santa Fe Weekly New Mexican,* September 9, October 21, 1873.
19. *Santa Fe Weekly New Mexican,* March 10, 1874; James K. Proudfit to R. Robertson, October 1, 1874 (F.R.C.); George W. Julian to O. P. McMains, September 24, 1886 (F.R.C.).
20. *Santa Fe Weekly New Mexican,* December 12, 1876, reported that the sale was to be held on December 16; Pearson, *Maxwell Land Grant,* p. 74, states that the sale was held on December 23.
21. Harold H. Dunham, *Government Handout: A Study in the Administration of the Public Lands, 1875–1891,* p. 226.
22. *Santa Fe Weekly New Mexican,* November 13, 1877.
23. *Ibid.,* July 22, 1873.
24. *Ibid.,* August 26, 1873.
25. *New York Sun,* October 15, 1875, as quoted in *Thirty-Four,* October 20, 1880.
26. Angel, *Report on Charges Against Axtell,* October 3, 1878 (N.A.R.G. 48).
27. Catron, *Affidavit Answering Interrogatories by Frank Warner Angel,* September 11, 1878 (N.A.R.G. 60). Catron explained that the record is to be found in Vol. 94, p. 614, U.S. Reports, United States vs. Joseph.
28. Catron to Attorney General Alfonso Taft, February 24, 1877 (N.A.R.G. 60).
29. Agnes Morley Cleaveland, *No Life For a Lady,* p. 8; *Ibid.,* p. 9.
30. *U.S. Attorney Reports — New Mexico* (N.A.R.G. 206).
31. Mary E. McPherson to Attorney General Alfonso Taft, February 7, 1877 (N.A.R.G. 60).
32. *Ibid.*
33. Catron to Taft, February 24, 1877 (N.A.R.G. 60).
34. *Ibid.*
35. W. R. Morley to Taft, September 3, 1877 (N.A.R.G. 60).
36. For example, see "A Friend of Reform to the Attorney General," April 21 and 28, 1877 (N.A.R.G. 60).
37. Angel, *Report on Charges Against Axtell,* October 3, 1878 (N.A.R.G. 48). See also Appendix 2 for summary.

NOTES FOR CHAPTER SEVEN
Pages 122 to 134

1. Acting Attorney General S. F. Phillips to Catron, March 18, 1878 (N.A.R.G. 60).
2. Victor Westphall, *Public Domain in New Mexico,* p. 55; William A. Keleher, *Violence in Lincoln County,* p. 246.
3. Catron to Attorney General Charles Devens, April 5, 1878 (N.A.R.G. 60).

4. *Santa Fe Weekly New Mexican,* March 23 and June 8, 1878.
5. Frank Warner Angel to Devens, July 10 and 16, 1878 (N.A.R.G. 60).
6. Angel to Devens, June 5, 1878 (N.A.R.G. 60).
7. *Ibid.,* July 16, 1878. Angel was still in Lincoln on July 6. *Santa Fe Weekly New Mexican,* July 6, 1878.
8. Angel, *Report on the Death of Tunstall and Troubles in Lincoln County,* October 7, 1878 (N.A.R.G. 60).
9. Frank Springer and Governor Axtell correspondence, April 4 through May 13, 1878 (N.A.R.G. 48).
10. Axtell to Angel, August 12, 1878 (N.A.R.G. 48); *Santa Fe Weekly New Mexican,* August 10, 1878.
11. Axtell to Angel, August 12, 1878 (N.A.R.G. 48).
12. Angel to Axtell, August 13, 1878 (N.A.R.G. 48).
13. Angel to Devens, August 24, 1878 (N.A.R.G. 60); *Santa Fe Weekly New Mexican,* September 21, 1878; Angel, *Report on Charges Against Axtell,* October 3, 1878 (N.A.R.G. 48).
14. Catron to Angel, August 10, 1878; Angel to Catron, August 12, 1878 (N.A.R.G. 60).
15. Angel to Devens, September 20, 1878; Devens to S. B. Elkins, September 16, 1878 (N.A.R.G. 60).
16. Mark G. Eckhoff, Acting Chief Diplomatic, Legal and Fiscal Branch, National Archives, to the author, August 9, 1966.
17. Catron to Elkins, September 26, 1892 (C.P. 105, Vol. 5); S. D. Miller (Elkins' secretary) to Catron, October 3, 1892 (C.P. 102, Box 16); Catron to Elkins, February 5, 1893 (C.P. 105, Vol. 6); Elkins to Catron, March 13, 1893 (C.P. 102, Box 18).
18. Angel to Attorney General Devens, August 24, 1878 (N.A.R.G. 60).
19. Catron to Attorney General Devens, October 10, 1878; Devens to Catron, October 19, 1878 (N.A.R.G. 60).
20. S. B. Elkins to Catron, August 15, 1879 (West Virginia University Library).
21. Devens to Catron, November 1, 1878; Catron to Devens, November 4, 1878; Devens to Catron, November 12, 1878 (N.A.R.G. 60); Sidney M. Barnes to U.S. Attorney General, January 20, 1879 (N.A.R.G. 60).
22. *Santa Fe Weekly New Mexican,* February 8, 1879.

NOTES FOR CHAPTER EIGHT
Pages 135 to 149

1. *Santa Fe Weekly New Mexican,* May 8, 1877.
2. For example, Catron to Jennie Walz, October 9, 1893 (C.P. 105, Vol. 7); Jennie Walz Turner to Catron, July 31, 1912 (C.P. 501, Box 8).
3. T. B. Catron to George Catron, April 15, 1890 (C.P. 105, Vol. 3); George Catron to T. B. Catron, April 22, 1890 (C.P. 102, Box 7).
4. Catron to W. E. Coons, April 25, 1890 (C.P. 105, Vol. 3).
5. Coons to Catron, June 6, 1890 (C.P. 102, Box 7); Catron to Coons, June 9, 1890 C.P. 105, Vol. 3).
6. L. E. Wolfe to Coons, December 5, 1892 (C.P. 102, Box 17).
7. R. P. Ingram to Catron, October 10, 1891 (C.P. 102, Box 12).
8. T. B. Catron to Julia Catron, September 15, 1894 (C.P. 105, Vol. 4).
9. *Ibid.,* February 26, 1895, Vol. 11.
10. Wendell M. Strong to Catron, February 15, 1898 (C.P. 103, Box 4); T. B. Catron to John Catron, February 24, 1898 (C.P. 109, Vol. 2).
11. T. B. Catron to George Catron, April 18, 1898 (C.P. 105, Vol. 15).
12. *Ibid.,* April 19, 1898.
13. T. B. Catron to Julia Catron, September 3, 1902 (C.P. 105, Vol. 20).
14. T. B. Catron to Thom Catron, June 8, 1903 (C.P. 105, Vol. 21).

15. T B. Catron to Charles Catron, September 30, 1893 (C.P. 105, Vol. 7).
16. Fletcher Catron to T. B. Catron, March 30, 1910 (C.P. 103, Box 35).
17. T. B. Catron to Fletcher Catron, June 6, 1911 (C.P. 105, Vol. 31).
18. *Ibid.*, May 18, 1908, Vol. 27.
19. Bernard S. Rodey to Catron, January 21, 1904 (C.P. 103, Box 19).
20. Catron to Rodey, January 26, 1904 (C.P. 105, Vol. 22).
21. Julia Catron to T. B. Catron, undated (C.P. 103, Box 1).
22. Catron to M. W. Mills, August 23, 1909 (C.P. 105, Vol. 28).
23. Catron to J. W. Schofield, August 24, 1893 (C.P. 105, Vol. 7).
24. T. B. Catron to Julia Catron, April 6, 1908 (C.P 105, Vol 27).
25. T. B. Catron to George Catron, May 26, 1908 (C.P. 105, Vol. 27).
26. T. B. Catron to Charles Catron, December 13, 1908 (C.P. 103, Box 33).
27. Charles Catron to T. B. Catron, May 3, 1909 (C.P. 110, Vol. 1).

NOTES FOR CHAPTER NINE
Pages 150 to 165

1. John P. Casey, *Statement.*
2. *Ibid.*
3. Catron to W. L. Rynerson, and Catron to Neill B. Field, September 22, 1892 (C.P. 105, Vol. 5).
4. El Caso Ranch, *Abstract of Title*, p. 31.
5. *Albuquerque Morning Journal*, June 12, 1883.
6. *Ibid.*, September 13, 1883.
7. Secretary of the Interior, *Fraudulent Acquisition of Titles to Land in New Mexico*, pp. 112, 123.
8. John P. Casey, *Statement;* El Caso Ranch, *Abstract of Title*, pp. 29, 30.
9. *Santa Fe Weekly New Mexican Review*, January 17, 1884.
10. John P. Casey, *Statement;* Ellen Salmon (Casey's granddaughter) to the author, September 16, 1964.
11. Chas. F. Easley, register of the land office, to William B. Slaughter, December 15, 1885 (C.P. 611, Box 2).
12. Catron to S. B. Elkins, April 4, 1901 (C.P. 105, Vol 8).
13. *Corporation agreement* (C.P. 611, Box 2).
14. C. H. Elmendorf to John D. Patterson, October 20, 1899 (C.P. 601, Vol. 1).
15. Catron to John P. Casey, May 31, 1887 (C.P. 105, Vol. 1); Catron to Neill B. Field, November 30, 1896 (C.P. 611, Box 2); Catron to Field, December 23, 1896 (C.P. 106, Box 1).
16. *Rio Grande Republican*, March 12, 1887; Catron to former Governor Lionel L. Sheldon, February 21, 1887 (C.P. 105, Vol. 1); Catron to Field, November 30, 1896 (C.P. 611, Box 2).
17. Catron to John P. Casey, August 23, 1887 (C.P. 105, Vol. 1); Catron to S. M. Folsom, June 29, 1887 (C.P. 105, Vol. 1).
18. El Caso Ranch, *Abstract of Title*, pp. 38, 39; Catron to Casey, December 28, 1887 (C.P. 105, Vol. 1); Catron to S. B. Newcomb, October 15, 1888 (C.P. 105, Vol. 2); C. H. Elmendorf to Clerk of Court, Socorro County, October 6, 1899 (C.P. 601, Vol. 1); Elmendorf to Frank W. Clancy, October 19, 1899 (C.P. 601, Vol. 1); Elmendorf to Casey, October 20, 1899 (C.P. 601, Vol. 1).
19. Elmendorf to Dr. H. M. Warren, June 30 and July 12, 1900 (C.P. 601, Vol. 1).
20. Frank W. Clancy to Catron, January 28, 1892 (C.P. 102, Box 13).
21. *Ibid.*, June 6, 1893 (C.P. 611, Box 2).
22. Neill B. Field to Catron, December 28, 1896, and February 25, 1897 (C.P. 106, Boxes 1 and 2).
23. Catron to Field, March 1, 1897 (C.P. 106, Box 2).
24. C. H. Elmendorf to William Watson, April 14, 1900 (C.P. 601, Vol. 1).

NOTES FOR CHAPTER TEN
Pages 166 to 182

1. Frank W. Clancy to Catron, May 19, 1899 (C.P. 103, Box 7).
2. C. H. Elmendorf to Ada I. Atkinson, June 16, 1899 (C.P. 105, Vol. 16).
3. Elmendorf expense statement, June 20–28, 1899 (C.P. 103, Box 8).
4. Elmendorf to J. F. Lederer, August 14, 1899 (C.P. 105, Vol. 15).
5. Elmendorf to George L. Brooks, October 6, 1899 (C.P. 601, Vol. 1).
6. Elmendorf to Richard L. Powell, October 2, 1899 (C.P. 601, Vol. 1).
7. Elmendorf to John E. Ryan, May 21, 1900 (C.P. 601, Vol. 1).
8. *Ibid.,* May 22, 1900.
9. Elmendorf to R. M. Barbour, April 11, 1900 (C.P. 601, Vol. 1).
10. Catron to Elmendorf, December 20, 1900 (C.P. 105, Vol. 24).
11. Elmendorf and Catron to First National Bank, February 17, 1900 (C.P. 601, Vol. 1).
12. Elmendorf to Catron, June 22, 1900 (C.P. 103, Box 10).
13. *Abstract of Title* (C.P. 611, Box 1).
14. S. B. Elkins to Catron, November 24, 1900 (C.P. 103, Box 11).
15. *Ibid.,* January 19, 1901.
16. Elmendorf to Catron, September 11, 1900 (C.P. 103, Box 11).
17. *Ibid.,* January 31, 1900.
18. El Caso Ranch, *Abstract of Title,* pp. 100, 102; Catron to W. N. Coler, May 15, 1901 (C.P. 105, Vol. 18).
19. Elmendorf to Catron, September 7, 1901 (C.P. 103, Box 13).
20. *Ibid.,* September 14, 1901.
21. Catron to Elmendorf, April 25, 1902 (C.P. 105, Vol. 19).
22. T. B. Catron to Julia Catron, May 16, 1902 (C.P. 105, Vol. 20).
23. Catron to Elmendorf, May 11, 1902 (C.P. 105, Vol. 20).
24. *Ibid.,* January 10, 1903, Vol. 21.
25. *Ibid.,* February 7, 1903.
26. Elmendorf to Catron, March 7, 1903 (C.P. 103, Box 17).
27. Catron to Elmendorf, March 19, March 30 and April 22, 1903 (C.P. 105, Vol. 21).
28. Elmendorf to Catron, April 28, 1903 (C.P. 103, Box 17).
29. *Statement,* May 12, 1906 (C.P. 105, Vol. 24); El Caso Ranch, *Abstract of Title,* pp. 103, 105.
30. Catron to Elmendorf, October 29, 1903, and April 4, 1904 (C.P. 105, Vol. 22).
31. *Ibid.,* April 14, 1904.
32. *Ibid.,* April 19, 1904.
33. Catron to Elmendorf, April 27, 1905 (C.P. 105, Vol. 23).
34. Elmendorf to Catron, September 30, 1905 (C.P. 103, Box 23).
35. *Catron-Elmendorf Agreement,* May 12, 1906 (C.P. 105, Vol. 24).
36. Newspaper clipping received by Catron, March 16, 1911 (C.P. 103, Box 26); Catron to L. C. Nelson, March 19, 1908 (C.P. 105, Vol. 27).
37. Fidelity Trust Company to Catron, November 16, 1911 (C.P. 103, Box 37).
38. Sidney P. Allen to Catron, July 6, 1911 (C.P. 103, Box 37).
39. Catron to Allen, August 5, 1911 (C.P. 105, Vol. 31).

NOTES FOR CHAPTER ELEVEN
Pages 183 to 207

1. *G.N.M.* 9/6/83, 48 Cong., 1 Sess., *H.E.D.* No. 1, p. 555 (2191).
2. *Thirty=Four,* October 27, 1880.
3. *Ibid.,* August 18, 1880.
4. *Ibid.,* October 6, 1880.
5. Miguel Antonio Otero, *My Life on the Frontier, 1882–1897,* p. 232.
6. *Albuquerque Daily Democrat,* November 28, 1882.

7. Lucretia Pittman, *Solomon Luna: Sheepmaster and Politician of New Mexico*, p. 80.
8. *Ibid.*
9. Otero, *My Life on the Frontier, 1882–1897*, pp. 232, 233.
10. Mabry, "New Mexico's Constitution in the Making," *New Mexico Historical Review*, 19: 172.
11. *Albuquerque Daily Democrat*, November 9, 1882.
12. *Santa Fe Daily Democrat*, July 22, 1882.
13. *Albuquerque Daily Democrat*, February 22, 1884.
14. *Santa Fe Weekly New Mexican Review*, February 21, 1884.
15. *Ibid., February* 28, 1884.
16. *G.N.M.* 10/6/84, 48 Cong., 2 Sess., *H.E.D.* No. 1, p. 570 (2287).
17. *Albuquerque Daily Democrat*, March 4, 1884.
18. *Santa Fe Weekly New Mexican Review*, February 28, 1884.
19. *Ibid.*, March 13, 1884.
20. *Ibid.*, March 20, 1884; *Albuquerque Daily Democrat*, March 24 and March 27, 1884.
21. *Santa Fe Weekly New Mexican Review*, April 3, 1884.
22. *McMains' Resolution* (University of New Mexico Special Collections, C302, Box 10). See Chapter 4 for the history of the Mora Grant.
23. *Santa Fe Weekly New Mexican Review and Livestock Journal*, March 20, 1884.
24. A. M. Gibson, *The Life and Death of Colonel Albert Jennings Fountain*, p. 178.
25. *Santa Fe Weekly New Mexican Review and Livestock Journal*, July 17, 1884.
26. *Ibid.*, August 28, 1884.
27. *Ibid.*, August 28 and September 4, 1884.
28. *Ibid.*
29. A. M. Gibson, *Life and Death of Colonel Fountain*, pp. 178, 179.
30. *Santa Fe Weekly New Mexican and Livestock Journal*, January 7, 1886.
31. *Ibid.*, December 9, 1886.
32. Catron to O. H. Platt, January 27, 1889 (C.P. 105, Vol. 2).
33. *Ibid.*
34. W. W. Griffin to Catron, September 24, 1888 (C.P. 102, Box 1).
35. Catron to Pedro Sanchez, October 27, 1888 (C.P. 105, Vol. 2).
36. J. A. Carruth to Catron, October 27, 1888 (C.P. 102, Box 1).
37. Undated manuscript in Prince's handwriting (Prince collection, State Records Center, Santa Fe).
38. Catron to S. B. Elkins, November 8, 1888 (C.P. 105, Vol. 2).
39. Ralph E. Twitchell, *Leading Facts of New Mexican History*, Vol. 2, p. 501.
40. For example, Howard Roberts Lamar, *The Far Southwest, 1846–1912*, p. 187.
41. Catron to Elkins, February 9, 1889 (C.P. 105, Vol. 2).
42. A. L. Morrison to Catron, May 31, 1890 (C.P. 102, Box 7).

NOTES FOR CHAPTER TWELVE
Pages 208 to 229

1. Miguel A. Otero, *My Life on the Frontier*, p. 171, *passim; Albuquerque Weekly Citizen*, September 5, 1891.
2. Miguel Salazar to Catron (with accompanying article from the *Las Vegas Optic*) August 22, 1890 (C.P. 102, Box 8).
3. W. J. Mills to Catron, July 19, 1890 (C.P. 102, Box 8).
4. O. D. Barrett to Catron, July 21, 1890 (C.P. 102, Box 8).
5. Catron to Wilson Waddingham, August 13, 1890 (C.P. 105, Vol. 3).
6. *Albuquerque Weekly Citizen*, August 8 and September 5, 1891.
7. *Black Range*, April 18, 1890.
8. S. Davis to Catron, August 14, 1890 (C.P. 102, Box 8).

9. Robert Gortner to parents, February 11, 1891 (C.P. 109, Vol. 1).
10. M. W. Mills to Catron, February 9, 1891 (C.P. 102, Box 11).
11. W. E. Broad to Catron, February 9, 1891 (C.P. 102, Box 11).
12. Elfego Baca to Catron, February 7, 1891 (C.P. 102, Box 10).
13. Thomas Branigan to Catron, February 17, 1891 (C.P. 102, Box 10).
14. R. Ewing to Catron, May 26, 1891 (C.P. 102, Box 11).
15. *Albuquerque Weekly Citizen,* August 22, 1891.
16. *Santa Fe Weekly New Mexican,* January 19, 1878; Catron to W. T. Thornton, January 31, 1887 (C.P. 105, Vol. 1).
17. *Catron-Thornton Agreement,* courtesy Thomas B. Catron III.
18. Catron to President of the United States, February 16, 1897 (C.P. 106, Box 2).
19. *Santa Fe Weekly New Mexican Review,* June 15 and August 3, 1893; February 22, 1894.
20. *Ibid.,* July 6, 1893; Catron to President of the United States, February 16, 1897 (C.P. 106, Box 2).
21. *Santa Fe Weekly New Mexican Review,* November 23 and December 7, 1893.
22. *Ibid.,* January 4, 1894; Porter A. Stratton, *The Territorial Press of New Mexico, 1834–1912,* pp. 86, 87.
23. *Santa Fe Weekly New Mexican Review,* January 11, 1894.
24. *Ibid.*
25. *Ibid.*
26. *Ibid.,* May 16, 1895.
27. *Ibid.,* January 18, 1894.
28. *Ibid.,* January 25, 1894.
29. *Ibid.,* February 8, 1894.
30. Juliana V. Chavez to Catron, March 2, 1894 (C.P. 102, Box 21).
31. Catron to H. B. Hamilton, April 14, 1895 (C.P. 105, Vol. 11).
32. Richard Hudson to Catron, May 14, 1895 (C.P. 102, Box 25).
33. *Santa Fe Weekly New Mexican Review,* June 6, 1895.
34. T. B. Catron to Julia Catron, June 1, 1895 (C.P. 105, Vol. 12).
35. *Santa Fe Weekly New Mexican Review,* June 20, 1895.
36. *Ibid.*
37. *Ibid.*
38. J. H. Knaebel to Catron, August 17, 1899 (C.P. 103, Box 8).
39. *Santa Fe Weekly New Mexican Review,* July 4, 1895.

NOTES FOR CHAPTER THIRTEEN
Pages 230 to 268

1. Frank W. Clancy to Geo. W. Fowle, August 2, 1889 (C.P. 604, Vol. 1); Edgar A. Walz, *Retrospections,* p. 8.
2. *Santa Fe Weekly New Mexican and Livestock Journal,* October 21, 1886.
3. Clancy to Fowle, August 2, 1889 (C.P. 604, Vol. 1).
4. *Ibid.*
5. W. E. Broad to T. B. Catron, January 24, 1889 (C.P. 102, Box 2).
6. Alex Read to Catron, February 11, 1889 (C.P. 102, Box 2).
7. Catron to Alex Bowie, August 27, 1889 (C.P. 604, Vol. 1).
8. Broad to Catron, December 4 and 28, 1891; August 16, 1895 (C.P. 102, Boxes 12, 13 and 26).
9. Catron to J. H. Knaebel, September 1, 1895 (C.P. 105, Vol. 12).
10. R. D. Thompson to Catron, Charles A. Spiess, and Robert C. Gortner, February 19, 1898 (C.P. 103, Box 4).
11. Catron to F. M. Cockrell, November 29, 1889 (C.P. 105, Vol. 2).
12. Catron to Wm. J. Mills, February 18, 1894 (C.P. 105, Vol. 9).
13. Catron to Chas. A. Johnson, September 17, 1895 (C.P. 105, Vol. 12).

14. *Ibid.,* August 20, 1895.
15. Johnson to Catron, September 20, October 3, and October 25, 1895 (C.P. 102, Boxes 26 and 27); Catron to Johnson, October 19, 1895 (C.P. 105, Vol. 13); Catron to H. L. Pickett, September 27, 1895 (C.P. 105, Vol. 12).
16. A. P. Morris to Catron, September 12, September 26, and October 9, 1895 (C.P. 102, Boxes 26 and 27).
17. Perfecto Padia to Catron, September 12, 1895 (C.P. 102, Box 26).
18. Catron to Alex Read, September 27, 1895 (C.P. 105, Vol. 12).
19. W. L. Stevens to Catron, September 13, 1895 (C.P. 102, Box 26).
20. Catron to Johnson, October 24, 1895 (C.P. 105, Vol. 13).
21. Catron to S. B. Elkins, August 24, 1895 (C.P. 105, Vol. 12).
22. *Ibid.,* F. W. Clancy to Catron, September 5, 1895 (C.P. 102, Box 26).
23. Catron to Elkins, August 24, 1895 (C.P. 105, Vol. 12).
24. *Ibid.*
25. Arie W. Poldervaart, *Black-Robed Justice,* p. 166.
26. Catron to S. B. Newcomb, Andreius A. Jones, and Bernard S. Rodey, August 25, 1895 (C.P. 105, Vol. 12).
27. Catron to Elkins, August 24, 1895 (C.P. 105, Vol. 12).
28. Elkins to G. D. Bantz, September 9, 1895 (C.P. 102, Box 26).
29. Elkins to Catron, September 25 and October 30, 1895 (C.P. 102, Boxes 26 and 27).
30. Catron to Elkins, April 9, 1893 (C.P. 105, Vol. 6).
31. A. M. Gibson, *Life and Death of Colonel Fountain,* p. 204; A. B. Fall to Catron, October 6, 1895 (C.P. 102, Box 27).
32. T. A. Finical to Catron, October 11, 1895 (C. P. 102, Box 27).
33. Catron to Albert B. Fall, October 9, 1895 (C.P. 105, Vol. 13); *Albuquerque Daily Citizen,* October 9, 1895.
34. W. S. Williams to Catron, August 26, 1895, and S. B. Newcomb to Catron, September 25, 1895 (C.P. 102, Box 26).
35. Catron to Thos. Hughes, October 10, 1895 (C.P. 801, Box 1).
36. Catron to Editor of *Citizen,* October 10, 1895 (C.P. 801, Box 1).
37. F. W. Clancy to Catron, October 11, 1895 (C.P. 102, Box 27).
38. Catron to T. W. Collier, November 1, 1895 (C.P. 105, Vol. 13).
39. *Ibid.;* Catron to A. L. Cristy, October 21, 1895 (C.P. 105, Vol. 13).
40. L. R. E. Paulin to W. B. Childers, October 11, 1895 (C.P. 801, Box 1).
41. Poldervaart, *Black-Robed Justice,* p. 168.
42. Paulin to Childers, October 11, 1895 (C.P. 801, Box 1).
43. Catron to W. H. Alley, October 24 and November 11, 1895 (C.P. 105, Vol. 13).
44. Catron to W. S. Williams, October 25, 1895 (C.P. 105, Vol. 13).
45. *Ibid.*
46. *Ibid.*
47. Catron to T. W. Collier, November 1, 1895 (C.P. 105, Vol. 13).
48. *Santa Fe Weekly New Mexican,* October 31, 1895.
49. Catron to J. J. Dickey, October 30, 1895 (C.P. 105, Vol. 13).
50. Napoleon B. Laughlin, *Dissenting Opinion* (C.P. 801, Box 1).
51. H. B. Hamilton, *Majority Opinion* (C.P. 801, Box 1).
52. Chas. A. Johnson to Catron, November 4, 1895 (C.P. 102, Box 27).
53. Catron to W. J. Mills, July 18, 1896 (C.P. 105, Vol. 13).
54. Catron to F. W. Clancy, September 23, 1895 (C.P. 105, Vol. 12); *Santa Fe Weekly New Mexican Review,* October 31, 1895.
55. Charles Spiess to Jerry Leahy, October 24, 1895 (C.P. 101, Vol. 4).
56. Catron to Walter C. Hadley, October 29, 1895 (C.P. 105, Vol. 13).
57. Catron to H. B. Hamilton, October 30, 1895 (C.P. 105, Vol 13).
58. William A. Keleher, *Fabulous Frontier,* p. 130; T. A. Finical to Catron, December 9, 1895 (C.P. 102, Box 27).
59. W. T. McCreight to Catron, November 5, 1895 (C.P. 102, Box 27); Catron to Hughes, July 11, 1896, and Catron to Hughes and McCreight, September 21, 1896 (C.P. 105, Vol. 13).

60. C. A. Spiess to Catron, December 29, 1897 (C.P. 103, Box 4); Catron to Spiess, December 29, 1897 (C.P. 105, Vol. 14).
61. Catron to R. E. Twitchell, September 22, 1892 (C.P. 105, Vol. 5).
62. Catron to Twitchell, January 15, 1900 (C.P. 105, Vol. 17).
63. Frank Springer, F. W. Clancy, Neill B. Field, and A. B. Fall to Catron, January 15, 1900 (C.P. 103, Box 9).
64. *Santa Fe Daily New Mexican,* September 11, 1896 (taken from the *Albuquerque Citizen*).
65. *Ibid.*
66. Catron to F. W. Clancy, September 16, 1896 (C.P. 105, Vol. 13).
67. Catron to W. E. Thornton, September 16, 1896 (C.P. 801, Box 1).
68. Catron to H. B. Hamilton, September 11, 1896 (C.P. 105, Vol. 13).
69. Catron to C. A. Spiess, January 12 and 24, 1897 (C.P. 103, Box 2).
70. Catron to president of the United States Grover Cleveland, February 16, 1897 (C.P. 106, Box 2).
71. Julia Catron to Mrs. Recarda Gonzales y Borrego, February 21, 1897 (C.P. 106, Box 2).
72. Thomas J. Curran to W. B. Childers, February 17, 1897 (C.P. 106, Box 2).
73. Catron to Robert Gortner, February 25, 1897 (C.P. 103, Box 2).
74. Francisco Gonzales y Borrego to his brother, Antonio, March 12, 1897 (Thornton Papers, State Records Center, Santa Fe).
75. Keleher, *Fabulous Frontier,* p. 126.
76. Francisco Gonzales y Borrego to Catron, July 23, 1890 (C.P. 102, Box 8).

NOTES FOR CHAPTER FOURTEEN
Pages 269 to 297

1. Catron to President Cleveland, September 16, 1896 (C.P. 801, Box 1).
2. Catron to Pedro Perea, March 1, 1897, and Catron to A. Staab, March 8, 1897 (C.P. 106, Box 2).
3. M. W. Mills to Catron, March 2, 1897 (C.P. 106, Box 2).
4. Perea to Catron, February 25, 1897 (C.P. 106, Box 2).
5. L. B. Prince to Catron, February 18, 1897 (C.P. 106, Box 2).
6. Catron to Prince, March 5, 1897 (C.P. 106, Box 2).
7. Ira M. Bond to Catron, May 2, 1897 (C.P. 103, Box 2).
8. *Ibid.,* May 7, 1897.
9. Miguel A. Otero, *Nine Years as Governor;* Catron to Elkins, June 3, 1897 (C.P. 105, Vol. 13).
10. Elkins to Catron, June 7, 1897 (C.P. 103, Box 3).
11. Howard Roberts Lamar, *The Far Southwest, 1846–1912,* p. 171.
12. Otero, *Nine Years as Governor,* p. 144.
13. Catron to Elkins, October 4, 1897 (C.P. 105, Vol. 14).
14. *Ibid.,* June 3, 1897, Vol. 13.
15. Catron to Perea and Solomon Luna, November 25, 1897 (C.P. 105, Vol. 14).
16. Catron charges against Otero, November 5, 1901 (C.P. 105, Vol. 19).
17. Otero, *Nine Years as Governor,* p. 7.
18. *Ibid.,* p. 8; Catron to S. B. Elkins, December 13, 1897 (C.P. 105, Vol. 14).
19. Catron to Otero, December 13, 1897 (C.P. 105, Vol. 14).
20. Catron to W. F. Allender, February 13, 1897; Catron to Secundino Romero, February 18, 1897 (C.P. 106, Box 2).
21. Catron to Elkins, August 4, 1897 (C.P. 105, Vol. 14).
22. *Ibid.,* November 18, 1889, Vol. 2.
23. Elkins to Catron, October 20, 1897 (C.P. 103, Box 3).
24. Catron to Jefferson Raynolds, December 16, 1897 (C.P. 105, Vol. 14); telegrams from Otero to Catron, December 6 and 18, 1897 (C.P. 103, Box 4).
25. Catron to Elkins, January 5, 1898 (C.P. 105, Vol. 14).
26. *Ibid.,* April 19, 1898.

27. Elkins to Catron, January 10, 1898 (C.P. 103, Box 4).
28. Otero, *Nine Years as Governor,* p. 144.
29. B. S. Rodey to J. W. Griggs, December 1, 1900 (C.P. 103, Box 11).
30. Otero, *Nine Years as Governor,* p. 142.
31. Ralph E. Twitchell, *Leading Facts of New Mexican History,* Vol. 2, p. 524.
32. Undated newspaper clipping, Laughlin Papers, State Records Center, Santa Fe.
33. Otero, *Nine Years as Governor,* p. 98.
34. Grand Jury Report, January 1899 (C.P. 103, Box 7); Catron to Thomas Hughes and W. T. McCreight, January 11, 1900 (C.P. 105, Vol. 17).
35. Otero, *Nine Years as Governor,* p. 149.
36. W. B. Childers to Catron, May 21, 1899 (C.P. 103, Box 7).
37. Otero, *Nine Years as Governor,* p. 132.
38. Catron to S. B. Elkins, January 13, 1901 (C.P. 105, Vol. 18).
39. *Ibid.,* January 30, 1901.
40. F. T. Tobin to Catron, June 1, 1901 (C.P. 103, Box 13).
41. Otero, *Nine Years as Governor,* p. 159.
42. Catron to Elkins, June 23, 1901 (C.P. 105, Vol. 18).
43. Catron to Joseph Reed, November 4, 1901 (C.P. 105, Vol. 19); Reed to Catron, November 8, 1901 (C.P. 103, Box 14).
44. Eugene Fiske to Catron, December 27, 1901 (C.P. 402, Box 1).
45. Catron to Dave Winters, September 20, 1902 (C.P. 105, Vol. 20).
46. *Ibid.*
47. Otero, *Nine Years as Governor,* p. 224.
48. Catron to Frank Hubbell, October 7, 1902; Catron to Eugenio Romero, November 21, 1902 (C.P. 105, Vol. 20).
49. Catron to J. R. Andrews, November 9, 1904; Catron to C. H. Harlee, March 10, 1905 (C.P. 105, Vol. 23).
50. Otero, *Nine Years as Governor,* p. 335.
51. W. A. Hawkins to Catron, December 2, 1904 (C.P. 103, Box 21).
52. Catron to President Theodore Roosevelt, October 28, 1901 (C.P. 402, Box 1).
53. Nelson Newell affidavit, March 24, 1905 (C.P. 402, Box 1).
54. I. Sparks to Catron, June 15, 1905 (C.P. 103, Box 23).
55. J. J. Hagerman to Catron, October 21, 1905 (C.P. 103, Box 23).
56. Catron to Hagerman, October 24, 1905 (C.P. 105, Vol. 24).
57. Hagerman to Catron, October 30, 1905 (C.P. 103, Box 23).

NOTES FOR CHAPTER FIFTEEN
Pages 298 to 307

1. Certificate of election as mayor, April 6, 1906 (C.P. 801, Box 1).
2. Catron to J. J. Hagerman, November 22, 1905 (C.P. 105, Vol. 24).
3. *Ibid.*
4. Catron to President of the United States, Theodore Roosevelt, November 24, 1905 (C.P. 105, Vol. 24).
5. Ralph E. Twitchell, *Leading Facts of New Mexican History,* Vol. 2, p. 551.
6. Robert Gortner to Governor Hagerman, September 21, 1906 (C.P. 109, Vol. 28).
7. Catron to Holm Bursum, November 12, 1906 (C.P. 105, Vol. 25).
8. Curry, *Autobiography,* pp. 232–33.
9. T. B. Catron to Fletcher Catron, November 11, 1909 (C.P. 105, Vol. 29).
10. *Ibid.*
11. Catron to Gortner, November 10, 1909 (C.P. 105, Vol. 29).
12. Gortner to Charles Catron, November 14, 1909 (C.P. 103, Box 34).
13. Charles Catron to Gortner, November 23, 1909 (C.P. 101, Vol. 10).
14. Catron to President Taft, November 19, 1909 (C.P. 103, Box 34).
15. Catron to R. A. Ballinger, November 27, 1909; Catron to President Taft, November 28, 1909 (C.P. 105, Vol. 29).

NOTES FOR CHAPTER SIXTEEN
Pages 308 to 347

1. Warren Beck, *New Mexico: a History of Four Centuries,* p. 226.
2. Catron to Joseph M. Carey, January 15, 1893 (C.P. 105, Vol. 6).
3. Catron to Alexander Arnuch, September 27, 1890 (C.P. 105, Vol. 3).
4. Adolph Bandelier to R. Oestrom, January 9, 1892 (C.P. 105, Vol. 4).
5. Catron to R. C. Kerens, February 3, 1894 (C.P. 105, Vol. 8).
6. Catron to Thomas B. Reed, August 2, 1895 (C.P. 105, Vol. 12).
7. Catron to Kerens, February 3, 1894 (C.P. 105, Vol. 8).
8. *Milwaukee Sentinel,* April 6, 1876 in Ritch Scrapbook, as quoted in Beck, *New Mexico,* p. 231.
9. Marion Dargan, "New Mexico's Fight for Statehood," *New Mexico Historical Review,* 14: 138; 18: 70.
10. S. B. Elkins to Catron, January 19, 1889 (C.P. 102, Box 2).
11. Catron to O. H. Platt, January 27, 1889 (C.P. 105, Vol. 2).
12. W. J. Mills to Catron, February 1, 1889 (C.P. 102, Box 2).
13. W. M. Stewart to Catron, February 6, 1889 (C.P. 102, Box 2).
14. Dargan, "New Mexico," *New Mexico Historical Review,* 15: 156.
15. W. L. Rynerson to Catron, February 11, 1890 (C.P. 102, Box 6); Dargan, "New Mexico," *New Mexico Historical Review,* 15: 158, 159.
16. W. H. H. Llewellyn to Catron, February 12, 1890 (C.P. 102, Box 6).
17. Dargan, "New Mexico," *New Mexico Historical Review,* 15: 160.
18. W. C. Hazeldine to Catron, March 7, 1890 (C.P. 102, Box 6).
19. Hazeldine to Catron and Clancy, March 26, 1890 (C.P. 102, Box 6).
20. Hazeldine to Clancy, March 26, 1890 (C.P. 102, Box 6).
21. *Ibid.,* April 4, 1890.
22. *Ibid.*
23. Llewellyn to Catron, February 12, 1890 (C.P. 102, Box 6).
24. Dargan, "New Mexico," *New Mexico Historical Review,* 15: 165.
25. S. B. Axtell to Catron, July 12, 1890; L. A. Hughes to Catron, July 21, 1890 (C.P. 102, Box 8).
26. Catron to W. M. Stewart, October 6, 1890 (C.P. 105, Vol. 3).
27. Catron to Nestor Montoya, September 20, 1890 (C.P. 105, Vol. 3).
28. *Ibid.*
29. Catron to R. C. Kerens, August 10, 1892 (C.P. 105, Vol. 5).
30. Kerens to Catron, August 16, 1892 (C.P. 102, Box 15).
31. R. B. Thomas to Catron, August 18, 1892 (C.P. 102, Box 15).
32. E. R. Chapman to Catron, August 31, 1892 (C.P. 102, Box 16).
33. W. H. Newcomb to Catron, September 1, 1892 (C.P. 102, Box 16).
34. P. R. Smith to Catron, September 8, 1892 (C.P. 102, Box 16).
35. See also Chapter 9 herein.
36. See also Chapter 7 herein.
37. Catron to S. B. Elkins, October 3, 1894 (C.P. 105, Vol. 10).
38. Elkins to Catron, October 30, 1894 (C.P. 102, Box 23); Catron to A. J. Fountain, Jr., February 15, 1897 (C.P. 106, Box 2).
39. Ralph E. Twitchell, *Leading Facts of New Mexican History,* Vol. 2, p. 520.
40. M. W. Mills to Catron, August 2, 1892 (C.P. 102, Box 15); January 11, 1897 (C.P. 106, Box 1).
41. Beck, *New Mexico,* p. 234.
42. B. S. Rodey to Catron, May 27, 1902 (C.P. 103, Box 15).
43. John Paul Wooden, *Thomas Benton Catron and New Mexico Politics, 1866–1921,* pp. 93, 94.
44. Beck, *New Mexico,* p. 235.
45. *Detroit Journal,* October 30, 1905. Clipping enclosed with letter from E. Van Schick to Catron, October 31, 1905 (C.P. 103, Box 23).

46. *Ibid.*
47. Catron to Matthew Quay, January 6, 1903 (C.P. 105, Vol. 20).
48. *Ibid.* See Appendix 3 for the contents of this letter.
49. Rodey to Catron, March 14, 1904 (C.P. 103, Box 19).
50. Catron to T. D. Burns, August 6, 1906 (C.P. 105, Vol. 25).
51. Catron to Elkins, April 13, 1904 (C.P. 105, Vol. 22).
52. Elkins to Catron, April 21, 1904 (C.P. 103, Box 20).
53. Frank D. Reeve, *History of New Mexico,* Vol. 2, p. 331.
54. Joseph Foraker to A. L. Morrison, September 1, 1906 (C.P. 103, Box 26).
55. George Curry to Catron, January 31, 1908 (C.P. 103, Box 31).
56. Catron to Curry, February 6, 1908 (C.P. 105, Vol. 27).
57. Curry to Catron, February 11, 1908 (C.P. 103, Box 21); Catron to Charles P. Taft, April 28, 1908 (C.P. 105, Vol. 27).
58. Catron to A. J. Beveridge, February 6, 1909 (C.P. 105, Vol. 28).
59. *Ibid.*
60. *Ibid.,* February 10, 1909; Elkins to Catron, February 13, 1909 (C.P. 103, Box 33).
61. W. H. Andrews to Catron, February 13, 1909 (C.P. 103, Box 33); Catron to Andrews, February 18, 1909 (C.P. 105, Vol. 28).
62. Curry, *Autobiography,* pp. 244–46.
63. Andrews to Catron, June 27, 1910 (C.P. 103, Box 35).
64. *Ibid.*
65. *Ibid.,* August 16, 1910, Box 36.
66. Catron to Hallie D. Elkins, March 28, 1912 (C.P. 105, Vol. 31).
67. Mary Elizabeth Sluga, *The Political Life of Thomas Benton Catron, 1896–1921,* p. 110.
68. Mabry, "New Mexico's Constitution," p. 170.
69. *Ibid.,* p. 175.
70. Catron to Elkins, undated letter of 1912 (West Virginia University Library).
71. Andrews to Catron, March 11, 1911 (C.P. 103, Box 36).
72. Catron to Andrews, July 29, 1911 (C.P. 105, Vol. 31).
73. *Ibid.,* August 22, 1911.
74. *Ibid.,* September 1, 1911.

NOTES FOR CHAPTER SEVENTEEN
Pages 348 to 383

(Notes credited "Stratton" are letters provided by David H. Stratton, biographer of Albert B. Fall, which are now in the Henry E. Huntington Library, San Marino, California.)
1. T. B. Catron to W. H. Andrews, February 18, 1909, August 15, 1910 (C.P. 105, Vols. 28, 30); Andrews to Catron, August 16, 1910 (C.P. 103, Box 36).
2. Catron to Andrews, September 1, 1911 (C.P. 105, Vol. 31).
3. Catron to Charles E. Leonard, March 23, 1912 (C.P. 105, Vol. 31).
4. Catron to M. W. Mills, September 10, 1911 (C.P. 105, Vol. 31).
5. A. B. Fall to W. J. Mills, September 20, 1911 (Stratton).
6. Frank Lavan to Thom Catron, October 3, 1911 (C.P. 101, Vol. 13).
7. Andrews to Catron, October 11, November 15, 1911 (C.P. 103, Box 37).
8. A. B. Fall to Charles Springer, April 24, 1912 (Stratton).
9. Catron to M. W. Mills, September 10, 1911 (C.P. 105, Vol. 31).
10. Catron to Rev. Thomas Harwood, March 20, 1912 (C.P. 105, Vol. 31).
11. George Curry, *Autobiography,* pp. 265, 266.
12. See Chapter 16.
13. Catron to Andrews, March 2, 1911 (C.P. 105, Vol. 30).
14. *Ibid.,* September 1, 1911, Vol. 31.
15. Catron to James F. McCleary, April 5, 1912 (C.P. 501, Box 10).
16. M. W. Mills to Catron, March 28, 1912 (C.P. 501, Box 10).

17. Catron to Hallie D. Elkins, March 28, 1912 (C.P. 105, Vol. 31).
18. Catron to Charles E. Leonard and Walter Williams, March 28, 1912 (C.P. 105, Vol. 31).
19. Mary Elizabeth Sluga, *The Political Life of Thomas Benton Catron*, p. 127.
20. Catron to Tremont Medical Co., October 16, 1893 (C.P. 105, Vol. 7).
21. T. B. Catron to Julia Catron, August 22, 1895 (C.P. 105, Vol. 12).
22. *Santa Fe New Mexican*, October 10, 1913.
23. Catron to Arthur Garland, August 8, 1895 (C.P. 105, Vol. 12).
24. Interview with Mrs. Sue Catron Bergere, May 17, 1966.
25. *Albuquerque Morning Journal*, February 12, 1912.
26. W. A. Keleher to the author, September 15, 1965.
27. General Thomas B. Catron II to the author, October 4, 1965.
28. Frank F. Catron to the author, September 21, 1965.
29. Frank Lavan to Catron, April 4, 1912 (C.P. 101, Vol. 14).
30. A. B. Fall to Solomon Luna, April 9, 1912 (Stratton).
31. T. B. Catron to C. C. Catron, April 7, 1912 (C.P. 104, Box 1).
32. Catron to Elkins, April 9, 1893 (C.P. 105, Vol 6).
33. T. B. Catron to C. C. Catron, April 25, 1912 (C.P. 104, Box 1).
34. Catron to Luna, May 30, 1912 (C.P. 501, Box 9).
35. T. B. Catron to C. C. Catron, June 3, 1912 (C.P. 104, Box 1).
36. *Ibid.*
37. C. C. Catron to T. B. Catron, June 10, 1912 (C.P. 110, Vol. 2).
38. Catron to Andrews, September 12, 1914 (C.P. 101, Vol. 19).
39. C. C. Catron to Charles Safford, February 17, 1921 (C.P. 101, Vol. 29).
40. C. C. Catron to H. O. Bursum, April 6, 1921 (C.P. 101, Vol. 29).
41. A. B. Fall to Charles Springer, April 24, 1912 (Stratton).
42. Keleher, *Fabulous Frontier*, p. 117.
43. Catron to W. C. Gordon, April 4, 1912 (C.P. 501, Box 6).
44. A. B. Fall to Solomon Luna, April 9, 1912 (Stratton).
45. A. B. Fall to Charles Springer, April 24, 1912 (Stratton).
46. T. B. Catron to C. C. Catron, June 3, 1912 (C.P. 104, Box 1).
47. A. B. Fall to H. B. Holt, July 22, 1912 (Stratton).
48. *Ibid.*
49. *Albuquerque Morning Journal*, August 8, 1913.
50. Catron to Jesus Romero, July 19, 1912 (C.P. 501, Box 1).
51. *Farmington Enterprise*, July 8, 1913.
52. *Questa Gazette*, September 20, 1912.
53. *Baltimore Sun*, January 21, 1913.
54. *Washington Herald*, September 6, 1914.
55. *El Paso Times*, September 1, 1913.
56. *Ibid.*
57. *Albuquerque Morning Journal*, November 17, 1913.
58. *Albuquerque Herald*, August 17, 1914.
59. Catron to H. M. Crist, July 10, 1915 (C.P. 501, Box 49).
60. *Washington Herald*, September 6, 1914.
61. A. B. Fall to Charles Springer, August 10, 1914 (Stratton).
62. A. B. Fall to H. B. Holt, January 4, 1916 (Stratton).
63. A. B. Fall to W. A. Hawkins, January 4, 1916 (Stratton).
64. Catron to S. B. Elkins, April 9, 1893 (C.P. 105, Vol. 6).
65. Fall to C. L. Parsons, March 23, 1918 (Stratton).

NOTES FOR CHAPTER EIGHTEEN
Pages 384 to 398

1. C. C. Catron to Stephen B. Davis, Jr., September 14, 1921 (C.P. 101, Vol. 30).
2. C. C. Catron to Thom Catron, January 30, 1920 (C.P. 101, Vol. 28).

3. C. C. Catron to John W. Catron, March 14, 1921 (C.P. 101, Vol. 29).
4. C. C. Catron to Fletcher Catron, November 22, 1912 (C.P. 110, Vol. 2).
5. C. C. Catron to Fletcher Catron, May 29, 1914 (C.P. 101, Vol. 18).
6. C. C. Catron to T. B. Catron, July 28, 1914 (C.P. 108, Box 1).
7. T. B. Catron to Julia Catron, November 27, 1894 (C.P. 105, Vol. 10).
8. *Ibid.*
9. C. C. Catron to Thom Catron, November 27, 1912 (C.P. 110, Vol. 2).
10. C. C. Catron to T. B. Catron, January 10, 1920 (C.P. 101, Vol. 28).
11. C. C. Catron to Major Harry F. Cameron, June 3, 1921 (C.P. 101, Vol. 29).
12. C. C. Catron to T. B. Catron, June 25, 1912 (C.P. 110, Vol. 2).
13. C. C. Catron to Thom Catron, November 27, 1912 (C.P. 110, Vol. 2).
14. C. C. Catron to T. B. Catron, March 6, 1914 (C.P. 108, Box 1).
15. Catron to P. F. Garrett, June 1, 1904 (C.P. 105, Vol. 23).
16. Garrett to Catron, August 12, 1904 (C.P. 103, Box 21).
17. Catron to Garrett, January 20, 1906 (C.P. 105, Vol. 24).
18. Catron to R. E. Twitchell, January 22, 1901 (C.P. 105, Vol. 18).
19. William A. Keleher, *Fabulous Frontier,* p. 139.
20. S. D. Lasier to Catron, January 12, 1899 (C.P. 103, Box 7).
21. *Ibid.,* December 4, 1901, Box 14.
22. *Santa Fe New Mexican,* May 16, 1921.
23. George W. Prichard, *Thomas Benton Catron,* May 17, 1921 (C.P. 801, Box 1).
24. Editorial by E. Dana Johnson, *Santa Fe New Mexican,* May 16, 1921.
25. B. S. Rodey to Catron, April 13, 1912 (C.P. 501, Box 1).
26. *Santa Fe New Mexican,* May 16, 1921.

Bibliography

1. Archives
2. Government Publications
3. Personal Interviews
4. Letters of Information
5. Maps and Diagrams
6. Newspapers
7. Dissertations and Masters' Theses
8. Other Publications
9. Periodicals

ABBREVIATIONS

(B.L.M.) Bureau of Land Management, Santa Fe., N.M.
(C.P.) Catron Papers
(F.R.C.) Federal Records Center, Denver, Colo.
G.N.M. Annual Reports of the Governor of New Mexico Territory.
H.E.D. House Executive Document
(L.C.) Library of Congress, Washington, D.C.
L.O.R. Annual Reports of the Commissioner of the General Land Office of the United States.
(N.A.) National Archives, Washington, D.C.
(N.A.R.G.) National Archives Record Group.
S.E.D. Senate Executive Document.
S.G.R. Annual Reports of the Surveyor General of New Mexico Territory.
S.I.R. Annual Reports of the Secretary of the Interior of the United States.

[423]

1. ARCHIVES

A. The National Archives (Washington)

Commissioners of the General Land Office. *Correspondence.* To Surveyors General of New Mexico and others, 4 vols., 1854–1891.

Registers and Receivers of District Land Offices in New Mexico. *Monthly Abstracts of Original and Final Entries under the Various Land Laws,* 36 vols., 1861–1891.

United States Adjutant General's Office. Document File (N.A.R.G. 94).

United States Department of Interior. Frank Warner Angel. *Report and Testimony in the Matter of Charges Against Samuel B. Axtell, Governor of New Mexico,* October 3, 1878 (N.A.R.G. 48).

————. Records of the General Land Office Relating to Private Land Claims (N.A.R.G. 49).

United States Department of Justice. Frank Warner Angel. *In the Matter of Examination of the Causes and Circumstances of the Death of John H. Tunstall, a British Subject, and Troubles in Lincoln County, New Mexico,* October 7, 1878 (N.A.R.G. 60).

————. Source Chronological File (N.A.R.G. 60).

United States Department of State. Temporary and Permanent Attorney's Commissions (N.A.R.G. 59).

United States Quartermaster General's Office. Consolidated Correspondence File.

United States Solicitor of the Treasury. U.S. Attorney Reports (N.A.R.G. 206).

B. Library of Congress (Washington)

Albert Bacon Fall Papers. Manuscripts Division.

C. Federal Records Center (Denver)

Surveyors General of New Mexico. *Correspondence.* To Commissioners of the General Land Office and others, 2 vols., 1887–1895.

————. *Correspondence.* To Commissioners of the General Land Office, private individuals and surveyors, 117 vols., 1884–1910.

————. *Correspondence.* To various persons concerning land grants and small holding claims, 1 vol., 1885–1893.

D. Bureau of Land Management (Santa Fe)

Commissioners of the General Land Office and others. *Correspondence.* To Surveyors General of New Mexico and others, 1 vol., 1854–1876.

Deputy Surveyors in New Mexico. *Field Note Books.*

Registers and Receivers of District Land Offices in New Mexico. *Tract Books.*

Surveyors General of New Mexico. *Correspondence.* To Commissioners of the General Land Office and others, 8 vols., 1854–1887.

————. *Survey Plats of Townships.*

E. *United States Court House* (Santa Fe)

United States. *Territorial District Court Records.* Criminal Cases.

F. *State Records Center and Archives* (Santa Fe)

Adjutant General Files.

Herbert J. Hagerman Papers.

Napoleon B. Laughlin Papers.

Miguel A. Otero Papers.

L. Bradford Prince Papers.

Edmund G. Ross Papers.

William T. Thornton Papers.

G. *Museum of New Mexico Library* (Santa Fe)

Edwar A. Walz. *Retrospections, 1931.*

H. *Henry E. Huntington Library* (San Marino)

Robert Alonzo Brock Collection.

Albert Bacon Fall Collection.

William Gillet Ritch Collection.

I. *University of New Mexico Library* (Albuquerque)

William H. Andrews Papers.

Bell Ranch Papers.

Joseph H. Blazer Business Records.

Holm O. Bursum Papers.

John P. Casey. Oath of Office and Bond.

Thomas B. Catron Papers.

Albert Bacon Fall Papers.

First National Bank of Santa Fe Records.

Fred Fornhoff Papers.

Oscar P. McMains Resolution.

Miguel A. Otero Papers.

J. *West Virginia University Library* (Morgantown)

Stephen B. Elkins Papers.

K. *Vicksburg National Military Park* (Vicksburg)

Miscellaneous letters concerning Thomas B. Catron.

L. *Missouri Historical Society* (Saint Louis)

Eighteenth Annual Catalogue of the Officers and Students of the University of Missouri, for the Year Ending July 4, 1860, Saint Louis, 1860.

Hugh McKay. *University of Missouri Alumni Directory,* Saint Louis, 1915.

M. *Miscellaneous*

Abstract of Title. *El Caso Ranch.*

————. *La Majada Grant.*

————. *Pablo Montoya Grant and Baca Location No. 2, in San Miguel County.*

Casey, John P., Sr. *Notarized Statement,* October 15, 1892. This is an unsigned copy of the typewritten original possessed by Mrs. Myrtle Cox, Quemado, New Mexico. The original was not found.

Catron, Thomas B. *In Memoriam, Eulogy by Thomas B. Catron at the Funeral Services of his Wife.*

————. Agreement with William T. Thornton concerning gambling.

————. Confederate Battle Flag.

————. Scrapbooks. These six volumes were made available through the courtesy of Thomas B. Catron III, Santa Fe. They contain newspaper clippings and miscellaneous items.

————. Major Thomas B. II. *Notes and Observations on the Espiritu Santo Grant.* Courtesy Manuel P. and Jane Sanchez.

Catron Family *Holy Bible.* Genealogical Pages.

New Mexico Cattle Corporations, 1871–1900. Western Range Cattle Industry Study, State Museum, Denver.

2. GOVERNMENT PUBLICATIONS

Attorney General of the United States (United States Attorney for the Court of Private Land Claims). *Annual Reports,* 14 vols., Washington, 1891–1904.

Commissioner of the General Land Office. *Annual Reports,* 38 vols., Washington, 1854–1891.

Governor of New Mexico. *Annual Reports,* 50 vols., Washington, 1855–1904 (called *Annual Messages* prior to 1879).

Kenyon, William S. *Report on Land Claims in New Mexico,* 36 Cong., 1 Sess., *H.E.D.* No. 321 (1068).

McKinney, William M., and Peter Kemper, Jr., Compls. *The Federal Statutes Annotated Containing All the Laws of the United States of a General and Permanent Nature in Force on the First Day of January, 1903,* Vol. VI, Northport, L.I., N.Y., 1905.

Secretary of the Interior. *Annual Reports,* 38 vols., Washington, 1854–1891.

————. *Fraudulent Acquisition of Titles to Lands in New Mexico, 1885,* 48 Cong., 2 Sess., *S.E.D.* No. 106.

Stone, W. F. "The Only Court of its Kind in the World," *Report of the Governor of New Mexico to the Secretary of the Interior, 1903,* 378–386, Washington, 1903.

Surveyor General of New Mexico. *Annual Reports,* 50 vols., Washington, 1855–1904.

The War of the Rebellion. A compilation of the official Records of the Union and Confederate Armies, Washington, 1880.

3. PERSONAL INTERVIEWS

Armijo, Frank. Native of Quemado, N.M.
Bergere, Sue (Catron). Granddaughter of T. B. Catron, Santa Fe.
Catron, Fletcher A. Attorney. Son of T. B. Catron, Santa Fe.
————, John B. Builder. Grandson of T. B. Catron, Santa Fe.
————, John S. Attorney. Grandson of T. B. Catron, Santa Fe.
————, General Thomas B. II. Retired. Son of T. B. Catron, Baltimore.
————, Thomas B. III. Attorney. Grandson of T. B. Catron, Santa Fe.
Feather, Adlai. Historian, Mesilla.
Genta, Tony. Native of Alamogordo.
Hartmann, Reverend Julius. Catholic clergyman. Chaplain for the 1910 constitutional convention of the Territory of New Mexico, Albuquerque.
Keleher, William A. Attorney and historian, Albuquerque.
Otero, Miguel A. III. Attorney, Santa Fe.
Padilla, Celestino. Native of Quemado, N.M.
Riley, Genevieve. Daughter of John H. Riley, Las Cruces.
Sanchez, Manuel A. Abstracter, Mora.
Staab, Dr. Edward A. Albuquerque.
Watson, John C. Attorney, Santa Fe.

4. LETTERS OF INFORMATION

These letters are to the author unless otherwise noted. Dates are for the first letter received, and the number in parentheses at the end of an entry indicates additional letters from that person.

Adams, E. S. Adjutant General, War Department, Washington, D.C., to Vioalle Hefferan, March 20, 1939.
Armijo, Luis E. District Judge, Las Vegas, November 13, 1964.
————, to Fletcher A. Catron, December 5, 1959 (3).
Bell, Mrs. Robert K. Relative of Richard Hudson, Silver City, June 8, 1965.
Bilisdly, Mrs. E. E. Niece of Clemente (Pourade) Grossetete, Portsmouth, Virginia, April 2, 1960.
Brockenbrough, Eleanor S. Assistant Director, Confederate Memorial Literary Society, Richmond, Virginia, March 29, 1965 (1).
Brothers, Mary Hudson. Writer. Daughter of Bell Hudson, Farmington, February 9, 1960.
Bryan, Howard. Editor, "Off the Beaten Path," *Albuquerque Tribune,* March 9, 1959.

Calley, Mrs. Tommie. Owner El Caso Ranch, Quemado, N.M., January 26, 1964.

Catron, Fletcher A. To Luis E. Armijo, District Judge, Las Vegas, N.M., December 9, 1959 (2).

————. To Robert C. Gortner, former partner of T. B. Catron, January 4, 1960.

————. To Dick House, June 16, 1961.

————, Mrs. Fletcher A. October 19, 1964 (6).

————, Frank F. Attorney, Lexington, Missouri, September 3, 1964 (5).

————, John S. Attorney. Grandson of T. B. Catron, Santa Fe, August 11, 1964.

————, Robert C. President, Tavern Talk Publishing Company, Kansas City, Missouri, November 7, 1965 (3).

————, General Thomas B. II. Son of T. B. Catron, Baltimore, July 15, 1964 (12).

————, Thomas B. III. Attorney. Grandson of T. B. Catron, Santa Fe, November 16, 1965 (2).

Crocchiola, Reverend Stanley (F. Stanley). White Deer, Texas, February 15, 1960.

Davis, Les. Charles Springer Cattle Company, Raton, August 16, 1967.

Feather, Adlai. Historian, Mesilla, January 9, 1964 (18).

Gold, Robert B. Nephew of Robert C. Gortner, West Corina, California, April 29, 1966.

Gortner, Robert C. To Fletcher A. Catron, son of T. B. Catron, January 10, 1960 (1).

Grisso, W. D. Historian, Oklahoma City, February 3, 1965.

Hayden, Senator Carl. Washington, October 31, 1967.

Keleher, William A. Attorney and historian, Albuquerque, September 15, 1965.

Ketring, Lewis, Jr. Distant relative of T. B. Catron, Monterey Park, California, January 12, 1966.

Lamar, Howard Roberts. Director of Graduate Studies, Department of History, Yale University, New Haven, July 2, 1965 (2).

Lee, Susan. Author, Los Lunas, October 22, 1960 (1).

————, Thomas Davis. Relative of Stephen B. Elkins, Elkins, West Virginia, July 20, 1964.

Letarte, A. N. Relative of Clemence (Pourade) Grossetete, Phoenix, March 30, 1960 (1).

Mullin, Robert N. Historian, South Laguna, California, December 24, 1964 (1).

Murphy, Lawrence R. Department of History, Texas Christian University, Fort Worth, December 2, 1965 (1).

Newman, Ralph G. Abraham Lincoln Book Shop, Chicago, May 24, 1965.

————, Simeon H. Administrative Assistant, University Archives, University of Texas, El Paso, February 9, 1967 (13).

Rasch, Philip J. Historian, Sneads Ferry, North Carolina, December 6, 1964.

Sanchez, Jane. Historian, Albuquerque, July 6, 1965 (4).

Salmon, Ellen Gene. Granddaughter of John P. Casey, April 15, 1964 (1).

Stratton, David H. Albert B. Fall's biographer, also provided copies of several letters to and from Fall which are now in the Henry E. Huntington Library, San Marino, California. These are cited in the notes as (Stratton).

————. Professor of History, Washington State University, Pullman, April 27, 1964 (17).

Turner, Mrs. Jennie Walz. To Thomas B. Catron II, October 22, 1964.

Watson, John T. Attorney, Santa Fe, June 3, 1964.

Williams, John Alex. New Haven, Connecticut, July 3, 1965.

5. MAPS AND DIAGRAMS

Diagram of New Mexico Showing Public Land Surveyed, Private Land Claims Confirmed and Surveyed under Act of Congress, also, Confirmed and Surveyed under Decree of Court of P.L.C., Indian Reservations, Forest Preserves and Reservoir Sites. Drawn by Norman King in the early 1900s (Santa Fe, Bureau of Land Management, Survey Records Section).

State of New Mexico. Compiled from the official records of the General Land Office and other sources, 1936.

Surveys Around Vicksburg showing the Rebel Defenses and Federal Works. Vicksburg National Military Park.

Ojo del Espiritu Santo Grant, 1885. Courtesy Manuel P. and Jane Sanchez.

6. NEWSPAPERS

Albuquerque Citizen, 1891–98 (daily and weekly).

Albuquerque Daily Democrat, 1882–92.

Albuquerque Evening Democrat, 1884.

Albuquerque Evening Herald, 1912–14.

Albuquerque Morning Journal, 1882–1916.

Albuquerque Review, 1876–80.

Baltimore Sun, 1913.

Black Range (Chloride), 1885–97.
Carlsbad Argus, 1896.
Chronicle-News (Trinidad), 1916.
Clovis News, 1912.
Deming Graphic, 1916.
Deming Headlight, 1896.
Denver News, 1913.
Detroit Journal, 1905.
El Fenix (Clayton), 1912, 1913.
El Monitor (Taos), 1896.
El Paso Herald, 1913.
El Paso Times, 1913.
Endee Enterprise, 1912.
Era Southwestern (Santa Fe), 1880.
Farmington Enterprise, 1912, 1913.
Grant County Herald (Silver City), 1876–78.
Great Falls Tribune, 1913.
Kingston Weekly Shaft, 1891.
La Bandera Americana (Albuquerque), 1912–14.
La Opinion Publica (Albuquerque), 1893, 1914.
Las Animas, Col., Leader, 1875.
Las Cruces Borderer, 1872.
Las Cruces Citizen, 1912.
Las Vegas Gazette, 1877.
Las Vegas Optic, 1884, 1895–96, 1912, 1913.
Leslie's Weekly, 1912.
Louisville Courier-Journal, 1912.
Mesilla News, 1883.
Mesilla Valley Independent (Mesilla), 1879.
Milwaukee Sentinel, 1876.
New York Advertiser, 1896.
New York American, 1916.
New York Commercial, 1913.
New York Herald, 1896, 1912.
New York Mercury, 1896.
New York Sun, 1875, 1896, 1912–13.
New York Town and Country, 1914.
Otero County Advertiser (Alamogordo), 1912.
Portales Times, 1912.
Progress (Obar), 1912.
Questa Gazette, 1912.
Raton Range, 1895–96, 1912–13.
Republican Review (Albuquerque), 1870–76.

Rio Grande Republican (Las Cruces), 1887–1912 (title varies).
Rock Island Tribune, 1912–13.
Roswell News, 1913.
St. Louis Daily Globe, 1896.
St. Louis Globe Democrat, 1914.
San Marcial Bee, 1895–96.
Santa Fe Daily Democrat, 1882.
Santa Fe Eagle, 1912–13.
Santa Fe New Mexican, 1863–1921 (title varies, daily and weekly).
Santa Fe Weekly Gazette, 1864–69.
Santa Fe Weekly Leader, 1885–86.
Santa Fe Weekly Sun, 1891.
Santa Rosa Sun, 1912.
Seattle Post-Intelligencer, 1912.
Silver City Eagle, 1895.
Silver City Enterprise, 1895–96, 1912.
Silver City Independent, 1912.
Socorro Chieftain, 1895–96, 1912–16.
Taos Valley News, 1912.
Texico Trumpet, 1912.
Thirty=Four (Las Cruces), 1879–80.
Topeka State Journal, 1912.
University Missourian (Columbia), 1912.
Washington Herald, 1912–14.
Washington Post, 1912–16.
Washington Star, 1912–16.
Washington Times, 1912–16.
West Coast Monthly (Los Angeles), January, 1912.
Western Liberal (Lordsburg), 1896, 1913.
Westgate [California] News, 1913.
Worth While (Washington, D.C.), 1912.

7. DISSERTATIONS AND MASTERS' THESES

Heath, Jim F. *A Study of the Influence of the Atchison, Topeka, and Santa Fe Railroad upon the Economy of New Mexico,* University of New Mexico, 1955, Ms. (MA thesis).

Hefferan, Vioalle Clark. *Thomas Benton Catron.* University of New Mexico, 1940, Ms. (MA thesis).

Leonard, Olen E. *The Role of the Land Grant in the Social Organization and Social Processes of a Spanish-American Village in New Mexico.* Louisiana State University and Agricultural and Mechanical College, 1943, Ms. (PhD dissertation).

Moorman, Donald. *A Political Biography of Holm O. Bursum, 1899–1924*. University of New Mexico, 1962, Ms. (PhD dissertation).

Paulus, Lena. *Problem of the Private Land Grant of New Mexico*. University of Pittsburgh, 1933, Ms. (MA thesis).

Pittman, Lucretia. *Solomon Luna: Sheepmaster and Politician of New Mexico*. Saint Louis University, 1944, Ms. (MA thesis).

Sluga, Mary Elizabeth. *The Political Life of Thomas Benton Catron, 1896–1921*. University of New Mexico, 1941, Ms. (MA thesis).

Waldrip, William I. *New Mexico During the Civil War*. University of New Mexico, 1950, Ms. (MA thesis).

Wooden, John Paul. *Thomas Benton Catron and New Mexico Politics, 1866–1921*. New Mexico State University, 1959, Ms. (MA thesis).

Willoughby, Roy. *The Range Cattle Industry in New Mexico*. University of New Mexico, 1933, Ms. (MA thesis).

8. OTHER PUBLICATIONS

Anderson, G. B., Compl. *History of New Mexico: Its Resources and People,* 2 vols. Los Angeles: Pacific States Publishing Co., 1907.

Bancroft, Hubert Howe. *History of Arizona and New Mexico*. San Francisco: The History Co., 1889.

Beck, Warren. *New Mexico: A History of Four Centuries*. Norman: The University of Oklahoma Press, 1962.

Billington, Ray Allen. *The Far Western Frontier, 1830–1860*. New York: Harper, 1956.

Blackmar, Frank W. "The Land Question," in *Spanish Institutions of the Southwest*. Baltimore: The Johns Hopkins Press, 1891.

Brayer, Herbert O. *William Blackmore: A Case Study in the Economic Development of the West*. Denver: Bradford-Robinson Printing Co., 1949.

Brevoort, Elias. *New Mexico: Her Natural Resources and Attractions*. Santa Fe: E. Brevoort, 1874.

Brothers, Mary Hudson. *A Pecos Pioneer*. Albuquerque: The University of New Mexico Press, 1943.

Bureau of Immigration. *The Resources of New Mexico, Prepared for the Territorial Fair to be held at Albuquerque, N.M., October 3d to 8th, 1881*. Santa Fe, 1881.

Catron, Henry Hardy. *Kettenring Family in America*. Mount Pulaski, Illinois, 1956.

Cleaveland, Agnes Morley. *No Life for a Lady*. Boston: Houghton, 1941.

Coan, Charles F. *A History of New Mexico*, 3 vols. Chicago and New York: The American Historical Society, 1925.

Culley, John H. (Jack). *Cattle, Horses and Men of the Western Range.* Los Angeles: The Ward Ritchie Press, 1940.

Curry, George. *George Curry, 1861–1947: An Autobiography.* Albuquerque: The University of New Mexico Press, 1958 (Edited by H. B. Hening).

Davis, W. W. H. *El Gringo: or, New Mexico and Her People.* Santa Fe: Rio Grande Press, 1938 (first published in 1857).

Donnelly, Thomas C. *The Government of New Mexico.* Albuquerque: The University of New Mexico Press, 1953.

Duffus, R. L. *The Santa Fe Trail.* New York: Longman, Green and Co., 1930.

Dunham, Harold H. *Government Handout: A Study in the Administration of the Public Lands, 1875–1891.* New York: Columbia University, 1941.

French, William. *Some Recollections of a Western Ranchman.* London: Neuthen & Co., Ltd., 1927.

Fulton, Maurice G. *Roswell in its Early Days.* Roswell: Maurice G. Fulton, 1963.

———. *History of the Lincoln County War.* Tucson: The University of Arizona Press, 1968.

Garrett, Pat F. *The Authentic Life of Billy the Kid.* Albuquerque: Horn and Wallace, 1964.

Gibson, A. M. *The Life and Death of Colonel Albert Jennings Fountain.* Norman: The University of Oklahoma Press, 1965.

Hagerman, Herbert J. *A Statement in Regard to Certain Matters Concerning the Governorship and Political Affairs in New Mexico, 1906–1907.* Printed for private circulation, 1908.

Hamlin, William Lee. *The True Story of Billy the Kid: A Tale of the Lincoln County War.* Caldwell, Idaho: Caxton Printers, 1959.

Hendron, J. W. *The Story of Billy the Kid: New Mexico's Number One Desperado.* Santa Fe: The Rydal Press, 1948.

Hinkle, James F. *Early Days of a Cowboy on the Pecos.* Roswell: James F. Hinkle, 1937.

Holmes, Jack E. *Politics in New Mexico.* Albuquerque: The University of New Mexico Press, 1967.

Horn, Calvin. *New Mexico's Troubled Years: The Story of Early Territorial Governors.* Albuquerque: Horn and Wallace, 1963.

Hunt, Frazier. *The Tragic Days of Billy the Kid.* New York: Hastings House, 1956.

Julian, George W. *Political Recollections, 1840–1872.* Chicago: Jansen, McClurg & Company, 1884.

Keleher, William A. *The Fabulous Frontier.* Albuquerque: The University of New Mexico Press, 1962 (first published in 1945).

———. *Maxwell Land Grant.* Santa Fe: The Rydal Press, 1942.

———. *Turmoil in New Mexico, 1846–1868.* Santa Fe: The Rydal Press, 1952.

———. *Violence in Lincoln County, 1869–1881.* Albuquerque: The University of New Mexico Press, 1957.

Kull, Irving S. and Nell M. *A Short Chronology of American History, 1492–1950.* New Brunswick: Rutgers University Press, 1952.

Lamar, Howard Roberts. *The Far Southwest, 1846–1912: A Territorial History.* New Haven: Yale University Press, 1966.

Lambert, Oscar Doane. *Stephen Benton Elkins: American Foursquare.* Pittsburgh: The University of Pittsburgh Press, 1955.

Larson, Robert W. *New Mexico's Quest for Statehood, 1846–1912.* Albuquerque: The University of New Mexico Press, 1968.

Lee, Susan. *These Also Served.* Los Lunas: Susan Lee, 1960.

Lorant, Stefan. *The Presidency: A Pictorial History of Presidential Elections from Washington to Truman.* New York: Macmillan, 1951.

Marshall, James. *Santa Fe: The Railroad that Built an Empire.* New York: Random House, 1945.

Moore, John C. *Confederate Military History (Missouri).* Atlanta: Confederate Publishing Company, 1899.

Morrow, W. W. *Spanish and Mexican Private Land Grants.* San Francisco: Bancroft, Whitney Co., 1923.

Nevins, Allan. *Fremont: Pathfinder of the West.* New York, London and Toronto: Longmans, Green and Co., 1955.

———. *Grover Cleveland: A Study in Courage.* New York: Dodd, Mead and Co., 1933.

Nolan, Frederick W. *The Life and Death of John Henry Tunstall.* Albuquerque: The University of New Mexico Press, 1965.

Otero, Miguel Antonio. *My Life on the Frontier, 1864–1882.* New York: The Press of the Pioneers, 1935.

———. *My Life on the Frontier, 1882–1897.* Albuquerque: The University of New Mexico Press, 1939.

———. *My Nine Years as Governor of the Territory of New Mexico, 1897–1906.* Albuquerque: The University of New Mexico Press, 1940.

Pearson, Jim Berry. *The Maxwell Land Grant.* Norman: The University of Oklahoma Press, 1961.

Poldervaart, Arie W. *Black-Robed Justice: A History of the Administration of Justice in New Mexico from the American Occupation in 1846 Until Statehood in 1912.* Santa Fe: Arie W. Poldervaart, 1948.

Portrait and Biographical Record of Lafayette and Saline Counties, Missouri. Chicago: Chapman Bros., 1893.

Read, Benjamin M. *Illustrated History of New Mexico.* Santa Fe: New Mexico Printing Co., 1912.

Reeve, Frank D. *History of New Mexico,* Vol. 2. New York: Lewis Publishing Co., 1961.

Reynolds, Matthew G. *Spanish and Mexican Land Laws.* St. Louis: Buxton and Skinner Stationery Co., 1895.

Rippy, J. Fred. *The United States and Mexico.* New York: A. A. Knopf, 1926.

Siringo, Chas. A. *A Lone Star Cowboy.* Santa Fe: C. A. Siringo, 1919.

Smith, Edward C. *The Borderland in the Civil War.* New York: Macmillan, 1927.

Sonnichsen, C. L. *Tularosa: Last of the Frontier West.* New York: The Devin-Adair Company, 1961.

————, and William V. Morrison. *Alias Billy the Kid.* Albuquerque: The University of New Mexico Press, 1955.

Stratton, David H., Ed. *The Memoirs of Albert B. Fall.* El Paso: The University of Texas, 1966.

Stratton, Porter A. *The Territorial Press of New Mexico, 1834–1912,* Albuquerque: The University of New Mexico Press, 1969.

Thompson, Albert W. *They Were Open Range Days: Annals of a Western Frontier.* Denver: The World Press, 1946.

Thorp, N. Howard (Jack). *Pardner of the Wind: Story of the Southwestern Cowboy.* Caldwell, Idaho: The Caxton Printers, 1945.

Twitchell, Ralph E. *The Leading Facts of New Mexican History,* Vol. 2. Cedar Rapids, Iowa: Torch Press, 1912.

————. *Old Santa Fe; The Story of New Mexico's Ancient Capital.* Santa Fe: Santa Fe New Mexico Publishing Corp., 1925.

Waters, L. L. *Steel Trails to Santa Fe.* Lawrence: The University of Kansas Press, 1950.

Westphall, Victor. *The Public Domain in New Mexico, 1854–1891.* Albuquerque: The University of New Mexico Press, 1965.

9. PERIODICALS

Anderson, Clinton P. "The Adobe Palace," *New Mexico Historical Review* 19: 97–122, April, 1944.

Bloom, Lansing. "The Governors of New Mexico," *New Mexico Historical Review* 10: 152–157, April, 1935.

Chauvenet, Beatrice. "The Title of Dona Sofia," *New Mexico Magazine* 15: 35, 36, August, 1937.

————. "Titles from the King of Spain," *New Mexico Magazine* 15: 45–47, September, 1936.

"Catron and Renehan Sued by Lobato Heirs," *Santa Fe New Mexican,* September 30, 1912.

"Tom Catron Gained Fame, Fortune as Early-Day New Mexico Lawyer," *West Texas Livestock Weekly,* August 15, 1968.

Dargan, Marion. "New Mexico's Fight for Statehood, 1895–1912," *New Mexico Historical Review* 14: 1–33; 121–42; 15: 133–87; 16: 379–400; 18: 60–96, 148–75, January, April, 1939; April, 1940; October, 1941; January, April, 1943.

Dorsey, Stephen W. "Land-Stealing in New Mexico, A Rejoinder," *North American Review* 145: 396–409, October, 1887.

Dunham, Harold H. "New Mexican Land Grants With Special Reference to the Maxwell Grant," *New Mexico Historical Review* 30: 1–22, January, 1955.

Espinosa, Gilberto. "About New Mexico Land Grants," *The State Bar of New Mexico Bulletin* 6: 258–63, November 2, 1967.

Hinton, Harwood P., Jr. "John Simpson Chisum, 1877–84," *New Mexico Historical Review* 31: 177–205, 310–37, 32: 53–65, July, October, 1956; January, 1957.

Julian, George W. "Land-Stealing in New Mexico," *North American Review* 145: 17–31, No. 368, 1887.

———. "Our Land Grant Railways in Congress," *International Review* 14: 198–212, February-March, 1883.

———. "Railway Influence in the Land Office," *North American Review* 136: 237–56, March, 1883.

Keleher, William A. "Land Law of the New Mexico Land Grant," *New Mexico Historical Review* 4: 350–71, October, 1929.

Lamar, Howard R. "Edmund G. Ross as Governor of New Mexico: A Reappraisal," *New Mexico Historical Review* 36: 177–209, July, 1961.

Leopard, Donald D. "Joint Statehood, 1906," *New Mexico Historical Review* 34: 241–47, October, 1959.

Mabry, Thomas J. "New Mexico's Constitution in the Making — Reminiscences of 1910," *New Mexico Historical Review* 19: 168–84, April, 1944.

"Missouriana," *Missouri Historical Review* 29: 74, 75, October, 1934; 33: 394–97, April, 1939.

Newman, S. H. III. "The Las Vegas Weekly Mail," *New Mexico Historical Review* 44: 155–66, April, 1969.

Nolan, Frederick W. "A Sidelight on the Tunstall Murder," *New Mexico Historical Review* 31: 206–22, July, 1956.

Parish, William J. "The German Jew and the Commercial Revolution in Territorial New Mexico, 1850–1900," *New Mexico Historical Review* 35: 1–29, 129–50, January, April, 1960.

Potter, Chester D. (Paige W. Christiansen, Ed.) "Reminiscences of the Socorro Vigilantes," *New Mexico Historical Review* 40: 23–54, January, 1965.

Rasch, Philip J. "The Rustler War," *New Mexico Historical Review* 39: 257–73, October, 1964.

Stone, W. F. "The United States Court of Private Land Claims," *Minutes of the New Mexico Bar Association, 1904,* 6–26.

Tracy, Francis G., Sr. "Pecos Valley Pioneers," *New Mexico Historical Review* 33: 187–204, July, 1958.

Walter, Paul A. F. "New Mexico's Pioneer Bank and Bankers," *New Mexico Historical Review* 21: 209–25, July, 1946.

———. "The First Civil Governor of New Mexico Under the Stars and Stripes," *New Mexico Historical Review* 8: 98–129, April, 1933.

Westphall, Victor. "The Public Domain in New Mexico, 1854–1891," *New Mexico Historical Review* 33: 24–52, 128–43, January, April, 1958.

Index